Christ the Gift and the Giver

Christ the Gift and the Giver

Paul's Portrait of Jesus as the Supreme
Royal Benefactor in Romans 5:1–11

Enoch O. Okode

Foreword by Joshua W. Jipp

⁌PICKWICK *Publications* • Eugene, Oregon

CHRIST THE GIFT AND THE GIVER
Paul's Portrait of Jesus as the Supreme Royal Benefactor in Romans 5:1–11

Copyright © 2022 Enoch O. Okode. All rights reserved. Except for brief quotations in critical publications or reviews, no part of this book may be reproduced in any manner without prior written permission from the publisher. Write: Permissions, Wipf and Stock Publishers, 199 W. 8th Ave., Suite 3, Eugene, OR 97401.

Pickwick Publications
An Imprint of Wipf and Stock Publishers
199 W. 8th Ave., Suite 3
Eugene, OR 97401

www.wipfandstock.com

PAPERBACK ISBN: 978-1-6667-1577-4
HARDCOVER ISBN: 978-1-6667-1578-1
EBOOK ISBN: 978-1-6667-1579-8

Cataloguing-in-Publication data:

Names: Okode, Enoch O., author | Jipp, Joshua W., foreword

Title: Christ the gift and the giver : Paul's portrait of Jesus as the supreme royal benefactor in Romans 5:1–11 / by Enoch O. Okode; foreword by Joshua W. Jipp.

Description: Eugene, OR: Pickwick Publications, 2022 | Includes bibliographical references.

Identifiers: ISBN 978-1-6667-1577-4 (paperback) | ISBN 978-1-6667-1578-1 (hardcover) | ISBN 978-1-6667-1579-8 (ebook)

Subjects: LCSH: Bible. Romans, V, 1-11—Criticism, interpretation, etc. | Jesus Christ—Teachings.

Classification: BS2665.2 O363 2022 (print) | BS2665.2 (ebook)

01/13/22

For VG, CJ, & BJ

Contents

Foreword by Joshua W. Jipp | ix
Acknowledgments | xi
List of Abbreviations | xiii

1. Introduction and Methodology | 1
2. Royal Benefaction in the Greco-Roman Context | 25
3. Royal Benefaction in Jewish Writings | 67
4. The Messiah's Supreme Royal Benefaction in Romans 5:1–11 | 104
5. The Messiah's Supreme Royal Benefaction in Romans 5:12—8:39 | 172
6. Summary and Conclusion | 222

Bibliography | 235

Foreword

IS THERE A THREAD that holds together the variety of christological images Paul uses throughout Romans 5–8? In this extraordinary stretch of Romans, Paul speaks of Jesus as shedding his blood for his people, as a king who secures justice for his kingdom, as a military figure who calls his people to wield weapons of righteousness, and a heavenly agent who protects and intercedes for his people. In this book Enoch Okode makes a strong case that one of the most significant conceptual frameworks for understanding Paul's argument in Romans 5–8 is that of royal benefaction. Christ is depicted as a kingly figure who gives his life as a gift to rescue his royal subjects. The argument is characterized by clear writing, robust historical analysis, and careful exegesis of Pauline texts. Enoch's study provides a historically grounded thematic unity for Romans 5—8, and the argument is timely in light of recent research on Paul and messianism and discussions of how grace/gift-giving calls for a reciprocal response of allegiance. Readers will find plenty of significant insights into Romans when read in light of the proposed framework of royal benefaction including making sense of the difficult claim that "scarcely will someone die on behalf of a righteous person but for the sake of a good person someone may dare to die" (Rom 5:7). What follows is an excellent study that will illuminate Paul's world and his argument in Romans 5–8 but most importantly offers a memorable contribution to Paul's messianic Christology.

Joshua W. Jipp

Acknowledgments

I AM GRATEFUL TO God for enabling me to complete this work. He granted me strength, concentration, insights, creativity, and endurance. The whole project was delightful because God's grace abounded to me.

This work would not have been possible had it not been for the love and encouragement of my wife VG and my daughters CJ and BJ. You taught me to remain focused, love God fervently, and serve the church faithfully. On many occasions, you pleasantly surprised me when you stopped by my study carrel to put a smile on my face and remind me that I was never alone in this journey. Thank you for the unceasing gift of your love and support.

I am grateful to Dr. Joshua W. Jipp for serving as my doctoral advisor. You offered insights that challenged and sharpened my argument. You directed me to relevant and important resources, and you challenged me to think creatively and critically. Thank you for the gifts of your counsel, friendship, and hospitality. I am also indebted to Dr. Richard E. Averbeck and Dr. Constantine R. Campbell for their input as members of my doctoral committee.

God used many others as mediators of his benefactions that ensured the completion of this project. I thank my parents and siblings for their prayers and encouragement. I am grateful to all the friends whom God gave the desire to support me. I thank Ronald Kneezel and Daniel Fiester who interacted with my work and provided thoughtful feedback and insight. I will discharge my duty to reciprocate by remaining loyal to the Messiah wherever he may lead me.

List of Abbreviations

1 Regn.	Dio Chrysostom, Kingship 1	ALGHJ	Arbeitenzur Literatur und Geschichte des hellenistischen Judentums
2 Regn.	Dio Chrysostom, Kingship 2		
2 Tars.	Dio Chrysostom, Second Tarsic Discourse	Alleg. Interp.	Philo, Allegorical Interpretation
3 Regn.	Dio Chrysostom, Kingship 3	Anab.	Arrian, Anabasis
		Anab.	Xenophon, Anabasis
4 Regn.	Dio Chrysostom, Kingship 4	AnBib	Analectabiblica
AB	Anchor Bible	Ann.	Tacitus, Annales
ABR	Australian Biblical Review	ANRW	Aufstieg und Niedergang der römischen Welt
Aen.	Virgil, Aeneid		
Ag. Ap.	Josephus, Against Apion	Ant.	Josephus, Jewish Antiquities
AJ.	Sophocles, Ajax	ASBT	Acadia Studies in Bible Theology
AJP	American Journal of Philology		
		Aug.	Suetonius, Divus Augustus
Alex.	Plutarch, Alexander		

BDAG	Walter Bauer, Frederick W. Danker, W. F. Arndt, and F. W. Gingrich. *Greek-English Lexicon of the New Testament and Other Early Christian Literature*. 3rd ed. Chicago: University of Chicago Press, 2000.	*Clem.*	Seneca, *De Clementia*
		CQ	*Classical Quarterly*
		Creation	Philo, *On the Creation of the World*
		CTM	*Concordia Theological Monthly*
		CV	*Communio Viatorum*
		Cyr.	Xenophon, *Cyropaedia*
Ben.	Seneca, *De Beneficiis*	*De lege*	Dio Chrysostom, *Law*
BETL	Bibliotheca ephemeridum theologicarum lovaniensium	*Decal.*	Philo, *On the Decalogue*
		Dreams	Philo, *On Dreams*
Bib	*Biblica*		
BJS	Brown Judaic Studies	*Drunkenness*	Philo, *On Drunkenness*
BNTC	Black's New Testament Commentaries	*EFN*	*Estudios de filologíaneo testamentaria*
BTB	*Biblical Theological Bulletin*	*Embassy*	Philo, *On the Embassy to Gaius*
BZNW	Beiheftezur Zeitschriftfür die neutestamentliche Wissenschaft	*Ep.*	Pliny the Younger, *Epistulae*
		Ep.	Seneca, *Epistulae Morales*
Carm.	Horace, *Carmina*	*Epict. diss.*	Arrian, *Epicteti Dissertationes*
CBQ	*Catholic Biblical Quarterly*	*Epigr.*	Martial, *Epigrams*
Cher.	Philo, *On the Cherubim*	*Eth. nic.*	Aristotle, *Nichomachean Ethics*
CIG	*Corpus Inscriptionum Graecarum*	*Fam.*	Cicero, *Epistulae ad Familiares*

List of Abbreviations

Flaccus	Philo, *Against Flaccus*	JBL	*Journal of Biblical Literature*
Geogr.	Strabo, *Geography*	JESHO	*Journal of the Economic and Social History of the Orient*
Grat.	Dio Chrysostom, *Friendship for His Native Land*	JETS	*Journal of the Evangelical Theological Society*
HBT	*Horizons in Biblical Theology*		
Her.	Philo, *Who Is the Heir?*	JGRChJ	*Journal of Greco-Roman Christianity and Judaism*
Hist.	Herodotus, *Histories*	*Joseph*	Philo, *On the Life of Joseph*
HKAT	Handkommentarzum Alten Testament	JRS	*Journal of Roman Studies*
HNTC	Harper's NT Commentaries	JSJ	*Journal for the Study of Judaism in the Persian, Hellenistic, and Roman Periods*
Hom.	Dio Chrysostom, *Homer*		
HTR	*Harvard Theological Review*	JSNT	*Journal for the Study of the New Testament*
HUCA	*Hebrew Union College Annual*		
ICC	International Critical Commentary	JSNTSup	*Journal for the Study of the New Testament: Supplement Series*
Id.	Theocritus, *Idylls*		
IGR	*Inscriptiones Graecae ad res Romanas pertinentes*	JSOT	*Journal for the Study of Old Testament*
ILS	*Inscriptiones Latinae Selectae*	JSPSup	*Journal for the Study of the Pseudepigrapha: Supplement Series*
Imm	*Immanuel*		
Inv.	Cicero, *De Inventione Rhetorica*		

JTI	*Journal of Theological Interpretation*	NSBT	New Studies in Biblical Theology
JTS	*Journal of Theological Studies*	NTOA	Novum Testamentum et Orbis Antiquus
Life	Josephus, *The Life*	NTS	*New Testament Studies*
Mem.	Xenophon, *Memorabilia*	Off.	Cicero, *De Officiis*
Merc. Cond.	Lucian, *Salaried Posts in Great Houses*	OGIS	*Orientis Graeci Inscriptiones Selectae*
MNTC	Moffat New Testament Commentary	Oth.	Plutarch, *Otho*
		Pan.	Pliny the Younger, *Panegyricus*
Mor.	Plutarch, *Moralia*	Phil.	Plutarch, *Philopoemen*
Mos.	Philo, *On the Life of Moses*	Planc.	Cicero, *Pro Plancio*
Nat.	Pliny the Elder, *Natural History*	Plant.	Philo, *On Planting*
Neot	*Neotestamentica*		
NICNT	The New International Commentary on the New Testament	Pol.	Aristotle, *Politics*
		Post.	Philo, *On the Posterity of Cain*
		PRSt	*Perspectives in Religious Studies*
NIDNTT	The New International Dictionary of New Testament Theology	QE	Philo, *Questions and Answers on Exodus*
NIGTC	New International Greek Testament Commentary	Res Gestae	Augustus, *Res Gestae Divi Augusti*
		Resp.	Cicero, *De Republica*
NovT	*Novum Testamentum*	Resp.	Plato, *Republic*
NovTSup	Supplements to Novum Testamentum	Rewards	Philo, *On Rewards and Punishments*
		Rhet.	Aristotle, *Rhetoric*

Rhod.	Dio Chrysostom, *To the People of Rhodes*		ies Monograph Series
RILP	Roehampton Institute London Papers	SPhilo	*Studia Philonica Annual*
		Spec. Laws	Philo, *On the Special Laws*
RTR	*Reformed Theological Review*	ST	*Studia Theologica*
Saec.	Horace, *Carmen Saeculare*	SVTQ	*St. Vladimir's Theological Quarterly*
SBJT	*The Southern Baptist Journal of Theology*	TDNT	*Theological Dictionary of the New Testament*
SBLSP	Society of Biblical Literature Seminar Papers	TynBul	*Tyndale Bulletin*
		Unchangeable	Philo, *That God is Unchangeable*
SBLSymS	Society of Biblical Literature Symposium Series	VC	*Vigiliae Christianae*
		Ven.	Dio Chrysostom, *The Hunter*
SBT	Studies in Biblical Theology	Virt.	Philo, *On the Virtues*
SEG	*Supplementum epigraphicum graecum*	Vit. Apoll.	Philostratus, *Vita Apollonii*
SGBC	Story of God Bible Commentary	VT	*Vetus Testamentum*
SIG	*Sylloge inscriptionum graecarum*	VTSup	Supplements to Vetus Testamentum
Sir	Sirach	War	Josephus, *The Jewish War*
SJOT	*Scandinavian Journal of the Old Testament*	WBC	Word Biblical Commentary
SJT	*Scottish Journal of Theology*	WUNT	Wissenschaftliche Untersuchungenzum Neuen Testament
SNTSMS	Society of New Testament Stud-		

1

Introduction and Methodology

Paul and Royal Christology in Romans 5:1–11

RECENT ARGUMENTS HAVE SUGGESTED that one of the main threads of Paul's Christ-language is royal discourse.[1] This discourse is inspired by Paul's conviction that Jesus is Israel's Messiah and that, by his descent and ascent, he has been publicly revealed as the singular king of both Israel and the world. In his letter to the Romans, Paul introduces Jesus Christ as a descendant of David and as one who has been installed as the son-of-God-in-power by the resurrection from the dead (Rom 1:3–4).[2] Jesus is not only the promised royal Messiah of David's line but he has also been enthroned in power. He is the Lord (κύριος, 1:4, 7) who has entrusted his slave Paul with χάρις ("grace") and apostleship, leading to the

---

1. A broad modern consensus is that Χριστός is more of a proper name than a royal title in Paul. But a growing number of scholars argue that Davidic Messianism is more fundamental to Paul's Christology than this consensus admits and that Χριστός retains its messianic import. Among those who argue that royal ideology is a key thread in Paul are Agamben, *Time That Remains*; Hurtado, "Paul's Messianic Christology"; Jipp, *Christ Is King*; Juel, *Messianic Exegesis*; Novenson, *Christ among the Messiahs*; Smith, *Christ the Ideal King*; Tilling, *Paul's Divine Christology*; Wright, *Climax of the Covenant*; Wright, *Paul and the Faithfulness of God*, 815–36. For another helpful essay on Paul's use of "Christ," see Dahl, "Messiahship of Jesus," 37–47. For a brief discussion of the title "Messiah," see Cullmann, *Christology of the New Testament*, 111–36.

2. In these two verses Paul states his definition of the gospel as the proclamation of the enfleshed, risen, and enthroned king. For a brief reception history of this text, see Jipp, "Ancient, Modern, and Future Interpretations," 241–59. Another helpful discussion can be found in Whitsett, "Son of God, Seed of David," 661–81. For a discussion of Jesus' divine sonship in Romans, see Hurtado, "Jesus' Divine Sonship," 217–33.

obedience of the nations (1:5). This royal depiction of Jesus is also found towards the end of the letter, thus forming an inclusio for the body of the letter (1:1–7 with 15:7–13). In 15:12, Paul invokes Isaiah 11 to declare that Jesus Christ is the root of Jesse who comes as the ruler and the hope of the nations. Jesus is the hope of the destiny of Israel and the nations. His suffering and vindication demonstrate God's faithfulness, whereby God grants him sovereignty over the universe. The christological inclusio of Rom 1:1–7 and 15:7–13 shows Paul's deliberate portrayal of Jesus as the royal Messiah and thereby suggests the intriguing possibility, and perhaps even the likelihood, that the body of Romans also contains messianic discourse.[3]

And indeed some have argued convincingly that the body of Romans is also permeated with royal motifs, language, and concepts.[4] Unlike Adam's dominion, which is characterized by disobedience, sin, and death, Christ's dominion is characterized by obedience, righteousness, and life (5:12–21). His crucifixion is the means by which he conquers sin and death (6:9–10) and secures liberation for humanity (6:11–14). The Messiah alone can rescue humanity "from the body of death" (τοῦ σώματος τοῦ θανάτου, 7:24). Jesus Christ is God's son who identifies with humanity to secure their redemption (8:1–4). God delivers him up to death (8:32); and, because death could not hold him, he is now enthroned at God's right hand (8:34). His victory over suffering, sin, and death guarantees the victory of his followers (8:37; cf. 8:17). Thus Paul's royal ideology is programmatic for his messianic discourse in Romans 5–8 and in the entire letter.[5]

---

3. For further discussion on this inclusio as it relates to Paul's messianic Christology, see Hays, "Christ Prays the Psalms," 122–36; Novenson, "Jewish Messiahs, the Pauline Christ," 357–73; Wagner, "Christ, Servant of Jew and Gentile," 473; Walker, *Paul's Offer*, 167–74.

4. For example, Campbell rightly argues that Romans 8 is "a story of descent by a Father's own Son through obedience to suffering and death" as well as "a story of ascent through resurrection to glorification and heavenly enthronement ... explained by royal messianic theology, and in particular by the Old Testament's enthronement texts, among which Psalm 89 is outstanding" ("Story of Jesus," 97–124, especially 114, 116). Jipp asserts that "Romans 5–8 is essentially a cosmic and apocalyptic development and application of the soteriological significance of Christ's regal identity as set forth in 1:3–4" (*Christ Is King*, 179–97, especially 180). Wright states, "The Messiah himself is one of the main themes of 5–8 as a whole, whose every section ends with a refrain, like a great bell: *through our lord Jesus the Messiah; in the Messiah Jesus*" (*Paul and the Faithfulness of God*, 1012; italics original).

5. In Rom 5–8, Paul uses κύριος 6x in reference to Jesus Christ: 5:1, 11, 21; 6:23;

Introduction and Methodology

We may then ask: Is royal Christology present within Paul's discourse in Rom 5:1–11? Romans 5:1–11 has rightly been viewed as a summary of Paul's preceding argument (1:1—4:25) and a thesis for what follows (5:12—8:39). The argument in these verses is framed by the prepositional phrase "through our Lord Jesus the Messiah" (διὰ τοῦ κυρίου ἡμῶν Ἰησοῦ Χριστοῦ) in 5:1 and 5:11. This framing replicates the same pattern as Paul's christological inclusio for the whole letter (1:1–7 with 15:7–13). Therefore, if Paul is deliberately presenting Jesus as the Davidic Messiah whose eschatological reign incorporates Jews and gentiles, then we might expect the same intention to be prominent in this key passage. This study proposes that Paul's christological discourse in 5:1–11, which he then expands upon in 5:12—8:39, makes better sense when interpreted through the framework of royal benefaction.[6] That is to say, Paul depicts Christ as a royal benefactor whose superior gift delivers, empowers, and sustains his followers.[7] Greco-Roman benefaction may be defined as a system of calculated gift exchange that seeks to enhance social cohesion by the ethic of reciprocity.[8] Seneca states that gift-giving and its rules

---

7:25; 8:39. And he also uses βασιλεύειν ("to reign") in various forms 6x in the same chapters: 5:14, 17 (2x), 21 (2x); 6:12. The only other occurrences of the verb βασιλεύω in Paul's undisputed letters are: 1 Cor 4:8; 15:25 (2x).

6. "Benefactor" is the English rendition of the Greek technical term εὐεργέτης, which is also translated as "euergetism." Although Paul Veyne did not coin the term euergetism, he popularized it in his book *Bread and Circuses*. For a brief history of the term, see Garnsey, "Generosity of Veyne," 164–68. Other technical terms for 'benefactor' include προστάτης, πρόξενος, δεσπότες, ἐπίκουρς, προστασία, προστατεία, εὐεργεσία, and ἐπικουρία. Some of the synonyms for 'benefactor' are φίλος, σωτήρ, κτίστης, πάτηρ; *patronus, patrocinium, amicus, praeses, clientele; praesidium,* and *beneficum*. For a helpful general discussion on εὐεργέτης, see Spicq, *Theological Lexicon*, 107–13.

7. Since the publication of Marcel Mauss's classic work within sociology and anthropology ("Essai sur le Don," 145–279), there has been a growing interest in the theme of benefaction in Pauline letters. Mauss argues that the notion of a "pure gift" is alien to the ancient practice of gift exchange as the gift was somehow inseparable from the giver. For English translation, see Mauss, *Gift*. Apart from the works discussed below in the section on review of literature, some of the recent works that engage the language and metaphor of benefaction and patronage in Paul include Crook, "Divine Benefactions," 9–26; Danker, *Benefactor*; Hendrix, "Benefactor/Patron Networks," 39–58; Horsley, *Paul and Empire*; Malina and Neyrey, *Portraits of Paul*; Martin, *Slavery as Salvation*.

8. There is debate as to whether benefaction is identical to patronage. Broadly speaking, patronage may denote a long-term, inegalitarian social control system in which gifts and favors are exchanged between patrons and clients (Saller, *Personal Patronage*, 1). Many scholars use benefaction and patronage interchangeably and see little or no distinction between them. For instance, Moxnes maintains that benefaction is a form of patronage in the ancient world. In his discussion of Luke's view of God

"constitutes the chief bond of human society" (*Ben.* 1.4.2–4).[9] Aristotle maintains that wealth must be put to work in the form of beneficence, the doing of good (ἡ εὐεργεσία), and that such beneficence may include the preservation and means of life, the bestowal of wealth itself, or providing anything good which may be hard to obtain (*Rhet.* 1.5.7–9). He discusses two forms of benefaction in ancient Greece. The first is the noble individual who provides important benefits for the community as a whole (also known as collective benefaction or euergetism), and the second is the one who exchanges goods and services on an individual level with others who are equals, or nearly so, in status (*Eth. nic.* 4.2.5; 4.3.1). We are mainly concerned with the former, with focus on royal benefaction.

The ideal king is a generous benefactor who is committed to the welfare of his subjects.[10] Julien Smith states that "the Hellenistic monarch's efforts to cast himself as the benefactor of his people was largely successful to the extent that the ideal king came to be viewed as the source of a city's benefits."[11] Dio Chrysostom writes that the good king receives his scepter from Zeus and finds great pleasure in using it for the welfare of his subjects (*1 Regn.* 12–13). Such a king delights in bestowing benefits (*2 Regn.* 26) and governs as a father, with kindness, affection, and protective care (*Hom.* 53:12). Pliny notes in *Panegyricus* for Trajan that the ideal emperor is not necessarily an efficient administrator, but a benefactor and paternal protector (e.g., 2, 21, 28–31, 50). The good king toils endlessly for the sake of his subjects (Pliny, *Pan.* 7). Augustus's *Res*

---

and Jesus, he interchangeably refers to God as "benefactor and patron," "exclusive patron," "benefactor-patron," and "benefactor" ("Patron-Client Relations," 241–70). But Joubert is representative of those who reject such an assimilation of concepts as he argues that "'[p]atron-and-client language' is almost entirely absent from ancient Greek texts to our disposal" (*Paul as Benefactor*, 59). The goal of the present work is not to resolve this debate. As we recognize this ongoing discussion with respect to the extent to which the Roman patronage was adopted in eastern areas of the Mediterranean, we need to remember that "[w]hile in broad historical terms this distinction may be useful, one cannot maintain a strict distinction when one comes to the situation in the Hellenistic cities during the early imperial period" (Pao, *Thanksgiving*, 165–66). Also see Elliott, "Patronage and Clientage," 151. In this work, we will be using the term benefaction (as defined above) while acknowledging that at times we might use it where some would prefer patronage.

9. Unless otherwise noted, the editions and translations consulted for Greek and Roman sources are from the Loeb Classical Library, often with slight modification.

10. See Bringmann, "King as Benefactor," 7–24; Erskine, "Romans as Common Benefactors," 70–87; Stevenson, "Ideal Benefactor," 421–36.

11. Smith, *Christ the Ideal King*, 40.

Gestae recounts his benefactions and services to the Roman people as the emperor portrays himself as a generous benefactor and an effective agent of the *Pax Romana*. Horace praises Augustus's guardianship which has restored plentiful harvests to the fields and eradicated civil war, riots, and hatred (*Odes* 4:15). Arrian writes that Alexander sparingly used money "for his own pleasures, but most liberal in employing it for the benefit of others" (*Anab.* 7.28.3). Among other things Seneca states that the good king ensures that his subjects lack nothing, and adorns them by his kindness (*Ep.* 90:5). Josephus lists several benefactions which Herod made to the cities throughout Syria and Greece, including a Pythian Temple for Rhodes, construction of public works, contribution to civic functions, colonnades and paving for a street in Antioch of Syria, and sponsoring Olympic games (*Ant.* 16:146-49). Philo lists benefaction among the three qualities which "make a government secure from subversion" and win the affection and obedience of the subjects (*Rewards* 97).[12] In brief, the good ruler is generous, kind, and philanthropic.

Benefactions are in turn reciprocated by honoring the benefactor since in Greco-Roman society gifts come with inalienable ties of obligation.[13] Reciprocity is simply a conventional structure of exchange that is necessary for the maintenance of social cohesion as the beneficiaries discharge their obligation to the benefactor by rendering gratitude and loyalty. Reciprocity also consolidates the relative status of the benefactor and the beneficiaries.[14] So at the heart of generosity is the benefactor's

12. The other two qualities are dignity and strictness.

13. For further discussion on the obligations created by gifts, see Hands, *Charities and Social*, 26-48; Bourdieu, *Le Sens Pratique*, 167-231; Bourdieu, "Marginalia," 231-41; Irigaray, "Selections," 190-230.

14. Joubert rightly states, "The person in ancient Graeco-Roman society was a reciprocal being, *homo reciprocus*" ("One Form of Social Exchange," 24; italics original). According to Stegemann and Stegemann there were four main forms of ancient reciprocity: (1) "*Familiäre Reziprozität*," which was operative at the household and clan level, with brotherly love as social form of expression; (2) "*Ausgeglichene Reziprozität*" or egalitarian reciprocity, which was found between friends and neighbors, with hospitality, friendship, and benefaction as social forms of expression; (3) "*Generelle Reziprozität*" or inegalitarian reciprocity, such as found between patrons and clients, or rich and poor, with almsgiving, patronage, religious service, and discipleship as social forms of expression; and (4) "*Negative Reziprozität*," which existed between strangers and enemies, with hospitality and love as social forms of expression (*Urchristliche Sozialgeschichte*, 43). Also see Sahlins who suggests that there were three forms of reciprocity in the ancient world: generalized reciprocity ("selfless"), balanced reciprocity ("commercial"), and negative reciprocity ("self-interested") (*Stone Age Economics*, 191-96).

love of honor as he seeks to maintain his elevated status through publicized reciprocity and ongoing dependency of the subjects.[15] To underline the need for reciprocity, Sophocles states that "it is always one kindness (χάρις) that begets another, and if a man allows the memory of a kindness to slip away, he can no longer be accounted noble" (*AJ*. 522–24). Xenophon writes that Socrates recommends friendships in which one receives favors (εὐεργετούμενον) from honest men and offers favors in return (*Mem.* 2.9.8).[16] Aristotle states that "in the interchange of services, justice in the form of reciprocity is the bond that maintains the association" (*Eth. nic.* 5.5.6). Josephus notes that the king of Ethiopia was under obligation to the king of Egypt as an expression of gratitude (*Ag. Ap.* 1:246). According to Lucian, "(T)he king's most important reward (μισθὸς μέγιστος) is praise, universal fame, reverence for his benefactions, statues, and temples and shrines bestowed on him by his subjects." He adds that such rewards "are payment (μισθοί) for the thought and care which such men evidence in their continual watch over the common weal and its improvement" (*Merc. Cond.* 13). Failure to give appropriate honor to a benefactor is disgraceful, and might be viewed as a manifestation of impiety towards the gods, who are the ultimate benefactors.[17] As Thomas R. Blanton states, the sanctions of the obligation of reciprocity in gift exchange "reside in social disapproval and the weakening or dissolution of social bonds."[18] Thus without reciprocity benefaction would collapse, leading to social disintegration.[19] Honors and expressions of gratitude may be in the form of honorary inscriptions, public praise, social or political support, statues, crowns, and seats of honor among others.

15. Gordon writes that "generosity is one of the subtlest means of maintaining lasting asymmetrical relationships between social unequals" ("From Republic to Principate," 194).

16. The implication here is that one needs to choose friends who would be willing to repay services in full. See Millett, *Lending and Borrowing*, 118. To show that in the ancient world gift-giving was not disinterested, it was not unusual for the giver to remind the receiver to return a favor. Herodotus's Croesus reminded Adrastus of how he had helped him, and then said to Adrastus that he now owed him "a return of good service for the benefits I have done you" (*Hist.* 1:41). Thucydides's Themistocles said to Artaxerxes that "there is a kindness due me" (καί μοι εὐεργεσία ὀφείλεται, *Hist.* 1:137).

17. See Harland, *Associations, Synagogues, and Congregations*, 79; Hoklotubbe, *Civilized Piety*, 118–19.

18. Blanton, *Spiritual Economy*, 3.

19. Mott rightly states that reciprocity is the dynamic factor in the "phenomenon of benefactor and beneficiary relationships" that ensures its social impact ("Power of Giving and Receiving," 60).

Interpreting Rom 5:1-11 within the context of benefaction enables us to provide a coherent interpretation of the text as well as make headway in our understanding of three textual conundrums. These exegetical challenges function as the impetus for further research. The first problem is lexical in nature: Why are benefaction terms and motifs predominant in this passage? Paul speaks of peace, access, boasting, glory, shame, enmity, reconciliation, giving, suffering, hope, love, sacrifice, and "the good." Additionally, χάρις, which is one of the most important technical terms within the Greco-Roman benefaction system, occurs once in 5:2 as well as seven other times in various forms in the rest of the chapter (15 [3x], 16, 17, 20, 21).[20] Χαρ-root words continue to play a determinative role in Romans 6-8, where they occur seven times (6:1, 14, 15, 17, 23; 7:25; 8:32). Likewise, when Paul uses the word βασιλεύειν ("to reign") in connection with χάρις in Romans 5-6, he is not thinking merely of χάρις as a transformative power but as a conquering and renewing agent. The reign of χάρις is the reign of Jesus Christ, whose story culminates with his enthronement (cf. 1:1-4). By using these terminologies, Paul intends to invoke specific cultural symbols in order to accomplish his goal of presenting Jesus Christ as the singular king of Israel and the nations. Thus, there is need for an interpretive framework that adequately accounts for the frequent benefaction language as well as Paul's aim of depicting Jesus Christ's superior reign.

The second question is: What is the relationship between χάρις as used in 5:2a and Jesus Christ's self-sacrifice as described in 5:6-10? Paul states that Jesus Christ is the agent who grants believers access "into this grace" (εἰς τὴν χάριν ταύτην). But how does Christ accomplish this? It appears that this is one of the questions that 5:6-10 addresses. Christ offers his own life as χάρις and thereby ushers his followers into his domain, whereby they can enjoy the benefits of his reign. The prevalent sacrificial imageries in this passage coupled with the use of προσαγωγή ("access")[21] strongly suggests that Paul might be playing upon some aspects of Greco-Roman benefaction practices by depicting Jesus Christ as a royal priestly

---

20. Paul also uses various forms of the synonym δωρεά in 5:15-17 and the motif of περισσεία ("superabundance") in 5:15, 17, 20.

21. The noun προσαγωγή signifies privilege of approach to the royal chamber or to a person of high rank. Xenophon (*Cyr.* 7.5.45) writes about how Cyrus expected his friends to act as intermediaries between him and his supplicants: "Now what I expected all such [supplicants] to do, if any one wanted anything from me, was to get into favor with you as my friends and ask you for an introduction" (προσαγωγῆς).

benefactor who offers his own life as a sacrificial gift.[22] Christ offers this gift, not as a heroic act of reciprocity to the benefactor as would be expected in the ancient world (cf. 5:7), but to sinners and the unworthy as a demonstration of love and commitment. This interpretation illumines our understanding of 8:31–39. God did not spare his own son but gave him up as a sacrifice. Jesus Christ was then raised from the dead, and is now at the right hand of God, where he intercedes for the saints. The reference to Christ being at God's right hand (which suggests a heavenly throne) as well as his intercessory ministry explicitly echo LXX Ps 109:1, 4, where God's royal son is designated priest. Christ's sacrificial death, resurrection, and ascension as well as his enthronement at the right hand of God suggest that he is a king whose mediatorship guarantees eschatological security to his followers, and thereby relieves them of anxieties that might be caused by the future wrath of God. Therefore, in light of Paul's use of προσαγωγή, ὁ ἀγαθός, and sacrificial imagery, this study argues that Paul portrays Christ as a royal benefactor in ways that surprise the Greco-Roman notion of brokerage and the expectation that a beneficiary would be willing to die for the sake of his benefactor.

The final question is: How does Paul define how the believer lives in the realm of χάρις? Differently stated, does Paul view the Messiah's χάρις as obligatory, and if so, then how do believers discharge their obligation to the Messiah? In 5:2–4, Paul describes the relationship between the Messiah's benefaction and suffering even as he defines the shape that reciprocating χάρις takes in suffering. Paul's assertion that suffering accrues benefits that ultimately strengthen hope implies that suffering has a positive role within the domain of χάρις. Paul insists that believers must reciprocate χάρις by "boasting" (καυχᾶσθαι) in suffering. This "boasting" is another way of describing obedient response to Christ's beneficence. Honorable conduct—here defined as "boasting"—in suffering reveals the extent to which believers ought to express allegiance to their divine benefactor. Because Christ rules over the realms of life, suffering, sin, and death, his followers have the certain hope of glory since they faithfully participate in his pattern of dying and rising (5:5; 8:17). They will mightily prevail over every form of adversity (8:35) and conquer mortality because the Spirit of resurrection dwells in them (8:11). Rather than leading to disappointment, reciprocal obedience to Christ in suffering yields benefits in the present life and glory in the eschaton (5:5). It is, therefore, vital to provide a reading that situates

---

22. For a brief essay on the priestly or sacrificial role of the emperor, see Gordon, "Veil of Power," 201–31.

Paul's theology of suffering as found in Romans 5–8 within the context of benefaction since, for Paul, suffering is intricately related to χάρις.

In brief, this work provides a close look at how Paul uses the Greco-Roman royal benefaction system in Rom 5:1–11 as well as 5:12—8:39 to accomplish his theological purpose of portraying Jesus Christ as the supreme royal benefactor so that the Roman believers might faithfully respond to his reign now even as they anticipate glorification. We will consider three related questions. First, what benefaction motifs does Paul use in 5:1–11 to depict Jesus Christ's superior royal benefaction, and how does such a depiction serve as a helpful context for understanding Paul's argument in 5:12—8:39? Second, how does Jesus Christ's benefaction integrate the Greco-Roman royal benefaction system while at the same time offering a variant form of benefaction? Lastly, is the Messiah's benefaction obligatory? If so, what does giving loyalty and obedience to the Messiah entail in suffering?

Review of Literature

Recent scholarship on Rom 5:1–11 as well as scholarship on Paul and benefaction tends to emphasize either a prominent theme in the text or an aspect of benefaction, but no single work has been devoted to investigating whether, and if so, how Paul is seeking to articulate his messianic discourse in Romans 5–8 through the Greco-Roman royal benefaction system. Many commentaries discuss the rhetorical function of 5:1–11 and the themes introduced therein, yet very few pay attention to the pervasive benefaction terminologies. Apart from a few exceptions, pertinent works that consider some aspect of benefaction usually revolve around whether χάρις is obligatory. We can summarize these recent trends on 5:1–11 into five main sub-points: (1) concerns with structure and themes; (2) Paul as benefactor; (3) χάρις as unilateral; (4) χάρις as reciprocal; and (5) χάρις as leading to honor.

Concerns with Structure and Themes

There is general agreement among scholars that the first major section of Romans ends at Rom 4:25 and that Rom 5:1 marks the beginning of the second major movement that runs from 5:1 to 8:39.[23] In this section,

---

23. See Dahl, "Two Notes on Romans 5," 37–48; Byrne, *Romans*, 162–64; Cranfield,

5:1–11 both recapitulates the preceding argument and previews the themes for 5:12—8:39.[24] The view that 5:1–11 is a thesis statement for 5:12—8:39 provides the rationale for examining how Paul expands upon the themes of the former in the latter. There is, however, no consensus with regard to the main theme(s) of 5:1–11. The commonly suggested themes include hope,[25] reconciliation,[26] peace,[27] and the implications of God's righteousness for the individual believer.[28] So while there is general agreement regarding the function of 5:1–11 as a transitional and thesis passage, there is still need for a study that explores how readers familiar with the Greco-Roman benefaction system might have understood Paul's royal discourse.

Paul as Benefactor

An ongoing debate in Pauline studies is the extent to which Paul adapts and adopts the ancient practice of gift exchange. Does he present himself to his communities as benefactor, and if so, what are the implications? In a monograph that was published as the culmination of a doctoral dissertation, Gerald W. Peterman examines Jewish and Greco-Roman sources pertinent to monetary giving and receiving as he contends that, for Paul,

---

Critical and Exegetical Commentary, 253–54; Käsemann, *Commentary on Romans*, ix–x; Moo, *Epistle to the Romans*, 290–95; Schreiner, *Romans*, 245–49.

24. A related view is that Rom 5:11 marks the end of the first major section of the letter. A representative of those who see the passage as the conclusion to the first major section is Elliott, *Rhetoric of Romans*, 226–27. For the argument that the passage is transitional and a preview of succeeding themes, see Sanders, *Paul and Palestinian Judaism*, 486–87; Kaye, *Argument of Romans*, 1–13; McDonald, "Romans 5:1–11," 81–96; Longenecker, *Epistle to the Romans*, 538–66. For an overview of why 5:1—8:39 should be considered as a unit, see Longenecker, "Focus of Romans," 64–66. Dahl rightly argues for the close thematic connection between Rom 5:1–11 and 8:1–39, with the former stating the themes and the latter providing a fuller exposition of the themes ("Two Notes on Romans 5," 37–48). But his assertion that Romans 6–7 are digressions necessitated by Paul's anticipation of misunderstandings of his statement about the law in 5:20–21 is disputable on many grounds. For instance, the divine χάρις enacted through the death and resurrection of Jesus Christ is a key pillar that holds together the key themes of the second major section of Romans (5:15–21; 6:1, 14–17, 23; 7:25; 8:32). Similarly, Paul's discourse on sin and death, the two leading cosmic powers which Christ subdues, can be traced throughout these four chapters. There is, therefore, hardly any justification for treating the middle chapters as digressions.

25. Schreiner, *Romans*, 253–58; Moo, *Epistle to the Romans*, 295–414.

26. Martin, "Reconciliation," 36–48; Pulcini, "In Right Relationship," 83.

27. Byrne, *Romans*, 163; Cranfield, *Critical and Exegetical Commentary*, 255.

28. Dunn, *Romans 1–8*, 242–43.

gospel proclamation is an act of beneficence, which implies that his converts are spiritually indebted to him.[29] Although he is free to request repayment (Phlm 17–19; 2 Cor 6:13), Paul often refuses to enter into contracts of social obligations which might hinder the propagation of the gospel. In a similar vein, Stephan Joubert argues that as Paul seeks to help the poor believers in Judea he assumes the social status of a benefactor.[30] Yet, in Rom 15:25–33 Paul, in anticipation of a negative response to his collection, emphasizes sacrificial giving instead of the common practice that gifts must be reciprocated with counter gifts. Whereas Peterman and Joubert are not concerned with Paul's royal discourse as we are, their observation that Paul does not uncritically embrace the Greco-Roman benefaction system is relevant for the current project as it resonates with our assertion that Paul depicts the Messiah's benefaction in ways that are both conventional and yet surprising.

Χάρις as Unilateral

Apart from the question as to whether Paul is a benefactor, any study on gift exchange in Paul must investigate how he uses the term χάρις. While this study aims to show that for Paul divine χάρις evokes an obligatory relational response marked by enactment of the Messiah's rule, James R. Harrison[31] and Judith Gundry[32] are representative of those who assert that χάρις is unilateral. Harrison states that God's "free," "sovereign," "unilateral," and "unmerited" grace is given to the unworthy and ungrateful. God's gift of righteousness in Jesus Christ the "dishonoured and impoverished Benefactor," supersedes the beneficence of Augustus, provides better security for the beneficiaries, and inaugurates the eschatological reign of grace.[33] Although Harrison is right to underscore the fact that God's gift is incongruous, he fails to sufficiently address whether χάρις is obligatory. He acknowledges that Paul endorses the conventions that the beneficiary is obliged to "respond worthily of the Benefactor,"[34] yet his discussion becomes confusing and unclear when he also states that

29. Peterman, *Paul's Gift*.
30. Joubert, *Paul as Benefactor*.
31. Harrison, *Paul's Language of Grace*.
32. Gundry, "'Or Who Gave First to Him,'" 171–95.
33. Harrison, *Paul's Language of Grace*, 287, 226–34.
34. Harrison, *Paul's Language of Grace*, 287.

Paul's soteriology and pneumatology eschew loyalty oaths.[35] Harrison's argument, therefore, minimizes the value of χάρις as a relational thing that demands unwavering commitment to the giver.[36]

According to Gundry, Paul depicts God as a sovereign benefactor who does not reciprocate as is expected of human benefaction since God's gift is *free*. This portrayal is a critique of the gentile believers' view of God founded on the ethic of reciprocity, according to which gentile believers might have thought of themselves as worthy clients of God. Paul needs to take this critical stance against the ethic of reciprocity since it leads to gentile believers' boasting over Jews. Gundry's argument seems to suggest that Paul rejects reciprocity in its entirety, but this is highly disputable, especially in light of the need for obedient response to χάρις. Moreover, Paul explicitly uses the language of obligation (ὀφειλέτης) in Rom 8:12 as he urges the Romans to live appropriately as those who have received the Holy Spirit. Likewise, Paul characterizes his proclamation of the gospel as an obligation (1:14) and states that his gentile converts are under obligation to the Jerusalem church for the spiritual blessings they have received (15:27). So it seems more accurate to assert that Paul encourages a different kind of "boasting," namely, confidence in Christ's benefaction that transforms Jews and gentiles and enables them to participate in his eternal dominion.

Χάρις as Reciprocal

Unlike Harrison and Gundry, Troels Engberg-Pedersen[37] and John M. G. Barclay[38] convincingly argue that χάρις is reciprocal. Engberg-Pedersen

---

35. Harrison, *Paul's Language of Grace*, 241. Harrison's argument here seems completely opposite of Bates, *Salvation by Allegiance Alone*.

36. Harrison writes that "Paul spotlights the fact that the grace of Christ expected no requital. The humiliation and self-sacrifice of the incarnation is totally other-centred" (*Paul's Language of Grace*, 266). Yet this is a misconstrual of how χάρις functions in Greco–Roman society. The fact that as Christ offers χάρις he looks to the interests of others does not imply that he is less concerned with magnifying his own glory as humanity responds to his gift by giving obedience to him. Similarly, incongruity does not nullify reciprocity. As Barclay writes, "The gift of God in Jesus Christ has established not liberation from authority or demand, but a new allegiance, a new responsibility, a new 'slavery' under the rule of grace. Although not itself an imperative, grace is imperatival: it bears within itself the imperative to obey" ("Under Grace, 60").

37. Engberg-Pedersen, "Gift-Giving and God's Charis," 95–111.

38. Barclay, *Paul and the Gift*. Also see Barclay, "Under Grace," 59–76.

claims that reading Paul in close analogy with Seneca's *De Beneficiis* shows that to think of χάρις in Paul as an unconditionally given and received gift is misleading because it undermines personal interests that characterize divine-human relationship. God, who wants to save human beings and who wants to be honored, expects human beings to react to his grace with trust, hope, and love.[39] Engberg-Pedersen's thesis is very persuasive as it offers a more comprehensive and accurate interpretation of texts such as Rom 2:7–10, where Paul seems to imply that eschatological judgment will be based on works—which shows that "works" are just as important as "faith." We will build on Engberg-Pedersen's argument by relating reciprocity to Paul's royal discourse, with a close look at the relationship between χάρις and suffering in 5:1–11 (and 8:17–39).

Like Engberg-Pedersen, Barclay asserts that in ancient times gifts were always relational. Paul in Galatians and Romans demonstrates that the divine gift in Jesus Christ is the ultimate incongruous gift that radically transforms Jews and gentiles.[40] In his discussion of Rom 5:5–11, Barclay characterizes God's gift in Jesus Christ as a "strange and nonsensical phenomenon" due to its incongruity.[41] The Christ-gift is given in the "abject worthlessness" of the recipients.[42] This gift evokes a relational reciprocation of obedience. That is to say, the Christ-gift is "*unconditioned* (based on no prior conditions) but not *unconditional* (carrying no subsequent demands)."[43] A question that Barclay inadequately addresses is how believers enact χάρις in suffering. His only note on Paul's theology of suffering as found in Romans 5 reads, "Despite suffering, hope is secure, because the heart, transformed by the gift of the Spirit (cf. 2:15, 29), has been filled with the love of God."[44] The suffering of believers is integral to Paul's theology of χάρις, and therefore demands an elaborate discussion. In fact, the way Paul writes about suffering suggests that it is an indispensable component of believers' hope. That is part of the reason why we will contend that those who have been brought into the realm of χάρις and who therefore participate in Christ's pattern of death and

---

39. Engberg-Pedersen, "Gift-Giving and God's Charis," 105.

40. For further discussion on χάρις as a re-creative power in Christians, see Wetter, *Charis*, 195–98.

41. Barclay, *Paul and the Gift*, 478.

42. Barclay, "Under Grace," 59.

43. Barclay, "Under Grace," 64.

44. Barclay, *Paul and the Gift*, 477.

resurrection, must demonstrate their allegiance to their supreme benefactor by responding appropriately in suffering.

Χάρις as Leading to Honor

In addition to the studies mentioned above, there are also concerns with the relationship between χάρις and status. The main question here is: How does the divine gift affect the status of believers before God? Raymond Pickett maintains that Paul's description of Christ's death in Rom 5:1–11 should be interpreted against the backdrop of the social institution of patronage and the mythic pattern of honor.[45] Humanity is at enmity with God due to dishonor, which in turn incurs God's wrath. God, who is the divine patron, solves this human predicament through the death of Jesus Christ so that those who have been justified might gain a new status of glory. Ultimately, the ethic of reciprocity collapses "because the gift which God gives in the death of Christ is Godself."[46] Pickett rightly emphasizes God's faithfulness to humanity as demonstrated through the death of Jesus Christ, but his assertion that the divine gift collapses the ethic of reciprocity not only leads to a less persuasive account of how believers ought to enact Christ's rule but also fails to recognize that for Paul Christ's χάρις is an obliging, superior gift. While Pickett is right to maintain that those who are justified gain a new status of glory, he does not go a step further to look at how this honorable status is only realized through being mapped onto Christ's trajectory of dying and rising through the gift of the Spirit. Similarly, his assertion that the letter of Romans is more theocentric than christocentric leads to a less robust engagement with Paul's christological discourse. For instance, although he recognizes that "in his blood" (ἐν τῷ αἵματι αὐτοῦ, 5:9) points to the "sacrificial significance of Christ's death,"[47] he neither considers how this might relate to Christ's mediatorial role nor what light it might shed on our interpretation of 5:2. Because he is less interested in Paul's christological agenda, Pickett does not discuss how Christ's pattern of death and resurrection shapes the believer's boastful allegiance in sufferings.

In a sharp critique of Jacques Derrida's claim that the gift is an impossibility since it can only exist where there is no exchange, reciprocity,

---

45. Pickett, "Death of Christ," 726–39.
46. Pickett, "Death of Christ," 739.
47. Pickett, "Death of Christ," 733.

and debt,⁴⁸ Blanton maintains that the gift of salvation produces affective bonds between believers and their God, who grants them the gift of status through Jesus Christ. The donor and the donees enter into a persistent circle of reciprocity whereby "worshippers give of themselves because their savior first gave of himself."⁴⁹ Within this context of gift exchange, Paul's proclamation of the gospel renders symbolic gifts of Israel's God accessible while those offered to Paul in return could be viewed as gifts to Israel's God.⁵⁰ Blanton is right to assert that gifts are relational and that they produce ties between the parties involved. His point on how the divine gift produces positional status of honor and prestige for the recipients is persuasive, yet his discussion here with regard to Romans is only limited to 13:1–7 as well as Paul's relation with Phoebe (16:1–2). This means that, among other things, his work does not discuss how the Christ-gift enables believers to come into the royal domain whereby they can enjoy the benefits of Christ's rule.

Summary of Recent Scholarship

The preceding review of literature shows that no recent scholarship has applied theological exegesis and sociological studies to Paul's christological discourse as expressed through royal benefaction in Rom 5:1–11, and how that discourse operates in 5:12—8:39. A number of these works discuss several aspects of gift-giving in Paul, including (1) whether or not divine χάρις demands reciprocity; (2) Paul's role as a benefactor; (3) the privileged status of the beneficiaries of χάρις; and (4) the incongruous nature of divine χάρις. Yet, none of these works specifically examine how Paul might be intending to portray Jesus Christ as the supreme royal benefactor. This means that important questions remain regarding (1) the significance of the presence of benefaction language and metaphors,

---

48. Derrida, "Time of the King," 121–47. Derrida embraces the notion of a "pure" gift as he postulates that the gift is "aneconomic" since it falls outside of the circle of reciprocal exchange that governs the marketplace. He writes, "If the other *gives* me back or *owes* me or has to give me back what I gave him or her, there will not have been a gift" (129; italics original). Many have rightly pointed out that Derrida's view of economy is narrow as it limits it to circulation and mercantile exchange.

49. Blanton, *Spiritual Economy*, 4.

50. By symbolic gifts Blanton is referring to gifts mediated by the power of a divine being.

(2) how divine benefaction reverses the status of Christ's followers, and (3) Paul's argument on what reciprocity entails for Christ's followers.

The Argument

This study argues that Paul portrays Jesus Christ as the supreme royal benefactor whose commitment to his followers guarantees their eternal honorable status before God and demands faithful response to his rule even in suffering. Believers reciprocate divine benefaction by enacting the rule of Christ. That is to say, those who have accepted the Messiah's χάρις subsequently recognize his lordship over every aspect of human life and seek to remain loyal and obedient to him as their supreme ruler. In general, there are at least four components of benefaction: generosity, discrimination, status, and reciprocity. The ideal ruler is indeed generous, yet he must also judiciously identify worthy (ἄξιοι) recipients of his good deeds (Cicero, *Off.* 1:42). In contrast, Paul shows that Christ offers a non-calculating and indiscriminate benefaction to all people. Social, moral, or ethnic worth and the ability to offer counter-gifts of value do not form the basis of Christ's act of kindness.[51] Similarly, benefactors are usually anxious for honor and maintenance of status, but Paul demonstrates that Christ willingly shares in the disgrace of humanity to reverse their dishonorable status. Due to this reversal, believers now enjoy an unbroken intimacy and friendship with God even as the gift of the Spirit grants them assurance of deliverance from the eschatological wrath. Paul also shares in the Greco-Roman convention that χάρις demands reciprocity.[52] As believers participate in Christ's pattern of dying and rising they enact the rule of Christ by boasting in suffering, which is designed to yield eternal dividends. Believers faithfully enact Christ's rule now even in affliction since suffering, as an inevitable reality within the domain of χάρις, strengthens hope rather than jeopardizes their glorious status before God.

---

51. See Barclay, *Paul and the Gift*, 72–73. Barclay rightly notes that in the ancient world gifts are given to "suitable, worthy, or appropriate recipients." In another essay, Barclay describes the Christ-gift as "the shocking, and in ancient terms bizarre, fact" due to its incongruity ("Under Grace," 64). Also helpful here is Mott, "Power of Giving and Receiving," 60.

52. To reciprocate the Messiah's benefaction is to respond appropriately as the Messiah's followers. In other words, believers' reciprocity is their grateful, loyal, fitting, and transformative participation in the Messiah's rule.

In sum, there are at least eight ways in which Paul portrays Jesus Christ as a royal benefactor in Rom 5:1–11: First, he establishes peace and reconciliation (5:1, 10–11). Second, he provides access into his royal presence whereby his followers can now enjoy the benefits of his reign (5:2). Third, he gives gifts (5:1–10). Fourth, he brings boasting (5:2–5, 11). Fifth, he offers sacrifice (5:6–10). Sixth, he promises immortality and an honorable status (5:2, 4, 9). Seventh, he brings deliverance (5:6–8). Lastly, he transforms the character of his followers (5:3–4). Yet as much as there are parallels between Christ's benefaction and what we find in Greco-Roman society, there are also striking discontinuities, which suggest that Christ is not just another ruler in the Greco-Roman sense. There are at least five surprising elements of Christ's benefaction. First, Jesus Christ offers his own life as a gift. He is both the gift and the giver. Second, unlike the ideal Greco-Roman ruler who judiciously identifies the recipients of his good deeds, Paul shows that Christ offers a non-calculating and indiscriminate benefaction to all people. In fact, Christ would be termed as an unwise and wasteful benefactor who sows his seed in "worn-out and unproductive soil" (Seneca, *Ben* 1.1.2). His gift is indeed unfitting. Third, Christ offers this gift, not as a heroic act of reciprocity to the good benefactor as would be expected in the ancient world (cf. Rom 5:7), but to sinners and the unworthy as a demonstration of love and commitment. Fourth, whereas benefactors are usually anxious for honor and maintenance of status, Paul demonstrates that Christ willingly shares in the disgrace, weakness, and fleshly existence of humanity to reverse their disgraceful status. One may argue that with Christ's benefaction comes democratization of honor, whereby rather than being limited to the emperor and the elite, all followers of Christ are assured of eternal honorable status before God through participation in the Messiah's resurrection life and rule.

Lastly, Christ's benefaction transforms believers' view of suffering. Christ offers his gift to the weak and godless, and then designs suffering for shaping their character so that through suffering they might attain true virtue. Christ's followers, who were formerly weak, dead, and godless, have now been brought into the realm of virtue, into the domain of Christ.[53] We may then ask: How do believers grow in piety in the face of suffering, and how do they honor their Lord when they are afflicted? By the Holy Spirit Christ maps his followers onto his pattern of death and

---

53. For a helpful discussion on the relationship between benefaction and piety, see Hoklotubbe, *Civilized Piety*, 1–54.

resurrection, and as they participate in this pattern they enact the rule of Christ by boasting in suffering. Paul views suffering, not negatively as something that impugns Christ's love and commitment to his followers, but as something to anticipate in light of Christ's story. In other words, for Paul, χάρις is indeed incongruous yet incongruity does not nullify reciprocity; instead, χάρις demands obedient response. Those who accept χάρις must live in ways that are befitting their new identity in Christ. The shape that this appropriate conduct or obedient response takes in suffering is not only confident assurance in the lordship of Christ over the realms of life, sin, suffering, and death but also the unwavering conviction that Christ is able to transform character and strengthen hope through adversity.

Plan of Study

The methodology applied in this study is a multidisciplinary comparative study involving both socio-historical and theological analyses. We use comparative analysis in this work with the understanding that contextual (or background) studies examine the extant literature of Greco-Roman society and Second Temple Judaism in order to reconstruct as best we can the values, culture, beliefs, and worldview of the people so that we may have a better understanding of the Scriptures.[54] Jonathan A. Linebaugh writes, "Texts look different when they are allowed to talk" as familiar passages become "strange and come alive."[55] One of the premises of contextual studies is that the meaning of the text is inextricably embedded in how the text interacts with its socio-historical context. Texts are cultural artifacts whose meaning may not be apparent to those who read them hundreds of years after composition. Because no text is composed in a historical vacuum, it is necessary to investigate how the author might be interacting with his contemporary values and worldview. Contextual study not only helps us to guard against anachronism but it also helps us to uphold the integrity of the text as a product of its own time and culture.[56] The

---

54. Bakhtin articulates the need for comparative studies when he writes, "The text lives only by coming into contact with another text . . . Only at the point of this contact between texts does a light flash, illuminating both the posterior and anterior, joining a given text to a dialogue" ("Toward a Methodology," 162).

55. Linebaugh, *God, Grace, and Righteousness*, 20.

56. In essence, reading the NT is a cross-cultural experience that is often exciting and yet challenging. Rohrbaugh asserts, "Understanding another culture is never easy.

Bible and other ancient texts are bound to their respective cultures. The interpreter therefore needs to study the culture of an ancient text and carefully evaluate how the author's discourse might be engaging various social structures, metaphors, idioms, and lexemes. By its very nature, comparative study juxtaposes data from the ancient world with the biblical text in order to assess how the ancient lens might illumine our reading of the Scriptures. In this work, we are mainly interested in how understanding the Greco-Roman royal benefaction system might illuminate our reading of Paul's royal discourse as found in the letter of Romans.

It is needless to state that there is hardly any monolithic culture. But as we will see, there is a consistent portrait of the ancient Mediterranean ideal ruler as a generous benefactor who demonstrates his commitment to the welfare of the people by giving gifts. The people are in turn expected to respond by giving gratitude and loyalty. The ancient authors that we will examine in the next two chapters sometimes emphasize different aspects of the benefaction system depending on their respective sociopolitical agenda, but they all agree that a reign is successful to the extent that it is marked by the ruler's liberality and the people's reciprocity.

There is a close relationship between Paul's royal discourse and the Greco-Roman social structure of benefaction. This relationship between theology and sociology implies that Paul actively participates in his social milieu even as he variously utilizes social structures therein to accomplish his theological agenda. Acknowledging Paul's embeddedness within the fabric of Greco-Roman society does not suggest that he uncritically embraces its structures. What is the theological basis for Paul's continuities and discontinuities with the values of Greco-Roman society? The extent to which Paul endorses or deviates from contemporary social norms is determined by his allegiance to Jesus Christ and his commitment to forming churches that are rooted in the gospel of God's son. At times there is explicit continuity between Paul's discourse and what we find in the ancient literature. For instance, when Paul portrays the Messiah as a gift-giver, he endorses the Greco-Roman portrait of the ideal ruler as a gift-giver. Similarly, Paul's argument that those who have

---

Not only does one have much new to learn, but also one frequently grows uneasy when one finally realizes that one's own familiar and much-loved culture is not the standard for all humanity. As anxiety over societal differences mounts, a profoundly unpleasant culture shock often sets in" ("Introduction," 2). The implication here is that when reading the NT, culture shock is inevitable if we recognize that it was not written by modern authors to modern readers.

received the Messiah's χάρις must live in a manner worthy of their identity in Christ (cf. Rom 16:2; 2 Cor 6:1; Phil 1:27; 1 Thess 2:12) is parallel to the Greco-Roman convention that χάρις bears inextricable ties of loyalty. Recognizing continuities implies that the text does not *always* have to be polemical; it is not always necessary for the authors of the Bible to be arguing against a set of assumptions so that their work might be regarded as sacred writings. Similarities do not detract from the theological nature of the biblical text. Paul can creatively incorporate or adapt the prevailing values without compromising loyalty to the Messiah.

Yet there are times when Paul surprises his readers by subverting the Greco-Roman value system.[57] This happens when Paul overturns the prevailing values by defining a counter-value system for his readers. Subversion is often necessary because unless human systems are brought to conformity to the redemptive power of the Messiah, they may not only be abusive and oppressive but they are also prone to distort the truth due to human rebellion and proclivity to sin. The new value system that Paul admonishes is founded on his conviction that Jesus is the Messiah and that by virtue of his death, resurrection, and enthronement, God's eschatological kingdom has been inaugurated. Those who have received the Messiah's χάρις have been brought into the realm of his dominion that has a different set of values. This means that because the new value system is often contrary to the prevailing culture, the readers must view reality in ways that might appear radical, strange, bizarre, or even nonsensical. The inversion of values points to the author's conviction that the Christ-gift has established the supreme way of living and that the readers' worldview must be aligned with their identity as loyal followers of the Messiah. An important aspect of the ancient benefaction system that Paul subverts is the belief that gifts should be selectively bestowed based on the worthiness of the beneficiaries. Virtue is rewarded with gifts while impiety is punished by withholding gifts. But Paul declares that the Messiah offers an indiscriminate benefaction to Jews and gentiles. No one can lay claim to the Messiah's benefaction based on some pre-existing moral, social, religious, ethnic, or biological values because the entire human race is morally base and "under sin" (Rom 3:9). The implication of this subversion of the criteria for worth is that believers must accept and serve each other, not based on some external human standards, but based on

---

57. For a brief survey of how Paul rejects Greco-Roman culture, see Johnson, *Among the Gentiles*, 2–9.

their common identity in Christ as those who have been liberated by the Messiah's indiscriminate gift.

It is therefore important to pay close attention to similarities and differences between the biblical text and other ancient literature.[58] Our task then is two-fold. First, we will describe the ancient system of royal benefaction and the ethic of reciprocity that sustains it. Second, we will read Rom 5:1–11 (and 5:12—8:39) through the lens of the Greco-Roman royal benefaction system to determine continuities and discontinuities. We will proceed in this interpretive task with the awareness that to understand the socio-theological relationship in Rom 5:1–11, we need a close examination of Paul's argument and a study of the economy of Greco-Roman society as seen through the phenomenon of royal benefaction.

At the exegetical level, a close examination of Paul's christological discourse demands that we investigate how the social and economic history of the Greco-Roman benefaction system lends insights into Rom 5:1–11. To this effect, our investigation embraces what Adolf Schlatter calls perceptive observation with "wide-open eyes and the sort of wholehearted surrender which perceives that with which it is presented."[59] Seeing what is in the text means that this project takes the descriptive task seriously. Additionally, we will also proceed hermeneutically with the conviction that the text in question is a theological composition that demands a response of its readers.

A pitfall that one needs to avoid is a totalizing reading that attempts to collapse everything in the text under the rubric of a single framework or paradigm. There is, of course, no single interpretive paradigm that can exhaust everything in a passage. A helpful paradigm needs to be simple even as it also makes room for exceptions. This methodology helps us to

---

58. Some of the recent works that examine continuities and discontinuities between the biblical text and other ancient literature include Barclay, "Unnerving Grace," 91–110; Dodson, *"Powers" of Personification*; Linebaugh, *God, Grace, and Righteousness*; Wells, *Grace and Agency in Paul*; McFarland, *God and Grace*. Barclay reads Rom 9:6–18 in conversation with the Wisdom of Solomon and concludes that "in contrast to *Wisdom*, with which he shares so much, Paul propounds a quite bizarre notion of Israel's story . . . What has twisted Paul's theology into this strange shape is his understanding of a 'gift' that has redefined the meaning of χάρις and ἔλεος and defies explanation or rationale" ("Unnerving Grace," 110). Barclay's argument is helpful because it rightly implies that continuities and discontinuities are inevitable due to the author's theological basis and hermeneutical rationale. For Paul, the Christ-event is the overarching and groundbreaking phenomenon through which he rereads his Jewish heritage and evaluates the contemporary culture.

59. Schlatter, "Theology of the New Testament," 121.

avoid this pitfall by drawing attention to benefaction motifs and metaphors as found in various ancient sources. Some of the key benefaction terms are χάρις, worth, honor/shame, peace, and friendship. Similarly, such concepts as privilege of approach and appropriate response also characterize benefaction. All these terms and concepts are present in Rom 5:1–11 as well as 5:12—8:39. As Paul writes in the Greco-Roman social context, there is every likelihood that his readers, who inhabit the same social context, would recognize that he is employing benefaction language and that his christological discourse presents Jesus Christ as the supreme royal benefactor whose followers must align themselves with his royal agenda.

Benefaction is a part of Paul's lived reality and an invaluable resource for his theologizing.[60] To substantiate our assertion that royal discourse as expressed through royal benefaction is a central interpretive framework for Rom 5:1–11, which previews the themes for 5:12—8:39, this introductory chapter will be followed by chapters 2 and 3 on contextual investigation. Chapter 2 will focus on Greco-Roman sources including Aristotle, Cicero, Seneca, Dio Chrysostom, Pliny the Younger, and epigraphic evidence. Chapter 3 will look at the theme of royal benefaction in Jewish writings, with special attention to the Old Testament, Ben Sira, Philo, and Josephus. The goal of these chapters is to describe the system

---

60. The interpretive framework used in this work is to some extent contrary to that suggested by Downs, "Is God Paul's Patron?," 129–56. Unlike those who contend that benefaction (or patronage) is a helpful lens for interpreting Paul's letters, Downs argues that "patronage is an unsuitable framework when it is applied to Paul's understanding of divine-human relations because appropriations of this model misconstrue some important things both about patronage and about Pauline theology" ("Is God Paul's Patron?," 132). He maintains that Paul avoids the terminology of patronage when discussing human and divine activity, and instead uses the metaphor of "father" to refer to God (Rom 1:7; 1 Cor 1:3; 2 Cor 1:2; Gal 1:3; Phil 1:2; Phlm 3). This metaphor of fatherhood "functions to frame the identity and character of God outside the Greco-Roman patronage" ("Is God Paul's Patron?," 132). But these assertions are problematic on many accounts. First, "Father" is an honorarium commonly applied to benefactors in Greco-Roman society. This suggests that methodologically—and bearing in mind that Paul is an apostle to the gentiles—we cannot exclusively limit the meaning Paul attaches to this title to its Jewish context. For a helpful discussion here, see Stevenson, "Ideal Benefactor," 421–36. Second, Paul in Rom 2:4 and 10:12 explicitly states that God is a generous benefactor, bestowing his riches on all who call on him. Finally, Crook rightly asserts that failure to engage the imagery and language of benefaction in Paul's letters undermines Paul's work since for Paul the imagery and language of benefaction and patronage is "more often than not a seamless part of Paul's epistolary discourse" ("Divine Benefactions," 9).

of royal benefaction and to demonstrate that gift-giving is discriminatory, obligatory, and a means of guarding status. The ideal ruler expresses generosity by providing medical services and reliefs, building cities, maintaining peace, supplying grain, sponsoring games, helping the city in time of upheaval, and lowering market price of commodities in time of need, among other efforts to help the populace. The beneficiaries are in turn obliged to reciprocate by offering gratitude, honor, and praise. Cicero, for example, admonishes that those who have been shown affection must be prepared to do most for him who loves them most. He adds that "if there shall be obligations already incurred, so that kindness is not to begin with us, but to be requited, still greater diligence, it seems, is called for; for no duty is more imperative than that of proving one's gratitude" (*Off.* 1:47). Although honor could take various forms, including counter-gifts, statues, front seats at public events, wreaths, and public decrees, it is the inscription of honor on stone or metal that immortalizes it as a public record of the people's gratitude and as a confirmation of the elevated status of the benefactor. Dio writes, "For the pillar, the inscription, and being set up in bronze are regarded as a high honor by noble men" (*Rhod.* 20). Inscriptions could be autobiographical (*OGIS* 383; *IGR* 3:159; *SIG* 814) or biographical (*OGIS* 90, 666; *SIG* 760; *SEG* 6:672). Augustus's *Res Gestae*, written both in Greek and Latin and posted in Ancyra and Pisidian Antioch and Apollonia, is a famous inscription that celebrates Augustus's benefactions, piety, and honors. Likewise, Augustus's accomplishments as savior and benefactor are celebrated across Asia Minor within the Priene Calendar Inscription (9 BCE), which is written in both Latin and Greek. The public display of inscriptions in places such as temples, marketplaces, or theaters is both a means of honoring benefactors and a strategic way of exerting pressure on them to offer more gifts.[61]

Chapters 4–6 form the core of this study as they discuss how Paul is using benefaction in Romans 5–8 to portray Jesus Christ as messianic king. Chapter 4 examines Rom 5:1–11 to demonstrate that Paul uses the conventional Greco-Roman cultural script of benefaction to make at least three related points: (1) Jesus Christ offers a non-calculating gift to the entire human race; (2) Jesus Christ's benefaction reverses the dishonorable status of the beneficiaries; and (3) those who have been brought into the realm of χάρις must reciprocate appropriately by enacting the

---

61. Rajak, "Benefactors," 308. Rajak observes that "the honors were a not-too-subtle statement to the donor that he had a reputation that could be kept up only by further benefaction."

lordship of Christ even in suffering. Chapter 5 examines how some of the benefaction themes introduced in Rom 5:1–11 are expanded upon in Rom 5:12—8:39. Specifically, it discusses Christ's reign over sin and death, the Holy Spirit and the status of believers as God's sons, and sharing in the Messiah's suffering. The final chapter will provide theological synthesis and conclusion by returning to the questions raised at the beginning of the study and summarizing the insights gained.

2

Royal Benefaction in the Greco-Roman Context

ONE OF THE CULTURAL scripts that Paul draws upon to construct his own royal Christology is the practice of gift-giving as found in the ancient system of royal benefaction. A close examination of how this system works and how ancient rulers use it to advance their aims will not only reveal Paul's familiarity with it but also enable us to gain further insight into resolving some of the textual conundrums in Rom 5:1–11.[1] Although we do not have any means by which to determine with certainty how Paul's original readers might have interpreted his discourse, given the prevalence of royal benefaction motifs within Romans 5–8, it is plausible that because they inhabited the same socio-historical context they interpreted his kingship discourse through the lens of royal benefaction. The close relationship between Paul's christological agenda and the benefaction system suggests that contemporary readers would benefit from using royal benefaction as an interpretive framework for Rom 5:1–11 (as well as 5:12—8:39).

Benefaction is a system of selective gift exchange that seeks to enhance social cohesion by the ethic of reciprocity. Broadly speaking, a gift may be defined as a voluntary bestowal of favor upon a significant individual or social group that in turn is obligated to reciprocate by honoring the benefactor.[2] There is a social convention that rulers

---

1. For a helpful discussion on good king *topoi* in Greco-Roman literature, see De Blois, "Traditional Virtues," 166–76; Walker, *Paul's Offer*, 91–140.

2. See Barclay, *Paul and the Gift*, 33.

possess an elevated status that obliges them to confer favors. The ideal ruler promotes the welfare of his subjects by providing medical services, overcoming enemies, building cities, constructing temples, maintaining peace, supplying grain, sponsoring games, renovating public buildings, remitting taxes and debts, and lowering market price of commodities in time of need. Rulers are responsible for undertaking these duties because the gods have entrusted them with great resources and power in order to benefit humanity. In turn, the beneficiaries must show loyalty, gratitude, and honor to their ruler. J. E. Lendon rightly states, "The Roman emperor and his subjects inhabited a world articulated in terms of honour and honouring, reciprocity and deference."[3] Barclay observes that the norms of reciprocation "were too deeply embedded, too obvious, and too incalculable for legal purposes" so that they became "the everyday etiquette of social communication as well as the formulaic language of civic proclamation."[4] The good ruler discharges his obligation by bestowing gifts while the subjects discharge their obligation by honoring their ruler. The ethic of reciprocity thus simultaneously confirms the elevated status of the benefactor as well as the dependent status of the beneficiaries. This ethic, whose leitmotif is gratitude, is the key pillar that sustains gift-giving and thereby enhances social cohesion.

The goal of the next two chapters is to describe the system of royal benefaction and to demonstrate that royal gift-giving in the ancient world is discriminatory, obligatory, and a means of asserting and guarding status. Five primary questions will guide our investigation. First, what elements and terminologies are involved in the practice of benefaction? Second, what kind of ruler is the ideal ruler in light of the benefaction system? Third, what motivates rulers' self-portrayal as beneficent and kind? Fourth, how do benefactors pick the beneficiaries of their good deeds? Lastly, what is expected of the beneficiaries? The present chapter, which focuses primarily on the Greco-Roman context, looks at the pertinent writings of Aristotle, Cicero, Seneca, Dio Chrysostom, and Pliny the Younger. Each work is examined under three subheadings: the ideal ruler, discrimination, and reciprocity. The chapter will conclude by considering epigraphic evidence, including *OGIS* 6, 90, *Res Gestae*, and Danker no. 39. By examining these authors as well as epigraphic evidence, we will provide a framework for reading Paul's royal discourse in Romans 5–8.

---

3. Lendon, *Empire of Honour*, 173.
4. Barclay, *Paul and the Gift*, 26.

Aristotle (384-322 BCE)

Aristotle was born in 384 BCE at Stagira in northern Greece.[5] His father Nicomachus was Philip of Macedon's court physician. After the death of his father, Aristotle went to Athens where he stayed for twenty years and was closely associated with the Academy of Plato. He left Athens after the death of Plato (347 BCE) and was later invited by Philip of Macedon to come to his court in Pella to become tutor for Alexander. After Philip's death in 335 BCE, Aristotle returned to Athens where he was devoted to the establishment of Lyceum, to speculation, research, writing, and teaching. He remained in Athens until the death of Alexander in 323 BCE, when his Macedonian connections forced him to flee to Chalcis, where he died in 322 BCE.

Aristotle was greatly influenced by his teacher Plato.[6] In the Platonic mold, Aristotle believed that the state should pursue the common good and inculcate social morality. He divided constitutions into the legitimate and illegitimate. The former, whose example is kingship, contributes to the common good; while the latter, whose example is tyranny, serves the interests of rulers at the expense of the common good. Legitimate constitutions create an environment that enables individuals to perform good deeds. And given that good deeds and the common good is the aim of political life, Aristotle believed that a ruler should be the most virtuous person in the society.

The Ideal Ruler

Aristotle's depiction of the ideal ruler is tied to his discussion on the central aim of society. The chief aim of society, the same aim which the government ought to pursue, is the good life, which can only be realized by promoting the welfare of the citizens (*Pol.* 3.4.20-30). Unlike the tyrant who pursues his own advantage, the good king understands that "beneficence is a function of the good man and of virtue" (ἐστὶ τοῦ ἀγαθοῦ καὶ τῆς ἀρετῆς τὸ εὐεργετεῖν, *Eth. nic.* 9.9.2). The good king is committed to the welfare of his subjects (*Eth. nic.* 8.10.1-2; cf. *Pol.* 3.1.14-15; 3.7.40-45; 4.8.1-24). For to "secure the good of one person only [as a

---

5. For introduction to Aristotle, see McKeon, *Introduction to Aristotle*, ix-xxix; Schofield, "Aristotle," 310-20.

6. On Plato's influence on Aristotle, see Ross, "Development of Aristotle's Thought," 63-78.

tyrant does] is better than nothing; but to secure the good of a nation or a state is a nobler and more divine achievement" (*Eth. nic.* 1.2.11–12). A king possesses independent resources and is better supplied "with goods of every kind than his subjects" (8.10.2). Because he lacks nothing, a king can advance the interests of his subjects (8.10.2) whom he loves like an artist loves his own handiwork (9.7.4) and a mother her children (9.7.7). His prosperity leads him to give glad benefactions (9.11.1), for "being wealthy consists in use rather than in possession" (*Rhet.* 1.5.7). The ideal king, therefore, serves as a father (*Eth. nic.* 8.10.4; 8.11.2–3) and a shepherd to his subjects (8.11.2).

The hallmark of this paternal and shepherd-like care is service to the citizens. Aristotle comments that in ancient times, kings would be appointed on the basis of public service or benefaction, and that doing this "is a task for the good men" (ἐστὶν ἔργον τῶν ἀγαθῶν ἀνδρῶν, *Pol.* 3.10.11–12). Such men excel in liberality (*Eth. nic.* 4.1.8; 9.7.5) and magnificence, which "consists in suitable expenditure on a great scale" (*Eth. nic.* 4.2.1, 5). A magnificent man engages in honorable acts such as votive offerings, sacrifices, public buildings, sponsoring games, equipping a ship of war, and giving a banquet to the public (*Eth. nic.* 4.2.11). Moreover, the ideal king brings freedom to his subjects, delivers them from any imminent external danger, and promotes internal cohesion by protecting private property of his subjects and dealing with every form of injustice (*Pol.* 5.8.33–46). In *Rhetoric*, Aristotle argues that benefaction "relates either to personal security and all the causes of existence, or to wealth, or to any other good things which are not easy to acquire, either in any conditions or at such a place, or at such a time" (1.5.9). He describes these public benefactions as "the greatest forms of expenditure and the ones most honored" (*Eth. nic.* 4.2.15). Additionally, in the interest of his friends and country the virtuous man is not afraid to lay down his own life if necessary. And by so doing, he wins the honor and praise of his friends (*Eth. nic.* 9.8.9). The ideal ruler, then, is a father, a guardian, and a shepherd who wins the praise of his subjects by maintaining peace and bestowing benefits generously on them.

Discrimination

To give rightly, a generous person needs to observe three basic guidelines: (1) carefully identify worthy recipients of benefactions; (2) give the right amount; and (3) give at the right time (*Eth. nic.* 4.1.7, 12). Whoever gives to the wrong people lacks the virtue of liberality (*Eth. nic.* 4.1.14, 22–23). A benefactor "will not give indiscriminately, in order that he may be able to give to the right persons (ἕξει) and at the right time, and where it is noble to do" (*Eth. nic.* 4.1.17–18). Aristotle states that the term "worthy" (ἀξία) "denotes having a claim to goods external to oneself" (*Eth. nic.* 4.2.10). Those worthy of receiving gifts are people of reputable character (*Eth. nic.* 4.1.34–35), for "only what is good is lovable" (*Eth. nic.* 9.3.3).[7] The implication here is that worthy beneficiaries would not subject their benefactor to disgrace (*Rhet.* 1.14.7).[8]

In addition to reputable character, Aristotle admonishes that benefactions should not be made to the poor, for the suitability of the expenditure is relative both to the spender and the object. Rather than "one who spends adequate sums on objects of only small or moderate importance," the term *magnificent* "denotes someone who spends suitably on great objects (*Eth. nic.* 4.2.3). Apart from their inability to offer commensurate return, the poor are "morally as well as economically at the bottom of the scale."[9] In short, the poor are incapable of being magnificent (*Eth. nic.* 4.2.13) and unworthy of the great expenditure of the magnificent man (*Eth. nic.* 4.2.6).[10]

Aristotle also notes that it is a great pleasure "to bestow favors and assistance on friends" (τὸ χαρίσασθαι καὶ βοηθῆσαι φίλοις) because this accords one the opportunity to express liberality and thereby leads to self-gratification (*Pol.* 2.2.5–10).[11] A king finds great security in having loyal friends (*Pol.* 5.9.30–33), who are also good men (*Pol.* 9.11.2). Friendship is not simply an indispensable necessity in life; rulers and the wealthy require friends to serve as outlets for their beneficence and as safeguards of their prosperity. Such beneficence "is displayed in its fullest and praiseworthy form towards friends" (*Eth. nic.* 8.1.1; cf. 9.9.2). A ruler

---

7. According to Aristotle, bestowing favors on the wrong people is ignoble because sometimes it makes rich those who ought to be poor (*Eth. nic.* 4.1.35).

8. Aristotle writes, "One who fears disgrace is an honorable man, with a due sense of shame; one who does not fear it is shameless" (*Eth. nic.* 3.6.3). He also argues that those who are morally inferior are worthless and incapable of true self-esteem and meaningful friendship (9.4.7–8).

9. Barclay, *Paul and the Gift*, 34.

10. A poor man who attempts magnificence is foolish because he lacks the means to undertake great expenditure (*Eth. nic.* 4.2.13).

11. Plato shares similar sentiments about benefiting one's friends when he writes that the just person does good to his friends and harm to his enemies (*Resp.* 2:262B–C).

must therefore identify friends who are both useful and pleasant (*Eth. nic.* 8.6.5; cf. 8.7.4), and love them accordingly because men who love their friends are worthy of praise (*Eth. nic.* 8.8.4).

Reciprocity

A generous giver wins the gratitude of the beneficiaries (*Eth. nic.* 4.1.8). To be grateful to a benefactor is a just action found in the category of rendering good for good (*Rhet.* 1.13.13). Failure to return a favor is disgraceful (*Rhet.* 2.23.8; cf. 2.2.26) for "in the interchange of services, justice in the form of reciprocity is the bond that maintains the association" (*Eth. nic.* 5.5.6–7). To underline the importance of reciprocity, Aristotle refers to the Graces (Χάριτες) that had been strategically erected to remind people of the justice of returning a favor: "This is why we set up a shrine of the Graces (Χαρίτων) in a public place, to remind men to return a kindness; for that is a special characteristic of grace (χάριτος), since it is a duty not only to repay a service (χαρισαμένῳ) done one, but another time to take the initiative in doing a service (χαριζόμενον) oneself" (*Eth. nic.* 5.5.7).[12]

The fact that Aristotle does not elaborate what these Graces are suggests that the ethic of reciprocity is more prevalent than subtle, and that everyone understands the significance of the Graces. Additionally, Aristotle clearly affirms that a proper understanding of the initial gift (χάρις) given would cause the recipient to return a favor. One ought to return the services received, and "do so willingly; for one ought not to make a man one's friend if one is unwilling to return his favors" (*Eth. nic.* 8.13.9; cf. 8.13.10–11).[13] In inegalitarian relationships such as found between the king and his subjects, reciprocity takes the form of honors. Aristotle defines honor as "a token of a reputation for doing good" (σημεῖον εὐεργετικῆς δόξης, *Rhet.* 1.5.9). Honors may take the form of "sacrifices, memorials in verse and prose, privileges, grants of land, front seats, public burial, state maintenance, and among the barbarians, prostration and giving place, and all gifts (δῶρα) which are highly prized in each country"

---

12. Leithart suggests that the "Graces" might refer to "three beautiful and utterly naked goddesses believed to be the dispensers of charis in all its senses. Originally fertility goddesses, they were later honored for their contributions to civic and social life. Youth, marriage, health, and other social benefits were under their bailiwick" (*Gratitude*, 25). Also see MacLachlan, *Age of Grace*, 4–5.

13. People often liken benefactors to creditors and beneficiaries to debtors and that the former wish the latter to live so that they may receive a return (*Eth. nic.* 9.7.1).

(*Rhet.* 1.5.9). The gift (τὸ δῶρόν), then, is simultaneously a giving of benefits and a token of honor (*Rhet.* 1.5.9).

Aristotle describes the needy as lovers of money and the wealthy as lovers of honor; he adds that the benefactor's gift brings to both what they desire (*Rhet.* 1.5.9).[14] The one who alone deserves honor is the good man (ὁ ἀγαθὸς μόνος τιμητέος, *Eth. nic.* 4.3.19–20), for honor is the prize of virtue and the tribute paid to the good (*Eth. nic.* 4.3.15). It is the greatest external good which men who are highly placed covet, and which is "the prize awarded for the noblest deeds" (*Eth. nic.* 4.3.10–17; cf. 8.14.3; 9.1.7; 9.2.3–4; *Rhet.* 1.5.9). Honor, therefore, is the appropriate requital to those who hold office and use their resources for societal welfare.

Cicero (106–43 BCE)

Born in January 106 BCE to a wealthy *eques* during the consulship of Gaius Marius, Cicero was not only highly educated in philosophy and rhetoric in Rome and in Greece but also served as a military officer, quaestor, praetor, and consul.[15] In his adult life, Cicero witnessed the recurrent civil wars that threatened the stability of the Roman Republic. He applied ethics in order to make sense of this changing historical situation. He was convinced that government instability was caused by the corruption of the rulers. As a political philosopher and a moralist, Cicero embraced an eclectic approach that allowed him to suspend judgment in questions of knowledge (hence yielding his intellect to Plato's Academy) but dogmatize on moral questions (hence showing sympathy for Stoic and Peripatetic traditions). Similarly, his works (most famous of which are *de Re Publica* and *de Officiis*) reflect aristocratic ideals. He was preoccupied with war and politics and he also supported the collective authority of the senate. He asserted that the virtues of courage, wisdom, and piety were indispensable in public service. Cicero believed that those who served the public were owed loyalty and gratitude.

---

14. Hands, *Charities and Social Aid*, 35.

15. *Eques* (plural *equites*) refers to a wealthy member of non-senatorial families. *Equites* were equal to the senators in social standing. For a brief discussion on Cicero's historical background, see Atkins, "Cicero," 477–516.

The Ideal Ruler

Cicero contends that wealth is a means of bestowing favors (*Off.* 1.8.25; 2.18.64), and that the most honorable thing to do with money is to devote it to beneficence and liberality (*Off.* 1.20.68). In contrast to a man who chooses the easier, safer, and less burdensome life of retirement, the one who is engaged in public service is more profitable to mankind and contributes more to his own greatness and fame (*Off.* 1.20.70; 1.26.92). Such a man devotes himself "unreservedly to his country" in order to "further the interests of all," and as a king, he is like a father to his subjects, providing for them and always eager to protect them (*Resp.* 1.35.54). He not only takes measures to ensure "an abundance of the necessities of life" (*Off.* 2.21.74) but he is also willing to face dangers and death for the sake of his country (*Off.* 1.25.86). Unlike the tyrant and despot whom people hate and wish to see dead due to his burdensome rule (*Off.* 3.6.32), the benevolent ruler's throne is kept safe by the affection of the subjects (*Off.* 2.7.23).

As "the best man," the king is the most pious among all humanity, and he is naturally inclined to generosity and enhancing the welfare and peace of the empire.[16] His commitment to justice and to the welfare of his subjects leads him to secure freedom for the oppressed, provide help for the helpless, and protect the weak (*Off.* 2.12.41–42; cf. *Resp.* 3.3.6).[17] Other benefactions may include sponsoring games and entertainment, offering public dinners, supplying grain (*Off.* 2.17.58), ransoming prisoners, relieving the poor (*Off.* 2.18.63), offering hospitality (*Off.* 2.18.64), constructing "walls, docks, harbors, aqueducts, and all those works which are of service to the community," including constructing temples, theatres, and colonnades (*Off.* 2.17.60).

Discrimination

The ideal ruler's zeal to advance the welfare of his subjects does not imply that he ought to confer favors indiscriminately. When a benefactor

---

16. Hoklotubbe, *Civilized Piety*, 6: "Roman emperors and Latin authors justified the legitimacy of the Roman Empire on the basis that the Roman people and its rulers were the most pious among all humanity, and so favored by the gods."

17. Aalders writes that the king is "a noble-minded and well-gifted person, toiling uninterruptedly for the common welfare and for the well-being of his subjects, as their benefactor, even their savior ... (whose gifts and indulgences are termed therefore *philanthropia*)" (*Political Thought*, 21; italics original).

intends to show kindness to individual citizens rather than to the community at large, he needs great discretion and moderation to avoid incurring loss due to indiscriminate giving (*Off.* 2.15.54).[18] Showing kindness to the reputable people ensures a "prompter and speedier return" (*Off.* 2.20.69; cf. 2.20.71). Even when Cicero concedes that there are no perfect men, he still insists that help should be given only to those who display virtue and that the more a man exemplifies justice, self-control, and temperance, the more he deserves to be favored (*Off.* 1.15.46). Additionally, the beneficiary must be a friend and a man whom the benefactor loves and whose requital of the favor shown promotes the reputation of the benefactor (*Inv.* 2.55.166; cf. *Off.* 1.14.43).[19] For the sake of the society and its common bonds, kindness ought to be shown to each individual in proportion to his closeness to the benefactor (*Off.* 1.16.50). What Cicero means by closeness is more than kinship and citizenship. Rather it is "when good men join together in intimate friendship" (*Off.* 1.17.55).

Unlike Aristotle who rejects benefiting the poor, Cicero argues that a poor man might not be able to return a favor in kind, but if he is a good man marked by self-control, justice, and temperance, he can reciprocate at least by expressing gratitude (*Off.* 2.20.69). When bestowing benefactions, the poor who are upright and honest should be preferred to one's favorites because by so doing "all the lowly who are not dishonest . . . look upon such an advocate [benefactor] as a tower of defense raised up for them" (*Off.* 2.20.70–71). So for Cicero, one's moral standing is more important than one's social status in the society.[20]

Calculated gift-giving is the only way benefactors can guard their own interests as they seek to identify recipients who will not fail to reciprocate. Cicero criticizes those who indiscriminately bestow gifts as such acts of generosity do not attract as high esteem as "those which are performed with judgment, deliberation, and mature consideration" (*Off.* 1.15.49; cf. 1.16.50). According to Ennius, whom Cicero quotes to underline the problem with indiscriminate liberality, "Good deeds misplaced

18. On service to individual citizens and to the community, see *Off.* 2.19.65; 2.21.72–73.

19. Cicero not only closely connects glory to generosity and friendship but also defines glory as consisting "in a person's having a widespread reputation accompanied by praise" (Inv. 2.55.166).

20. In *Off.* 2.20.69, Cicero writes that "in investing kindnesses we look not to people's outward circumstances, but to their character." A few lines down he adds that "in conferring favors our decision should depend entirely upon a man's character, not on his wealth" (2.20.71).

... are evil deeds" (*Off.* 2.18.63). But favor conferred on a good and grateful man elicits its reward from the man's goodwill as well as that of others. In a candid remark aimed at encouraging generosity as well as modesty and discretion, Cicero asserts, "One's purse, then, should not be closed so tightly that a generous impulse cannot open it, nor yet so loosely held as to be open to everybody" (*Off.* 2.15.55). In short, because gift-giving is a calculated move that considers the character of the beneficiary to ensure a return, three rules should be observed: (1) acts of kindness should never be done with the intention of harming others; (2) beneficence should be within the benefactor's means; and (3) the gift should be "proportioned to the worthiness of the recipient." Cicero emphasizes that these rules form the corner-stone of justice (*Off.* 1.14.42).

Reciprocity

Benefaction is an investment that anticipates returns (*Off.* 2.20.69). Generosity involves showing a kindness and requiting one, and "to fail to requite one is not allowable to a good man" (*Off.* 1.15.48). Mutual exchange of kind services strengthens fellowship and produces ties of enduring intimacy (*Off.* 1.17.56). Perhaps Cicero's entire approach to the ethic of reciprocity might be summarized as follows: "[I]t is the first demand of duty that we do most for him who loves us most" (*Off.* 1.15.47; cf. *Fam.* 3.5.1; 13.18.2). Through acts of kindness, the benefactor wins the goodwill of the people, which in turn contributes to his own glory (*Off.* 2.9.31–32).

At the heart of reciprocity is thankfulness, for there is no single duty (Latin, *pietas*; Greek, εὐσέβεια) that is more urgent and mandatory than that of demonstrating one's gratitude (*Off.* 1.15.47).[21] Gratitude is the greatest of all virtues, for it does not merely stand "alone at the head of all the virtues, but is even mother of all the rest" (*Planc.* 33:80). Even a poor man who cannot return a favor in kind is still under obligation to be thankful if he is a good man (*Off.* 2.20.69). Out of gratitude, the beneficiaries do not hesitate to support the benefactor in his hour of peril, holding his "safety dear above all things" (*Planc.* 28:69). And since service to the community wins lasting gratitude from posterity (*Off.* 2.17.60), care

---

21. Hoklotubbe notes that *pietas* denotes an affectionate service rendered to one's homeland, parents, and emperor (*Civilized Piety*, 6). For further discussion on "εὐσεβής, εὐσέβεια, εὐσεβέω," see Mikalson, *Greek Popular Religion*, 6–9, 140–86. On *pietas* in Latin literature, see Wagenvoort, *Pietas*, 1–20; Hoklotubbe, *Civilized Piety*, 1–54.

must be taken to be of service to the greatest number possible "so that the memory of them [services] shall be handed down to children and to children's children, so that they too may not be ungrateful" (*Off.* 2.18.63; cf. *Inv.* 2.22.66; 2.53.161; *Off.* 2.6.22).[22] Public service, then, is regarded as a pathway to immortality as posterity continues to memorialize and express gratitude to their benefactors.

The preceding discussion shows that the ideal ruler is a paternal figure, who uses his resources to protect and provide for his subjects. He brings freedom for the oppressed and help for the helpless, and through his service to humanity he wins the goodwill and affection of the masses. Given that the good ruler is also an exemplar of high moral character— he is the just and the good man—he must be careful to promote virtue by showing kindness to the pious, even if they are poor. Due to his benevolence, the people honor him by their unceasing loyalty and gratitude.

Seneca (ca. 4 BCE–65 CE)

Seneca's *De Beneficiis* ("On Benefits") was written between 56 and 62 CE.[23] How should Seneca be read?[24] At the surface level, Seneca might be accused of offering careless and contradictory solutions to problems surrounding gift-giving.[25] For instance, he admonishes liberal benefactors not to ask for a return (*Ben.* 1.1.13), yet they can still ask for it in times of crisis (5.20.7), and only if the recipient is able to make a return (5.21.3). Slow recipients should be admonished to make a return (5.22.1–3). A benefactor should give gifts discriminately in order to ensure reciprocity (1.10.5; 2.11.4–5), yet a good benefactor does not withhold favors in the face of ingratitude (2.11.5). These and similar examples might suggest frivolousness and inconsistency, but Seneca himself suggests how he should be interpreted: "Some of the utterances that we Stoics make avoid

---

22. Cicero tells of one Paulus who defeated the Macedonians and got all their wealth, which he brought into the treasury of Rome. Because of the spoils of this single general, property tax was completely eliminated in Rome. Consequently, Paulus brought to his own house "the glory of an immortal name" (2.22.76).

23. For further discussion on this consensus, see Griffin, *Seneca*, 399. For a recent introduction and translation, see Seneca, *On Benefits*.

24. Griffin and Inwood, *Lucius Annaeus Seneca*, 2; Inwood, *Reading Seneca*, 65–94.

25. MacMullen characterizes *De Beneficiis* as "high-minded nonsense" ("Personal Power," 521).

the ordinary meaning of the terms, and then by a different line of thought are restored to their ordinary meaning" (2.35.2).

As a Stoic philosopher, Seneca exercises great sensitivity due to complexities surrounding benefaction relationships even as he proposes paradox as a solution to the prevalent problems (2.31.1–2).[26] It appears that *De Beneficiis* ought to be read at two levels.[27] The first "level promotes the social ideal, while the other acknowledges the social reality."[28] The material and the intentional levels must be kept in perspective.[29] Seneca reveals prevalent cultural values and social codes by means of hyperbole.[30] He and other Stoics "overstate some rules in order that in the end they may reach their true value . . . Hyperbole never expects to attain all that it ventures, but asserts the incredible to arrive at the credible" (7.22.1—7.23.2). In the words of David E. Briones: "Seneca sets the bar of morality obscenely high so that his readers will reach an attainable goal and so perpetuate the fundamental practice of reciprocal exchange."[31]

De Beneficiis provides a description of the ideal conditions for giving, receiving, and returning a gift, and thereby offers a law for human life in order to strengthen the bond of human society (1.4.2–4). Seneca justifies this undertaking by asserting that in his day people "do not know how either to give or to receive benefits" (1.1.1).[32] To correct this situation, Seneca seeks to define *how* giving and receiving should be undertaken. He remains true to his Stoic heritage when he emphasizes that the essence of benefaction is *how* (*animus*) gifts are exchanged rather than *what* (*res*) is

---

26. Harrison, *Paul's Language of Grace*, 205.

27. According to Inwood *De Beneficiis* is "a two-level mode of discourse" with persuasive value (*Reading Seneca*, 90).

28. Briones, *Paul's Financial Policy*, 46.

29. Inwood, *Reading Seneca*, 89.

30. Griffin describes *De Beneficiis* as "the pedagogical technique of hyperbole" ("De Beneficiis and Roman Society," 94).

31. Briones, *Paul's Financial Policy*, 47. Barclay suggests that *De Beneficiis* should be read as: "(i) a selective restatement of largely common assumptions about gift-reciprocity; (ii) an intelligent analysis of the problems of gift exchange; and (iii) the provision of distinctively Stoic solutions to those problems, aimed at keeping the system of benefit exchange operational for the good of all" (*Paul and the Gift*, 45–46).

32. Seneca defines a benefit as "the act of a well-wisher who bestows joy and derives joy from the bestowal of it, and is inclined to do what he does from the prompting of his own will" (*Ben.* 1.6.1).

exchanged (1.5.1–3; 1.6.1–3; 6.2.1).[33] The giver is to be of service while "he who receives a benefit gladly has already returned it" (2.31.1).

The Ideal Ruler

The ideal ruler does not humiliate his subjects; instead, he cares for them with gentleness and tenderness. Seneca narrates a story whose main characters are Gaius Caesar and Pompeius Punnus to illustrate the marks of the beneficent ruler (2.12.1—2.13.3). Apparently, Pompeius, a senator, was granted life by Caesar who had orchestrated his acquittal. When Pompeius took the initiative to express his thanks as expected, the emperor "extended his left foot to be kissed." Seneca remarks that this was demeaning and servile, and that it amounted to "trampling upon the commonwealth . . . with the left foot." At best this was arrogant and disgraceful.[34] Against the backdrop of this negative illustration, Seneca writes, "The gifts that please are those that are bestowed by one who wears the countenance of a human being, all gentle and kindly, by one who, though he was my superior when he gave them, did not exalt himself above me" (2.13.2). From his inexhaustible wealth (cf. 4.40.2), the ideal emperor humbly cares for his subjects, uses his power for their well-being, and comes to their aid with timely assistance (2.13.2–3). His "care embraces all" and "fosters each and every part of the state as a portion of himself" (*Clem.* 1.13.4).

The good king is appointed by the gods because of his own virtue, or that of his ancestors if he is wanting in goodness (*Ben.* 4.32.1–3). The king upholds justice and sacrifices himself to the state through acts of kindness and steadfast care (*Ben.* 4.32.2). The gods entrust to the king an exalted position that enables him to give many gifts (*Ben.* 5.4.2; *Clem.* 1.3.3). The king's greatness means that he is superior to his subjects, but his commitment to their well-being assures them that he is still their friend. He is a "bright and beneficent star" who is daily concerned "for the safety of each and all" (*Clem.* 1.3.3). The civil law also states that everything belongs to the king (*Ben.* 7.4.2). In addition to monetary aid and political offices,

33. With regard to a gift offered as a requital, Barclay remarks that "since Stoics refer all things to the *animus* (2.31.1), what a benefit aims to achieve is not an external counter-gift, but an internal virtue, gratitude" (*Paul and the Gift*, 48).

34. Seneca describes Gaius Caesar as "a man so greedy of human blood that he ordered it to be shed in his presence as freely as if he intended to catch the stream in his mouth!" (*Ben.* 4.31.2).

a king may grant citizenship as well as an exemption from taxes (*Ben.* 6.19.2–5). He may fund public buildings and help in times of disaster (*Ben.* 6.32.3–4). He distributes grain and enhances peace and liberty (*Ep.* 73:8). His good deeds protect him so much that he "needs no bodyguard; the arms he wears are for adornment only" (*Clem.* 1.13.5). For a king's "one impregnable defense is the love of his countrymen" (*Clem.* 1.19.6).

Apart from the honorifics "bright and beneficent star" (*Clem.* 1.3.3), "the Great," "the Fortunate," and "the August," the good king also deserves the title "the Father of his Country" (*Clem.* 1.14.1–3; cf. 1.13.1). Seneca explains that the king is given the latter honorific "in order that he may know that he has been entrusted with a father's power, which is most forbearing in its care for the interests of his children" (*Clem.* 1.14.2–3; 1.15.1—1.16.1; 1.19.8). He wins the greatest glory by holding his power in check and by rescuing "many from the wrath of others" (1.17.3). And he shows by his constant goodness, not that the State belongs to him, but that he belongs to the State (1.19.8–9). In short, the ideal king is the greatest and the best man, who, like the gods that appoint him, is generous and beneficent, and uses his power and resources for the prosperity of his subjects.

Discrimination

The opening paragraph of *De Beneficiis* categorically asserts that gifts that are ill-placed are also ill-acknowledged (1.1.1). When a gift is bestowed carelessly without discrimination, the beneficiary will only thank himself rather than the unwitting giver (1.1.8). One of the causes of ingratitude is the failure by the benefactors to pick "those who are worthy of receiving our gifts" (1.1.2; cf. 1.10.5; 3.14.2). A gift given to one who is base is dishonorable (4.9.3). Benefits should be bestowed, not merely upon people, but *because of who they are* (6.18.2). Non-calculating gift-giving is "the thoughtless indulgence that masquerades as generosity" (1.4.3); it is like a farmer who sows seed in "worn-out and unproductive soil," and who inevitably suffers loss (1.1.2).[35] One needs to place gifts like a skilled player pitching the ball to a skilled catcher (2.27.3–5). A gift needs to "go by a path, and not wander" (1.14.2). Instead of scattering gifts indiscriminately, they should be given judiciously since "it is more important who

---

35. Seneca writes: "Thoughtless benefaction is the most shameful sort of loss" (*Ben.* 4.10.3).

receives a thing than what it is he receives" (*Ep.* 19:11–12). A poor man who is good, and who will subsequently show gratitude amidst extreme poverty should be picked for benefaction instead of an unworthy rich man (*Ben.* 4.10.4–5). A worthy person is sincere, upright, grateful, mindful, and kind to others (*Ben.* 4.11.1–2). A wise donor must, therefore, pick donees who are capable of reciprocating by expressing gratitude for the gift given (*Ben.* 1.10.5; 2.11.4–5; 4.27.5; 4.33.3; 4.34.2).[36]

But does discrimination not contradict divine beneficence, which should serve as a model for human beneficence? This is the question that Seneca tackles in *Ben.* 4.28.1–6.[37] The gods confer many blessings upon the ungrateful, not because they are indifferent to worthiness, but because it is impossible to separate the good from the bad when conferring certain blessings such as rains, the sun, seasons, and wind. When the gods give these seemingly indiscriminate favors, their ultimate intention is to benefit the good, yet in the process the bad also end up enjoying these blessings.[38] Likewise, kings grant largesse to the worthy and the unworthy, to everyone who is a citizen without shutting anyone out because some favors are given to all. Those of ignoble reputation receive these royal boons as citizens and not based on their flawed reputation.[39] But these general benefactions of the gods and of the kings are exceptional, and therefore do not nullify the need for judicious gift-giving. So on the one hand, favors "ought to be showered upon the mob"; on the other hand, being wasteful of anything, especially of benefits, is not right. A

---

36. Even kings divide their friends into three classes: (1) chief friends (who come into their presence first); (2) ordinary friends (who follow the first class); and (3) others (who are not true friends, hence are treated together with the masses). It is honorable to be permitted to sit "nearer the front door, and to be the first to set foot inside the [king's] house" (Seneca, *Ben.* 6.34.1–4). Seneca is critical of all these classes of friendship because they do not lead to gratitude. A true friend should be found in the heart rather than "in a reception hall." For "there [in the heart] must he be admitted, there retained, and enshrined in affection. Teach a man this—and you show gratitude!" (6.34.4–5).

37. Also see *Ben.* 1.1.9–13, where Seneca concludes that it is not enough to merely forestall the fault of the ingrates by withholding gifts, for whoever "does not return a benefit sins more; he who does not give one sins earlier."

38. Sometimes the gods confer benefits on the bad because of their virtuous parents, ancestors, or descendants (*Ben.* 4.32.1). Thus the gods do not ignore virtue when conferring benefits.

39. Barclay makes a similar note regarding the benefaction intended to meet an economic crisis, and which therefore does not discriminate between the poor and the rich (*Paul and the Gift*, 34).

giver who disregards discernment while bestowing benefits must find a different name for his acts; they are no longer benefits (*Ben.* 1.2.1–2). Benefactors must apply "the rule of censorship and of rating the person" because a favor "which must go to a beneficiary of my own choosing will not be given to a man whom I know to be ungrateful" (*Ben.* 4.28.5–6). Seneca concludes the first book thus, "A gift is not a benefit if the best part of it is lacking—the fact that it was given as a mark of esteem. Moreover, the gift of a huge sum of money, if neither reason nor rightness of choice has prompted it, is no more a benefit than is a treasure trove" (*Ben.* 1.15.16). In brief, benefactors must observe the rule of censorship by considering the reputation of the intended beneficiaries to ensure that their favors are appropriately received and returned.

Reciprocity

How should people receive benefactions? As we have noted, Seneca's *De Beneficiis* describes a system of reciprocity in which each gift should be reciprocated by the goodwill of the beneficiary and the return of a counter-gift (2.33.1–2; 5.11.5; cf. *Ep.* 36:5–6). The treatise is a strategy-book for the benefactor, giving counsel on how to "place" benefits to maximize the possibility of a return. Humans are like social animals whose welfare is maintained by the interchange of benefits (*Ben.* 4.18.1–4; 7.1.7). The exchange of benefits enhances the public good (7.16.2) by strengthening friendship between the parties involved (2.18.5) as each discharges his obligations (2.18.2). Because gift-giving is not a unilateral social act, it seeks to win the goodwill of the beneficiary and lays him under obligation to return a favor (2.35.1, 4; 5.11.5).

Like Aristotle (*Eth. nic.* 5.5.6), Seneca refers to the Roman *Gratiae* (Graces), which he traces back to Hesiod, and which remind people of the need to return a favor (*Ben.* 1.3.2–10). Why are the *Gratiae* young and three in number, and why are their hands interlocked? Their youthfulness signifies the constancy with which benefits ought to be remembered. They are three because "there is one for bestowing a benefit, another for receiving it, and a third for returning it." The Graces dance in a ring to visualize a benefit passing from one hand to another, ultimately returning to the initial giver. The benefactor or the initial giver is the older sister to whom special honor is due. If this circle of reciprocity is broken, then the beauty of the dance also collapses. In other words, the maxim of *do ut des*

("I gave that you may give") should always be maintained. The one word that sums up the expected goodwill and return is gratitude, which should be verbalized and publicized (2.23.2).[40] The one who is truly grateful must return a favor with a tangible, counter gift (2.25.3). That is why Seneca emphasizes that the "man who intends to be grateful, immediately, while he is receiving, should turn his thought to repaying" (2.25.3).

Ingratitude is both shameful and the worst of all vices.[41] Seneca states, "Homicides, tyrants, thieves, adulterers, robbers, sacrilegious men, and traitors there always will be; but worse than all these is the crime of ingratitude, unless it be that all these spring from ingratitude, without which hardly any sin has grown to great size" (1.10.4). Failure to express gratitude for benefits is disgraceful and the whole world judges it as such (3.1.1; cf. 1.6.1; 5.20.4). Some of the causes of ingratitude are pride, greed, jealousy, and the failure to understand one's place in relation to one's benefactor and peers (2.26.1—2.29.6). People should not tolerate ingratitude as it destroys social cohesion and weakens solidarity in times of disaster (4.18.1-2).[42] Even poverty and weakness do not justify ingratitude (2.30.2). Interestingly, Seneca exhorts that even in the face of ingratitude, a generous benefactor should persist in conferring benefits, hoping that "either shame or opportunity or example will some day make these grateful" (1.2.4-5; cf. 1.3.1). In keeping with his Stoic heritage, Seneca suggests the extreme ideal of persistent generosity as that seems to be the most effective way to shame the ingrates and thereby impart some sense of gratitude in them. Benefactors should take care of their gifts just as a farmer takes care of his crops to ensure fruition (2.11.5).[43] Like fathers who do not discontinue bestowing benefits upon their children while they

40. For further discussion on verbalized gratitude in Greco-Roman society, see Peterman, *Paul's Gift*, 73-83.

41. Inwood comments that "from the opening lines to the conclusion of book VII Seneca is persistently concerned with ingratitude and with the discouraging effect it has on the giving of benefits" ("Politics and Paradox," 263).

42. See Blanton, *Spiritual Economy*, 3. Blanton rightly observes that "refusal or reticence to reciprocate . . . constitutes a denial of social relations."

43. Seneca concludes *De Beneficiis* by stating that "what I have lost in the case of one man [who is ungrateful], I shall recover from others [who are grateful]. But even to him [who is ungrateful] I shall give a second benefit, and, even as a good farmer overcomes the sterility of his ground by care and cultivation, I shall be victor" (7.32). In *Ep.* 81:1-2, he writes, "Even after a poor crop one should sow again; for often losses due to continued barrenness of an unproductive soil have been made good by one year's fertility. In order to discover one grateful person, it is worthwhile to make trial of many ungrateful ones."

are still infants (3.11.2), benefactors must tend benefits by further benefits if they are to accomplish their ultimate goal, namely, gratitude.[44] For just as "nothing is more honorable than a grateful heart" (*Ep.* 81:30), so nothing is more shameful than failure to return a favor.

Sometimes reciprocity to "a bright and beneficent star," the ideal king and benefactor, demands readiness to pay the ultimate price:

> In his [the king's] defense they [the subjects] are ready on the instant to throw themselves before the swords of assassins, and to lay their bodies beneath his feet if his path to safety must be paved with slaughtered men; his sleep they guard by nightly vigils, his person they defend with an encircling barrier, against assailing dangers they make themselves a rampart (*Clem.* 1.3.3).

The one who throws himself "before the swords of assassins" is simply displaying his love for their king as well as asserting that he must guard the safety of a beneficent ruler at all costs (*Clem.* 1.3.4; 1.13.1; 1.19.7-8). Although some argue that such heroic acts show "self-depreciation or madness when many thousands meet the steel for the sake of one man, and with many deaths ransom the single life," those who do them are gladly publicizing their "protection and love to their kings" (*Clem.* 1.3.4). A king who rules well "is the bond by which the commonwealth is united, the breath of life which these many thousands draw, who in their own strength would be only a burden to themselves and the prey of others if the great mind of the empire should be withdrawn" (*Clem.* 1.4.1). For the sake of such a king, no sacrifice is too great to pay. So just as the king is under obligation to promote the welfare of his subjects, so the beneficiaries of a beneficent reign are obligated to reciprocate, even with their own lives.

For Seneca, therefore, benefactions are inextricably tied to virtue, especially as evident in the ruler's gentleness and kindness as well as in the subjects' gratefulness. As the benefactor aims to be of service to others through his inexhaustible wealth conferred on him by the gods, he must do it in such a way as to reward and enhance gratefulness in the society. The subjects regard a generous ruler as a father and a friend, whom they dearly protect with their affection, even to the point of death. Because such a king is both virtuous and liberal, he understands that the content

---

44. In another paragraph, Seneca urges: "In order to awaken some men, it is necessary only to shake, not to strike, them; in the same way, in the case of some men, their sense of honor about returning gratitude is, not extinct, but only asleep. Let us arouse it" (*Ben.* 5.23.1).

of what is given is not as important as how it is given.[45] Seneca's advice on how to pray for the benefactor offers an apt conclusion:

> I pray that he [the benefactor] may be in a position always to dispense benefits, and never to need them; that he may be attended by the means which he uses so generously in giving bounty and help to others; that he may never have lack of benefits to bestow nor regret for those bestowed; may his nature that of itself is inclined to pity, kindness, and mercy find stimulus and encouragement from a host of grateful persons, and may he be fortunate enough to find them without the necessity of testing them; may none find him implacable, and may he have need to placate none; may Fortune continue to bestow on him such unbroken favor that it will be impossible for anyone to show gratitude to him except by feeling it (*Ben.* 6.29.1).

Dio Chrysostom (ca 40–120 CE)

Born in Prusa of Bithynia around 40 CE, Dio Chrysostom writes at the end of the first-century CE.[46] Due to his friendship with Flavius Sabinus, Dio was banished from Rome and Bithynia by Domitian in 82 CE.[47] He then consulted the oracle at Delphi where he was instructed to continue wandering until he came "to the uttermost parts of the earth" (*Exil.* 9). He investigated the question of good and evil and did not reject being identified as a philosopher (*Exil.* 10–12). As Lau states, "[T]he exile compelled Dio to think deeply on moral questions and hastened his development as a Stoic philosopher."[48] Dio was recalled to Rome after the death of Domitian in 96 CE. He developed a close relationship with Nerva and Trajan, serving both as an intellectual adviser. He also secured many benefactions for Prusa. In his writings, Dio combines Stoicism with Cynicism

---

45. As Barclay observes, "Seneca's Stoic advice is subtle but realistic, sophisticated but designed for practice. It is a fine example of the Stoic ambition both to understand and to solve the problems that threaten both the individual psyche and the welfare of society" (*Paul and the Gift*, 50).

46. For a survey of secondary literature on Dio, see Swain, "Reception and Interpretation," 13–50. For a brief overview of Dio's background, see Lau, *Politics of Peace*, 157–59. A more detailed discussion of Dio's background and speeches has been provided by Jones, *Roman World*.

47. Flavius Sabinus was executed by Domitian (Dio, *Exil.* 1). For further discussion of Dio's friendship with Flavius Sabinus, see Sidebottom, "Dio of Prusa," 447–56.

48. Lau, *Politics of Peace*, 159.

and Platonism. Sometimes he accepts the validity of conventional political and social structures while at other times he questions their validity.[49]

The Ideal Ruler

Dio's *Kingship Orations* were perhaps dedicated to Trajan.[50] As Dio plays the role of a counselor to Trajan through praise and flattery, he articulates what is expected of the ideal king.[51] The good king receives his scepter from Zeus and must use it for the welfare of his people (*1 Regn.* 12-13; cf. 84). As the vicegerent of the gods, the good king is divinely equipped to show godlike care for humanity.[52] Instead of seeking to perfect himself in philosophy, the good king seeks to "live simply and without affectation, to give proof by his very conduct of a character that is humane, gentle, just, lofty, and brave as well, and, *above all, one that takes delight in bestowing benefits* (εὐεργεσίαις)—a trait which approaches most nearly to the nature divine" (*2 Regn.* 26; emphasis added). Whereas a bad king is a lover of pleasure (*1 Regn.* 21), the ideal king must be a lover of humankind (φιλάνθρωπος) and care for his people just as a shepherd cares for the sheep (*1 Regn.* 15-20; *2 Regn.* 6; cf. *3 Regn.* 39, 55-57; *4 Regn.* 43-44), and like the general on a campaign who ensures that his soldiers are equipped and well supplied with shelter and food (*3 Regn.* 67). The good king takes pleasure in toiling for his people (*1 Regn.* 21) because his kingship is "not for the sake of his individual self, but for the sake of all humanity" (*1 Regn.* 23).

Like Heracles, whom Dio holds up as worth emulating, Trajan should seek "to do the greatest good to the greatest number" (*1 Regn.* 65) and strive to be most fortunate by making his goodness known to all (*1 Regn.* 35).[53] Heracles "made presents to many men, not only of money without limit and lands and herds of horses and cattle, but also of whole kingdoms and cities." He did this because he "believed that everything

---

49. Gill, "Stoic Writers," 604.

50. Lau, *Politics of Peace*, 162.

51. On the question of whether Dio considers Roman monarchical rule to be ideal, see Swain, *Hellenism and Empire*, 192; Moles, "Date and Purpose, 252.

52. See Walbank, "Monarchies and Monarchic Ideas," 84-96.

53. Dio notes that the story about Heracles is a myth and an edifying parable that aptly illustrates what good kingship entails (*1 Regn.* 48-49). Heracles considered gold and silver as "worth nothing save to be given away and bestowed (δοῦναι καὶ χαρίσασθαι) upon others" (*1 Regn.* 62).

belonged to him exclusively and that gifts bestowed would call out the goodwill of the recipients" (*1 Regn.* 62–63). Likewise, every good king displays limitless generosity for Zeus has entrusted to him abundant resources and power.

The good king does not reject the title "'Father' of his people and his subjects" because his deeds of care and benefaction confirm that he is worthy of it (*1 Regn.* 22). He indeed is the savior and protector (σωτὴρ καὶ φύλαξ) of humanity (*3 Regn.* 6). As a generous benefactor, he finds pleasure in conferring benefits and considers benefaction as a voluntary and blessed royal function (*1 Regn.* 23–24). It is only when such a king is helping men that he thinks he is doing his duty (*3 Regn.* 55). Dio writes, "Blessings he [the good king] dispenses with the most lavish hand, as though the supply were inexhaustible" (*1 Regn.* 24). Like the sun, the ideal king does not grow weary of showering his blessings upon humanity (*3 Regn.* 73–81). And as he imitates Zeus, the good king creates harmony among the people (*1 Regn.* 41, 45; cf. *3 Regn.* 82–83). Unlike the bad king who alienates his friends, the good king makes his friends feel secure by his deep concern for them (*1 Regn.* 20, 25, 30–32) even as his enemies live in fear of him (*1 Regn.* 25; cf. *3 Regn.* 5).

Discrimination

Although Dio does not discuss discrimination at length, his few remarks indicate his belief that benefactions should be given judiciously. He writes that it is pleasurable both to show favor to good men and "to receive gifts when they are deserved and for merit" (δικαίως καὶ δι' ἀρετήν, *3 Regn.* 110). Like the ideal king, the good men recognize that happiness consists in excellence of character (καλοκἀγαθίαν, *3 Regn.* 123). These good men are the king's friends who reciprocate his gifts. In other words, the friends of the king cannot disappoint him: "[A]t no time has anyone been wronged by a friend, and that such a thing belongs to the category of the impossible" (*3 Regn.* 113). Thus friendship is the "noblest and most profitable possession" that a king can ever have (*1 Regn.* 30). Dio writes:

> Friendship, moreover, the good king holds to be the fairest and most sacred of his possessions, believing that the lack of means is not so shameful or perilous for a king as the lack of friends, and that he maintains his happy state, not so much by means of revenues and armies and his other sources of strength, as by the loyalty of his friends (*3 Regn.* 86–87).

The good king understands that although he cannot ignore kin, friendship is more important than kinship (3 *Regn.* 113–14).⁵⁴ Friends should be chosen not just from the king's inner circle, but from all over the world (3 *Regn.* 128–32). Where friendship is absent, life is insecure even in peace. The good king must therefore seek to share his pleasure with his friends (3 *Regn.* 95–96), for as a good man he delights in the happy experiences of his friends (3 *Regn.* 108).⁵⁵ Such a king, being ambitious for glory, achieves his goal through the endless eulogies of his friends. For if "wealth naturally gladdens its possessor, he can be rich many times over who shares what he has with his friends" (3 *Regn.* 109). So what stands out in Dio's brief remarks on discrimination is the need to show favor to one's friends, who are themselves good and honorable.

Reciprocity

Dio seems to endorse without reservation the ethic of reciprocity. He not only states that the good king understands that gifts bestowed win the goodwill of the recipients (1 *Regn.* 62–63), but he also identifies three social relationships that are marked by reciprocity: sons to fathers, beneficiaries to private benefactors, and cities to public benefactors (*De lege* 6). The ideal king who shares his largesse with his friends is simultaneously a giver and a receiver; he delights in loyal hearts as well as in the sweet praise of his friends (3 *Regn.* 110; cf. 1 *Regn.* 31–32).⁵⁶ He is "naturally covetous of honor" because he understands that men are inclined to honor the good (τους ἀγαθούς, 1 *Regn.* 27).⁵⁷ The rewards established by

---

54. While the king cannot sever kinship ties with unworthy relatives, he loves beyond others his kinsmen who live honorable lives (3 *Regn.* 119–21).

55. Like other ancient writers, Dio believes that "[c]ommon are the possessions of friends" and that "when the good have good things, these will certainly be held in common" (3 *Regn.* 110).

56. For further discussion on the relationship between rulers and their friends, see Friedländer, *Roman Life*, 70–82; Saller, "Patronage and Friendship, 49–62.

57. Dio's critique of Alexander in the fourth oration underlines man's inbuilt desire to be honored: "He [Alexander] was anxious to leave his name the greatest among all the Greeks and barbarians and longed to be honored, not only—as one might put it—by mankind the world over, but, if it were at all possible, by the birds of the air and the beasts of the mountains" (4 *Regn.* 4–5). In a similar vein, Dio criticizes rulers whose sole ambition is honor rather than the interests of their country: "And what is most serious is that these men [rulers], not for the sake of what is truly best and in the interest of their country itself, but for the sake of reputation and honors and the possession of greater

the law for benefactions are "crowns and public proclamations and seats of honor," and such things are worth everything for those who win them (*De Lege* 7–8). The law specifies the three words with which the good men (τῶν ἀγαθῶν) are publicly acclaimed, but Dio does not state what these words are (*De Lege* 7–8). H. Lamar Crosby suggests that perhaps the words are "he is a good man (ἀνὴρ ἀγαθός ἐστι)."[58] Additionally, honors may also be in the form of "statues, public burial, commemorative games, and many other valuable things" (*Grat.* 44:4).[59]

Perhaps the clearest mark of a true king is that "he is one whom all good men can praise without compunction not only during his life but even afterwards" (*1 Regn.* 33). Quoting Homer, Dio remarks that contrary to the bad king who is cruel and on whom "men call down evil from the gods," all mankind praises the good king due to his generosity and goodness (*1 Regn.* 47). Writing to the people of Rhodes, Dio affirms:

> [T]here is nothing nobler or more just than to show honor to our good men (τοὺς ἀγαθοὺς ἄνδρας) and to keep in remembrance those who have served us well . . . For those who take seriously their obligations toward their benefactors and mete out just treatment to those who have loved them, all men regard as worthy of their favor (χάριτος ἀξίους), and without exception each would wish to benefit them to the best of his ability (*Rhod.* 7–8).

---

power than their neighbors, in the pursuit of crowns and precedence and purple robes, fixing their gaze upon these things and staking all upon their attainment, do and say such things as will enhance their own reputations" (*2 Tars.* 34:29).

58. Crosby, *Dio Chrysostom LCL* V. 247n2.

59. In his *Speech of Greeting or Friendship for His Native Land* (*Grat.*), which was probably delivered when Dio returned from the embassy to Trajan, Dio thanks the people of Prusa for their love, friendship, and goodwill. Apparently, Prusa expressed their gratitude to Dio for bringing many benefits to them. Dio says that because of the profound love shown him, he does not need statues, proclamations, seats of honor, or even "if it be a portrait statue of beaten gold set up in the most distinguished shrines. For one word spoken out of goodwill and friendship is worth all the gold and crowns and everything else deemed splendid that men possess" (2). The implication here is that these items are common ways of demonstrating gratitude. Dio then adds that if he must be honored then the honors granted to his forebears are sufficient for him (3–4). As Jones observes, Dio's seeming refusal or polite show conforms to a common etiquette that "benefactors decline or moderate the rewards offered by grateful beneficiaries" (*Roman World*, 105). Dio admonishes Prusa to hope for imperial gifts even as they seek to excel in all virtues (*Grat.* 10). For further discussion of Dio's benefactions, see Jones, *Roman World*, 104–14.

Dio points out at least two advantages of honoring benefactors. First, it leads to further benefits as benefactors consider such recipients as "worthy of their favor" (χάριτος ἀξίους). Second, the maintenance of the reciprocity circle enhances social cohesion since there is security for all citizens. In other words, there is harmony and a sense of commitment when each side of the benefaction system discharges their respective obligations.

Failure to return a favor is both shameful and hurtful to peaceful coexistence. In this regard, Dio condemns the people of Rhodes for their ingratitude and envy as evident in their altering of the inscriptions on older statues to honor newer benefactors. This is a derogatory practice because it amounts to letting the "memory of the noblest men be forgotten and to deprive them of the rewards of virtue." It is an act that "cannot find any plausible excuse, but must be ascribed to ingratitude, envy, meanness and all the basest motives" (*Rhod.* 25). Changing inscriptions is disgraceful to benefactors as it amounts to rescinding honors previously bestowed (*Rhod.* 29). Given that there is nothing more sacred than honor or gratitude (*Rhod.* 37), failure to honor a benefactor is preposterous (*Rhod.* 27). This implies that altering previous inscriptions is tantamount to ingratitude and obliteration of the memory of the past benefactors from posterity. Moreover, since there are public records which contain the decrees by which honors are given, the inscriptions must be preserved for all time (*Rhod.* 53). To underline the value attached to honors, Dio elsewhere writes that although crowns, public proclamations, and seats of honor entail no expense for those who supply them, they are worth everything for those who win them (*De lege* 7).

Whereas Dio endorses the ethic of reciprocity, he also criticizes it, particularly when benefactors refuse to help the poor because of their inability to offer a commensurate return. Commenting on the Homeric account of Telemachus's refusal to assist a swineherd, Dio states that human benefaction is very calculating as benefactors only help the rich who can return a favor (*Ven.* 88–89). This criticism is not intended to nullify the need to honor benefactors, but to censor the rich who turn benefactions into loans, and who ignore the poor even when they are of reputable character. The crucial point for Dio is that benefactors who are genuinely concerned for the interest of humanity should be honored accordingly.

Overall, in addition to being the representative of Zeus, Dio portrays the ideal king as a shepherd, a father, a general, a savior, and a protector who does not withhold favors from good men, even if they are poor. The ruler's philanthropy elicits the goodwill and affection of his subjects.

Similarly, the ideal king highly values his friends and delightfully allows them to share in his resources. Such friends must be people of reputable character. The king's benefactions win the gratitude of his subjects, and the most endeared way of expressing gratitude is through inscriptions.

Pliny the Younger (ca. 61/62–113 CE)

Pliny the Younger was born in 61/62 CE into a landowning family in Comum, Italy. Because of his equestrian background, he rose in rank and entered the senatorial class in the 80s.[60] He served in prominent positions under the emperors Domitian (81–96), Nerva (96–98), and Trajan (98–117). He was named consul in 100 CE and continued to serve under Trajan as a judicial appointee and governor in Bythinia-Pontus, where he died sometime before the end of Trajan's rule (117 CE). Pliny's letters seek to instruct their recipients through praise. He delivered the *Panegyricus* in 100 CE upon his assumption of consulship. The speech offers thanks to Trajan and portrays him as the ideal example of a good ruler (*princeps*).

The Ideal Ruler

In the *Panegyricus* for Trajan, Pliny asserts that the ideal ruler is a generous benefactor (28–31, 37, 50) and a father of his people, not a tyrant and master (2:3; cf. 21:1–4; 91:4). He is also magnanimous and moderate (58:5).[61] The ideal king labors for the welfare of his people and ensures everyone's safety (44). He brings joy to everyone by his kindness (22). Pliny explicitly identifies Trajan as the benefactor of his people (6:3) and praises him for his generosity, which is like that of Trajan's father (43:4; cf. 28:4) and which motivates him to let the people enjoy his possessions as if they have a share in them (50:1). One of the emperor's benefactions is largesse distributed to all civilians (25:2). Pliny emphasizes that no one was excluded from the emperor's distribution (25:3–5).[62] Other imperial

---

60. On Pliny's background, see Krasser, "P. Caecilius Secundus," 390–92; Sherwin-White and Price, "Pliny the Younger," 1198.

61. For a helpful discussion on the portrait of the ideal ruler in Latin Panegyrists, see Born, "Perfect Prince," 20–35.

62. Pliny notes that the emperor's benefactions came from his own purse (e.g., *Pan.* 27:4).

benefactions included financial support to poor children (26:6),[63] the establishment of peace that created a conducive environment for the production of plentiful corn (29:1–5), supplying the needs of citizens and allies alike (33:1), sponsoring public entertainment and gladiatorial games (33:1–4; cf. 34:1–5), and repair and maintenance of buildings and temples (50:3–5; 51:3–5). Due to these benefactions, Trajan made every Roman citizen feel valued (25:5).

The emperor extended his benefactions abroad as he supplied grain to Egypt when the country looked to him for aid (30:1–5). Pliny praises Trajan for his quick and benevolent response to human need as exemplified in the case of Egypt (30:5). The plight of Egypt granted the emperor the opportunity to offer gifts and talents, and thereby obtain greatness (31:2; cf. 31:6). Indeed, it is a benefit for all provinces to have come under the rule and protection of Rome because Rome is "blessed with a prince who could switch the earth's bounty here and there, as occasion and necessity require, bringing aid and nourishment to a nation cut off by the sea as if its people were numbered among the humbler citizens of Rome!" (32:1). Pliny even implies that Trajan's generosity and care for the desperate surpasses that of the gods (32:2). Because Trajan is the source of every imaginable benefit for his subjects and beyond, Pliny says that it is apt to pray for "the safety of our prince" (94:2); he adds that the emperor ought to pray for himself alone since the state and the citizens alike depend on him (72:1). The *Panegyricus*, then, presents the ideal emperor as a universal benefactor who labors hard for the safety of humanity and whose generosity brings joy, relief, and prosperity to all.

Discrimination

Like the other authors discussed above, Pliny maintains that gift-giving needs to be calculated. He tells Trajan that those who are honest are rewarded with "honors, priesthoods, [and] provinces from your hands, and they flourish in your friendship and favor" (*Pan.* 44:7). Even in the Senate, there is an inner circle of the emperor's friends: "And to those of you in the Senate whom our Father deems worthy of his friendship and regard, I say: cherish the high opinion he has of you . . . for a prince may show that he can feel affection in one case without being blamed for not doing as much for others" (87:3–4). When the emperor rewards integrity

---

63. See Rawson, "Children as Cultural Symbols, 21–42.

with his friendship and attendant gifts, he implicitly rebukes those of bad character to change so that they too may be rewarded (44:8).

The emperor only employs those who have been carefully considered and selected based on their honesty and good character (88:1–3). His friends enjoy the ownership of princely possessions (50:7), for the emperor cannot withhold anything from a friend (86:1). Pliny stresses elsewhere the need to examine the character of the donees. In his letter to Priscus, whom he describes as commanding a large army that in turn gives Priscus a plentiful source of benefits to confer, Pliny writes about his friend Vocinius Romanus whose gratitude for the privileges granted by the emperor reveals that he is worthy of more favors: "It was to show you [Priscus] that he [Vocinius Romanus] is worthy of it [the highest office] and even of your closest intimacy that I have thus briefly described his interests and character, in short his whole life" (*Ep.* 2.13.11–12).[64] Writing to Statius Sabinus, Pliny notes that the people of Firmum are worthy of his care and attention because of their excellent reputation (*Ep.* 6.18.3). For Pliny, then, the benefactor cannot ignore the character of the beneficiaries even as he seeks to be of service to his friends, who reciprocate by giving loyalty.

Reciprocity

In one of the clearest assertions that a ruler expects his subjects to reciprocate his benefactions, Pliny states that the favors of the emperors and kings "resemble baited hooks or snares" that draw out with them whatever they touch (*Pan.* 43:5). The emperor seeks the affection of his people by his benefactions to them (28:2–3). In an interesting twist, albeit sarcastic, Pliny appears to suggest that Trajan is exceptional, for while he displays great generosity he is seemingly not too keen on returns:

> If someone dies now without showing gratitude, still he leaves heirs to his property, and nothing comes to you [Trajan] but an increase in reputation: for generosity may be more fortunate when it receives recognition, but is more glorious when it does

---

64. Pliny here acts as a broker. He states that if this request is granted then he would gladly be indebted to Priscus (*Ep.* 2.13.1). In a different place, Pliny assumes the role of a broker as he writes to the emperor Trajan when he was provincial governor of Bithynia in Asia Minor, asking the emperor to bestow more favors on Rosianus Geminus (*Ep.* 10.26.1–3).

not. Yet who before you chose this distinction in preference to additional wealth? (43:5).

We can infer at least three points from this text. First, showing gratitude for gifts is an indisputable social convention. Second, Trajan did not insist on reciprocity from his subjects, but this did not free them from this obligation. For even if one were to die without expressing gratitude, his heirs would still have to discharge this obligation. Lastly, Trajan still desires to be greatly honored because of his generosity. That is why Pliny maintains that delayed gratitude increases the reputation of the emperor as it indebts beneficiaries for a longer period. Thus, the emperor applies the ethic of reciprocity in ways that ultimately lead to self-aggrandizement and increase his subjects' dependency on him. Due to his exceptional rule, Trajan won the title *Optimus*, a title that "will never return to the memory of man without recalling you [Trajan], and whenever our descendants are called on to bestow it, they will always remember who it was whose merits won it as his due" (88:10; cf. 2:7–8).

Pliny praises Trajan as a lover of peace who comes home with true and genuine honor after ending strife and overcoming enemies (16:1–4). The people of Rome "are deeply in your [Trajan's] debt, and doubly so— for your own character, and even more for the improvement it has made in our own" (41:4).[65] As a result of the emperor's honesty and kindness demonstrated through generosity and rewarding good character, Trajan's "name is engraved not on beams of wood or blocks of stone but in the records of imperishable glory" (54:7). This might seem to suggest that through decreed honors, Trajan has attained immortality as his memory would be passed on from one generation to another, with his statues reminding everyone of his outstanding service to the empire and beyond (55:6–7). But that is not Pliny's point. Wherein lies the true and eternal glory of a prince? It must be a place where "devouring flames, passage of time, and the hands of a successor have no power" (55:9). Statues, altars, and temples can be destroyed, or be lost in oblivion, or be reviled or neglected by posterity (55:9).[66] In contrast, praise won by virtue and good deeds is the emperor's only secure pathway to lasting reputation. It is the

---

65. The Senate hailed Trajan as "fortunate," not because of his wealth, but on the basis of his inner self. Trajan writes that "genuine good fortune lies in being judged worthy of enjoying it" (*Pan.* 74:2). Because the emperor is the greatest of the blessings, the people of Rome appreciate the extent of their debt to him (86:3).

66. See *Pan.* 52:4–6, where Pliny writes about statues of Trajan's predecessors which were broken and destroyed by the people.

form of reciprocation expressed and retained, not in silver and gold, but in people's love (55:9–11). This is the kind of honor that Trajan has already won: "That happy fortune [eternal glory] is yours to enjoy, in every way you could desire, for your radiant face and beloved countenance dwell in the words, the looks, and the thoughts of all your subjects" (55:11). Nothing can bring Trajan greater glory than the people's thanks, which he has won by his true virtue and benevolence (56; cf. 52:7). And this glory will abide whether Trajan's successors follow his example or not (64:4).

As we have seen, Trajan's generosity extends to conquered territories such as Egypt. Because of the aid that Egypt received from Trajan when they were facing famine and starvation, they are indebted to Rome and her people. Using the imagery of farming, Pliny asks Egypt to ensure they return the king's favor: "[T]ake the seed sowed in your soft embrace and return it multiplied. We ask no interest, but remember that you have a debt to repay; redeem the broken promise of a single year in all the years and all the centuries to come, the more so as we are making no demands" (32:4). One cannot miss Rome's pride as conveyed in Pliny's words which are adorned with subtle sarcasm. Trajan's benefactions to Egypt are a hook that returns with whatever it touches. Rome is not asking for interest; nevertheless, the seed sowed should be multiplied when returned. Rome is not making any demands, yet Pliny sees no problem reminding Egypt that they have a debt to repay. This is a clear example of how the ethic of reciprocity pervades imperial benefactions. The implication is that the emperor's reputation is greatly diminished when the beneficiaries fail to acknowledge his good deeds and their continued indebtedness to him.

While Pliny's *Panegyricus* for Trajan is not void of flattery, it, like Seneca's *De Beneficiis*, which also utilizes hyperbole to describe the ideal, reveals social conventions that operate in gift-giving and in how rulers are keen on magnifying their honor through good deeds. The good ruler is magnanimous, generous, and paternal. He protects his subjects and brings them great joy. As a universal ruler, the emperor extends his watchful concern abroad and saves humanity from any adversity they might face. All these benefactions earn the emperor imperishable glory as his name is engraved in the immortal love of posterity.

Epigraphic Evidence

One way of expressing gratitude and honoring benefactors is through honorary inscriptions.[67] Paul Veyne notes that the real motivation of the benefactor "was not so much the honour itself as the engraving of the decree which awarded it and which posterity would be able to read."[68] Monumental statues would be erected in the public space such as temples and marketplaces, and an inscription containing the benefactor's name and the citizens' praise and gratitude would accompany each statue.[69] The honorific decree was the means by which "a grateful populace in the Graeco-Roman world recognized personal character or distinguished services."[70] When a polis issued decrees, it would justify them by such statements as "so that it may be manifest to all that the people know how to return . . . adequate thanks . . . to benefactors for the services they have performed," or "so that the people might be seen by all to be showing its gratitude."[71] Bruce W. Winter writes, "The Greek epigraphic benefactor *genre* conveyed the following information: Whereas A did X for our city, it is therefore resolved to honour A as follows . . . in order that all may see that the People appropriately honour benefactors commensurate with

---

67. See Danker, *Benefactor*. Danker provides an extensive epigraphic study of the phenomenon of benefaction as expressed through the honorific inscriptions. In addition to translating various texts and providing their respective historical and philological commentary, Danker discusses how the authors of Luke-Acts, the Pastorals, 2 Peter, and to a lesser extent Paul used the benefactor model in their theological discourse. For a general introduction to the epigraphic culture, see Meyer, "Explaining the Epigraphic Habit," 74–96; Macmullen, "Epigraphic Habit," 233–46. Other helpful recent works include Bodel, "Brief Guide," 153–74, which provides summaries of the respective contents of the various publications; Horsley and Llewelyn, *New Documents*, which provides updates on recent papyri and inscriptions that are relevant to biblical studies. Also relevant are Keppie, *Understanding Roman Inscriptions*; Woodhead, *Study of Greek Inscriptions*; McLean, *Introduction to Greek Epigraphy*; Hellerman, *Reconstructing Honor*.

68. Veyne, *Bread and Circuses*, 127.

69. Concerning the ubiquity of statues, Walker writes, "Imperial figures were everywhere, lining the streets, supervising the marketplaces and theaters, and residing in temples" (*Paul's Offer*, 112). On different categories of imperial statues in Greece and Asia Minor, see Vermeule, *Roman Imperial Art*, 6–7.

70. Danker, *Benefactor*, 30.

71. *SIG*.3 374 (Austin, *Hellenistic World*, no. 54) and *OGIS* 267 II (Austin, *Hellenistic World*, 229). Cf. *SEG* 35.744.

their benefactions" (italics original).⁷² In this way benefaction perpetuated the reputation and memory of the benefactor.⁷³

The desire to have one's name inscribed for posterity reveals benefactors' love of honor (φιλοτιμία). As a public display of gratitude, the honorific inscription "sets the official seal of approval on the benefactor's quest for φιλοτιμία in the public interest, encourages its continuance . . . and promises rewards commensurate with his beneficence."⁷⁴ Dio Chrysostom writes, "For the pillar, the inscription, and being set up in bronze are regarded as a high honor by noble men" (*Rhod.* 20). The honorific inscription was, therefore, perhaps the highest achievement one could accomplish because it was the most certain way of securing immortality. Acts of kindness and spectacular achievements in the interest of the public guaranteed victory over death through epigraphic memorialization. Similarly, displaying honor and praise to benefactors in public was not only a strategic way of exerting pressure on them to confer more gifts but also an inducement to those who saw it to emulate the original benefactor's virtue to earn similar recognition.⁷⁵ Inscriptions could be autobiographical or biographical. The four inscriptions examined below will illustrate how the concepts of gratitude (εὐχαριστία), honor (τιμή), and worth (ἄξιος) predominate the benefaction system and the ethic of reciprocity that sustains it.

---

72. Winter, *Seek the Welfare*, 27. Also see Harrison, *Paul's Language of Grace*, 39–40. Ma also provides a helpful discussion and relevant illustrations of honorific formula (*Statues and Cities*, 31–38, 56).

73. See Harland, *Associations, Synagogues, and Congregations*, 155–73.

74. Harrison, *Paul's Language of Grace*, 40.

75. Peterman, *Paul's Gift*, 86. Pliny's letter to Priscus illustrates this practice of soliciting further benefactions through gratitude. Soliciting for Voconius Romanus's promotion, Pliny asserts that Romanus's obligation to Pliny would be better maintained by additional favors, particularly because Romanus always receives Pliny's gifts with so much gratitude (*Ep.* 2.13.11–12). Stevenson aptly summarizes the function of honorary decrees: "The obvious meaning of these decrees was to honor and thank the benefactor in a public manner and with a tangible reward; yet the decrees also benefitted the giver in a somewhat self-aggrandizing fashion" ("Conceptual Background," 267). Lambert also summarizes this double duty of decrees as follows: "X benefits the city; the city honors X; because of the honor the city expects X to continue benefiting the city" ("What Was the Point of Inscribed Honorific Decrees?," 195).

Scepsians Honor Antigonus

In about 311 BCE, the Greek city of Scepsis honored Antigonus for his achievements and the benefits he brought to the city as follows:

> [S]ince Antigonus has been responsible for great benefits to the city and the other Greeks, [the people of Scepsis have resolved] to praise Antigonus and to rejoice with him in what has been accomplished; let the city also rejoice with the other Greeks that they shall live in peace henceforth enjoying freedom and autonomy; and so that Antigonus may receive honors worthy of his achievements and the people should be seen to be returning thanks for the benefits it has received, let it mark off a sacred enclosure . . . for him, build an altar and set up a cult statue as beautiful as possible, and let the sacrifice, the competition, the wearing of the wreath and the rest of the festival be celebrated every year in his honor as they were before. Let it crown him with a gold crown . . . and crown Demetrius and Philippus [sons of Antigonus] . . . and let it proclaim the crowns at the contest during the festival; let the city offer a sacrifice for the good tidings sent by Antigonus . . . and let the treasurer provide the money for this expense. Let . . . there be inscribed on a stele the text of the agreement . . . and place it in the sanctuary of Athena; let the secretary supervise the task, and let the treasurer provide the money for the expenditure.[76]

There are many points worth noting from this detailed declaration, but we will only draw attention to three. First, whereas Antigonus might have brought various kinds of benefactions to the city, the ones that really stand out as the most valuable are peace and freedom. Although the decree does not provide background details of wars or conflicts that the city might have faced, it is evident that prior to the achievements of Antigonus the people lacked liberty.[77] The highly regarded gifts of peace and freedom have brought the people of Scepsis to the same level of autonomy as the other Greeks so much that they can now "rejoice with the other Greeks." Second, gratitude for the benefits bestowed is not optional;

---

76. *OGIS* 6. The translation used here is from Austin, *Hellenistic World*, no. 39 (slightly modified).

77. In a brief section on Scepsis, Strabo states that the families of Scamandrius the son of Hector and Ascanius the son of Aeneias "held the kingship over Scepsis for a long time." Even after Scepsis became a democracy, the heirs of the royal family were still called kings and exercised some prerogatives. It was through Antigonus that the Scepsians were incorporated into Alexandreia (*Geogr.* 13:52).

rather it is a cultural obligation that must be discharged appropriately. That is why through the honors voted to Antigonus, which include sacred enclosure, altar, statue, and crown, the city wants to publicize its reciprocity so that all may recognize that Scepsis knows how to honor its benefactor. Finally, it is interesting to note that the honors of sacred enclosure, altar, and cult statue are all divine in nature. Moreover, the city would offer an annual sacrifice for Antigonus's benefactions, and the inscription should be kept in the sanctuary of Athena. These honors have clearly elevated Antigonus to a godlike figure worthy of veneration. His achievements on behalf of the city have transformed every aspect of the city's life. In turn, the city has discharged its obligation to return thanks and to ensure that posterity remembers their king and benefactor.

Egyptians Honor Ptolemy V

The reign of Ptolemy V Epiphanes (210–180 BCE) lavished the Egyptians with many gifts. In turn, the Egyptians issued a lengthy decree, acknowledging the king's worthiness and generosity as well as honoring him as their benefactor (196 BCE). Here are excerpts from the decree followed by Danker's translation:

> Βασιλεύοντος τοῦ νέου καὶ παραλβόντος τὴν βασιλείαν παρὰ Τοῦ πατρὸς κυρίου βασιλειῶν μεγαλοδόξου τοῦ τὴν Αἴγυπτον κατραστησαμένου καὶ τὰ πρὸς τοὺς θεοὺς εὐσεβοῦς ἀντιπάλων ὑπερτέρου, τοῦ τὸν βίον τῶν ἀνθπώπων ἐπανορθώσαντος, κυρίου τριακονταετηρίδων καθάπερ ὁ Ἥφαιστος ὁ μέγας, βασιλέως καθάπερ ὁ Ἥλιος ... Ἐπειδὴ βασιλυὲς Πτολεμαῖος αἰωνόβιος, ἠγαπημενος ὑπό τοῦ Φθᾶ, θεὸς Ἐπιφνὴς Εὐχάριςτος, ὁ ἐγ βασιλέως Πτολεμαίου καὶ βασιλίσσης Ἀρσινοης, θεῶν φιλοπατόρων, κατὰ πολλὰ εὐεργέτηκεν τά θ' ἱερὰ καὶ τοὺς ἐν αὐτοῖς ὄντας καὶ τοὺς ὑπο τὴν ἑαυτοῦ βασιλέιαν τασσομένους ἅπαντας, ὑπάρχων θεὸς ἐκ θεοῦ καὶ θεᾶς καθάπερ Ὧρος ὁ τῆς Ἴσιος καὶ Ὀσιριος υἱός, ὁ ἐπαμύνας τῶι πατρὶ αὐτοῦ Ὀσίρει, τὰ πρὸς θεούς.[78]

> In the reign of the young (King)—who has received the rule from his father—Glorious Lord of the Royal Crowns, who brought stability to the land of Egypt and showed his piety in everything that pertains to the Gods, supreme over his enemies, who improved the people's lot, Lord of the Thirty Years' Festival; Like Hephaistos the Great; a king like Helios ... Whereas Ever-Living King

78. OGIS 90, lines 1-2, 9-10. Also SEG 8232; CIG 3.4697.

Ptolemy Beloved-of-Phtah God Epiphanes Eucharistos, son of King Ptolemy (IV) and Queen Arsinoe, the Gods Philopatores, has in many ways showed generosity to the temples and to those who dwell in them and to all who are under his scepter, being a god, son of a god and a goddess—as is Horus, the son of Isis and Osiris, who avenged his father Osiris.[79]

The decree underscores the king's worthiness by asserting that he excelled in piety towards the gods and demonstrated great commitment to the people's welfare. He maintained peace and stability by prevailing over his enemies and destroying the impious.[80] He brought relief to the Egyptians by declaring amnesty and pardon, and some remission of rents, taxes, and debts (lines 9–21). He also gave liberally to the temples and provided certain tax and public service exemptions for the priests (lines 29–36). Ptolemy V also founded altars, shrines, and temples, and whenever necessary, he renovated them "with the zeal of a beneficent deity."[81] The king's care for Egypt at large and for the cult in particular is aptly summarized in lines 10–11: "[B]eing inclined with generosity toward the gods he has dedicated income of gold and grain in the temples and has borne many expenses in order to bring Egypt back to prosperity and to establish the shrines."[82] A few lines later, the decree reiterates that the king endured great expenses of grain and money to promote cultic observance and safety for the people (line 21).

Due to these benefactions the general council of Egyptian priests resolved "to multiply abundantly the honors that belong" to the king as a demonstration of their gratitude (lines 36–53).[83] Among other things, the statue of the king bearing the name "Ptolemy, Avenger of Egypt" (line 39), would be erected in each temple, and the priests would offer sacrifices daily before the statue. Additionally, the council resolved that the birthday of the king as well as the day he received the kingdom from his father would be commemorated "throughout the land of Egypt, with feasts and festivals." The reason for celebrating these two days was that they marked the beginning of good things for all Egyptians (lines 46–48). The final resolution was to inscribe the decree and place it in the temples near the statue of the immortal king. Towards the end, the decree asserts

---

79. Translated by Danker, *Benefactor*, no. 31.
80. On the King's victory over his enemies, see lines 22–28.
81. Danker, *Benefactor*, no. 31, line 34.
82. Danker, *Benefactor*, 208.
83. See Danker, *Benefactor*, 207–11.

its hortatory intention, namely, that the resolutions were passed "so that all might know that the people of Egypt do, with all legal right, magnify and honor God Epiphanes Eucharistos the King" (line 53). The goal of this decree then was to perpetuate the memory and the reputation of Ptolemy V as a victorious, pious, and generous benefactor, whose great deeds brought lasting prosperity to Egypt.

Res Gestae Divi Augusti

Augustus composed *Res Gestae Divi Augusti* to provide an account of his accomplishments as emperor. As has been pointed out by others, *Res Gestae* reflects Augustus's self-perception as Rome's ideal ruler.[84] Augustus wanted *Res Gestae* to be inscribed and displayed on bronze tablets that were to be set up at the entrance to his Mausoleum on the Field of Mars.[85] The emperor states that he wrote *Res Gestae* in his seventy-sixth year (35:2), which means that he composed it sometime between his last birthday (September 23, 13 CE) and his death (August 19, 14 CE). He portrays himself as a generous benefactor and an effective agent of the *Pax Romana*. For our purpose, we will discuss Augustus's role as benefactor followed by how the people honored him.

Augustus dispensed many benefactions to Rome and beyond. He supplied grain when the citizens were hit by grain shortage (5:2; 15:1; 18). His role as a provider of "bread" liberated "the people from the present fear and danger at my own expense in a few days" (5:2).[86] Apart from grain, the emperor gave gifts of money to the treasury (17:1–2; 18) and to the plebs (15:1–4), and constructed and repaired public buildings and temples (19–21; 24).[87] He rebuilt the city of Rome and so beautified it

---

84. For instance, Smith, *Christ the Ideal King*, 48.

85. Suetonius, *Aug.* 2.101.4; Cooley, *Res Gestae Divi Augusti*, 3. Cooley observes that the "use of bronze set the *RGDA* [*Res Gestae Divi Augusti*] on a par with Roman legal and other important official documents, and evoked ideals of sacrosanctity and durability."

86. All citations of *Res Gestae* are based on Cooley, *Res Gestae Divi Augusti*. Some other recent works on *Res Gestae* include Ridley, *Emperor's Retrospect*; Judge, *First Christians*, 182–223.

87. Augustus also served as chief priest. He became *pontifex maximus* in March 12 BCE after the death of its former bearer M. Aemilius Lepidus the previous year. He transformed chief priesthood into a "post of supreme religious authority in Rome" (Cooley, *Res Gestae Divi Augusti*, 148). To mark his election as *pontifex maximus*, the emperor donated to a great crowd that had assembled from the whole of Italy (*Res*

that "he could justly boast that he had found it built of brick and left it in marble" (Suetonius, *Aug.* 28). In his sixth consulship and in accordance with a decree of the senate he "repaired eighty-two temples in the city . . . leaving none that needed repair at that time (*Res Gestae* 20:4).[88] Augustus's cultic benefactions, including restoration of temples, rites, and priesthoods, as well as offering sacrifices to the gods, demonstrated his generosity and commitment to *pietas*.[89] Other benefactions included distribution of land to soldiers (16:1), cultic offerings (21:2), and gladiatorial games and other amusements (22–23).

Perhaps Augustus's leading benefaction was the establishment of the Augustan peace.[90] He brought freedom from enemies leading to peace in the entire empire (1:1; 2:5; 6:13; 26–33). Augustus boasts of extinguishing the flames of civil war after receiving by universal consent the absolute control of affairs. To underline the extent to which he brought peace, the emperor writes: "It is agreed that the gate of War, which our ancestors desired to be closed once all land and sea was at peace under the Romans, has before me, since the foundation of the city, in the whole era been closed twice only, whereas under my leadership the senate voted for it to be closed three times" (13).[91] The poet Horace celebrates the blessings of the *Pax Augusta* by noting that his reign has restored "rich harvests to the fields, and restored to our Jove the standards torn down from the proud doorposts of the Parthian." Moreover, the emperor has eliminated war, removed sin, renewed the ancient arts, and so extended the prestige

---

Gestae 10:2). Augustus writes, "I have been chief priest [*pontifex maximus*], augur, one of the Fifteen for conducting sacred rites, one of the Seven in charge of feasts, Arval brother, member of the fraternity of Titus, and fetial priest" (*Res Gestae* 7:3). Gordon states that about twenty of the 230 extant statues of Augustus represent him in the act of sacrificing ("Veil of Power," 212). Cooley notes that after Augustus's reign, all successive emperors until Gratian, who became emperor in 367 CE, held the office of *pontifex maximus* (*Res Gestae Divi Augusti*, 148). The emperor may thus be described as the hub and symbol of religious stability as well as the paradigm of virtuous devotion to the gods. Hoklotubbe states that imperial ideology "held that the emperor, in his capacity as the high priest (*pontifex maximus*) of Rome's state cult, was especially near to the gods and secured the gods' benefaction to the empire through his pious service toward them" (*Civilized Piety*, 71).

88. On how Augustus promoted cult and sacred traditions, see Galinsky, *Augustan Culture*, 295–96; Gradel, *Emperor Worship*.

89. On priesthoods that Augustus founded or reorganized, see Zanker, *Power of Images*, 118–35.

90. For a recent discussion on the *Pax Romana*, see Goldsworthy, *Pax Romana*.

91. Also see 26:2–3.

and majesty of the Empire that Horace can say, "With Caesar in charge of affairs, peace will not be driven out by civic madness or violence, or by the anger that beats out swords and makes cities wretched by turning them against one another" (*Carm.* 4.15.5–20). Horace praises Augustus for bringing peace to his subjects (*Saec.* 4.5.33–36) and enhancing abundant crop production (*Saec.* 4.5.37–41). Suetonius comments that Augustus made Rome safe "for the future, so far as human foresight could provide for this" (*Aug.* 28). In short, the *Pax Augusta* guaranteed the well-being and prosperity of the emperor's subjects.

What was the source of the emperor's largesse? Augustus continually reiterates that all these benefactions came from his own wealth, or from spoils taken in war (*Res Gestae* 1:1; 2:5; 5:2; 3:15; 15:1; 17:1–2; 18; 21:1–2). As Fergus Millar states, Augustus's enumeration of his largesse shows that in his estimation he succeeded in fulfilling the "role demanded of a true 'king' in Greek thought, in dispensing gifts."[92] Likewise, his establishment of peace within the empire and beyond demonstrates that he fulfilled the expectation that an ideal king must enhance social cohesion and harmony.[93] While Augustus himself did not claim the title of "king" (*rex*), his "superiority in benefactions, his military success and the production of peace, and his outstanding virtue show clearly his self-portrait as a Hellenistic king."[94] Horace aptly summarizes Augustus's benefactions:

> [F]or when your face shines like spring upon the citizens, the day passes more happily and the sun's radiance is brighter . . . For then the ox ambles over the pastures in safety; Ceres and kindly Prosperity give increase to the crops, sailors wing their way across a sea clear of lawlessness, fidelity takes care not to incur blame, the home is pure, unstained by any lewdness, custom and law have gained control over the plague of vice, mothers are praised for having similar children, punishment follows hard on the heels of guilt (*Carm.* 4.5.17–24).

How did the people honor Augustus for his benefactions? The historian Suetonius states that Augustus expected his friends to reciprocate his benefactions with affection "both in life and after death" (*Aug.* 66). The emperor scrutinized the deathbed utterances of his friends, expressing his satisfaction whenever he was shown gratitude and affection. But

---

92. Millar, *Emperor in the Roman World*, 190.

93. For a discussion of the emperor's role in establishing *concordia*, see Born, "Perfect Prince," 22–23.

94. Jipp, *Christ Is King*, 23.

whenever his friends failed to praise him, he did not hesitate to express his disappointment (*Aug.* 66). The emperor was not only honored as "Father of the Fatherland" (*Res Gestae* 35:1), but his name was also "incorporated into the hymns of the Salii by decree of the Senate" (10:1).[95] This is confirmed by an inscription stating that "the choir of all Asia, gathering at Pergamum on the most holy birthday of Sebastos Tiberius Caesar god, performs a task that contributes greatly to the glory of Sebastos in hymning the imperial house and performing sacrifices to the Sebastan gods."[96] Suetonius recounts an incident when the passengers and crew of an Alexandrian ship sang praises to Augustus:

> As he [Augustus] sailed by the gulf of Puteoli, it happened that from an Alexandrian ship which had just arrived there, the passengers and crew, clad in white, crowned with garlands, and burning incense, lavished upon him good wishes and the highest praise, saying that it was through him they lived, through him that they sailed the seas, and through him that they enjoyed their liberty and their fortunes (*Aug.* 98).

Augustus won praise and public acclamation by extinguishing hostilities, promoting freedom, and restoring peace and safety in Rome and abroad.

In brief, as a benefactor, Augustus is both a fatherly and a priestly figure who exemplifies devotion to the gods as well as commitment to the prosperity of humanity. His *pietas* towards the nation, the gods, and family demonstrated through generous benefaction toward temples, his subjects, and abroad means that he has the virtue which is necessary for winning the favor of the gods, enhancing the welfare of his subjects, promoting harmony, and securing the *Pax Romana*. Due to his benefactions, the emperor is highly honored as the founder of the *Pax Romana* and as the Father of the Fatherland.

Stratoniceans Honor Marcus Cocceius Nerva

The final inscription we are examining here is dated 96–97 CE, and it describes how the people of Stratonicea, the modern Lagina in Karia, honored Imperator Marcus Cocceius Nerva:

---

95. On encomia to kings, emperors, and heroes, see Jipp, *Christ Is King*, 86–100.
96. Quoted from Price, *Rituals and Power*, 59.

Royal Benefaction in the Greco-Roman Context

> Marcus Cocceius Nerva, Imperator and Consul Designate—
> who has been the benefactor, patron, and protector of our city
> and has restored to us our ancestral freedom and civil rights—
> was honored by the people for a second time with a panegyric,
> a golden crown of valor, and front seating at the contests, in
> appreciation of his arête [virtue], his goodwill, and generosity
> shown to the people of our city.[97]

Pliny the Elder refers to the town of Stratonicea twice (*Nat.* 5:109; 6:119). There is nothing in those references suggesting that the town had been under some duress. To the contrary, the former reference states that Stratonicea is a "free town." But as we see from this inscription the town lost its freedom under circumstances that we do not know, and is now grateful to the emperor for coming to their rescue and for restoring their former glory. Two points are worth noting from the inscription. First, due to the emperor's intervention leading to the restoration of the people's freedom and civil rights, he has been granted the honorifics "benefactor, patron, and protector." These are titles that describe outstanding, and sometimes heroic undertaking, for the good of the populace. It is possible that the people of Stratonicea might have faced war, dangers from surrounding enemies, or even civil unrest that rendered their life unbearable. In such circumstances the emperor took the necessary measures to restore peace and order, which the people describe as "our ancestral freedom and civil rights." The emperor therefore deserves the three honorifics as a way of recognizing how he has used his resources for the prosperity of the people. Second, in addition to the three honorifics, the people decree three specific acts in honor of the emperor: (1) a panegyric; (2) a crown; and (3) a front seating.[98] The people undertake these honorific acts in response to the emperor's virtue, goodwill, and generosity. The conspicuous triadic formula in this inscription might be a mere rhetorical embellishment, but it could also be a deliberate rhetorical strategy for emphasizing the emperor's beneficence as well as the people's enduring gratitude.[99] The overarching point is that Marcus showed great concern and generosity to the city of Stratonicea, and the people in turn reciprocated by conferring on him the highest honors possible.

---

97. Text and translation by Danker, *Benefactor*, no. 39.

98. For a brief discussion on hymns to rulers and kings, see Jipp, *Christ Is King*, 81–93.

99. Ma states, "An honorific decree was a highly stylized text, built according to a formalized, universally known schema" (*Statues and Cities*, 56).

All four inscriptions considered above clearly show that when rulers engage in various forms of good deeds, they are partly motivated by love of honor. The subjects too recognize their obligation to give loyalty and show gratitude by publicizing the worthiness of their rulers through decrees, statues, and inscriptions. Through inscriptions the people assert that their benefactor enjoys an elevated status that can only be maintained by further benefactions. In brief, inscriptions reveal three interconnected factors. First, when people issue an honorific decree they approve of the benefactor's quest for φιλοτιμία through kindness and philanthropy. Second, inscriptions both testify to the merit of the honorand and the worthiness of the honoring body. Lastly, as much as inscriptions express the beneficiaries' gratitude, they are also an indirect way of asking for continued philanthropy. Inscriptions, therefore, reveal how the concepts of φιλοτιμία, ἄξιος, and εὐχαριστία are intricately integrated in the warp and woof of the benefaction system and the ethic of reciprocity.

Summary of Royal Benefaction in the Greco-Roman Context

We can summarize this chapter by highlighting four main points. First, the ideal ruler is a benefactor who manifests love and concern for his subjects by conferring favors on them and by helping them in time of need. The writings and the inscriptions we have looked at employ various imageries to depict a king as beneficent. The ideal ruler is a father, a shepherd, a guardian, a savior, a general, and a friend. These imageries denote the ruler's love, generosity, concern, and philanthropy. Unlike a tyrant who ignores the interests and plight of the masses, the ideal ruler toils hard for his flock to ensure their prosperity. He distributes gifts, maintains peace, protects his people, delivers his subjects from enemies, funds public buildings, promotes cultic adherence by building temples and offering sacrifices, supplies grain, remits debts, provides tax reliefs, and offers medical services. As to his character, the ideal ruler is not just liberal and magnanimous; he is also the best (or "the good") and the most virtuous among men. This means that he promotes virtue by his kindness, gentleness, and piety. The ideal ruler, then, is the exemplar of a generous spirit and high moral character. And because he is the vicegerent of the gods, he serves as the agent through whom the gods dispense their gifts to humanity.

Second, gift-giving is discriminatory, which means that favors are proportionate to the worthiness of the beneficiary. The writings that we have considered above urge benefactors to apply the rule of censorship and of rating so that rather than wander, their gifts may proceed by a secure path. Benefactors should place their gifts strategically as a careful farmer who sows his seeds in productive soil to ensure plentiful harvest, and as a skilled player who pitches the ball to skilled catchers. The point of all these metaphors is that it is the benefactor's duty to carefully select the good and pious as recipients of his benefactions. Favors should not be conferred on the wrong people; it is evil and unacceptable to assist the base. But rewarding virtue with gifts both promotes piety and ensures that gifts are returned with gratitude. The ruler's purse is thus closed tightly towards the impious but loosely towards people of reputable character. While some writers like Aristotle maintain that benefactions should not be made to the poor because they are incapable of magnificence, others like Cicero and Dio argue that if the poor are pious then they too ought to be benefited. So although the motivation to give to the poor might be weak or completely lacking, there is general consensus that benefactors should promote the welfare of the virtuous.[100]

Third, related to the preceding point is the close relationship that a ruler maintains with his friends. A ruler's friends are the noblest and the best among men. They have an intimate access to the ruler and enjoy his special attention. Unlike the Roman plebs who receive benefits more broadly and collectively, and often through brokerage, the emperor's friends who enjoy an unhindered access to him receive benefits directly from him.[101] As Peter Garnsey and Richard Saller write, proximity to the emperor was the privilege of just a few, including members of his household, relatives, and friends of high rank.[102] The friends of a ruler are always convinced that, unlike the ignoble and enemies, the ruler can neither ignore their plight nor fail to grant their requests. By applying the rule of censorship, a ruler seeks to serve his friends *because of who they are*.

Finally, benefactions create reciprocal ties of obligation between the benefactor and the beneficiaries. The subjects are obligated to give loyalty

---

100. Barclay rightly notes that "since the destitute could give nothing worthwhile back to the donor (except the limited good of ceasing to 'hassle' them), the motivation for giving to the poorest members of society was comparatively weak" (*Paul and the Gift*, 43).

101. Garnsey and Saller, *Roman Empire*, 174.

102. Garnsey and Saller, *Roman Empire*, 174.

and obedience to their beneficent ruler. They are to honor their ruler by expressing gratitude publicly and in tangible ways. Both parties must discharge their respective obligation for the sake of social cohesion. A ruler discharges his obligation to bestow favors bearing in mind that the circle is incomplete unless he is duly honored. Rulers are thus motivated by both φιλανθρωπία ("love of humanity") and φιλοτιμία ("love of honor") in their self-portrait as kind, gentle, protective, generous, and caring. The importance of showing gratitude is underlined not just by identifying worthy beneficiaries, but by what Aristotle and Seneca refer to us the three Graces that had been strategically set up to remind the people to return a favor. Honors and expressions of gratitude may be in the form of public praise, social or political support, statues, crowns, and seats of honor among others. But the greatest of all these is the honorary inscription that publicizes the benefactor's virtues, achievements, and honors voted him. The inscription also testifies to the benefactor's victory over mortality as posterity memorializes his acts of kindness. The system of benefaction and the ethic of reciprocity that sustains it, therefore, enable rulers to obtain lasting glory by having their names inscribed on bronze tablets as well as on the immortal love of posterity.

3

Royal Benefaction in Jewish Writings

THE PRECEDING CHAPTER HAS described the system of royal benefaction in the Greco-Roman context, with emphasis on the ideal ruler, discrimination, and reciprocity. The Greco-Roman rulers were keen to portray themselves as beneficent, generous, and caring while the people sought to give the rulers appropriate honor and loyalty to avoid the charge of ingratitude, which was regarded as the worst of all evils. Gift-giving flourished due to the benefactors' liberality and discrimination as well as the beneficiaries' perpetual requital. The present chapter continues with the aim of describing the system of royal benefaction, specifically as found in Jewish writings. In addition to the five questions explored in the previous chapter,[1] the present chapter investigates whether the Jews embraced the ethic of reciprocity.[2]

In his book *Were the Jews a Mediterranean Society?* Seth Schwartz investigates the extent to which the Jews embraced, rejected, or subverted the Greco-Roman system of institutionalized reciprocity.[3] He argues that due to their "strongly antireciprocal cultural imperatives" it was

---

1. The five questions are: (1) What elements and terminologies are involved in the practice of benefaction? (2) What kind of ruler is the ideal ruler in light of the benefaction system? (3) What motivates rulers' self-portrayal as beneficent and kind? (4) How do benefactors pick the beneficiaries of their good deeds? (5) What is expected of the beneficiaries?

2. We are using "Jew" simply to refer to the people of Israel who trace their ancestry to Abraham, Isaac, and Jacob, and whose history, beliefs, values, and political allegiance are intricately tied to their covenantal relationship to Yahweh. By "Jewish writings," we are referring to the Old Testament and Second Temple Literature.

3. Schwartz, *Were the Jews a Mediterranean Society?*

more difficult for the Jews than other provincial populations to integrate in the Roman Empire.[4] Schwartz is mainly concerned with intrahuman reciprocity, hence he cannot be accused of ignoring deuteronomic theology that upholds the principle of retribution, whereby God blesses or curses Israel, depending on faithfulness to the covenant stipulations. Nevertheless, Schwartz's thesis that Torah is opposed to gift exchange and honoring humans is disputable. The question here is: Do later Jewish writers interpret Torah's vision within a reciprocity framework?[5] As we consider various Jewish writings, we will see that the expectation to honor rulers was tightly woven into the fabric of the Jewish royal narrative. Such honors could include loyalty, obeisance, encomia, prayers, sacrifices, and various other gifts.[6] So it would be more accurate to argue that whereas pre-common-era Palestine might have lacked a benefactor-client social structure, it never lacked intrahuman reciprocity.[7] Thus when Paul portrays Jesus as the supreme royal benefactor whose commitment to his followers demands faithful response to his reign, he is not introducing an entirely new concept to the Jewish ear. To gain a better understanding of royal gift-giving among the Jews, the chapter will proceed by examining the Old Testament, Ben Sira, Philo, and Josephus respectively.

Old Testament

Our reading of the OT will be a bit different from how we read the other writings discussed in this section. Unlike Second Temple Literature where we find explicit description of the system of royal benefaction, the OT does not explicitly portray the king as a benefactor in the Greco-Roman

---

4. Schwartz, *Were the Jews a Mediterranean Society?*, 10.

5. By Torah's vision for Israel, we are referring to complete dependence on God and honoring him alone as their provider, lover, friend, father, and Lord. This vision is opposed to gift exchange that perpetuates obsession with honor and promotes an inegalitarian and exploitative dependency. Instead of dependency based on personal ties, Torah commands love for neighbor (Lev 19:18) as a way of reflecting their solidarity and commitment to God.

6. Whereas the Greco-Roman rulers were usually motivated by love of honor and philanthropy, the Jewish rulers, especially those that were successful in their leadership, were driven by the desire to exemplify faithfulness to the covenant.

7. Crook, *Reconceptualising Conversion: Patronage*, 79. Crook argues that unlike the Greeks and Romans, Israel lacked the vocabulary as well as the social institution of benefaction/patronage. Instead, Israel had a covenantal relationship with their God. But Israel's interaction with Hellenism changed all this.

sense of the term. It would be anachronistic and a misreading of the OT to claim that the kings of Israel view themselves as benefactors. However, such benefaction themes as gift, honor, gratitude, loyalty, peace, and suffering are evident in the OT's portrait of the king and in how the king relates to the people. Our discussion will therefore primarily focus on relevant kingship motifs such as anointing, adoption, righteousness, peace, suffering, and deliverance.[8] The goal here is twofold: (1) to demonstrate that the king is Yahweh's representative who establishes a righteous reign; and (2) to show that the king serves as an agent of Yahweh's blessings to the people. Due to his righteous rule that brings peace and prosperity, the people honor and praise the king.

The roots of kingship in ancient Israel can be traced back to the Pentateuch. Yahweh promises Abraham that he would bless his seed and that kings would come from him (Gen 17:6, 17:16; 35:11).[9] In Gen 49:8–12, Jacob predicts that the scepter would not depart from Judah and that he would be honored by his brothers and receive tribute as well as the obedience of the nations. According to Balaam's oracle, a ruler would proceed from Jacob and destroy the enemies of Israel as he exercises his dominion (Num 24:17–19). Deuteronomy 17:14–20 envisages a monarchic Israel and warns the people against choosing as a king a foreigner who would inevitably lead them astray.[10] All these royal texts suggest that kingship was not a foreign concept in ancient Israel. Rather, Yahweh intended to use kingship as a means of accomplishing his purpose for Israel and for the nations. What shape, then, does kingship take in Israel? How does the OT portray the ideal king, especially in light of gift-giving? What is the relationship between Yahweh's rule and the king's rule? How do the people expect to be ruled, and what does the king expect from his subjects? As we consider these questions within the narrow framework of gift-giving and the ethic of reciprocity, our goal will be more illustrative than exhaustive. The two main texts discussed below—Samuel and Chronicles and the Psalter—show that the king is Yahweh's vicegerent who manifests Yahweh's righteous reign and serves as an agent of blessings to the people. Due to his righteous reign and gifts, the people praise and honor the king.

---

8. For a general discussion of the portrait of the king in the OT, see Joseph, *Portrait of the Kings*.

9. On Adam as a royal figure, see Hess, "Splitting the Adam," 1–15.

10. Horbury suggests that Gen 49:1–12; Num 23:21–23; Deut 17:14–20; and 33:4–5 anticipate an eschatological Davidic king (*Jewish Messianism*, 48–49).

Anointed and Adopted Ruler (Samuel and Chronicles)

The books of 1 and 2 Samuel and 1 and 2 Chronicles provide us with a detailed portrait of the king. As God's appointed ruler, the king is Yahweh's anointed one and adopted son. Hannah ends her song by looking forward to the promised king, who will be the Lord's "anointed one" (1 Sam 2:10). The first anointing that we see in Samuel is that of Saul as "the prince" over the Lord's inheritance (1 Sam 10:1).[11] Although Saul does not identify himself as Yahweh's anointed, Yahweh (9:16) and Samuel (10:1; 15:1) speak of his anointing. David himself repeatedly recognizes that Saul is Yahweh's anointed (24:10; 26:11; also see 2 Sam 1:14, 16). Whereas the entire narrative of Saul's rise and reign might have been "composed in ironical and farcical terms to serve as a foil against which to present David as Yahweh's anointed," the view of Yahweh, Samuel, and David that Saul is the Lord's anointed not only presents a high view of Saul but also affirms that whoever assumes the throne as king ought to be chosen by Yahweh.[12]

The one whom the narrator presents as the ideal anointed one is David (and his offspring). Following Yahweh's instruction, Samuel anoints David privately at Bethlehem (1 Sam 16:3, 12–13); henceforth, he is "Yahweh's anointed one," the Messiah of Yahweh.[13] According to Tryggve

---

11. The term that the narrator uses here is נָגִיד rather than מֶלֶךְ. Brooks argues that unlike *melekh* the term *nāgîd* is used of Saul with a favorable connotation (*Saul and the Monarchy*, 52). It is unlikely that *nāgîd* implies a status inferior to that of a king, for the term is also used of David (cf. 13:14; 25:30; 2 Sam 5:2; 6:21; 7:8). Mettinger states that generally *nāgîd* is a title applied to a future king before he begins to reign. Whoever is referred to by this title must become king since he has been divinely designated (*King and Messiah*, 87). The consensus among scholars is that the term means a king-designate. The son of Kish who left home to search for lost donkeys is returning as a prince. For further discussion, see McCarter, *I Samuel*, 186–87.

12. Block, "My Servant David, 38. Commenting on 1 Sam 9:17, Chapman writes, "Samuel's religious credibility, in combination with God's explicit direction . . . rules out any sense that the choice of Saul is a mistaken one" (*1 Samuel as Christian Scripture*, 106).

13. Collins notes that at minimum the term "messiah" refers "to a figure who will play an authoritative role in the end time, usually the eschatological king" (*Scepter and the Star*, 16). Rose defines "messiah" as "a future royal figure sent by God who will bring salvation to God's people and the world and establish a kingdom characterized by features like peace and justice" (*Zemah and Zerubbabel*, 23). Block states that "anointing with oil was a common ancient Near Eastern custom by which individuals were ritually purified and that conferred special power, authority, honor, and glory" ("My Servant David," 23–24). In the OT Hebrew, "messiah" simply means "anointed"

N. D. Mettinger, the term *Messiah* connotes "the king as very definitely set apart from the rest of the people, since it signifies his status as linked with God and thus inviolable."[14] Anointing confers special responsibility, authority, and honor. When representatives from the ten northern Israelites tribes came to Hebron and anointed David as king, they said, "And the Lord said to you, 'You shall be shepherd of my people Israel, and you shall be prince over Israel'" (2 Sam 5:2). Although this promise does not appear earlier in the narrative, it is more likely a reference to Samuel's anointing of David at Bethlehem (1 Sam 16:1–13). These leaders acknowledge that David is Yahweh's appointed king to rule over them (cf. Pss. 2:6–9; 89:26–28; 110:1–4). Their conviction together with the fact that Saul has already been rejected suggests that David is the anointed one of whom Hannah spoke (cf. 2 Sam 22:51; 23:1–7).[15] As Yahweh's anointed, the king receives the Spirit.[16] The narratives of Saul and David show that the anointing is the occasion/cause for the king's endowment with the Spirit of Yahweh (1 Sam 10:10; 16:13).[17] As one upon whom the Spirit rests, the king acts as a vicegerent of Yahweh; he has been divinely equipped to accomplish Yahweh's purposes as his representative.

Related to the preceding point is the assurance that Yahweh's presence abides with his anointed to grant him success for the sake of his people. After Saul unsuccessfully attempted to kill David, the narrator tells us that "Saul was afraid of David because Yahweh was with him but had departed from Saul" (1 Sam 18:12). David was successful in all his undertakings as a commander of Saul's army "because Yahweh was with him" (1 Sam 18:14; cf. 18:28; 2 Sam 5:10–12).[18] Yahweh's presence with

---

and does not necessarily refer to an anticipated figure. See Fitzmyer, *One Who Is to Come*, 8–25; Hess, "Image of the Messiah," 22–33.

14. Mettinger, *King and Messiah*, 199.

15. On David and his offspring as having been granted power to rule, see Collins and Collins, *King and Messiah as Son of God*, 25–30. For further discussion on David as the anointed historical figure par excellence, see Block, "My Servant David," 17–56. For the view that 2 Sam 22:51 and 23:1–7 express a messianic hope, see Satterthwaite et al., *Lord's Anointed*, 47; Watts, *Psalm and Story*, 105–6.

16. For further discussion on the Messiah as receiving Yahweh's Spirit, see Johnson, *Sacral Kingship*, 15–19.

17. According to Fox Saul was not able to handle the Spirit of Yahweh well (*Give Us a King*, 34).

18. See Chapman, *1 Samuel as Christian Scripture*, 151–52.

David is "the decisive influence of Yahweh's special favor for David" that enables him to succeed as a king.[19]

Divine sonship is also closely connected to the identity of the king as Yahweh's anointed. In the dynastic oracle of 2 Sam 7:1–17, God promises to establish an eternal dynasty for David through a son. This son will build a temple and reign forever over the kingdom of Israel. David is referred to both as a servant (vv. 5, 8) and son (v. 14).[20] Adela Y. Collins and John J. Collins argue that, rather than denoting the king's divine nature, adoption as son implies that the king "is empowered to act as God's surrogate on earth."[21] The promise of divine sonship is a common royal language. For instance, in Psalm 2 God says to the king, "You are my son, today I have begotten you." The LXX version of Ps 110:3 states, "I have begotten you from the womb before the morning." What seems clear is that the enthronement of the king is accompanied by a divine oath through which Yahweh begets the king. The sons of David, therefore, are divinely sanctioned as legal heirs of the throne of Israel. According to 1 Chr 28:5, the throne on which Solomon sits is "the throne of the kingdom of Yahweh over Israel" (cf. 1 Chr 16:31; 29:11, 23; 2 Chr 9:8).[22] The point here is that the Davidic kingdom manifests God's kingship over his creation. Yahweh's king occupies an exalted position as he shares Yahweh's throne as his vicegerent. Sharing Yahweh's throne implies that the king also receives divine honors (1 Chr 29:20–25).

In addition to anointing and sonship, Yahweh's appointed ruler also fights his battles and shepherds his flock. Saul successfully fought against the Ammonites and delivered Jabesh-Gilead (1 Sam 11:1–13). Yet more than Saul, David is the king-warrior par excellence. According to 1 Samuel 17, David who was just recently anointed as God's king challenges and kills Goliath. Because of this victory, Saul appoints David over the men of war (1 Sam 18:5). And as David, the army, and King Saul return from the battlefield, the women welcome them with songs of praise and

---

19. McCarter, "Apology of David," 503–4.

20. In his prayer in 2 Sam 7:18–29, ten times David refers to himself as "your [Yahweh's] servant," which reveals his identity as Yahweh's vassal.

21. Collins and Collins, *King and Messiah as Son of God*, 22.

22. On Davidic king as receiving the worship reserved for God, see Lynch, *Monotheism and Institutions*, 209–43. Also see Horbury, *Jewish Messianism*, 132; Hahn, *Kingdom of God*, 97; Jipp, *Christ Is King*, 99–100. On Solomon sharing the throne of Yahweh, see Throntveit, "Idealization of Solomon," 421–23.

celebration (1 Sam 18:6-8).[23] This presents clear evidence that hymning to the king who has acted victoriously to deliver the people is not an alien notion in Israel. The women's song, which ascribes to Saul victory over thousands and to David ten thousands, recognizes that David is more victorious in battle than Saul. David is victorious over the Philistines, Moabites, and Hadadezer among others (1 Sam 23:1-6; 27:8-16; 2 Sam 5; 8; 10; cf. 3:18).[24] God uses David's victories to validate and legitimize his (i.e., David's) kingship over Israel.

The king is also a shepherd of God's flock. As the northern tribes of Israel anoint David at Hebron, they recognize that Yahweh has chosen him to shepherd his people (2 Sam 5:2). Later Yahweh affirms the testimony of the leaders when he says, "Thus says the Lord of hosts, I took you from the pasture, from following the sheep, that you should be prince over my people Israel" (2 Sam 7:8). The Prophets pick up this imagery of the king as a shepherd. Jeremiah 23 condemns shepherds who scatter and destroy the sheep. In the place of these uncaring shepherds Yahweh promises that he will raise up shepherds who will care for and protect his flock. Ezekiel 34:1-31 portrays Yahweh as a benevolent shepherd who rescues his flock from shepherds who feed themselves only at the expense of the flock. These human shepherds are exploitative and ruthless; their actions expose Yahweh's flock to the wild beasts (vv. 5-8). But Yahweh promises to search for his sheep and rescue them. Yahweh's actions culminate with the appointment of a human shepherd over his flock (vv. 23-31). This singular shepherd, namely, "my servant David," will feed the people, restore peace and security, and serve as prince among the people. His reign shall be marked by prosperity as the Lord sends showers of blessing on the land so that the earth might yield abundant produce and the trees of the field their fruit. He will deliver the people from their enemies and from the yoke of oppression and cause them to dwell securely in the land. Ultimately through the benevolent care of this shepherd the people shall know that Yahweh is their God, and they are his people.[25]

Apart from the preceding points, the king also obeys the law (1 Chr 22:12-19; 28:7; 2 Chr 6:16; 7:17-18).[26] In 1 Chr 29:19, David prays

---

23. On encomia to Jewish rulers, see Horbury, *Jewish Messianism*, 127-40; Jipp, *Christ Is King*, 93-100.

24. Satterthwaite, "David in the Books of Samuel," 46.

25. For a helpful discussion of this text and how it contributes to the messianic hope, see Block, "Bringing Back David, 172-77.

26. See Joseph, *Portrait of the Kings*, 77-105.

that God would grant Solomon a "whole heart" so that he may keep the commandments and thereby construct the temple to completion. David implies that without keeping the commandments Solomon cannot succeed in constructing the temple.[27] This requirement to obey the law points back to Deut 17:18–20, which places the law at the center of the duty of the king. He is to write for himself a copy of the law, read it, meditate on it, and obey it so that he may abide in the fear of the Lord.[28] A king who forsakes the Lord's commandments suffers defeat and brings destruction to the land. But the one who is careful to follow the Lord brings prosperity and enjoys a peaceful reign.

Righteous and Universal Ruler (Psalm 72)

The book of Psalms provides a rich resource for royal discourse in ancient Israel. Since it is beyond the scope of this work to consider all of the so-called royal psalms, we will discuss Psalm 72 in detail before providing an overview of kingship discourse in the rest of the Psalter.[29] The goal here is to show that, similar to what we find in the Greco-Roman system of royal benefaction, the Psalter portrays the king as a highly exalted figure, a compassionate deliverer, and an agent of blessings to the people. This discussion will illumine our reading of Paul's portrait of the Messiah as the supreme royal benefactor who is not only exalted and loving but also a victorious deliverer and a generous gift-giver.

Psalm 72 celebrates as well as anticipates the reign of the singular ideal king whose rule fills the whole earth with the glory of God.[30] The

---

27. Throntveit, *When Kings Speak*, 89–96.

28. See Gerbrandt, *Kingship According to Deuteronomistic History*.

29. The so-called royal psalms include 2, 18, 20, 21, 45, 72, 89, 101, 110, 132, and 144. The enthronement psalms, which center specifically on the theme of Yahweh as king consist of 47, 93, 96, 97, 98, and 99. For further discussion on the royal psalms, see Eaton, *Kingship and the Psalms*, 1–86; Wilson, "Use of Royal Psalms," 85–94; Roberts, "Enthronement of Yhwh and David," 675–86; Mowinckel, *Psalms in Israel's Worship*; Jipp, *Christ Is King*, 32–37.

30. On the settings of this psalm, both as a cultic celebration of the new king's enthronement and as a messianic expectation, see Heim, "Perfect King of Psalm 72," 224–26. Kaiser writes that "Psalm 72 simultaneously celebrated an illustrious and exalted reign of that Israelite king in the day this psalm was written as one who also distinguished himself in peace, righteousness, and benevolent concern for the poor, miserable, and oppressed of his own times as well as final relief in the end times" ("Psalm 72," 259).

psalm may be divided into three strophes (vv. 1–7; vv. 8–14; vv. 15–19), but rather than providing a consecutive analysis of each strophe, for our purpose we will briefly discuss three themes that point to benefaction motifs as well as reciprocity.[31] To begin with, the king's reign is just and righteous. The psalmist requests God to endow the king, his royal son, with justice and righteousness (72:1). These are indispensable judicial powers that only God can grant by enabling the king to participate in his own righteous rule.[32] The king needs to embody righteousness so that he may in turn transform the people by his righteousness. Whereas the wicked, who are here depicted as the oppressor (72:4) and the enemies of the king (v. 9), will be defeated, the righteous will flourish in the days of the king (72:7). Through his righteous reign the king ensures justice for the people, promotes the fear of the Lord (72:5),[33] and acts as an agent of the wondrous things of the Lord (cf. 72:18).

As the king reigns righteously, he brings many benefits to the people—this is the second theme that we need to note. We have already seen in the preceding paragraph that the king blesses the people with his righteous rule (72:7). Similarly, he is an advocate for the poor and a defender of the needy (72:4, 12–14). This righteous king does not ignore the plight of the weak and the poor who might suffer injustice and oppression at the hands of the powerful and the rich (72:12). Instead, he ensures that justice prevails for the poor by crushing their oppressor.[34] He is compassionate toward the needy and redeems their life from oppression, for "their blood is precious in his sight" (72:14). The afflicted and the destitute who are often trampled by the society can find refuge in the king. Additionally, the king grants victory over the powers that threaten God's people (72:9). The imagery of the enemy of the king licking the dust depicts a people whose hostility has been rendered futile, and who can henceforth do nothing but surrender to the king and do

---

31. For further discussion on the structure of the psalm, see Heim, "Perfect King of Psalm 72," 226–29; Skehan, "Strophic Structure," 302–8.

32. Kaiser, *Messiah in the Old Testament*, 134.

33. The LXX reads συμπαραμενεῖ = he will endure (71:5), which might suggest a messianic reading of the psalm, asking for the unending reign of the king. The MT's reading ("they will fear you") implies that the righteous king's reign will transform the people, resulting in their submission to the Lord forever. For further discussion of this textual problem and why the MT's reading should be preferred, see Heim, "Perfect King of Psalm 72," 238–43.

34. According to Ps 101:5–8, the king protects and defends the righteous from their enemies.

his bidding.³⁵ Another kingly gift is the establishment of peace in the land (72:7). Peace and order reflect God's own heavenly rule that leads to cosmic stability.³⁶

In addition to the above benefits, the king also ensures abundant supply of "bread" (72:3, 6, 16; cf. Isa 25:6–9; Joel 2:24). The king's reign will be characterized by prosperity in perpetuity. His accession to the royal throne is like fresh rain falling on the earth and causing the land to produce abundant fruit. The king's righteous reign is likened to rain that falls on a mown field (Ps 72:6; cf. 2 Sam 23:3–4; Hos 6:3; Mic 5:7). The people enjoy abundance of grain and gold even as they thrive like "the grass of the field" (72:16).³⁷ Even the desolate places like the tops of the mountains and hills will produce bountifully. All these blessings show that this king is an agent of Yahweh's favor to the people, a fountain of righteousness, a compassionate redeemer, and a mighty warrior against whom no enemy shall prevail.

The third theme that we see in this psalm is giving obedience and loyalty to the king (72:8–11, 15–19). The king is not only honored in the Promised Land but also by the gentiles. His kingdom is universal in scope since he rules "from sea to sea, and from the River to the ends of the earth" (72:8; cf. Exod 23:31; Zech 9:9–10).³⁸ Those who dwell in the wilderness shall bow down before him, and the rulers of the nations shall bring tribute and gifts to him (72:9–10, 15). Verse 11 beautifully summarizes how the king shall receive universal honor: "Let all the kings give obeisance before him, and all the nations serve him." The basis for this invitation to the nations to serve the king is his righteous rule that brings deliverance to the defenseless and ensures impartial justice for all (72:12–14). Moreover, the king's life, rule, and honor are eternal. The psalmist prays that the king may live long (72:16), and that his name may endure forever and "abide as long as the sun," and that "may people be

---

35. On this imagery, see Gen 49:8–12; Num 24:17–19; Ps 89:23; Zech 9:10.

36. Whitelam, "Israelite Kingship, 129–30.

37. Mowinckel writes that in the context of the ancient Near East, the king "is the channel through which blessing and happiness and fertility flow from the gods" to the people (*Psalms in Israel's Worship*, 51).

38. Jipp observes, "One of the central hopes of the royal psalms is that God will establish God's kingdom by extending worldwide dominion over the people through God's 'chosen,' elected king" (*Christ Is King*, 34). The universal dominion of the king is also the subject of Ps 89:25–27: "I will set his hand on the sea and his right hand on the rivers. He shall cry to me, 'You are my Father, my God, and the Rock of my salvation!' I will make him the firstborn, the highest of the kings of earth."

blessed through him; all nations call him blessed" (72:17).[39] As he blesses the nations by his righteous and benevolent reign, the king receives obedience and homage. Similarly, prayers are offered and blessings are invoked on behalf of the king (72:16). In fact, the whole psalm is composed as an intercessory prayer for the royal son (72:1). All this shows that the king is highly exalted, and therefore worthy of honor, for he is merciful and compassionate, and brings deliverance to the needy.[40] He reveals the wonderful works of God, leading ultimately to the whole earth being filled with God's glory (72:18–19).[41]

Kingship Discourse in the Rest of the Psalter

The preceding discussion has highlighted three main themes in Psalm 72: (1) the king's righteous reign; (2) the king as an agent of Yahweh's blessings to the people; and (3) the king's high exaltation. These themes are found elsewhere in the Psalter. Like Psalm 72, the rest of the Psalter envisages the king's righteous and universal reign.[42] The king is Yahweh's Messiah (2:2; 89:20; 132:10) and son (2:7) whose enthronement (2:6; 110:2) bears at least three implications. First, the king triumphs over his enemies as he establishes his righteous reign (2:9; 110:2). Those who had plotted against Yahweh's Messiah and subjected him to a situation of distress are utterly defeated as Yahweh rescues his son (2:1–3; 20:6–9; 21:8–12; 22:22–24; 89:22–23; 110:5–7; 144:9–11). After he has been vindicated and enthroned, the king now executes righteousness, which according to Psalm 2 means the shameful destruction of his enemies (cf. 132:18). Psalm 97:2–3 (98:2–3 MT) proclaims how the Lord has made known his salvation and revealed his righteousness in the presence of the nations. This psalm, along with LXX Pss 92 and 94–98, celebrates the

---

39. This prayer clearly echoes the Abrahamic promise of Gen 12:3; 22:18; and 26:4, whereby God promises to bless all the nations of the earth through Abraham's descendant. Ps 2:9–10 declares that those who take refuge in the king will be blessed, and not perish.

40. See LXX Ps 44 which praises the king and concludes by declaring that the peoples will praise the king forever.

41. Heim writes, "[The doxology] highlights that the consequences arising from the righteous king's actions culminate in a universal and unending praise of the Lord" ("Perfect King of Psalm 72," 238).

42. For a brief overview of kingship discourse in the Psalter, see Jipp, *Christ Is King*, 32–37. Also see Mitchell, "Lord, Remember David," 526–48; Starling, "Messianic Hope in the Psalms," 121–34.

kingship of Yahweh over all creation and the nations. The Lord rules in righteousness as he delivers his people and judges their enemies. He is the lover of justice, establishing equity and doing justice and righteousness in Jacob (LXX Ps 98:4). He judges the world with righteousness (LXX Ps 97:9) for "righteousness and justice are the foundation of his throne" (LXX Ps 96:2). He saves his people from the wicked and shames the idolatrous (LXX Ps 96:7-12). Elsewhere the Psalter declares that the king rides victoriously for the sake of righteousness, for he loves righteousness and hates wickedness (45:4-7). He is the guardian of integrity and the exemplar of righteousness (101:1-4). He promotes righteousness by rewarding the faithful and punishing the wicked (101:5-8). Thus there is an intricate relationship between Yahweh's righteous reign and salvation for his people and judgment against the wicked.

Second, the king brings blessings to the people. Psalm 2:12 warns against rebelling against the king, for this would incur his fierce wrath. Instead, the psalmist urges the readers to embrace the king and take refuge in him. Psalm 22 summarizes the king's blessings to the people in terms of food and worship. Having been delivered from his enemies and from death (22:1-21), the king now proclaims Yahweh's name to humanity (22:22). Those who are afflicted can eat and be satisfied even as they worship Yahweh under the king's dominion (22:25). Indeed, "All the prosperous of the earth eat and worship" (22:29). Yahweh's son satisfies the poor with bread, procures salvation for the people, and brings great joy to Zion (132:15-16). According to Psalm 144:13-14, the king transmits such blessings as full granaries, healthy and productive flock and cattle, and a peaceful existence. The king also stabilizes the cosmos by reigning over the sea and the rivers (89:25).[43]

Third, the king is highly exalted. He sits at Yahweh's right hand and shares his throne (2:6; 110:1). Yahweh has made him "the highest of the kings of the earth" (89:27) and bestowed on him splendor and majesty (21:5). He rules over all the nations of the earth (2:8, 10-11). Through him all the ends of the earth shall turn to Yahweh "and all the families of the nations shall worship before you" (22:27). The entire human race shall bow before him (22:29; cf. v. 30). Yahweh has made all the nations his heritage, and the ends of the earth his possession. People will bring him gifts to find favor with him (45:12). The rulers of the earth are warned to act wisely (2:10), which probably means that they should

---

43. On Psalm 89 as a messianic Psalm, see Pohl, "Messianic Reading of Psalm 89, 507-25.

recognize Yahweh's Messiah, submit to his authority, and serve him joyfully. Yahweh sets a crown of gold on the king's head and grants him everlasting life; hence, his reign has no end (21:3–4; 89:29). The throne of this Davidic king shall endure "as the days of the heavens" (89:29) and "as long as the sun" before Yahweh (89:36). The Psalter, therefore, portrays the king as righteous, victorious, and highly exalted. He is Yahweh's Messiah, who both reigns universally and through whom divine blessings flow to the people.

The OT texts discussed above show that the king is Yahweh's vicegerent, extending Yahweh's righteous reign on earth. He is anointed and empowered by the Spirit to accomplish Yahweh's will. He exemplifies devotion to Yahweh, for his heart delights in Torah. As he rules, divine blessings flow to the people. He fights Yahweh's battles; he brings deliverance from the enemies; he establishes peace; he delivers the destitute and the afflicted from their oppressors; and he transforms the people by his righteousness, leading to the fear of the Lord in the land. His universal dominion is marked by a fourfold extension: (1) geographically, it extends from sea to sea; (2) militarily, he triumphs over all his enemies; (3) economically, tribute and gifts are brought to him from all over the world; and (4) politically, rulers of the world submit to him and serve him. The land produces bountifully under his reign, leading to the flourishing of the people. Due to his righteous rule, which manifests God's beneficence and wondrous deeds, the king receives honor and praise from Israel as well as the nations of the earth. All these points will shed light on our understanding of Paul's christological discourse in Romans 5–8. We will see that Paul portrays Jesus as the righteous sufferer and as God's enthroned son who delivers his followers from sin and death and from all sorts of threats. The Messiah also gives gifts to his followers, gifts which include his own life, the Holy Spirit, peace, life, and a glorious status among others. Similarly, we will see that Paul asserts that the Messiah's reign is universal since he delivers and exercises lordship over Jews and gentiles. And due to his benefaction to humanity, the Messiah's followers are to give him loyalty and obedience.

The next section will focus on Second Temple Literature, including Ben Sira, Philo, and Josephus, to assess the reception of Jewish gift-giving against the backdrop of the Greco-Roman royal benefaction system. Given that the Jews have a shared kingship tradition within the covenantal framework, how does their encounter with Greco-Roman practices, especially royal benefaction and the ethic of reciprocity, affect kingship discourse in Second Temple Judaism? To what extent does Second Temple Judaism strictly adhere to its tradition, or how much is it willing to integrate the Greco-Roman royal benefaction notions?

Ben Sira

Jesus Ben Sira lived in Jerusalem at the end of the third to the beginning of the second century BCE, when the Ptolemaic and the Seleucid kings controlled Palestine, and just a few decades before the Hasmonean revolt against Antiochus IV. He composed the apocryphal wisdom literature of Sirach sometime between 190 and 175 BCE. Sirach was translated into Greek by Ben Sira's grandson in Alexandria at some point after his emigration there in 132 BCE.[44] Although Sirach might have been written before the Hellenization in Jerusalem had reached its climax, there are indications that the pressure to assimilate the Hellenistic culture was already being felt and that Ben Sira was endeavoring to combat such influence.[45] The situation was in many ways one of an identity crisis. What provides stability and authenticity when the popular culture, which seems to be promising greater stability, success, and hope, is challenging one's ancestral values? Against this backdrop, Ben Sira writes to reinvigorate the confidence and faith of his fellow Jews by directing their attention to an acceptable and honorable conduct as defined by Torah. Ben Sira adopts a twofold strategy to accomplish his aim: (1) he lays out obedience to Torah as the foundation for attaining wisdom and lasting reputation; and (2) he supplies his readers with a list of moral exemplars in order to admonish obedience to Torah and honorable conduct. As we investigate how Ben Sira seeks to foster fidelity to Torah against the backdrop of gift-giving and reciprocity, we will discover that he is both assimilative and subversive; he embraces certain aspects of benefaction and rejects others.

---

44. DeSilva, *Introducing the Apocrypha*, 156–57. On the texts and versions of Sirach, see Di Lella, *Hebrew Text of Sirach*; Yadin, *Ben Sira Scroll from Masada*; Wright, *No Small Difference*; Nelson, *Syriac Version of the Wisdom of Ben Sira*; Rey and Joosten, *Texts and Versions of the Book of Ben Sira*. Unless indicated otherwise, all quotations of Sirach are from Skehan and Di Lella, *Wisdom of Ben Sira*.

45. See Siebeneck, "May Their Bones Return to Life," 411; Di Lella, "Wisdom of Ben-Sira," 933.

How to Obtain Honor

Honor and praise are fundamental values in the ancient society.[46] It is therefore not surprising that Ben Sira discusses how one might obtain glory and immortality. The sage believes that whoever pursues wisdom finds honor and a good reputation. The wise recognize that "the human body is a fleeting thing," yet their "virtuous name will never be annihilated" (41:11). Whereas an ungodly name will be purged out or remembered as a curse (41:9–10), the name of the wise will stand by them as a great treasure (41:12) and will be remembered "for days without number" (41:13b). Social and economic prosperity lasts only "a number of days" (41:13a), but a good name abides forever. Whoever clings to wisdom obtains gladness and an everlasting name (15:6; 37:26). Wisdom brings peace, perfect health, and "heightens the glory of those who possess her" (1:18–19). The Lord bestows his blessing on the wise (4:13). Wisdom leads to the throne of majesty and glorious adornment (6:29–31); it is a tree whose branches are honor and grace (24:16–17).

To obtain wisdom and thereby live honorably, one must obey Torah and walk in the fear of the Lord (1:26; 19:20). Because of the indispensability of the law in the pursuit of wisdom, Ben Sira castigates those who have abandoned Torah, presumably in favor of Hellenistic ideas (41:8–9). The Hellenizing Jews who have compromised their faith by assimilating pagan practices and customs are "a reprobate line" and "witless offspring" (41:5). They are like the faithless kings of Judah (49:4–5). Whoever hates the law is not wise (33:2). And the only way to acquire wisdom and to fear the Lord is to keep the commandments (1:26). In short, the sage's ethical approach intricately links wisdom to Torah and to the fear of the Lord. To obtain honor and a lasting reputation, one must live wisely by following the Lord. If wisdom is the only pathway to honor, then how does this affect Ben Sira's kingship discourse?

Portrait of the King

Although Israel did not have a king during the life of Ben Sira, the sage is keenly interested in political leadership. The theme of kingship permeates Ben Sira's poem on skill, arrogance, and pride (9:17—10:18) as well as the Praise of the Ancestors (44:1—50:24). A prudent ruler brings order

---

46. Neyrey, "Lost in Translation," 8.

and stability to the nation (10:1). Whereas a wanton ruler destroys his people, a wise prince brings prosperity (10:3). God appoints a wise ruler and grants him splendor to rule "for the time" (10:4–5). Ben Sira here seems to offer a critique of the pagan rulers who thought of themselves as gods and against whom the sage invokes destruction, for they claimed, "[T]here is no one besides me!" (36:12). In keeping with the teaching of the OT (e.g., Dan 2:21; 4:14, 31–34; Ps 113:4–8), Ben Sira asserts that a ruler is a mere human being chosen by God as his vicegerent (cf. 17:17). God reigns sovereignly over the nations; he is seated upon his throne and is greatly to be feared (1:1). He is Lord, king, and savior, redeeming his own from danger and adversity (51:1–2). He is the ideal king who exercises sovereignty over all. Yet, he is pleased to rule humanity through his vicegerent, who is expected to imitate the divine paradigm.[47] The Lord's appointee rules diligently and does not allow anything to tarnish his glory (33:19–24).

To illustrate what wise leadership entails, Ben Sira presents his students with the Praise of the Ancestors (44:1—50:24).[48] He employs encomium as a rhetorical tool to reinforce fidelity to the Jewish values. The encomium begins with an invitation to "praise those godly people, our ancestors, each in his own time" (44:1). It proceeds by including Israel's great ancestors from Adam, whose splendor was beyond that of any living being, to Simon II, the high priest whom Ben Sira himself observed ministering in the Temple "wearing his splendid robes, and vested in sublime magnificence" (50:11). To underscore his interest in these illustrious men's leadership, Ben Sira states that they were "[r]ulers of the earth, of royal rank, persons renowned for their valor" (44:1). They governed the people resolutely (44:4) and were all "glorious in their time, each illustrious in his day" (44:7). Owing to their outstanding reign, "Some of them have left behind a name so that people recount their praises" (44:8). How, then, did these figures rule? What did they do or not do that won them such lasting glory and praise (cf. 44:13–14)? To answer these questions, we will limit our discussion to two exemplars: David and Simon II.

David is praised for his victories in battle and his loyalty to the Lord as seen in his cultic participation (47:1–12).[49] Four points stand out in this

---

47. For further discussion of God as the ideal king in Ben Sira, see Wright, "Ben Sira on Kings and Kingship," 78–80.

48. On the form of Ben Sira 44–50, see Lee, *Studies in the Form of Sirach 44–50*.

49. For further discussion of the portrait of David in Ben Sira, see Marttila, "David in the Wisdom of Ben Sira," 29–48.

depiction. First, David saved Israel from humiliation by defeating Goliath. Ben Sira narrates David's encounter with Goliath in colorful detail (vv. 4–6). Having noted David's courage as a shepherd (v. 3), Ben Sira proceeds swiftly to how, as a youth, David killed the giant "and did away with the people's disgrace" (v. 4). By destroying the pride of "the skilled warrior," David restored "the eminence of his own people" (vv. 4–5). Second, David prevailed over his enemies throughout his reign. After David became king, "he fought and subdued the enemy on every side" and completely put an end to the Philistines' power (v. 7). Third, David exemplified cultic adherence. He called on the Lord to grant him victory over his foes (v. 5) and sought to proclaim the Lord's glory in every deed (v. 8). He thanked God, sang praises to him, and loved him. He led the Israelites in singing praises to the Lord (vv. 8–10). Lastly, David was honored by the people and by God. Ben Sira notes that the women praised David for having killed tens of thousands (v. 6). But it is the Lord's exaltation of David that points to how he obtained lasting glory. The Lord exalted his horn forever and bestowed on him royal authority; his throne is firmly established in Israel (v. 11). In sum, as a king, David fights against Israel's enemies, restores Israel's glory, and exemplifies devotion to the Lord. In turn, the people praise him even as the Lord promises him an everlasting dynasty.

Simon II is another exemplar whom Ben Sira praises for his kingly roles (50:1–24). Ben Sira introduces Simon as an exalted figure: "Greatest among his kindred, the glory of his people" (v. 1). His kingly benefactions included renovating the temple (v. 1), building the wall (v. 2), providing the city with water (v. 3), and protecting the city from enemies (v. 4). Simon was faithful in his role as high priest, leading the people in sacrificing to the Lord and praising him (vv. 5–21). Unlike David whose roles are mainly defined by his courage in battle and devotion to the commandments, Ben Sira's portrait of Simon is much closer to the Hellenistic depiction of king as benefactor. Simply stated, Simon acts like the prudent ruler of 10:3; he cares for the city of Jerusalem and for the people even as he also promotes religious observance.

Discrimination and Reciprocity

So far, we have seen that Ben Sira believes that wisdom is the only pathway to lasting honor and that wise leaders are caring, courageous, successful in battle, and exemplary in cultic adherence. There are two other aspects of benefaction which we also need to consider. First, how should gifts be bestowed? Second, what is Ben Sira's attitude towards the ethic of reciprocity?

Ben Sira's discussion of how gifts should be given is closely linked to his teaching on wisdom. He maintains that how one gives a gift affects how it is received. A foolish person spoils a gift by harsh words (18:15), but a kind word transforms a gift like the "dew that abates a burning wind" (18:16). Unlike a fool who "upbraids before giving" (18:18), a wise person offers gracious words as well as the gift (18:17). But being wise does not imply that gifts should be given indiscriminately; instead, Ben Sira admonishes a careful selection of the recipients of good deeds: "If you do good, know for whom you are doing it, and your kindness will have its effect. Do good to the just and reward will be yours, if not from him, then from the Lord (12:1–2)."[50] According to 12:2, the intended effect of kindness is reward, which implies returning a favor (cf. 20:10). The just man, who alone can reciprocate, understands the conventions of gift exchange; hence he will not be ungrateful. The wicked, however, will only repay the generosity of the righteous with evil. The wicked can attack the giver with the giver's own weapons (12:5). Whoever shows kindness to the wicked receives no reward in return; he should not even think that he is merciful (12:3). Only the good person ought to be picked for good deeds (12:4).[51] Ben Sira provides two further reasons for his advice against helping the wicked: (1) they are proud (12:5); and (2) God hates them and requites them with vengeance (12:6). According to 12:5, the pauper is not able to reciprocate with counter gifts, but unlike the wicked he will not attack the giver. The one who gives to the poor should expect divine reciprocation.

It is evident here that care is necessary when choosing friends and beneficiaries of good deeds. Whoever shows mercy indiscriminately would suffer loss since there is no guarantee that his acts would be reciprocated.[52] In fact, indiscriminate gift-giving does not reflect God's pattern, for he too hates sinners and blesses the righteous. Ben Sira therefore

---

50. Skehan and Di Lella, *Wisdom of Ben Sira*, 242. The Greek text of 12:1a clearly shows that discriminatory gift-giving ensures that gifts are given to those who can reciprocate by showing gratitude: καὶ ἔσται χάρις τοῖς ἀγαθοῖς σου ("and you shall be thanked for your good deeds").

51. Ben Sira also urges his students to not only do good to themselves (14:11) but also be generous, particularly to their friends (14:13; 29:10).

52. See 11:29–34, where Ben Sira states that indiscriminate hospitality to strangers may lead to unpleasant consequences.

has embraced the Hellenistic ethic of intrahuman reciprocity even as he also continues to champion the Jewish belief that God blesses those who show kindness to others. But Ben Sira is also critical of how intrahuman reciprocity might be abused.[53] A gift that must be paid back double does not do anyone good (20:10). The gift of a fool does not benefit the receiver because the giver parades the one gift like seven gifts (20:14). Due to the one gift, the fool criticizes much and expects immediate repayment (20:15). The fool lacks friends and complains that he does not receive gratitude for his generosity (20:16). All this is because he is hateful, for he expects to be repaid for every gift he gives (20:15; cf. 20:10). A wise person, however, looks to God for requital.

God repays everyone without partiality (17:23; 35:24). Whoever is generous to the poor and kind to his kindred and friends obeys God's commands. Such a person will be rewarded with things more precious than gold; his almsgiving will save him from evil and fight for him against his enemies (29:8-13; cf. 3:30-31; 7:32-33). Likewise, a person who shows hospitality and who is generous with food wins lasting praise (31:23; 32:1-2). A generous person understands that "God always repays, and he will give back to you seven times over" (35:13). And since God is the ultimate reciprocator, showering favors upon his children, he alone should be praised above all (32:13).

The above discussion shows that Ben Sira's attitude is characterized by rejection and approval of the value of the gift even as he also affirms the inferiority of the gift to wisdom. He rejects the gift as the exclusive means of obtaining glory; instead, he argues that lasting reputation comes through wisdom and the fear of God. He rejects the notion that it is the beneficent wealthy alone who can obtain immortality through memorialization; instead, he posits that wealth without the fear of God leads to destruction. In fact, he asserts that the poor who observe Torah will be remembered forever. He criticizes those who insist that their gift must be repaid; instead he points to God as the ultimate reciprocator. But the sage also approves of some aspects of reciprocity. Like his Hellenistic contemporaries, Ben Sira argues that gift-giving should be discriminative, for only the righteous should be benefited. He also maintains that people duly honor a king who is committed to Torah, caring for the people,

---

53. Ben Sira also cautions against relying on wealth as the source of power (5:1). Wealth is deceitful and offers no help on the day of wrath (5:8). Wealth ruins many princes by perverting their character (8:2), and because of wealth sovereignty passes from one nation to another (10:8).

maintaining peace and stability, fighting the Lord's battle, and promoting cultic adherents. Whereas in Greco-Roman society honor would be in the form of decrees, inscriptions, statues, and seats of honor among others, Ben Sira nowhere writes about these forms of honor. He most likely refrains from talking about inscriptions and statues owing to the second commandment that prohibits images of living beings (Exod 20:4). For Ben Sira, rulers are honored by obeisance, perpetual memorialization, and encomia.

Philo

Philo Judaeus of Alexandria was a Jewish scholar, philosopher, politician, and an author who lived approximately between 30 BCE and 50 CE. He was part of the Jewish leadership of the diaspora community in Alexandria in the Roman province of Egypt.[54] His extant works, all of which are written in Greek, evince the attempt to merge Greek philosophy with Judaism within a Platonic and Stoic framework. Philo believed that the Pentateuch was the basis of Plato's philosophy and that Holy Scripture was the source of all wisdom, which implies that true philosophy could only be found in Judaism.[55] Following the Alexandrian school of Hellenistic Judaism, Philo applied Platonic allegorical method to his commentaries on the Pentateuch; consequently, he was able to explain away difficult statements in the OT by arguing that they had a hidden meaning of spiritual significance.[56] His treatises that are relevant for kingship (especially *On the Life of Joseph*, *On the Life of Moses*, and *On the Embassy to Gaius*) reveal his acquaintance with the system of benefaction as he tries to integrate Hellenistic concepts with Judaism.[57]

---

54. For helpful introduction to Philo's background and methodology, see Borgen, "Philo of Alexandria," 233–82; Borgen, *Philo of Alexandria*; Mondésert, "Philo of Alexandria," 877–900; Seland, *Reading Philo*; Sterling, "Philo," 789–93. Also helpful is Hadas-Lebel, *Philo of Alexandria*.

55. Goppelt, *Typos*, 42; Bray, *Biblical Interpretation*, 82.

56. Philo explicitly asserts that "broadly speaking, all or most of the law-book is an allegory" (*Joseph* 6:28).

57. Harrison comments that Philo is "intimately acquainted with the terminology and ideology of benefaction." He notes that in addition to fundamental benefaction terms such as δωρέα, εὐεργέτης, λειτουργία, and χάρις, Philo uses words and phrases commonly found in honorific inscriptions such as ἀρετή, εὔνοια, εὐσέβεια, ζῆλος, ἴσος, σωτήρ, τιμή, φιλία, φιλανθρωπία, and φιλοτιμία among others (*Paul's Language of Grace*, 120). On Philo and kingship, see Goodenough, *Politics of Philo Judaeus*,

Joseph, Moses, and Augustus as Ideal Rulers

Philo presents Joseph, Moses, and Augustus as exemplars of the ideal rule. *On the Life of Joseph* is a biographical treatise that depicts Joseph as typical Hellenistic ideal king. Based on his allegorical method, Philo argues that the name Joseph, which literally means "addition of a lord," is a significant title indicating that Joseph was invested with universal lordship to rule over the whole world (*Joseph* 6:28–29).[58] While serving in Potiphar's house, Joseph learned how to manage the great city, for "a city too is a great house and statesmanship the household management of the general public" (8:38–39). In addition to household management, Joseph started acquiring the skills needed to lead well at the age of seventeen when he was shepherding his father's flock. Shepherding trained Joseph on how to care for "the noblest flock of living creatures—mankind" (1:2–3). Joseph was committed to ruling as a good guardian and an affectionate father (14:67). Expounding on this father analogy, Philo writes that "the good rulers may be truly called the parents of states and nations in common, since they show a fatherly and sometimes more than fatherly affection" (*Spec. Laws* 4:184). As the father-king, Joseph neither allowed craving for honors nor longing for reputation to subdue him (*Joseph* 14:70). Instead, he endeavored to benefit all and to legislate for the common good, bearing in mind that the interests of the people were committed to him (14:73–77).

When Joseph was put in charge of Egypt after he had interpreted Pharaoh's dream, Philo comments that rather than being a viceroy, Joseph actually became king while Pharaoh only reserved to himself the name of the office. Joseph exercised sovereignty over the whole land and did everything that brought him honor (21:119–21). He served the people "with pure and guileless good faith" (25:148), remembering that "the excellence of wealth consists not in a full purse but in helping the needy" (24:144). Quoting Joseph's speech to his brothers, Philo writes: "Silver and gold are stored in my [Joseph's] keeping alone, and, what is more necessary than these, the means of sustenance, which I distribute and parcel out to those who ask, according to their necessary requirements, so that they have no superfluities . . . nor lack of what may satisfy

---

86–120; Barraclough, "Philo's Politics," 418–551. For a recent work that examines χάρις in Philo and Paul, see McFarland, *God and Grace*.

58. On Joseph as king in Philo, see Goodenough, *Politics of Philo Judaeus*, 44–63; Barraclough, "Philo's Politics," 491–506.

actual want" (40:243). And since the one who is highly reputed receives honor (24:144), Joseph not only rode on the king's chariot but he was also "dignified and honored by the multitude" (25:150), by his brothers (28:163–64; 41:246–49), and by the king of Egypt (40:242). He presented himself warmly to his subjects through his appearance and "the benefits which they received from him" (27:157). As he told his brothers, Joseph was convinced that God had appointed him to take charge of "his boons and gifts" (τῶν αὐτοῦ χαρίτων καὶ δωρεῶν) which he provided for humanity in their greatest need (40:241). He managed Egypt and the other lands and nations that were devastated by famine as though they were a single household; he distributed the lands and food as was suitable (43:259). In turn, the people honored Joseph and "requited the benefits which they had received from him in the times of adversity" (44:267–68).

In addition to Joseph, Moses also excelled as a ruler. The biographical treatise *On the Life of Moses* traces Moses' life from his childhood to his offices even as it presents him as a philosopher-king. The first volume focuses on Moses' accomplishments as king while the second discusses his priestly, prophetic, and legislative responsibilities. Like Joseph, Moses was the shepherd-king who received his initial training in leadership while he was tending his father-in-law's flock (*Moses* 1.11.60–62).[59] Philo writes that "the shepherd's business is a training-ground and a preliminary exercise in kingship for one who is destined to command the herd of mankind, the most civilized of herds" (1.11.60). The king is the good shepherd who cares for the weakling, especially the widow, the unfortunate, and the orphan (*Decalogue* 10:40–43).[60] As Moses chased wild animals, he gained the skills necessary for waging war against the enemy and establishing peace. And pasturing the flock enabled him to acquire the tenderness necessary for dealing with his subjects. By referring to Moses as the shepherd-king, Philo is not reproaching Moses; rather, he is ascribing to him a term of "the highest honor" (ὑπερβάλλουσα τιμή) since "the only perfect king . . . is one who is skilled in the knowledge of shepherding" (*Moses* 1.11.62).

---

59. On Moses as the ideal king in Philo, see Barraclough, "Philo's Politics," 487–91; Meeks, "Moses as God and King," 354–71; Feldman, *Philo's Portrayal of Moses*, 280–89. On Moses' birth and upbringing, see Feldman, "Philo's View of Moses' Birth and Upbringing," 258–81.

60. This emphasis on caring for the widows and fatherless is most likely based on Hebrew tradition as found in such texts as Exod 22:22–24; Deut 10:18; 24:17; 27:19; Isa 1:17, 23; Ezek 22:7.

Moses' greatest task as a king was liberating his subjects from the oppressive reign of Pharaoh into the Promised Land. God invested Moses with the royal office "on account of his goodness and his nobility of conduct and the universal benevolence which he never failed to demonstrate" (ἀρετῆς ἕνεκα καὶ καλοκἀγαθίας καὶ τῆς πρὸς ἅπαντας εὐνοίας, ᾗ χρώμενος ἀεὶ διετέλει, *Moses* 1.27.148). As a beneficent and incorruptible king, Moses neither sought to exalt himself nor his own household. Instead, his sole aim was to benefit his subjects and to promote their interest in word and deed. He did not overlook "any opportunity that would advance the common well-being" (1.27.151). Contrary to the tyrant who treasures up gold and silver, and whose rule is burdensome to the subjects, Moses was "generous in the truly royal expenditure of those treasures which the ruler may well desire to have in abundance" (1.27.152–53).[61] Given that Moses did not set his heart upon amassing gold, God rewarded him by allowing him to share his possession as his own friend. He exercised authority over the wealth of the whole earth, sea, and rivers, and received the title "god and king of the whole nation" (1.28.155–58). Each element of the earth "obeyed him as its master, changed its natural properties, and submitted to his commands" (1.28.156). Thus, Philo depicts Moses as the ideal king appointed by God to rule victoriously and benevolently by liberating his subjects and promoting their welfare.

Apart from Joseph and Moses, Philo also presents Augustus as a perfect ruler in the treatise *On the Embassy to Gaius*. The treatise describes Philo's diplomatic mission to Gaius to plead with the emperor to save the Alexandrian Jews from sufferings and to grant their rights. As he writes, Philo makes a clear distinction between tyrants and good emperors. Gaius represents the former while Augustus the latter. Although Gaius is accorded the title "savior and benefactor (ὁ σωτὴρ καὶ εὐεργέτης), who would pour new streams of blessings on Asia and Europe, giving happiness indestructible to each singly and all in common," he fails miserably and resorts to savagery and brutality (*Embassy* 4:22). Gaius does not heed his advisor's word that an emperor ought to rejoice and delight "in nothing so much as in benefiting your subjects" (7:50; cf. 7:52). In contradistinction to the title "savior and benefactor," Gaius "rained miseries untold one after the other as from perennial fountains

---

61. These royal treasures are "self-restraint, continence, temperance, shrewdness, good sense, knowledge, endurance of toil and hardships, contempt of pleasures, justice, advocacy of excellence, censure and chastisement according to law for wrongdoers, praise and honor for well-doers, again as the law directs" (1.27.154).

on every part of the inhabited world" (13:101) and "brought disease to the healthy" (14:107). He "filled every house and city throughout Greece and the outside world with intestine wars!" (13:102). He was so obsessed with vengeance (42:330) and vice (13:98) that "if he did commit any kind action he immediately repented of it and sought some means of cancelling it, thus causing increased affliction and injury" (43:339). Gaius is the antithesis of a beneficent emperor.

In contrast, Philo praises Augustus as the "great benefactor," "the source and fountain-head of the Augustan stock," "the first and the greatest," and "the common benefactor of all" (22:148–49). Augustus is "the averter of evil;" he brought peace to the whole human race when it was on the verge of complete destruction (21:144). Philo hails him for calming "torrential storms on every side" and for healing "the pestilences common to Greeks and barbarians" (21:145). This encomium clearly portrays Augustus as the ruler of the cosmos who deserves to be venerated (cf. 21:143).[62] Additionally, Augustus "cleared the sea of pirate ships," "reclaimed every state to liberty," and "led disorder into order and brought gentle manners and harmony to all unsociable and brutish nations" (21:146–47). Philo further writes, "[Emperor Augustus is] the guardian of the peace, who dispensed their dues to each and all, who did not hoard his gifts (ὁ τὰς χάριτας) but gave them to be common property, who kept nothing good and excellent hidden throughout his life" (21:147). In brief, Augustus exemplifies the ideal kingship. He brings harmony within and without, promotes good health for his subjects, and displays great liberality.

The Basis of Divine Favor

Does Philo share the Hellenistic view that gift-giving ought to be discriminative? The answer to this question is implicit in Philo's discussion of divine favors. In his allegorical interpretation of Genesis 3, Philo seeks to determine the basis on which blessings were pronounced upon Noah, Melchizedek, Abraham, Isaac, Jacob, Ephraim, and Bezalel (*Alleg. Interp.* 3:77–103). He argues that the only convincing explanation for such blessings is found in the meaning of these names. For instance, Noah, who found favor with God, represents a praiseworthy constitution and nature, for his name means rest or righteousness (*Alleg. Interp.* 3:77).

---

62. See Price, *Rituals and Power*, 52–55.

Melchizedek is worthy of priesthood because his name indicates nobility (*Alleg. Interp.* 3:79–82). Likewise, Moses is "deemed worthy of the boon" (ἀξιοῦται μέντοι τῆς χάριτος) due to his virtue and tactical withdrawal from Pharaoh (*Alleg. Interp.* 3:14). Joseph too is a worthy man, for he refuses to take vengeance against his brothers. Joseph's brothers praised him for his fairness and kind behavior; he "treated them as worthy of his favor" (*Joseph* 41:249). The pattern found in each of these cases is that God recognizes the inner quality of the individual and considers them worthy of favor.

Using the adjective ἄξιος and its cognates (e.g., *Alleg. Interp.* 3:25; 3:27–28; 3:30; 3:34), Philo implies that divine gift is bestowed depending on the fittingness of the recipient.[63] When Moses requests God to reveal himself, God denies the request but both praises Moses' zeal and explains the basis of his benefaction:

> Your zeal I approve as praiseworthy, but the request cannot fitly be granted to any that are brought into being by creation. I freely bestow what is in accordance with the recipient; for not all that I can give with ease is within man's power to take, and therefore to him that is worthy of my grace (τῷ χάριτος ἀξίῳ) I extend all the boons which he is capable of receiving (*Spec. Laws* 1:8).

The implication here is that divine gift-giving, like that of any other wise giver, is fitting, appropriate, and reasonable (cf. *Post.* 42:139). Indeed, "God proportions the things which he gives to the strength of those who receive them" (*Post.* 43:145). And just as God dispenses favors in a way corresponding "to the ever-varying capacity of those whom he would benefit," so human liberality should correspond to how much "the man in want is capable of receiving" (*Post.* 43:142–43). In brief, Philo believes that intrahuman gift-giving should be patterned after divine beneficence, meaning that gifts must be appropriate to the worthiness of the receiver.

Honoring Benefactors

In keeping with the contemporary philosophy of kingship, Philo states that the ideal king creates love and goodwill in his subjects' soul through benefactions (*Planting* 21:90). He writes, "For respect is created by dignity, fear by strictness, affection by benevolence, and these when blended

---

63. On Philo's use of the adjective ἄξιος and its cognate verb ἀξιόω, see Barclay, "Grace Within and Beyond Reason," 11–13.

harmoniously in the soul render subjects obedient to their rulers" (*Rewards* 97). Those who fail to demonstrate affection to their benefactors are perverse, and inevitably face the harsh consequences of their ingratitude (*Embassy* 9:60). Commenting on the chief butler who failed to show gratitude to his benefactor, Philo states that "the ungrateful are always forgetful of their benefactors" (*Joseph* 19:99). When the daughters of the priest of Midian returned home after Moses had protected them from the unkind shepherds and watered their flock (*Moses* 1.10.51-58), they narrated the incident to their father, who immediately censored them for their ingratitude (1.11.58). By failing to invite Moses to their home, they contravened societal ethics and did not remember that people "who forget kindness (χαρίτων) are sure to lack defenders" (1.11.58). To correct this error, the father commanded his daughters to run after Moses and bring him home so that he might receive "some requital of the favor which we owe to him (ὀφείλεται γὰρ αὐτῷ χάρις). They hurried back and found him . . . and . . . persuaded him to come home with them" (1.11.58-59). Philo's rendition of this incident adds details that are not found in the Hebrew and LXX versions of Exod 2:16-22. The Exodus account makes no reference to favor, requital, gratitude, social convention, and cultural obligation. All these show that Philo is reinterpreting and recasting this account through the lens of Hellenistic benefaction. Gratitude, then, is the appropriate response to favors bestowed.[64]

Philo laments that Augustus, whom he praises as the great and the common benefactor, was not appropriately honored during his reign:

> This great benefactor (τὸν τοσοῦτον εὐεργέτην) they ignored during the forty-three years in which he was sovereign of Egypt, and set up nothing in our meeting houses in his honor, neither image, nor bust, nor painting. And yet if it was right to decree new and exceptional honors to anyone, he was the proper person to receive them. He was what we may call the source and fountain-head of the Augustan stock in general. He was also the first and the greatest and the common benefactor (κοινὸς εὐεργέτης) in that he displaced the rule of many and committed the ship of the commonwealth to be steered by a single pilot, that is himself, a marvelous master of the science of government (*Embassy* 22:148-49).

---

64. Elsewhere Philo implies that whoever fails to show gratitude is no longer worthy of receiving benefits (*Virtues* 165-66).

Several points are apparent in Philo's complaint. First, he describes the Greco-Roman ethic of reciprocity, particularly regarding emperors who use their position and attendant resources to establish peace and bring relief to their subjects. A few lines later, Philo delightfully recognizes that "the whole habitable world voted him [Augustus] no less than celestial honors" (*Embassy* 22:149). In *Against Flaccus*, Philo asserts that the Alexandrian Jews use Jewish houses of prayer as the essential means of showing devotion or piety to their benefactors (*Flaccus* 7:49). Second, Philo maintains that failure to confer honors on Augustus as expected reflects ingratitude and lack of goodwill. Those who ignore their duty to honor the emperor as far as the law permits deserve "utmost penalty for not tendering our requital with all due fullness" (*Flaccus* 7:50). Philo emphasizes that Augustus's achievements, which exceed those of his predecessors, means that he deserves "new and exceptional honors."[65] Lastly, it is surprising that being a Jew, Philo is not opposed to erecting statues or images in honor of the emperor. Philo depicts Jews as loyal Roman subjects whose religious meetings are compatible with the imperial practice of honoring the emperor as savior and benefactor.[66]

But Philo is also critical of reciprocity (*Cher.* 122–23). Due to the obligation to return a favor, benefaction has been reduced to a financial transaction whereby the benefactor and the beneficiary perceive of their roles as a seller and a buyer respectively. Benefactors are usually anxious to be honored. Although acts of beneficence are still designated as "gift" or "benefit," the transaction is incomplete unless the receiver offers due praise to the giver. Philo seems to lament that human benefaction has been reduced to a means of satisfying the elite's love of honor rather than a genuine concern for those in need. In contrast to this transaction-like practice, Philo states that God is not a hawker, but a free giver who is not motivated by the desire to be honored. Because he is the creator of all things, God has no need; rather, he generously offers all things that his creation needs without seeking returns.[67] Philo's understanding of divine benefaction is partly influenced by his Jewish heritage, yet as much as he is critical of the abuse of the ethic of reciprocity Philo does affirm the need

---

65. Philo writes elsewhere thus: "The ruler should preside over his subjects as a father over his children so that he himself may be honored in return as by true-born sons" (*Spec. Laws* 4:35).

66. See Hoklotubbe, *Civilized Piety*, 70.

67. Seneca shares similar sentiments in relation to divine benefaction (*Ben.* 4.25.1–2). Also see Plutarch, *Mor.* 423D.

to honor those who contribute to the sustenance of humanity. In brief, as Peter Leithart puts it, Philo *de*-triangulates the triangular relationship found in the Torah, according to which Yahweh requites the generous benefactor who shows kindness to the poor.[68] Apparently, Philo does not have significant problems in relation to the contemporary practice of showing honor and gratitude to the ruler whose reign is marked by peace, benefactions, philanthropy, and goodness.

Josephus

Josephus was a Jerusalem-born historian who lived from 37/38 CE to 120 CE.[69] He was born from a priestly family and claimed that he was of royal blood through the Hasmonean lineage of his mother. At the age of nineteen, Josephus began to govern his life "by the rules of the Pharisees, a sect having points of resemblance to that which the Greeks call the Stoic school" (*Life* 2:12). At the outbreak of the Jewish revolt in 66 CE, Josephus served as a general, fighting on behalf of the Jewish rebels in defense of Galilee (*War* 2:562–82). He surrendered to Vespasian in 67 CE and prophesied to him that he would become the emperor of Rome (*War* 3:400–402). Vespasian became the emperor in 69 CE. During the Jewish war, Josephus served Vespasian and his son Titus as an interpreter, pleading with the Jews inside the walls of Jerusalem to surrender. But they refused and were consequently destroyed in 70 CE. Josephus was then taken to Rome, released from his chains, and appointed by Vespasian to serve as a court historian. He received Roman citizenship and took the name Flavius. He then spent the next twenty-five years or so writing. His extant works include *The Jewish War, Jewish Antiquities, The Life,* and *Against Apion.*

The integrity of Josephus's historical witness and methodology has been questioned due to many discrepancies that exist between his account in *Jewish Antiquities* and *The Jewish War*.[70] But given how much

---

68. Leithart, *Gratitude*, 68.

69. On Josephus's life and career, see Attridge, "Josephus and His Works," 185–232; Bilde, *Flavius Josephus*; Cohen, *Josephus in Galilee and Rome*; Ferguson, *Backgrounds*, 485–89; Neyrey, "'Josephus' Vita," 177–206.

70. Cohen specifically points to the differences between numbers and proper names (*Josephus in Galilee and Rome*, 7). Ben Zvi is representative of scholars who point to internal inconsistencies in Josephus's writings ("Josephus' Account of the Destruction of the Temple," 62–63). Also see Rappaport, "Josephus' Personality," 79–80;

the patristic writers draw from him as well as the fact that he continues to be a significant source for understanding Second Temple Judaism, an understanding of his historical method is vital.[71] Josephus is most forthright about his historical method when he introduces the power struggles which followed the death of Queen Alexandra (*Ant.* 14:1–3). He follows Thucydides's model, whereby the veracity of the facts becomes the measure of a historian's success.[72] Josephus applies two major principles in his historical accounts. First, he mainly focuses on a single individual at a time (or on a group of people functioning as a single character).[73] Second, he seeks to explain how these figures caused the events that he recounts. Due to the complexity surrounding Josephus's methodology, it would be naïve to assume that he provides an objective window into the events of the Second Temple period.[74] He needs to be read critically, in context, and at times with suspicion.

Solomon and Agrippa I as Benefactors

Josephus is undoubtedly well-versed in the benefaction system, including its terminologies and expectations. Apart from Herod (*Ant.* 16:212), other emperors whom Josephus calls εὐεργέτης include Trajan (*War* 3:459), Titus (*War* 4:113), Vespasian (*War* 7:71), and Caesar Augustus (*Ant.* 16:98). He lists several projects that each of these emperors undertook as they were motivated by love of honor (e.g., *Ant.* 15:267–79). To get a better understanding of Josephus's portrayal of rulers as benefactors, we will mainly discuss his relevant accounts of the leadership of Solomon and Agrippa I.

Josephus portrays Solomon as a great ruler who manifests courage, gratefulness, piety, and generosity.[75] In his retelling of David's instructions to Solomon concerning the construction of the temple (1 Chr 22:6–19), Josephus quotes David telling Solomon not only that God chose him

---

Mason, *Josephus, Judea, and Christian Origins*, 103–37; McLaren, *Turbulent Times*.

71. On the patristic writers' interaction with Josephus, see Hardwick, *Josephus as an Historical Source*, 124–25.

72. Hadas-Lebel, *Flavius Josephus*, 211.

73. Pere Villalba i Varneda, *Historical Method of Flavius Josephus*, 69.

74. Mason, *Josephus, Judea, and Christian Origins*, 112–13.

75. See Feldman who asserts that Josephus portrays Solomon as a great man in order to respond to the charge that "the Jews had failed to produce great men" ("Josephus' Portrait of Solomon," 103).

to be king even before his birth but also that God would bring prosperity to the Hebrews in his reign. To succeed as king, Solomon must be pious, brave, just, and obedient to God's commandments (*Ant.* 7:337–39). The greatest of all blessings to characterize Solomon's reign would be "peace and freedom from war and civil dissension" (*Ant.* 7:338). Josephus also portrays Solomon as wealthy. Whereas the Bible states that Solomon's daily provisions consisted of, among other things, a hundred sheep (1 Kgs 5:2–3), Josephus has a hundred fatted sheep together with birds and fish (*Ant.* 8:40). Solomon's great wealth manifested his unprecedented glory (cf. *Ant.* 8:190).[76]

Solomon showed great concern for his subjects. This is seen at the close of the dedication of the temple (*Ant.* 8:124). Unlike 1 Kgs 8:66 which attributes the favors received by Israel to God, Josephus attributes them to King Solomon. Similarly, whereas 1 Kgs 8:66 simply states that the people blessed the king and then gladly departed, Josephus adds their gratitude to the king for his "providential care of them and for the display he had made, praying to God to grant them Solomon as king for a long time." In addition to caring for his subjects, Solomon was also brave and victorious in battle. God promised to grant Solomon riches, honor, and victory over his enemies (*Ant.* 8:24).[77] Solomon conquered "the Canaanites who were still unsubmissive" (*Ant.* 8:160). He subjugated many nations (*Ag. Ap.* 2:132) who brought daily provisions to him (*Ant.* 8:40). He made the walls of Jerusalem much greater and stronger than they had been previously "and thereafter governed the state in perfect peace" (*Ant.* 8:21; cf. 8:150). And as a military strategist, Solomon built Gezer because it was naturally strong and could serve as a stronghold in times of war or revolution (8:152). Together with Gezer, Solomon also built Hazor and Megiddo—all these cities are counted among the most powerful (8:151). Solomon's other benefactions included building many ships in the Egyptian gulf and making provisions for their needs (8:163–64), sending yearly gifts of grain, wine, and oil to Hiram (8:141), and giving gifts to the Queen of Sheba (8:175). Moreover, owing to his concern for the welfare of his subjects, Solomon built many cities "that were conveniently placed for enjoyment and pleasure and were naturally favored with a mild temperature and seasonable fruits and irrigated with

---

76. Josephus often juxtaposes wealth and glory (e.g., *Ant.* 8:129, 166, 394; 10:272; *War* 6:442).

77. The biblical account does not mention Solomon's victory over his enemies (1 Kgs 3:5–9).

streams of water" (8:153). The Solomonic peace brought great prosperity and wonderfully increased the population of the Hebrews as they turned to husbandry and the cultivation of land and enjoyed the fullest and most desirable freedom (8:38).

Like Solomon, Agrippa I was also a beneficent ruler. Agrippa gained power by cultivating the friendship of emperors (18:167-68, 289-300).[78] Early in his life, Agrippa was infamous for his debts and irresponsible spending (18:143-44, 160). But later in life, Agrippa's generosity endeared the people to him (16:65; 18:144).[79] Unlike Herod I whom Josephus castigates for constructing temples, baths, and theaters in foreign cities, Agrippa who also undertook construction projects in foreign countries receives praise rather than condemnation:

> Now King Agrippa was by nature generous in his gifts (εὐεργετικὸς εἶναι ἐν δωρεαῖς) and made it a point of honor to be high-minded towards gentiles; and by expending massive sums he raised himself to high fame. He took pleasure in conferring favors and rejoiced in popularity, thus being in no way similar in character to Herod, who was king before him ... Agrippa, on the contrary, had a gentle disposition and he was a benefactor to all alike. He was benevolent to those of other nations and exhibited his generosity to them also; but to his compatriots he was proportionately more generous and more compassionate (19:328-30).

Agrippa, driven by philanthropy and love of honor, presented himself as a universal benefactor, showing generosity to Jews and gentiles alike (cf. 16:40-41, 46). Josephus writes, "For it is not only to us [Jews] but to almost all men that you have been benefactors in your rule ... and one might make an endless speech if one were to enumerate each of the benefits which they have received from you" (16:49-50). Agrippa also exemplified gentleness and compassion and presented himself as a friend of Herod and of the Jews (e.g., 16:60-62). Indeed, Agrippa's story is remarkable, for he rose "from a position of no distinction" to a "high and mighty exaltation" (18:129).

Josephus also portrays Agrippa as a protector of the Jews (18:289-91; 19:278-91; 19:300-311) and a prolific builder (19:335-37). Concerning the latter, Josephus notes that Agrippa both fortified the walls of Jerusalem (19:326) and constructed many buildings in many places

---

78. Braund, *Rome and the Friendly King*, 44; Schwartz, *Agrippa I*, 40.
79. Agrippa brought "great joy" to the people by his kindness (*Ant.* 16:65).

(19:335–37). He particularly singles out Berytus where Agrippa built a theater, amphitheater, baths, and porticoes. Agrippa likewise provided generously for the dedication of these buildings by sponsoring gladiatorial games and spectacles. He offered tax remission (16:64) and held lavish banquets and parties, including a birthday celebration (19:321). It is clear that Josephus portrays Agrippa as one who understood the Greco-Roman reciprocal terms and who projected himself as a benefactor to all.

Benefiting Worthy Recipients

Josephus undoubtedly embraced the ancient practice of benefiting worthy people. This is well illustrated by his account of the exchange between Agrippa and Nicolas, with the latter representing the Jews of Ionia (*Ant.* 16:31–62).[80] Apparently, the Jews are victims of violence and mistreatment because their opponents are envious of their prosperity. Nicolas asserts that the Jews have been the recipients of the imperial favors (χάριτας) and acknowledges that Agrippa has the power to grant such favors. One of the present concerns of the Jews is that their opponents, who share the same status as the Jews as subject to the king, are depriving them of the imperial munificence. On their part, the Jews have shown themselves worthy (ἀξίους) of imperial benefaction, so that it is improper to deny them further favors. In fact, those who are mistreating the Jews are committing an offense because they are not considering "worthy the people to whose worth their rulers have testified by granting them such favors" (16:34). The opponents of the Jews are the ones who are contravening the conventions governing royal benefaction. Nicolas praises and thanks the king for the happiness, protection, and blessings that he has brought to the whole human race (16:36, 38–39).

In reply, Agrippa grants the request of the Jews because of Herod's goodwill and friendship, which implies that as a worthy and trustworthy client-king of Rome, Herod does not cause the Roman government any trouble (16:60). Agrippa therefore reciprocates by upholding the Jewish rights and granting them the imperial favors even as he maintains that "if they were to ask for still more, he would not hesitate to give them this" (16:60). Although it would be naïve to ignore the fact that Agrippa's

---

80. Grant observes, "Most of the orations of Josephus, as in other ancient historians, are more or less fictitious ... But since Nicolaus was Josephus' principal source, and is specifically stated by him to have written about this whole occasion at length, the speech is probably authentic" (*Herod the Great*, 182).

generosity is partly motivated by his love of honor, it is clear from this incident that the primary basis for the Jews' petition is their merit as loyal and peaceful subjects. It is because of their outstanding reputation that past rulers have bestowed favors upon them.

Josephus elsewhere writes that Joseph was worthy of God's favors. Reuben, the eldest of Joseph's brothers, warns his brothers that killing Joseph would incur God's wrath because God had adjudged him worthy (ἄξιον) of coveted blessings, and that by killing him they would "rob God of the recipient of his favors" (*Ant.* 2:27–28). Josephus is certainly influenced by his Hellenistic context since he incorporates benefaction motifs that are absent from the Hebrew and the LXX text of Gen 37:21–22. In short, Josephus believes that gift-giving must consider the character of the recipients.

Honoring Benefactors

Josephus shares the same convention found in Greco-Roman society that gratitude, which he says is a natural duty (*Ant.* 4:212), is the proper reciprocation of a good deed. In *Ant.* 19:183–84, he writes about a speech that Sentius Saturninus made in the Senate. Sentius praises Cassius Chaerea for his deeds, especially in overthrowing the tyrant, and asserts that it is their duty to "confer the very highest honors" on people like Cassius. He adds, "It is a most noble deed, and such as becomes free men, to requite a benefactor, such as this man has now shown himself in relation to all of us." Elsewhere, Josephus writes that while at Rephidim, the Israelites, who are in acute distress due to lack of water, vent their wrath on Moses, who then pleads with God to maintain his generosity by offering a new boon of water so that the Israelites may be continually grateful. Josephus comments, "Nor did God long defer this boon (τὴν δωρεάν), but promised Moses that he would provide a spring with abundance of water" (*Ant.* 3:34–35). The implication here is that gratitude is the appropriate response to favors and that where favors have ceased gratitude might subsequently stop.

Writing to Hiram, Solomon asserts that he now gives thanks to God for the peace that he enjoys and that has now created a conducive environment for the construction of the temple (*Ant.* 8:52). It is interesting to note that 1 Kgs 5:18 does not mention that Solomon gives thanks for the peace that he is enjoying. This is another indication that Josephus is reinterpreting this account through the lens of reciprocity; he implies that God is the ultimate king whose benefactions are reciprocated with gratitude.[81] Solomon understands that although "it is impossible by deeds for men to return thanks to God for the benefits they have received" (οὐ δυνατὸν ἀνθρώποις ἀποδοῦναι θεῷ χάριν ὑπὲρ ὧν εὖ πεπόνθασιν), for God does not need anything, humanity must praise God's greatness and thank him for his favors (*Ant.* 8:111–12).

The same theme of gratitude to beneficent rulers is seen in Ptolemy's royal correspondence. When King Ptolemy promised to confer a favor both on the Jews and on all those throughout the habitable world, he dispatched emissaries (Andreas and Aristaeus) to the high-priest Eleazar to convey this royal promise (*Ant.* 12:48). In his reply, Eleazar expressed the Jews' obligation to the king as well as their willingness to reciprocate in every way possible:

> Be assured that we shall submit to anything that is of benefit to you, even though it exceeds our nature, for we ought to make a return (ἀμείβεσθαι) for the kindness (εὐεργεσίας) which you have shown our fellow-citizens in various ways. We therefore promptly offered sacrifices on behalf of you and your sister and children and friends, and the people offered up prayers that your plans may be realized and that your kingdom may be preserved in peace (*Ant.* 12:53–56).

The Jews understand their obligation to return the favors they have been shown. And to demonstrate that they do not delay in expressing gratitude, they sacrificed and prayed for Ptolemy.

But Josephus is also critical of some aspects of reciprocity. In *Against Apion*, Josephus criticizes the value of public honors thus: "For those . . . who live in accordance with our laws the prize is not silver or gold, no crown of wild olive or of parsley with any such public mark of distinction" (*Ag. Ap.* 2:217–18). Instead of such awards, those who adhere to the law anticipate the gift of a better life, which God alone will award. Likewise, Josephus states that although the Romans and the Greeks are fond of making statues of their rulers, the law forbids the Jews from the making

---

81. On God as benefactor/patron in Josephus, see Spilsbury, "God and Israel in Josephus," 172–91. Spilsbury argues that Josephus replaces covenant language with terminology drawn from patron-client relations since that is more understandable to his audience in the ancient Mediterranean world. Through the paradigm of this dominant form of social relations in the Roman world, God is Israel's patron while Israel is God's client.

of images of God or any living creatures, hence they cannot honor the Roman authority by erecting statues (*Ag. Ap.* 2:73–75) or conspicuous monuments (*Ag. Ap.* 2:205). It was because of the law against erecting images and statues that Agrippa asked Gaius to refrain from erecting his statue in the Jerusalem temple (*Ant.* 18:297–98). As Tessa Rajak states, this abstention from "social competition and from its various manifestations was a way of marking out a community from its civic environment and binding it together."[82] This, however, does not imply that the Jews do not honor the emperor and the people of Rome. Josephus writes, "For them we offer perpetual sacrifices; and not only do we perform these ceremonies daily at the expense of the whole Jewish community . . . we jointly accord to the emperors alone this signal honor which we pay to no other individual" (*Ag. Ap.* 2:77). In principle, then, Josephus upholds the ethic of reciprocity and giving gratitude to those who are committed to the welfare of humanity. He believes that the Jews do certainly honor their benefactors, but only so far as the law permits.

Summary of Royal Benefaction in Jewish Writings

The portrait of the king in Jewish writings reveals that just as we find in the Greco-Roman world, the Jews expected their rulers to govern with great benevolence and care. The OT depicts the king as Yahweh's earthly representative through whom he reveals his righteousness and channels his blessings. As Yahweh's appointed ruler and representative, the king acts "on God's behalf by bestowing divine benefits to God's subjects. He is the royal agent who *shares in* God's *rule* and acts as the channel through whom God acts" (italics original).[83] The king is Yahweh's anointed, servant, and adopted son whose reign is without end. Yahweh's Spirit empowers him to fight Yahweh's battles and deliver the people from their enemies. He is compassionate toward the afflicted and the destitute, and rescues them from their oppressors. As a shepherd he cares for the flock and ensures that the people flourish.

The king is the righteous one whose heart delights in the commandments of Yahweh. He invites the people to share in his righteousness and transforms them so that they might walk in the fear of God. He establishes peace and prosperity for the people. He brings stability and order

---

82. Rajak, "Benefactors," 306.
83. Jipp, *Christ Is King*, 34.

to the cosmos. His reign is universal, extending from sea to sea. The king also receives tribute and gifts from the rulers of the world. The nations give obeisance before him, and the people of the earth serve him. Because he triumphs over all his enemies, the king is highly exalted; he shares in Yahweh's rule even as he reveals Yahweh's glory. Due to his righteous reign and divine benefactions, the people praise and honor the king.

The portrait that we find in Second Temple Judaism is not sharply different from the one in the OT and Greco-Roman writings. Although Ben Sira does not explicitly portray the king as benefactor, it is apparent that his portrait of the ideal ruler shares some of the ancient notions of king as benefactor. As the Lord's representative, the king leads the people in battle; he protects and delivers his subjects; he cares for his subjects; and he exemplifies devotion to the Lord. In turn, such a king wins lasting glory as posterity memorializes him. Since the only way to defeat death is by living virtuously in accordance with the law, Ben Sira's illustrious rulers have attained immortality. Yet, Ben Sira also manifests an attitude characterized by rejection and approval of benefaction. Lasting glory comes through wisdom and the fear of the Lord, and not through the gift. He criticizes those who give gifts arrogantly as they insist on repayment; instead, he points to God as the ultimate reciprocator. But the sage also embraces some aspects of reciprocity. Gift-giving should be selective, for only the righteous ought to be benefited. He also believes that people duly honor a wise leader who models cultic devotion and promotes peace, stability, and prosperity.

Employing specific gift-giving terminology such as benefactions, favors, kindness, generosity, philanthropy, love of honor, and gratitude, Philo and Josephus depict the ideal ruler in ways that are typical of Hellenistic kings. The king is divinely chosen. He is wealthy, caring, generous, and brave. He brings great prosperity and peace to his subjects. He exerts universal influence through benefactions and the subjugation of the nations. Both writers also believe that intrahuman gift-giving should be patterned after divine beneficence, meaning that gifts must be appropriate to the worthiness of the receiver.

Whereas both Greco-Roman and Jewish sources agree in principle that rulers who promote the welfare of their subjects should be honored, they do not entirely agree on *how* to honor benefactors. Both sources agree on such forms of reciprocation as obeisance, sacrifices, prayers, counter gifts, encomia, and memorialization. Where we see a major disjunction is with regard to statues. Statues and their accompanying inscriptions are a prominent way of reciprocating royal benefactions in Greco-Roman society. The Jews, however, are opposed to erecting statues and images of humans. Ben Sira does not write anywhere about statues and inscriptions. Philo is surprisingly more tolerant of statues while Josephus is vehemently opposed to them. The Jews' opposition to statues is due to the second commandment that prohibits the setting up of images of living beings (Exod 20:4). But this objection does not nullify their belief that humans are under obligation to honor rulers for their gifts as well as for their commitment to the welfare of their subjects.

The next chapter will examine how Paul might be drawing upon the system of royal benefaction in his christological discourse of Rom 5:1–11. If Paul is indeed portraying Jesus as the supreme royal benefactor whose gift delivers, empowers, and sustains his followers, then how does he use the cultural script of royal benefaction to accomplish this goal? Are there benefaction motifs that Paul invokes to portray Jesus Christ as the supreme royal benefactor? And if benefaction motifs are present in Paul's christological discourse, then are there ways in which his argument surprises his readers who are familiar with the ancient practice of royal benefaction?

4

The Messiah's Supreme Royal Benefaction in Romans 5:1–11

IN THIS CHAPTER, WE will analyze Rom 5:1–11 to see how Paul's christological discourse might be drawing upon the system of the ancient Mediterranean royal benefaction. Differently stated, how does the ancient royal benefaction system shape Paul's construal of Christ's kingship? We have seen in chapters 2 and 3 that the ancient rulers offer various kinds of gifts to the people as a demonstration of their concern for their well-being. Because of their exalted position, rulers have been entrusted with resources that they are expected to use to enhance communal flourishing. The ruler's benefactions might include building cities, providing medical services and reliefs, maintaining peace, supplying grain, sponsoring games, helping the city in time of upheaval, and lowering market price of commodities in time of need. The ideal king delights in bestowing benefits and governs as a father, a shepherd, and a guardian. The people are in turn expected to show gratitude and loyalty to their benefactor. That is why Aristotle maintains that "in the interchange of services, justice in the form of reciprocity is the bond that maintains the association" (*Eth. nic.* 5.5.6). How, then, might Paul's argument in Rom 5:1–11 be drawing upon the Greco-Roman royal benefaction system?

The main goal of this chapter is to demonstrate that Paul's argument engages the ancient economy of royal benefaction in ways that are both conventional and subversive. For Paul, Jesus Christ is the supreme royal benefactor whose commitment to his followers guarantees their eternal honorable status before God and demands faithful enactment of his rule

The Messiah's Supreme Royal Benefaction in Romans 5:1-11

even in suffering. At the level of literary analysis, we will draw attention to the benefaction motifs which Paul is invoking to portray Jesus Christ as the supreme royal benefactor whose gift delivers and sustains his followers. But it is necessary to move beyond mere recognition of the presence of the motif. In what ways does Paul's christological discourse surprise his readers who understand the ancient practice of royal benefaction? How does the Messiah's gift reverse the status of his followers? What is the relationship between the Messiah's benefaction and believers' affliction? How should believers reciprocate the Messiah's benefaction? The present chapter addresses such questions by providing a close analysis of Rom 5:1–11. It also provides the framework for the discussion in the next chapter which focuses on how some of the themes of 5:1–11 are developed in 5:12—8:39.

Our argument will build on the works of Troels Engberg-Pedersen and John M. G. Barclay, both of whom contend that χάρις demands reciprocity.[1] Engberg-Pedersen argues that to think of χάρις in Paul as an unconditionally given and received gift detaches Paul's letters from their social context and undermines personal interests that characterize the divine-human relationship. Barclay points out that in ancient times gifts were always relational, meaning that gift-giving created ties of obligation between the giver and the receiver. He adds that for Paul the divine gift in Jesus Christ is the ultimate incongruous gift that radically transforms Jews and gentiles. Barclay characterizes God's gift in Jesus Christ as a "strange and nonsensical phenomenon" due to its incongruity.[2] We will build on these and similar works by looking at how Paul depicts Jesus Christ as the supreme royal benefactor and by examining Paul's argument on the shape that reciprocity takes in suffering.

The chapter will proceed by first situating Rom 5:1–11 in its literary context. The aim here is to see how the passage both summarizes the preceding themes of 1:1—4:25 and previews 5:12—8:39. The second section will provide a detailed discussion of the Messiah's substitutionary death as the ultimate incommensurable benefaction to humanity. This benefaction that does not fit with humanity's unworthiness both delivers from sin and death and guarantees eternal life. Sections three to six will focus on how the Messiah's singular benefaction of himself in turn brings the gifts of eschatological life, peace, status, and the Holy Spirit respectively.

---

1. Engberg-Pedersen, "Gift-Giving and God's Charis"; Barclay, *Paul and the Gift*; and Barclay, "Under Grace."

2. Barclay, *Paul and the Gift*, 478.

The Greco-Roman system of royal benefaction shows that benefits come with ties of obligation. In this regard, the final section discusses what reciprocating the Messiah's benefaction entails. Throughout our discussion in this chapter, we hope to demonstrate that Paul depicts Jesus as the supreme royal benefactor whose benefaction both delivers humanity and demands faithful allegiance to him as king.

Romans 5:1-11 as Recapitulation and Preview

We have argued that Paul's royal discourse is one foundational thread for his argument in the letter of Romans. By discourse, we are referring to an interdisciplinary model of linguistic investigation that unites semantics, syntax, and pragmatics. It is a synthetic approach whose primary premise is that because meaning is a function of the context, the text must be interpreted in its social environment.[3] Royal discourse investigates how Paul's first-century readers might have understood how he uses various social scripts to present Jesus Christ as king. Our concern is with how Paul employs the script of royal benefaction to depict Jesus as the singular royal Messiah of Jews and gentiles. The discourse persuades the readers that by virtue of the resurrection from the dead, Jesus has been installed as the son-of-God-in-power (1:3-4). Through his death, he provides atonement for the sinful humanity, and by his resurrection he prevails over all opposing powers; hence he alone can deliver humanity. He is the son of God (1:3, 9; 5:10; 8:3, 29) and the Lord (1:4, 7; 5:1, 11, 21; 6:23; 7:25; 8:39) who commands obedience from the nations (1:5; cf. 15:7-13). He conquers sin and death by means of crucifixion (4:25; 6:9-10; 8:32) and brings liberation to humanity (3:21-26; 6:11-14). His rule is marked by life and righteousness (5:12-21). His enthronement (8:34) means that he now exercises dominion over the entire human race even as he rescues those who were formerly subdued by sin and death. The question, then, is: How does 5:1-11 function within this royal discourse? Many have rightly noted that 5:1-11 both recapitulates the preceding argument (1:1—4:25) and previews what follows (5:12—8:39).[4] To understand

---

3. Westfall, *Discourse Analysis*, 22-23; Reed, "Discourse Analysis," 223-40.

4. Dodd states that Rom 5:1-11 "contains in brief the theme of the whole argument down to viii. 39" (*Epistle of Paul to the Romans*, 93). Also Wright, "Letter to the Romans," 397, 508. For alternative views that either include 5:1-11 in the preceding unit or contend that the first major unit runs through 5:21, see the discussion in Moo, *Epistle to the Romans*, 290-95.

this passage's double duty as transition and thesis, we will briefly discuss three themes which this text recapitulates before turning to four themes which it previews.

One of the themes that Paul discusses in 1:1—4:25 and that is integral to his argument in 5:1-11 is humanity's complete moral incapacitation due to sin and death. Human sinfulness and the consequential wrath of God dominate Paul's discussion in 1:18—3:20. In 1:17, Paul writes that the righteousness of God (δικαιοσύνη θεοῦ) is revealed (ἀποκαλύπτεται) in the gospel; in 1:18 he uses the same verb to describe the revelation of the wrath of God (ὀργὴ θεοῦ). The gospel reveals both the righteousness and the wrath of God. The verses that follow paint a horrible scene of utter wickedness against which God's wrath burns. Paul's rhetorical strategy in 1:18-32 is to elicit indignation in order that he may turn that indignation against his interlocutor when he comes to 2:1-16. He says three times that God "handed them over" (1:24, 26, 28).[5] Because of humanity's refusal to acknowledge and honor God, he has handed them over to the dominion of sin. Moreover, Paul charges his audience with three types of exchanges (1:23, 25, 26). The first two exchanges basically point to their idolatry while the last exchange describes their immorality. The threefold description of being handed over and of exchange accentuates the audience's inability to rescue themselves from the dominion of sin and death.

Paul further emphasizes the gentiles' unrighteousness by means of alliteration in 1:31. They are ἀσυνέτους ἀσυνθέτους ἀστόργους ἀνελεήμονας ("foolish, faithless, heartless, unmerciful"). Perhaps Paul uses alliteration here to show that the list of gentile vices is inexhaustible and that whatever he has stated is enough to prove their wickedness. Paul also underscores the gentile predicament by the inclusio of 1:18 and 1:32. In 1:18, he mentions "unrighteousness of men" (ἀδικίαν ἀνθρώπων) against which the wrath of God is revealed; he ends the section in 1:32 by referring to "the righteous decree of God" (τὸ δικαίωμα τοῦ θεοῦ), which pronounces a death sentence against the unrighteous. The placement of the theme of righteousness both at the beginning and at the end demonstrates that the leading gentile predicament is ἀδικία. At the end of Romans 1, Paul's audience certainly agrees with his assessment that the accused stands

---

5. See Gaventa, "God Handed Them Over," 42-53. Gaventa has persuasively argued that παρέδωκεν αὐτοὺς ὁ θεός ("God handed them over") is apocalyptic language that highlights both human rebellion against God and God's active role in cosmic conflict.

condemned because of his idolatry and immorality. Similarly, the accused is plagued with complete moral incapacitation, for having been "handed over" he acts dishonorably and ungratefully to God.

Romans 2 focuses on the relationship between divine justice and universalism to assert that humanity lacks righteous standing before the eschatological judge.[6] Paul, by means of diatribe, turns the verdict on the imaginary interlocutor who has just voiced his approval of the preceding sermon and thereby reacted with indignation.[7] The interlocutor condemns those who commit the sins of 1:18-32 yet he himself is guilty of such sins. Unlike human judgment, God's judgment is based on truth (2:2), and it is inescapable (2:3). God's judgment is also righteous because people will be judged according to their deeds (2:5-16). Moreover, this judgment, which is through Jesus the Messiah (2:16), is preceded by God's patient plea intended to lead humanity to repentance (2:4-5). Whoever rejects God's mercy is storing up wrath against himself for the day when God's righteous judgment will be revealed, when he will render to each person according to his deeds (2:6), to the Jew first then also to the gentile, for God does not show partiality (2:11).[8]

It is futile to attempt to solve the problem of ἀδικία by circumcision, for what Jews and gentiles need is the transformation of the heart rather than an outward mark of identification (2:17-29). To prove his declaration that "both Jews and gentiles are all under sin" (3:9), Paul unleashes a catena of scriptural quotations (3:10-18).[9] One of the main points of the quotations is that the distinction between the righteous and the unrighteous collapses because the whole human race is plagued by sin.[10] Observing the law cannot solve humanity's problem since man cannot secure his own deliverance from the slavery of unrighteousness.

---

6. The courtroom setting, which is prevalent in this whole section, is dominated in 2:11-29 by the juridical concept of the law. The term νόμος occurs nineteen times in various forms in this section: Rom 2:12 (2), 13 (2), 14 (2), 15, 17, 18, 20, 23 (2), 25 (2), 26, 27 (2).

7. Campbell, *Deliverance of God*, 547-50; Stowers, *Rereading of Romans*, 97-118.

8. See Bassler, *Divine Impartiality*, 77-119. Bassler seeks to show how the theological axiom of divine impartiality plays a central role in Paul's argument.

9. This catena of scriptural quotations is from the following Jewish Scriptures: Eccl 7:20; Ps 14:1-3 (cf. 53:2-4; Ps 5:10); Ps 10:7; Isa 59:7-8; and Ps 36:2. For further discussion of the quotations, see Keck, "Function of Rom 3:10-18," 141-57.

10. In 3:19-20 Paul uses πᾶς three times to highlight humanity's accountability before God.

The Messiah's Supreme Royal Benefaction in Romans 5:1-11

Romans 5:1–11 restates this problem of complete moral incapacitation due to sin and death. In 5:6, Paul describes humanity as "weak" (ἀσθενῶν) and "ungodly" (ἀσεβῶν). Romans 5:7 implies that humanity is neither "righteous" (δίκαιος) nor "good" (ἀγαθός), and 5:8 explicitly asserts that we are "sinners" (ἁμαρτωλοί). Humanity is helpless, fragile, and sinful; it is at enmity with God and the object of divine wrath (5:9–10). Humans cannot do anything to deserve the Messiah's gift. Complete moral incapacitation renders humanity unworthy of the Messiah's benefaction. God takes the initiative through Jesus Christ to overcome the dominion of sin and death, reconcile humanity to himself, and restore humans to an honorable embodiment. Paul's discourse contends that the royal son of God exercises sovereignty over the realms of life and death even as he liberates humanity so that they may participate in his righteous rule.

The second theme that Paul recapitulates in 5:1–11 is the Messiah's death and resurrection. Paul speaks of Jesus' Davidic descent in 1:3–4, hence his messiahship, as well as his installation as "the son-of-God-in-power according to the Spirit of holiness by means of the resurrection from the dead." Although this summary of the Messiah's descent and ascent does not explicitly mention Christ's death, it is implicit in terms of "corpses" language, as Paul writes in 1:4 of "the resurrection from the dead ones" (ἀναστάσεως νεκρῶν)—which implies that prior to his resurrection, the Messiah's body was among the corpses. Paul describes Christ's death in 3:21–26. The passage marks a new chapter in Paul's articulation of the human predicament and the solution that God has provided. The section begins with an emphatic νυνὶ δέ ("but now") to draw attention to how God has demonstrated his righteousness. The christological emphasis cannot be clearer: God presented the Messiah as a sacrifice of atonement for a demonstration of his righteousness. Notwithstanding its highly debated details and imagery, this passage is a bold and celebratory declaration of God's act in Christ. That is to say, God has manifested his righteousness through the faithfulness of Jesus Christ for the liberation of women and men who share in the faithfulness of the martyred and vindicated redeemer. In 4:25, Paul writes that Jesus our Lord "was handed over for our trespasses and raised for our justification." The solution to the human predicament comes by participating in the revelation of God's righteousness through his Messiah. Christ's death and resurrection continue to permeate Paul's argument in 5:1–11. Believers obtain righteousness through Jesus the Messiah (5:1, 9) who died for them (5:6–8). Through his death they are reconciled to God (5:1, 10) and enjoy close communion with him (5:2). And his sacrifice is efficacious because he was raised to life; Paul, therefore, asserts that "we shall be saved by his life" (5:10).

The last theme that Paul restates in 5:1-11 is hope. Abraham trusted God and received the promise of progeny; he never wavered in his conviction that God was able to bring life out of death (4:16-22). Likewise, Jesus faced the situation of death, yet he was vindicated when God raised him to life (4:24-25). Abraham's descendants and the Messiah's followers must be marked by complete trust and hope in the resurrecting God. Just as Abraham and the Messiah were vindicated, so believers too will be vindicated by being raised from the dead. The Pauline hope is also related to the coming judgment. Paul leaves no doubt that for those who have experienced liberation in Christ Jesus, God's judgment does not cause anxiety but hope-filled anticipation; God's wrath no longer hangs over those who are in Christ. This confident assurance is rooted in what God has done in providing redemption (3:21-26). In Romans 5, Paul writes that believers "boast in the hope of the glory of God" (5:2), that this hope will not put them to shame (5:5), and that we are confident that we will be saved from the future wrath through Jesus the Messiah (5:9-10). In brief, considering the three themes of moral incapacitation, Christ's death and resurrection, and hope in 1:1—4:25, there are good reasons for viewing 5:1-11 as a recapitulation of the preceding argument, with a strong emphasis on what God has accomplished through the Messiah.[11]

Yet, 5:1-11 is more than a restatement of the previous argument; it also previews at least four themes.[12] The first theme is suffering, which Paul introduces in 5:3-5 and then expands upon in 8:17-39. Paul argues in 5:3-5 that suffering has been designed for producing endurance, which in turn shapes character. As believers "boast in afflictions" they demonstrate their faithfulness to the Messiah. Ultimately, suffering strengthens rather than weakens the hope of resurrection (5:5). In Romans 8, Paul states that suffering is inevitable for Christ's followers; because we suffer with Christ, we will also be glorified with Christ (8:17). Suffering

---

11. Pickett rightly suggests that the narrative structure of Romans 1-5 could be summarized thus: "[A]ll human beings have alienated themselves from God, but God has taken the initiative to provide the basis for a new relationship through the death of Christ" ("Death of Christ," 729).

12. On the parallels between 5:1-11 and chapter 8, see Dahl, "Two Notes on Romans 5," 37-42. Dahl (here p. 39) notes that "chapter 8 contains a fuller development of the themes which are briefly stated in 5:1-11."

cannot separate believers from the love of God; rather, Christ's followers mightily prevail over all sufferings and oppositions through Jesus Christ (8:31–39).

The second theme is the gift of the Holy Spirit. Paul writes in 5:5 that God's love has been poured out in the heart of believers through the Holy Spirit. In chapter 8, Paul states that the Spirit gives life and empowers believers' walk (8:1–4); he grants victory over sin (8:5–9, 11–12); he unites us with Christ and assures us of resurrection (8:10–11); and he intercedes for us (8:26–27). By the Spirit, believers are adopted into the family of God (8:14–17).

The third theme is the dominion of grace. Paul writes in 5:2 that through Christ believers have access into χάρις; he then picks up this theme in 5:12–21 where he depicts χάρις as reigning over sin and death.[13] As those who have been brought into the realm of χάρις, Christ's followers must not allow sin to reign in their mortal bodies; instead, they must present their "members to God as instruments for righteousness" (6:11–14) even as they remember that it is through "Jesus the Messiah our Lord" that there is deliverance from the body of death (7:24–25). Rather than promoting sin, the dominion of χάρις is characterized by "newness of life" (6:1–4), obedience (6:16), and "eternal life in Jesus the Messiah our Lord" (6:23).

The final theme that Paul previews in 5:1–11 is peace and reconciliation. There is peace with God through the Messiah (5:1). Those who have been reconciled to God through the death of the Messiah have confidence that they will be saved through him from the coming wrath (5:9–11). Because Christ's followers have been reconciled to God, they can no longer be condemned (8:1), and no one can successfully bring any charge against them (8:31–34). The one who did not spare his own son is for us (8:32); he is the one who justifies (8:33). And since he has given himself to us in friendship, nothing "will be able to separate us from the love of God in the Messiah Jesus our Lord" (8:39).

In sum, just as Paul's recapitulation of 1:1—4:25 in 5:1–11 serves to emphasize what God has accomplished through the Messiah, so the parallels between 5:1–11 and 5:12—8:39 emphasize the consequences of the Messiah's death and resurrection for believers. It is therefore not surprising that just as the prepositional phrase "through our Lord Jesus the Messiah" (διὰ τοῦ κυρίου ἡμῶν Ἰησοῦ Χριστοῦ) bookends Paul's discussion

---

13. See Dahl, "Two Notes on Romans 5," 43–48.

in 5:1–11, so does it continue to frame his proceeding discussion (5:21; 6:23; 7:25; 8:39).[14] The focus is on Jesus Christ as the king who invites his subjects to participate in his trajectory of dying and rising in this life even as they anticipate the redemption of their bodies. We want to suggest that one of the ancient socio-economic systems that Paul is using to construct this christological discourse is royal benefaction. In the section that follows, we will discuss how Paul uses the Greco-Roman benefaction system in 5:1–11 to accomplish his theological purpose of portraying Jesus Christ as the supreme royal benefactor so that Roman believers might participate faithfully in his lordship now even as they anticipate glorification. We will proceed by discussing the Messiah's substitutionary death before turning to the gifts of eschatological life, peace, status, and the Holy Spirit respectively. We will conclude by looking at how Christ's followers might reciprocate his benefaction.

The Messiah's Substitutionary Death

How does the Messiah liberate humanity from sin and death, secure humanity's peace with God, grant access into grace, provide eschatological assurance, and enable his followers to boast? This question is one of the main problems which Paul addresses in Rom 5:6–11. The shortest answer is that "the Messiah died for us" (Χριστὸς ὑπὲρ ἡμῶν ἀπέθανεν, 5:8). But Paul's answer is more nuanced and presented in explicit benefaction motifs. In these six verses, Paul explicitly refers to the Messiah's death four times (5:6, 8, 9, 10) and implicitly once (5:7). This suggests that the focus is heavily on the Messiah's sacrifice on the cross. The Messiah, the supreme royal benefactor, offered his life *for us* as a gift. But who are we that the Messiah would die *for us*?

The Messiah's Non-Calculating Gift

Gift-giving in Greco-Roman society is deeply discriminative as benefactors must judiciously identify worthy (ἄξιοι) beneficiaries. Benefactors must apply the rule of censorship and of rating to place their gifts strategically. They must act as careful farmers, sowing their seed in productive

---

14. Wright notes that the christological formula that rounds off 5:1–11; 5:12–21; 6:1–11; and 6:12–23 "is not just added on for effect but sums up the paragraph" ("Letter to the Romans," 509).

soil, and as skilled players, pitching the ball to skilled catchers. Favors conferred on the wrong people do not yield returns; in fact, it is thoughtless and unacceptable to assist the base. Aristotle writes that whoever gives to the wrong people is not generous (*Eth. nic.* 4.1.14, 22–23). Cicero insists that a man should be favored to the extent that he exemplifies justice, self-control, and temperance (*Off.* 1.15.46). Seneca writes that to give to the base is dishonorable (*Ben.* 4.9.3). Gifts are bestowed on people *because of who they are* (Seneca, *Ben.* 6.18.2). Benefactors must, therefore, carefully select the good and the pious as beneficiaries. This is the only way to promote piety and ensure that gifts are reciprocated. Cicero not only urges that the gift should be "proportioned to the worthiness of the recipient" (*Off.* 1.14.42) but also that one's purse should not be "so loosely held as to be open to everybody" (*Off.* 2.15.55). Plutarch argues that it is honorable for the statesman to help reputable friends (*Mor.* 582F). Whereas requests from enemies should be rejected because they are not in accord with excellence and reputation, those from friends should be granted because a man's friends ought to enjoy his "good and kindly acts of favor" (Plutarch, *Mor.* 808D–E).[15]

Ben Sira, Philo, and Josephus also argue that gift-giving must be calculated. Ben Sira writes, "If you do good, know for whom you are doing it, and your kindness will have its effect. Do good to the just and reward will be yours, if not from him, then from the Lord" (Sir 12:1–2). Whoever assists the wicked ignores God's pattern because he too hates sinners and blesses the righteous (Sir 12:6). Such a person should not think that he is showing mercy to the needy (Sir 12:3). Philo uses the adjective ἄξιος and its cognates to assert that God bestows favors depending on the fittingness of the recipients (*Alleg. Interp.* 3.25.79; 3.27.83; 3.28.87; 3.30.93–94; 3.34.106). For instance, Moses is "deemed worthy of the boon" (ἀξιοῦται μέντοι τῆς χάριτος) based on his virtue and tactical withdrawal from Pharaoh (*Alleg. Interp.* 3.14). Joseph's worthiness is evident in his refusal to take vengeance against his brothers (*Joseph* 41:249). Josephus writes that the Jews have demonstrated that they are worthy (ἀξίους) of imperial benefaction, which means that they should not be denied additional favors (*Ant.* 16:31–62). He asserts that those who are withholding the imperial munificence from the Jews are committing an offense because

---

15. Plutarch argues that while the ideal ruler seeks to show concern for all his subjects, he, like God who is "indeed a common father of all mankind" and yet makes "peculiarly his own the noblest and the best of them" (*Alex.* 27:6), must use his resources to cultivate an intimate relationship with good and reputable men (*Mor.* 808B).

they are not considering "worthy the people to whose worth their rulers have testified by granting them such favors" (*Ant.* 16:34). The implication in all this is that a ruler should withhold favors from the impious and unworthy but show generosity towards people of reputable character.

Selective gift-giving also touches on one's social status. Some writers like Aristotle maintain that the poor should not be benefited since they are unable to return a favor. But others like Cicero, Dio Chrysostom, and Ben Sira state that the poor who are of reputable character can be given favors because they are able to express gratitude. The underlying point is that benefactors should promote the welfare of good people and punish the impious by withholding gifts from them.

Does the Messiah's benefaction meet the ancient stipulation that favors ought to be conferred on the worthy? The answer to this question is found in how Paul describes those *for whom* the Messiah died. Paul uses four key words to describe humanity. First, Rom 5:6 states that the Messiah died for the weak (ἀσθενῶν). The adjective ἀσθενής means "weak" or "powerless." More specifically, it can denote "suffering from a debilitating illness," or "experiencing some incapacity or limitation."[16] Paul often uses the noun ἀσθένεια and the adjective ἀσθενής and related terms in a general sense "to characterize the human inability that is an inevitable part of life—even redeemed life—on this earth" (e.g., Rom 8:26; 1 Cor 15:43; 2 Cor 11:21—13:9).[17] But Paul does not seem to use this term here to describe human limitation in general. Contrary to James D. G. Dunn who argues that "ἀσθενής does not have any particular theological overtones here" and that Paul uses it to characterize "the weakness of the creature over against the omnipotence of the Creator,"[18] the broader context of Romans 1–5 suggests that the term bears a negative connotation.

We have already seen that in Romans 1–3, Paul declares that humanity is so enslaved to sin that they cannot rescue themselves. It is a situation marked by complete moral incapacitation.[19] If Paul is simply

---

16. BDAG 142.

17. Moo, *Epistle to the Romans*, 306n63. Also see Dunn, *Romans 1–8*, 254. Sometimes Paul uses the adjective ἀσθενής along with its cognates to describe physical illness (1 Cor 11:30; Gal 4:13; Phil 2:26–27; cf. 1 Tim 5:23; 2 Tim 4:10), but that is certainly not how it functions in Rom 5:6.

18. Dunn, *Romans 1–8*, 254.

19. See Rom 7:7–25 where Paul describes human weakness as revealed by the law. He basically tells gentiles that fixing their eyes on the law only flames their desires. Faced with his inability to meet the law's demands, the Judaizer cries out, "O wretched man that I am! Who will rescue me from this body of death?" (7:24). Deliverance only

describing humanity's limited power "over against the omnipotence of the Creator," then this term hardly contributes any point to his argument. For the goal of redemption is not to rescue humanity from its limitation and make it as powerful as God. The weakness that this term implies is something from which humanity needs deliverance. Thus humanity is weak, not in the general sense of human finiteness, but in the negative sense of moral helplessness and inability to secure one's own righteousness.[20] Or as Moo puts it, "weak" as used here "designates that 'total incapacity for good' which is characteristic of the unredeemed."[21] The genitive absolute ὄντων ἡμῶν ἀσθενῶν ("we being weak"), therefore, points to a condition of moral powerlessness that continually marks the life of the unredeemed. Paul probably uses the double ἔτι ("still") in this verse to emphasize that Christ died for humanity when it was in a state of helpless existence.[22]

The remaining three terms (ἀσεβῶν [5:6], ἁμαρτωλῶν [5:8], and ἐχθροί [5:10]), which Paul uses to describe those for whom the Messiah offered his life, are less problematic to understand. The adjective ἀσεβής literally means "irreverent, impious, ungodly"; it pertains to "violating norms for a proper relationship to a deity."[23] Paul uses the same word in 4:5 when he declares that God makes the ungodly righteous. In 1:18, the cognate noun ἀσέβεια is used almost synonymously with ἀδικίᾳ ("unrighteousness"): "For the wrath of God is revealed from heaven against all ungodliness and unrighteousness of men." Beverly R. Gaventa notes that "ungodly" is a term that "epitomizes the depiction of humanity in the second half of Romans 1 and recalls the scriptural quotations in 3:10–18."[24] The adjective ἀσεβής thus designates a relational deficiency

---

comes through the Messiah: "Thanks (χάρις) be to God through Jesus the Messiah our Lord" (7:25a).

20. BDAG 143. Pulcini states: "Human beings were unable, on their own, to rectify their relationship with God; that necessitated an unmerited divine initiative. Paul here points to that initiative: that Christ died for us when we could do nothing for ourselves" ("In Right Relationship," 73). But his suggestion that Paul might also be using "weak" to designate a group within the Roman community is less convincing.

21. Moo, *Epistle to the Romans*, 306. Fitzmyer rightly states that "weak" implies that humanity is "incapable of doing anything to achieve rectitude in the sight of God" (*Romans*, 398–99). Also see Schreiner, *Romans*, 260–61.

22. On the textual problem regarding the double ἔτι, see Schreiner, *Romans*, 265–66.

23. BDAG 141.

24. Gaventa, *When in Romans*, 35.

characterized by irreverence to God. It is closely related to the third term ἁμαρτωλός ("sinner"). Paul has already declared not only that the whole human race is under sin (3:9), but also that those who sin, whether without the law or under the law, will perish (2:12). The godless and sinners deserve death rather than the gift of life. The final word ἐχθρός ("enemy") points to a situation characterized by hostility (cf. 1:30) and wrath. It recalls both humanity's deliberate rebellion and God's just wrath against that rebellion (1:18—3:20). The fact that Paul has chosen this word to climax his description of the condition of the unredeemed implies that unless rescued by the Messiah, the wrath of God painfully hangs over Jews and gentiles.

Taken together, the terms "weak," "ungodly," "sinners," and "enemies" underscore the complete unworthiness of humanity as recipients of the Messiah's gift. Commenting on these terms, Barclay states, "The variety of terms, portraying the absence of value from multiple perspectives, seems designed to underline as emphatically as possible that the conditions for the gift were anything but positive."[25] Barclay adds that "no fitting features can be traced in the recipients of God's love, not even in their hidden potential."[26] Paul is depicting Christ's royal benefaction in conventional and yet surprising ways. What appears conventional is that a great gift has been given to the people. The one who offers his life as a gift is "Χριστός" (the Messiah, 5:6, 8). For the first time in Romans, Paul simply refers to the Messiah by the title Χριστός by itself in 5:6 and repeats it in 5:8. In both cases, the main statement is: Χριστὸς ἀπέθανεν ("the Messiah died"). Longenecker comments that this double occurrence of Χριστός by itself "seem[s] somewhat strange in this passage."[27] Dunn suggests that the statement "Christ died" "may well reflect the summary assertion of earliest Christian apologetic that Jesus' crucifixion was no disproof of his messiahship: it was precisely as the crucified that he was the Messiah."[28] By employing the title Χριστός, Paul does not leave his political agenda in doubt; failure to recognize this is to miss the central pillar of Paul's Christology.[29] Paul wants to be clear to his readers that the

25. Barclay, *Paul and the Gift*, 477.
26. Barclay, *Paul and the Gift*, 477.
27. Longenecker, *Epistle to the Romans*, 563.
28. Dunn, *Romans 1–8*, 254.
29. Bird contends, "The title *Christos* (Messiah) in Paul has routinely been de-Judaized and depoliticized in Pauline scholarship by those who want to show that Paul did not have a messianic faith. Yet the evidence overwhelmingly points in the other

one who died vicariously is the Davidic king and Yahweh's anointed one who brings eschatological deliverance to the oppressed and establishes righteousness and peace.

When read against the backdrop of the Greco-Roman royal benefaction system, this point is conventional and yet surprising because the king is both the giver and the gift. It is not unusual for the Greco-Roman ruler to demonstrate kindness and steadfast care to his subjects by sacrificial distribution of resources (cf. Seneca, *Ben.* 4.32.2). Aristotle writes that sometimes a person may even die for others:

> But it is also true that the virtuous man's conduct is often guided by the interests of his friends and of his country, and that he will if necessary lay down his life in their behalf. For he will surrender wealth and power and all the goods that men struggle to win, if he can secure nobility for himself; since he would prefer an hour of rapture to a long period of mild enjoyment, a year of noble life to many years of ordinary existence, one great and glorious exploit to many small successes. And this is doubtless the case with those who give their lives for others; thus they choose great nobility for themselves. Also the virtuous man is ready to forgo money if by that means his friends may gain more money; for thus, though his friend gets money, he himself achieves nobility, and so he assigns the greater good to his own share (*Eth. nic.* 9.8.9).

The Aristotelian virtuous man is willing to die for others because that is how he attains greater nobility for himself. It is a "glorious exploit" to safeguard the interests of others by substitutionary death. The Athenians declared in their praise of Demetrios the Great that in his bid to secure freedom for the Hellenes he "endured danger and hardship."[30] The historian Dio Cassius writes that the Roman emperor Otho refused to continue to wage war against Vitellius, and instead opted to commit noble suicide for his supporters:

> Surely it is far better and far more just that one should perish for all than many for one, and that I should refuse on account of one man alone to embroil the Roman people in civil war and cause so great a multitude of human beings to perish . . . I shall free myself [i.e., commit suicide], that all men may learn from the event that you chose for your emperor one who would

---

direction with messianism forming the hub of Paul's Christology" ("One Who Will Arise," 154).

30. Danker, *Benefactor*, no. 30.

not give you up to save himself, but rather himself to save you (63.13.2–3).

According to Plutarch, Otho would not listen to the soldiers who "begged him not to abandon them, and not to betray them to their enemies, but to use their lives and persons in his service as long as they had breath" (*Oth.* 15:3). Rather than allowing the many to die for him, the emperor asked them not to rob him "of a greater blessedness—that of dying nobly on behalf of fellow citizens so many and so good. If I was worthy to be Roman emperor, I ought to give my life freely for my country" (*Oth.* 15:4).[31] Although "the dominant transcript" is for the many to sacrifice their life on behalf of the one, it is not entirely unheard of in the ancient world, whether hypothetically or in reality, for rulers to express the willingness to die for their subjects.[32] Thus Paul is depicting the Messiah as having offered the greatest gift that one could ever imagine in the ancient world. Yet this gift is very surprising, not just because it is contrary to the dominant transcript but also because of *how* and *for whom* it is given!

The Messiah offers a non-calculating gift. The ideal ruler is indeed generous, yet he must also judiciously identify worthy (ἄξιοι) recipients of his good deeds. In contrast, Paul shows that the Messiah offers a non-calculating and indiscriminate benefaction to all people. Leithart rightly states that Jesus' act of giving gifts to those who could not repay is "revolutionary in the Greco-Roman world," where one gives gifts to those who are able to repay.[33] The Messiah does not strategically place his gifts to maximize the possibility of a return; he does not carefully pitch the ball to skilled catchers; and he does not choose the productive soil in which to sow his seeds. In fact, Christ would be termed as an unwise and wasteful benefactor who sows his seed in "worn-out and unproductive soil" (Seneca, *Ben.* 1.1.2). His failure to apply the rule of censorship means that he confers his favor on the wrong people. Aristotle would tell the Messiah that he should never think that he is being generous by giving to the unworthy. Seneca would accuse him of committing a dishonorable deed.

---

31. Also see Tacitus, *Ann.* 2:46; Martial, *Epigr.* 6:32; Suetonius, *Otho* 10:1–2.

32. Scott, *Domination and the Arts*. For further examples of noble, vicarious deaths in the classical literature, see Danker, "Endangered Benefactor," 40–43; Danker and Jewett, "Jesus as the Apocalyptic Benefactor," 489–90; Gathercole, *Defending Substitution*, 85–102; Thiessen, "Many for One," 455–56. Consider also Seneca's *De Clementia*, which urges Emperor Nero not to worry about his subjects who sacrifice their lives on his behalf.

33. Leithart, *Gratitude*, 7.

Cicero would condemn him for acting foolishly by making his purse accessible to the morally base. Plutarch would excoriate the Messiah for acting disgracefully (*Mor.* 582F). And Ben Sira would tell the Messiah that he is not wise because he ignores God's pattern for gift-giving and does not understand that the wicked only repay the kindness of the righteous with evil. Because of the indiscriminate nature of the Messiah's gift, one may justifiably characterize it as a "strange and nonsensical phenomenon" and "*the ultimate incongruous gift*" (italics original).[34]

According to the Greco-Roman benefaction system, the only way to ensure reciprocity is by benefiting the virtuous. To give gifts to those who are morally wanting erodes social cohesion and weakens moral standards since it amounts to rewarding vice with favors. So what Paul says in this text is very radical. The Messiah is neither indifferent to humanity's moral standing nor does he lack the discernment needed to identify worthy recipients. Instead, he understands more than anybody that "no one is righteous" and that "all are under sin." He knows that humanity's condition only merits wrath, yet he comes to their rescue by dying for them.

To emphasize further the Messiah's indiscriminate gift to the undeserving, Paul writes in Rom 5:6 that the Messiah died "at that time" (κατὰ καιρόν).[35] The phrase κατὰ καιρόν has elicited various interpretations, most of which highlight God's ordained time. It has been taken as indicating "the time of decision concerning the success of the work of Jesus,"[36] "the eschatological time as that to which God's purpose has been moving and in which he has acted decisively,"[37] "the fitting character of the time when Jesus died for human sinfulness,"[38] or "the culminating, eschatological 'time' of God's intervention in Christ."[39] Syntactically, the phrase modifies what follows, namely, the Messiah died for the ungodly. Considering the context, the temporal appropriateness of the Messiah's

---

34. Barclay, *Paul and the Gift*, 478–79.

35. BDAG 512. This is a less common expression in Paul. Whenever he uses the noun καιρός it is usually with the prepositions πρό ("before"; cf. 1 Cor 4:5), περί ("concerning"; cf. 1 Thess 5:1), πρός ("for"; cf. 1 Cor 7:5; 1 Thess 2:17), or ἐν ("in"; cf. Rom 3:26; 11:5; 2 Cor 8:14; 2 Thess 2:6). The only other occurrence of κατά with καιρός is in Rom 9:9.

36. *TDNT* 3:460.

37. Dunn, *Romans 1–8*, 255.

38. Fitzmyer, *Romans*, 399.

39. Moo, *Epistle to the Romans*, 307.

death is intricately linked to the identity of the beneficiaries as ungodly (as well as weak, sinners, and enemies).

Aristotle gives three basic guidelines for bestowing benefits: (1) carefully identify worthy recipients of benefactions; (2) give the right amount; and (3) give *at the right time* (*Eth. nic.* 4.1.7, 12). To elaborate, Aristotle writes:

> He [the generous person] will not be careless with his property, inasmuch as he wishes to employ it for the good of others. He will not give indiscriminately, in order that he may be able to give to the right persons and *at the right time*, and where it is noble to do so (ἵνα ἔχῃ διδόναι οἷς δεῖ καὶ ὅτε καὶ οὗ καλόν, *Eth. nic.* 4.1.17-18).

Although Paul uses the prepositional phrase κατὰ καιρόν rather the adverb ὅτε as we find in Aristotle, both share the same concept. Discriminatory gift-giving takes place *when* the beneficiary has demonstrated his worthiness. Otherwise, any gift given would be at the wrong time, hence unfit. Paul's assertion that the Messiah died *at that time*, therefore, implies that having taken perfect cognizance of human unworthiness, the Messiah did not, for a moment, contemplate withholding his gift until such a time as would be more fitting. According to the norms of the ancient benefaction, the Messiah's gift was *untimely*, but according to God's plan, the Messiah death was necessary to rescue the unworthy. So the Messiah's gift of his own life that brings peace with God breaks all the three basic guidelines for calculated gift-giving: (1) the Messiah offers his life to the entire sinful human race; (2) the Messiah gives more than "the right amount," for he offers the unquantifiable gift of his own life; and (3) the Messiah's gift comes *at the right time*, not in the Greco-Roman sense of being offered selectively to the virtuous people who are able to return a favor, but in the sense of being offered to a people completely lacking in merit and worthy of death.

The Messiah's Death as a Subversion of a Heroic Act of Reciprocity

Apart from indiscrimination, the Messiah's benefaction overturns the values of Greco-Roman society because his death is not a heroic act of reciprocity. This seems to be the point of 5:7: "For scarcely would anyone die for a righteous person (δικαίου); though perhaps for the sake of the good person (τοῦ ἀγαθοῦ) one would dare even to die." Romans 5:7 is an expansive comment on the main statement of 5:6 and highlights the extraordinary character of Christ's sacrifice.[40] But what exactly does Paul mean in this verse? Many interpreters skip over this verse, or say little about it, claiming that the gist of Paul's argument is clear enough even without 5:7.[41] Yet to treat this verse as an unnecessary parenthetical comment is to miss out a key point of Paul's goal to depict the Messiah as the supreme royal benefactor.[42]

Clarke provides a helpful summary of the six main interpretations of this verse, especially regarding the relationship between δίκαιος and ἀγαθός:

> (i) [T]here is no intended distinction between δίκαιος and ἀγαθός. Rare occurrences of personal self-sacrifice on behalf of the good and righteous man are possible; (ii) ἀγαθός is a stronger term than δίκαιος, and it depicts a warmer and more genial character than the merely law-abiding citizen; (iii) the two terms are virtually synonymous; Paul has overstated his case, and retracts it in verse 7b; (iv) τοῦ ἀγαθοῦ is taken in the neuter sense of a 'good cause'—a more compelling ground for self-sacrifice than to die on behalf of a fellow human-being; (v) τοῦ ἀγαθοῦ is taken in the technical sense of a patron or benefactor to whom one has greater obligations; and (vi) the text of Romans 5:7 is in some way not original.[43]

To substantiate our claim that this verse subverts a key aspect of the Greco-Roman ethic of reciprocity, we need to consider one main question: Why does Paul imply that there are greater obligations to the good person than to a righteous person? The terms δίκαιος and ἀγαθός are distinct and yet related.[44] In Greco-Roman usage, a δίκαιος person "is one

40. Cranfield, *Critical and Exegetical Commentary*, 264.

41. Landau, "Martyrdom in Paul's Religious Ethics," 25. Landau laments how the exegetical difficulties of 5:7 are often overlooked. Kümmel states that there can never be certainty regarding the meaning of 5:7 (*Exegetical Method*, 63). Barrett suggests that the details of the verse "are insignificant" (*Epistle to the Romans*, 99). Käsemann asserts that the analogy of 5:7 "is of no help" since it "pushes Christ's death into the sphere of the heroic" (*Commentary on Romans*, 137). McFarland states that in 5:7 "Paul digresses from 5.6 to set up an antithesis with 5.8" (*God and Grace*, 119).

42. In addition to the commentaries, some of the relevant resources here are Wisse, "Righteous Man and the Good Man," 91–93; Landau, "Martyrdom in Paul's Religious Ethics"; Clarke, "Good and the Just," 128–42; Bammel, "Patristic Exegesis of Romans 5:7," 532–42; Martin, "Good as God," 55–70.

43. Clarke, "Good and the Just," 132–33.

44. See for example Luke 23:50 where both terms are used in reference to Joseph

who upholds the customs and norms of behavior."[45] The righteous one is indeed a law-abiding citizen, but he does not necessarily care about the welfare of the city. The one who is ἀγαθός meets "a high standard of worth and merit," particularly due to his "usefulness to humans and society in general."[46] Adkins comments that beginning with Homeric days, ἀγαθός was among the highly valued words of praise in Greek society.[47] As Clarke notes, the term "described one who was valued because of considerable benefit to his immediate society."[48] This person used his wealth to assist and offer protection to others. The term, therefore, was closely associated with the wealthy and ruling elite.[49] The good person's concern for the welfare of others explains why people would feel more obligated to him. Adkins writes:

> To be *agathos* had always been more important than merely to be *dikaios,* and one's injustice did not traditionally . . . impair one's *arete.* Again, to be *agathos* was to be a specimen of the human being at his best, making to society the contribution that society valued most; and the poorer citizens could not deny this, nor yet that they were not *agathoi* themselves. In accepting *arete* as more important than *dikaiosune* they were of course not letting their hearts run away with their heads, but treating the well-being of the city as more important than the injustice of an individual: a calculation of advantages.[50]

As a technical description of the wealthy and elite, ἀγαθός is often employed in reference to benefactors. The good man bestows favors on the people, who in turn are expected to reciprocate. Dio castigates the people of Rhodes for their failure to honor their benefactors:

> It is in regard to these matters, men of Rhodes, that I ask you to believe that the situation here among you is very bad and unworthy of your state, your treatment, I mean, of your benefactors (τοὺς εὐεργέτας) and of the honors given to your good men (τῶν ἀγαθῶν ἀνδρῶν), although originally you did not handle the matter thus—most assuredly not! (*Rhod.* 8; cf. 14, 27, 65).

---

who was from the Jewish town of Arimathea.

45. BDAG 246.
46. BDAG 3.
47. Adkins, *Merit and Responsibility,* 30–31.
48. Clarke, "Good and the Just," 134.
49. Clarke, "Good and the Just," 135.
50. Adkins, *Moral Values,* 124.

Concerning his father as a benefactor, Dio writes that "there is no need for me to tell whether he was a good (ἀγαθός) citizen, for you are always singing his praises, both collectively and individually, whenever you refer to him, as being no ordinary citizen" (*Tumult.* 2-3). Plutarch equates benefactors to good men who ought always to receive reward and gratitude from their beneficiaries (*Phil.* 21:6). The good man "cannot escape the thanks" of the beneficiaries (*Mor.* 1098E) for he is a benefactor to his friends (*Mor.* 218A). Aristotle states not only that "beneficence is a function of the good man and of virtue" (ἐστὶ τοῦ ἀγαθοῦ καὶ τῆς ἀρετῆς τὸ εὐεργετεῖν, *Eth. nic.* 9.9.2) but also that kings would be appointed on the basis of benefaction (δ' ἀπ' εὐεργεσίας), and that doing this "is a task for the good men" (ἐστὶν ἔργον τῶν ἀγαθῶν ἀνδρῶν, *Pol.* 3.10.11-12). Due to his great resources, the king is committed to the welfare of his subjects (*Eth. nic.* 8.10.1-2). The good man is the only one who deserves honor (*Eth. nic.* 4.3.19-20) because honor is the prize of virtue and the tribute paid to the good (*Eth. nic.* 4.3.15; cf. Dio, *De Lege* 7-8). Dio writes that nothing is nobler "than to show honor to our good men (τοὺς ἀγαθοὺς ἄνδρας) and to keep in remembrance those who have served us well" (*Rhod.* 7-8).

Sometimes honoring the good man calls for a heroic act such as the willingness to die. It would be shameful for a beneficiary to refuse to suffer to death on behalf of the good benefactor. Dio writes:

> For whereas in the cause of justice and virtue and ancestral rights and laws and for a good king, a noble soul, one that does not cling to life, will, if need be, suffer and even die; yet if a man hangs himself for the sake of his chorus-girl, a low-born outcast, not fit to live, what depths of disgrace does that betoken! (*Alex.* 50).

Seneca shares similar sentiments concerning paying the ultimate price as a form of reciprocity to the good king: "In his [the king's] defense they [the subjects] are ready on the instant to throw themselves before the swords of assassins, and to lay their bodies beneath his feet if his path to safety must be paved with slaughtered men . . . against assailing dangers they make themselves a rampart" (*Clem.* 1.3.3). Seneca adds that when the subjects ransom a single life with many deaths, they are publicizing their love to the king (*Clem.* 1.3.4). No sacrifice is too great to pay for the sake of the good king.[51]

---

51. Valerius Maximus writes about L. Petronius who showed loyalty to his benefactor by taking his own life and that of Caelius, thereby saving his benefactor from

This background to the use of ἀγαθός within the Greco-Roman benefaction system sheds light on Paul's argument. Contrary to Barclay who maintains that "the labels appear to be general, and there is no good reason to take the second as a benefactor,"[52] there appears to be a distinction between the terms, with ἀγαθός denoting one's benefactor. Whereas δίκαιος simply refers to a law-abiding citizen who is not necessarily committed to the welfare of others, ἀγαθός refers to a benefactor whose concern for the well-being of others wins him great honor.[53] Rafael Rodríguez writes, "The social value of being *agathos* tapped into the cultural script of *benefaction*, in which the wealthy and élite members of a city provided goods and services to the city's population in exchange for public recognition, honor, and praise" (italics original).[54] We may, therefore, paraphrase the verse as follows: "For scarcely would anyone be willing to die on behalf of a law-abiding person, although[55] perhaps for the sake of his[56] benefactor one might even dare to die."[57] Paul knows that such a vicarious death for one's benefactor is rare, but it is not inconceivable, especially due to the ethic of reciprocity.[58] But what the Messiah does completely overturns this expectation. For he lays down his life, not as

---

dying at the hands of his enemies (*Memorable Doings and Sayings*, 4.7.5). For additional examples of vicarious deaths in Classical tradition, see Gathercole, *Defending Substitution*, 90–102. For more evidence of one's willingness to lay down his life for his friends or relatives, see Arrian, *Epict. diss.* 2.7.3; Philostratus, *Vit. Apoll.* 7:12. Also relevant here is Seeley, *Noble Death*, 83–112.

52. Barclay, *Paul and the Gift*, 477–78n71.

53. For the possible use of ἀγαθός to refer to a benefactor in the LXX, see Pss 72:1; 117:1.

54. Rodríguez, *If You Call Yourself a Jew*, 103.

55. The Greek word here is γάρ, which would normally mean "for." But when the particle is repeated after a clause with a similar assertion it might have a concessive force (cf. BDAG 189).

56. The article has a possessive force here. Gathercole (*Defending Substitution*, 89), however, suggests that the article specifies "death on behalf of a particular *type* rather than necessarily seeing a specific individual in view."

57. Cranfield comments, "We understand Paul's meaning then to be that, whereas it is a rare thing for a man deliberately and in cold blood to lay down his life for the sake of an individual just man, and not very much less rare for a man to do so for the sake of an individual who is actually his benefactor, Christ died for the sake of the ungodly" (*Critical and Exegetical Commentary*, 265).

58. Rodríguez writes, "Paul moves *up to the top* of the social scale to find a person for whom someone might possibly give his life" (*If You Call Yourself a Jew*, 103; italics original).

a heroic act of reciprocity to the good benefactor, but for the sake of the unworthy to rescue them from sin and death. It is not the many who are ransoming the life of the one good benefactor (cf. Seneca, *Clem.* 1.3.3–4), but the one righteous and supreme benefactor who ransoms the life of the many who are weak, ungodly, sinful, and enemies by dying *for us*.

The Messiah's Gift of Eschatological Life

If the Messiah's substitutionary death is *for us*, then we should be assured of conquering death and obtaining lasting glory. How to conquer mortality and obtain imperishable glory was a major concern of the ancients. In Greco-Roman society, the way to conquer death was by performing good deeds to humanity. Benefactors attained immortality through the perpetual gratitude of the beneficiaries. Cicero asserts that service to the community wins lasting gratitude from posterity (*Planc.* 2.17.60; cf. 2.18.63; *Inv.* 2.22.66; 2.53.161; *Off.* 2.6.22). Pliny writes that Trajan has won eternal glory through good deeds that have secured for him the praise of the people. The emperor's name is now engraved in the records of the imperishable glory, namely, in the people's love and memorialization (*Pan.* 54:7—55:11). In a carefully composed lyrical piece, Plutarch underscores the immortal value of expressing kindness to humanity by deeds and benefactions. The benefactor is motivated by the love of honor and philanthropy, and this motivation fulfills his desire to be memorialized for eternity: "[T]he love of honor and beneficence (τὸ φιλότιμον καὶ φιλάνθρωπον) reaches out to eternity as it strives for the crown by deeds and benefactions (χάρισιν) that bring the doer a pleasure impossible to describe" (*Mor.* 1098E).

Benefactors were often praised through statues and their accompanying inscriptions. As we have seen in chapter 2, the honorific inscription was perhaps the highest achievement one could accomplish because it was the most certain way of securing immortality. Acts of kindness and spectacular achievements in the interest of the public guaranteed victory over death through epigraphic memorialization (cf. Dio, *Rhod.* 20). The Priene Calendar Inscription (9 BCE) both honors Augustus for his great achievements and immortalizes him as posterity marks his birthday as a shared day of celebration for all.[59] The autobiographical inscription *Res Gestae* reveals Augustus's desire to be remembered by posterity as

---

59. For the Greek text, see *OGIS* 458, here lines 34–42.

a generous benefactor and an effective agent of the *Pax Romana*. Thus, the system of benefaction and the ethic of reciprocity enabled rulers to obtain lasting glory by having their names inscribed on bronze tablets as well as on the unending love of posterity.

One of the problems that Paul addresses in our passage is how humanity can be assured of life beyond death. Paul opens Romans 5 by summarizing the preceding argument as follows: "Therefore, having been justified by faith" (Δικαιωθέντες οὖν ἐκ πίστεως).[60] This verse clearly picks up on Paul's argument in Romans 4, especially 4:16-25. Abraham's justification (4:16-23) and the Messiah's acquittal (4:24-25) provide a significant context for understanding how Paul uses δικαιόω in 5:1 and how it relates to the Messiah's gift of eschatological life.[61] Faced with the deadness of his own body and that of Sarah's womb, Abraham trusts in hope that God can raise one from the dead. He receives Isaac through faith and gives glory to God (4:16-21). Because of his unwavering trust in God "it was reckoned to him as righteousness" (ἐλογίσθη αὐτῷ εἰς δικαιοσύνην, 4:22; cf. 4:3). Abraham's "justification" is therefore linked to righteousness and creating life out of deadness. Like Abraham, Jesus faces the situation of death.[62] Paul writes in 4:25 that Jesus our Lord "was handed over for our transgressions (παρεδόθη διὰ τὰ παραπτώματα ἡμῶν) and raised for our justification" (ἠγέρθη διὰ τὴν δικαίωσιν ἡμῶν). This verse both summarizes Jesus' downward trajectory, leading to his crucifixion, and upward trajectory, which is inaugurated by his resurrection. The διά prepositions indicate that both Christ's death and resurrection are for our benefit (4:25).[63]

There is likely an echo here of Isaiah's fourth Servant Song (Isa 52:13—53:12).[64] The song graphically depicts the servant's sacrificial

---

60. The inferential conjunction οὖν ("therefore," "consequently," or "accordingly") often introduces a summary of the preceding discussion. See Wallace, *Greek Grammar*, 673. The participle δικαιωθέντες is a passive adverbial participle of cause, from δικαιόω.

61. This work will not seek to provide an overview of scholarship on Paul's δικ- words. Some of the helpful works here include Cremer, *Die paulinische Rechtfertigungslehre*; Ziesler, *Meaning of Righteousness*; Reumann, *Righteousness in the New Testament*; Campbell, *Rhetoric of Righteousness*; Seifrid, "Righteousness Language in the Hebrew Scriptures, 415-42.

62. On how Paul reads Abraham's story christologically, and how that story relates to believers, see Jipp, "Rereading the Story of Abraham," 217-42.

63. On why διά + accusative clauses of 4:25 should be translated as "for us," see Lowe, "Oh διά!," 152-55.

64. Shum, *Paul's Use of Isaiah in Romans*, 189-93.

suffering as he bears the sins of many and intercedes for the transgressors.[65] Isaiah's servant suffers as a substitute because "the Lord has laid on him the iniquity of us all" (53:6). Isaiah 53:12b states that "for our sins he was handed over" (διὰ τὰς ἁμαρτίας αὐτῶν παρεδόθη). Yahweh's servant thus suffers rejection and great violence as he bears the iniquities of humanity. He is the subject of ridicule and scorn, and to highlight the magnitude of his pain, the song states that he is "a man of sorrows and acquainted with grief" (53:3). Yet, contrary to the perception of the general population (53:4b), the affliction of the servant is not due to his own sinfulness. In fact, the text clearly asserts his innocence. He would act prudently, wisely, and skillfully (52:13); he would not act violently nor speak deceit (53:9). Yahweh explicitly refers to him as "the righteous one, my servant" (53:11). So if the servant is innocent, then there must be another reason why Yahweh designs suffering for him, a suffering for which his innocence uniquely qualifies him. That reason is the subject of 53:4–6 and 53:10–12. Simply stated, the servant suffers for humanity as our substitute. The first person plural pronominal suffix occurs seven times in 53:4–6 to underline the fact that the servant suffers *for us*.[66] The same concept is reiterated in 53:12, where the servant is closely associated with the wicked as he bears "the sin of many, and makes intercession for the transgressors." He submits to his suffering, trial, death, and burial (53:7–9) to accomplish the Lord's purpose, for he is "the arm of Yahweh" (53:1) who "will not grow faint or be discouraged till he has established justice in the earth" (42:4). Isaiah 53:11 suggests that the righteous servant's justification will lead to the justification of many. His martyrdom

---

65. The song can be divided into five stanzas: (1) 52:13–15; (2) 53:1–3; (3) 53:4–6; (4) 53:7–9; and (5) 53:10–12). See Blocher, *Songs of the Servant*, 61. For a summary and bibliography of the leading positions regarding the identity of the servant of Yahweh, see Hugenberger, "Servant of the Lord," 106–19; Rae, "Texts in Context," 23–45. My view regarding the servant's identity has been largely influenced by Block, "My Servant David." Whereas Hugenberger contends that the messianic servant in the Servant Songs refers to Moses, Block convincingly argues for the Davidic interpretation of the fourth song. Others who see the servant as a royal figure, particularly the messianic king, include Allis, *Unity of Isaiah*, 87–101; Schultz, "King in the Book of Isaiah," 154–59; Alexander, *Servant King*, 108–12; Walton, "Imagery of the Substitute King Ritual," 734–43; Gentry, "Atonement in Isaiah's Fourth Servant Song," 20–47; Story, "Another Look at the Fourth Servant Song," 100–110; Treat, *Crucified King*, 68–86. Treat laments that the Isaianic song of the suffering servant "has often been torn from its royal context and turned instead into another barrier between atonement and kingdom" (*Crucified King*, 68).

66. On the use of pronouns in Isaiah 53, see Clines, *I, He, We and They*.

and acquittal are intended for the benefit of humanity. This "for us" language closely parallels Paul's language in Rom 4:24–25.

Paul argues in Rom 4:23–24 that the statement "it was reckoned to him" (Gen 15:6) was written for Abraham's sake "and for us to whom it is about to be reckoned" (Rom 4:24). God did something for Abraham that he will also do for us, but what is it?[67] That which was reckoned to Abraham, and which will also be reckoned to us is certainly δικαιοσύνην. How, then, is it reckoned to us? Like Abraham, it is reckoned to us based on trust: "to those who trust in the one who raised Jesus our Lord from the dead" (τοῖς πιστεύουσιν ἐπὶ τὸν ἐγείραντα Ἰησοῦν τὸν κύριον ἡμῶν ἐκ νεκρῶν). Like Abraham whose body was as good as dead yet he received the promise of future progeny, his descendants continue to face the situation of death, but their faith does not waver since they trust a God who is able to raise one from the dead. The one whom God has climactically raised from the dead is the Messiah. Paul defines the gospel as concerning the royal son of God who was raised from the dead (1:3–4). The Christ-event climaxing with his resurrection and enthronement provides the immediate context for interpreting justification-language in Romans.[68]

What, then, does the Messiah's resurrection have to do with our δικαιοσύνην? God has done something for the Messiah which he will also do for us, namely, he raised him from the dead. As Douglas A. Campbell writes, the participle δικαιωθέντες in 5:1 refers "in the first instance to Christ's resurrection that effects the deliverance of all those participating in him—ἡμῶν."[69] We have been justified in the sense that the Messiah has delivered us from the enslavement to sin and death and brought us under his victorious reign. But since we are still facing the situation of death, our justification is not complete unless we are raised from the dead. For those who are in Christ, the eschatological life has been inaugurated, and it will surely come to completion. That which is true for the Messiah must also be true for his followers—believers need deliverance from mortality. We may, therefore, assert that based on Romans 1–5, justification is sharing in Christ's acquittal or resurrection even as we look forward to our own

---

67. The term μέλλω often refers to a future occurrence, but it may also denote a logically subsequent event or a destined action (BDAG 627–28). Paul typically uses μέλλω to point to a future event. See Rom 5:14; 8:13, 18, 38; 1 Cor 3:22; Gal 3:23; Eph 1:21; Col 2:17; and 1 Thess 3:4.

68. See Campbell, *Rhetoric of Righteousness*, 155–56; Jipp, *Christ Is King*, 214–15.

69. Campbell, *Deliverance of God*, 824.

resurrection and acquittal.[70] In other words, justification is grounded in Christ's victory over sin and death and how that victory brings liberation to humanity. Moreover, justification is oriented towards the future as it anticipates our own victory over death.

To underline this future perspective, Paul states in Rom 5:2b that "we boast in the hope of the glory of God" (καυχώμεθα ἐπ' ἐλπίδι τῆς δόξης τοῦ θεοῦ). The term καυχᾶσθαι ("to boast," "to exult," or "to rejoice") and its cognates occur sixty-four times in the NT, out of which ninety percent are found in the Pauline corpus. Boasting in God finds precedence in the OT. For example, LXX Ps 5:12 says, "But let all who take refuge in you rejoice (εὐφρανθήτωσαν); let them ever sing for joy (ἀγαλλιάσονται), and spread your protection over them, that those who love your name may boast (καυχήσονται) in you." We find a similar expression in LXX Ps 31:11: "Be glad (εὐφράνθητε) in the Lord, and rejoice (ἀγαλλιᾶσθε), O righteous, and boast (καυχᾶσθε), all you upright in heart!" These references show that boasting is justifiable if it has the right object. Paul, therefore, can boast in the cross of Jesus Christ (Gal 6:14), in his service for God (Rom 15:17; 2 Cor 1:12), and in his converts in faith (2 Cor 7:4, 14; 10:16–18; Phil 2:16; 1 Thess 2:19).

Paul has already used καυχᾶσθαι four times in Romans, all in the negative sense of "to brag" (2:17, 23; 3:27; 4:2). This boasting denotes the interlocutor's confidence before God and how he is distinct from the immoral and idolatrous gentiles.[71] In 2:17–24, Paul condemns his interlocutor's boasting, owing to the interlocutor's failure to keep the law; he is guilty of what he criticizes in others. The imaginary interlocutor "boasts in God" (καυχᾶσαι ἐν θεῷ) and in the law yet he dishonors God (2:17, 23). The law of faithfulness, however, excludes all boasting (3:27; 4:2).[72] Justification, as Paul understands it, nullifies human pride before God since works, ethnicity, religion, or social privileges contribute nothing to his being established in righteousness. So what Paul says in 5:2b (as well as in 5:3, 11) is a redefinition of boasting in light of what God has accomplished through the Messiah.[73]

---

70. Jipp rightly maintains that "God's righteousness is revealed and established over the people by means of resurrecting from the dead his *righteous*, faithful, and obedient Messiah" (*Christ Is King*, 215; italics original).

71. See Gathercole, *Where Is Boasting?*, 194.

72. Eph 2:8–9 makes the same point: man is saved by grace alone through faith, hence there is no boasting.

73. Translating καυχᾶσθαι as "to rejoice" rather than "to boast," though true, fails to

According to 5:2b, the glory which God will bestow on all believers is the ground for boasting. To what does this glory refer? The broader context of Romans 2–4 sheds light on this question. Given that 3:27–28 and 4:2 connect boasting with justification, one might assert that even in 2:17–24, boasting points to the Judaizer's confidence that God will vindicate him at the eschaton on the basis of his obedience to the law (cf. 2:13).[74] Paul states in 2:7 that "to those who by perseverance in good deeds seek for glory and honor and immortality (δόξαν καὶ τιμὴν καὶ ἀφθαρσίαν) he [God] will give eternal life." He adds in 2:8–10 that those who do evil will face wrath and indignation, but those who do good will receive "glory, honor, and peace" (δόξα δὲ καὶ τιμὴ καὶ εἰρήν). These verses undoubtedly point to the future judgment. We see a similar future orientation in Romans 4 where Paul writes that Abraham trusted in "hope against hope" (4:18). And Paul uses the verb μέλλω in 4:24 to point to a future event of God reckoning righteousness to believers.

Paul summarizes the human predicament in 3:23 by declaring that all sinned "and fall short of the glory of God" (τῆς δόξης τοῦ θεοῦ). He then adds that the solution comes "by being justified freely by God's grace through the redemption which is in the Messiah Jesus" (3:24). The explicit connection between the glory of God and justification strongly suggests that falling short of the glory of God is to be devoid of life and to be held captive to sin and death. That is why Paul depicts humanity in 1:18–32 (cf. 2:1–6, 17–24) as utterly without a God-honoring life. To be justified, then, is to restore the glory of God to humanity. It means that humanity must be set free from the slavery of sin and death so that we may live a perfect life as God intends.[75] This hope of liberation and a perfect life is a ground for boasting. In light of this broader context, there is a strong likelihood that the boast of 5:2 is oriented towards the resurrection life.[76] The futuristic orientation shows that those who trust God are yet to attain some dimension of justification; we are yet to be physically raised from

---

capture Paul's echo and reversal of 2:17–24.

74. Stendahl, *Final Account*, 24; Gathercole, *Where Is Boasting?*, 201.

75. Commenting on Rom 3:21–26, Campbell states that "Paul's use of δικαιο-terminology probably carries strong connotations of 'life' and resurrection. The release that it speaks of is precisely the release from the oppressed Adamic age, ruled by Sin and Death, into the life of the world to come" (*Deliverance of God*, 665).

76. Moo writes that "'the glory of God' is that state of 'God-like-ness' which has been lost because of sin, and which will be restored in the last day to every Christian" (*Epistle to the Romans*, 302). But Moo does not discuss how "the glory of God" relates to the eschatological justification of believers.

the dead. But there is hope because God has demonstrated δικαιοσύνη θεοῦ by delivering the Messiah from the dead ones (1:3-4).

The Greco-Roman ruler's love of glory and the pursuit of immortality offer an illuminating context for understanding Paul's discussion of glory. Like what we find in the ancient context, the Pauline glory refers to attaining immortality, hence being raised from the dead. But unlike the ancient practice where there was no actual bodily resurrection—lasting glory was attained by perpetual memorialization by posterity—the Pauline glory is patterned after the resurrection of the Messiah (cf. 4:24-25), which means that Christ's followers are assured of victory over death. King Jesus is the supreme royal benefactor for he has dealt death a resounding blow. He alone can grant his subjects victory over the powers that threaten God's people (cf. Ps 72:9). Moreover, whereas in Greco-Roman society only rulers and the elite were certain of attaining glory through memorialization, Paul shows that all followers of Christ, regardless of their present social status, will be glorified. Their glory will come, not through perpetual memorialization, but by being mapped onto the Messiah's upward trajectory of resurrection. That which is true for the Messiah's body will also be true for his followers' bodies. The hope of the glory of God is certain because the Messiah will grant eschatological life to all his followers.

Kingship discourse in the OT also sheds light on how the Messiah brings life to his people. The Israelite king is responsible for administering justice and righteousness to the people (e.g., 2 Sam 8:15; 1 Kgs 10:9; 2 Chr 9:8; Prov 8:15-16; Isa 11:1, 3b-5; Jer 23:5-6). He defends the weak, exemplifies righteous devotion to Yahweh, and vindicates the righteous. Jeremiah 23:6 states that the king's name shall be called, "The Lord is our righteousness." The psalmist prays for the royal figure of Psalm 72 that he may live long (72:16) and that his name may endure forever and "abide as long as the sun" (72:17). He adds that "may people be blessed through him; all nations call him blessed" (72:17). Psalm 2:9-10 states that those who take refuge in the king will never perish. The king faces great distress, yet he is rescued by Yahweh and enthroned so that he might establish righteousness (LXX Pss 2:1-3; 20:6-9; 21:8-12; 22:1-24; 89:22-23; 101:1-8; 110:5-7; 144:9-11). The king not only obeys God but also trusts him for deliverance (LXX Pss 2:12; 117:8-9). The king's vindication is his justification, which in turn enables him to save his people from their enemies and establish them as righteous.⁷⁷ Isaiah's righteous servant is violently martyred, yet he triumphs over evil and death, and divides the spoil with the numerous (50:7–9; 53:12). The servant's restoration to life points to his resurrection and exaltation (53:10–11). The righteous servant can now rescue others because Yahweh has vindicated him.

Which king other than Jesus the Messiah was violently executed and yet was vindicated by being rescued from death? Having conquered death, the Messiah can now guarantee his followers victory over death and establish them forever as righteous. Boasting in the hope of the glory of God underlines the believer's confidence in a resurrecting God, as demonstrated in the story of the Messiah whom God rescued from all his enemies, especially death. Christ's followers confidently anticipate their future vindication since the resurrected Messiah grants eschatological life to his subjects.

The prepositional phrase ἐκ πίστεως ("by faith" or "on the basis of faithfulness") in Rom 5:1a specifies the means by which believers are established in righteousness. Does this phrase refer to Christ's faithfulness or to the believer's faith in God?⁷⁸ Our understanding of this phrase as used here should be informed by how God has demonstrated his righteousness to solve the human predicament. The term δικαιοσύνη ("righteousness") occurs for the first time in 1:16–17, which describes the revelation of δικαιοσύνη θεοῦ ("the righteousness of God") within which πίστις ("faith" or "faithfulness") has an instrumental function. God's righteousness leads to salvation for Jews and gentiles. Richard B. Hays and others have argued that this text alludes to LXX Ps 97:2–3: "The Lord has made known his salvation (τὸ σωτήριον αὐτοῦ), he has revealed (ἀπεκάλυψεν) his righteousness (τὴν δικαιοσύνην αὐτοῦ) before the nations. He has remembered his mercies to Jacob and his truth to the house of Israel; all the ends of the earth have seen the salvation of our God."⁷⁹ This psalm contains some of the key terms that Paul uses in Rom 1:16–17,

---

77. Jipp, *Christ Is King*, 223.

78. The question we are raising here is contrary to the argument of Westerholm that πίστις χριστοῦ is "not an issue here" ("Righteousness, Cosmic and Microcosmic," 23).

79. Hays, *Echoes of Scripture*, 36. Also see Jipp, *Christ Is King*, 246–49; Burk, "Righteousness of God," 356–57; Campbell, *Deliverance of God*, 688–89; Seifrid, *Justification by Faith*, 215–17.

a point which leads Hays to rightly assert that the terms "converge in ways that prefigure Paul's formulation strikingly."[80]

As we have seen in chapter 3, LXX Psalms 92 and 94–98 celebrate the kingship of the Lord over all creation and the nations. The Lord does not just love righteousness (LXX Pss 96:2; 97:9; 98:4); he also demonstrates his righteousness by saving his people (LXX 96:10; cf. Ps 103:6–7 MT) and judging their enemies (LXX 96:3, 7). If Paul is alluding to the Psalter (especially LXX Ps 97) in Rom 1:16–17, then God's righteousness should be understood as God's eschatological intervention to establish his dominion over all creation and to deliver his people and judge his enemies.[81] The groundbreaking event that reveals God's righteousness is the death, the resurrection, and the enthronement of Jesus the Messiah (Rom 1:3–4). This implies that we have in Rom 1:17 a messianic reading of Hab 2:4. In other words, Hab 2:4 is a prophetic anticipation of the gospel and of the revelation of the righteousness of God it envisions. Stephen L. Young contends that "Paul uses Hab. 2:4 to legitimate his position that the righteousness of God is revealed in the gospel through Christ's faithfulness (ἐκ πίστεως, Rom. 1:17a)."[82] By means of his faithfulness to the point of death on a cross, the Messiah shall live because he will be vindicated and resurrected.[83]

The same instrumental function of πίστις is found in Rom 3:22, where Paul writes that God's righteousness has been manifested "through the faithfulness of Jesus the Messiah" (διὰ πίστεως Ἰησοῦ Χριστοῦ). Paul has already declared that both Jews and gentiles are "all under sin" (3:9) and hence in need of justification/righteousness. God has provided the solution, not on the basis of man's faith, whether Jew or gentile, but through Christ's faithfulness.[84] It does not make sense that the solution would come through the faithfulness of those who have sinned and fall

80. Hays, *Echoes of Scripture*, 36.

81. See Jipp, *Christ Is King*, 247–49.

82. Young, "Romans 1.1–5 and Paul's Christological Use of Hab. 2.4," 281.

83. The Wisdom of Solomon also speaks of a righteous one who suffers, but later is vindicated and granted life by God (2:12–20; cf. 3:1–9; 4:7–16; 5:1, 15). This may corroborate the argument that the Habakkuk text was read, not as a narrative of how Christians are justified by faith, but as a narrative of a righteous sufferer who was granted eschatological vindication by means of resurrection.

84. For further discussion on the faithfulness of Christ, see Johnson, "Rom 3:21–26 and the Faith of Jesus," 77–90; Longenecker, "Pistis in Romans 3.25," 478–80; Wright, "Letter to the Romans," 469–70; Campbell, *Deliverance of God*, 601–76. Also see the essays in Bird and Sprinkle, *Faith of Jesus Christ*.

short of God's glory (3:23). Human faith cannot be the necessary precondition for the establishment of God's cosmic rule and the enactment of divine justice.[85] Thus given (1) Paul's understanding of God's righteousness as intricately connected with God's eschatological revelation of his dominion, which leads to salvation for his people and judgment against his enemies, (2) Paul's definition of the gospel as centered on God's royal son, (3) humanity's lack of righteousness, and (4) the role of πίστις in the revelation of δικαιοσύνη θεοῦ, there is a strong ground for connecting ἐκ πίστεως in 5:1 (and τῇ πίστει in 5:2) to God's act of handing over the Messiah to death and raising him back to life.[86]

How, then, is Paul using ἐκ πίστεως in 5:1 (and τῇ πίστει in 5:2)? Based on the context and argument of Romans 1–4, the phrase most likely refers to Christ's faithfulness.[87] It is evident from many ancient authors that beneficence reflects the ruler's faithfulness while reciprocity demonstrates the beneficiary's fidelity. According to Aristotle, the good king understands that "beneficence is a function of the good man and of virtue" (ἐστὶ τοῦ ἀγαθοῦ καὶ τῆς ἀρετῆς τὸ εὐεργετεῖν, *Eth. nic.* 9.9.2). Marcus Aurelius identifies faithfulness or fidelity as one of the virtues demanded of him as an emperor (*Meditations* 3.11.2). If the beneficiary is unfaithful, then the emperor should blame himself for having judged the man trustworthy:

> But above all, when you find fault with a man for faithlessness or ingratitude (ἀπίστῳ ἢ ἀχαρίστῳ), turn your thoughts to yourself. For evidently the fault is your own, whether you had faith (ἐπίστευσας) that a man with such a character would keep faith

---

85. But it is also important to note that the subjective reading does not eliminate Christian faith from Paul's logic. As in 1:16b and 17a, Paul uses εἰς construction in 3:22 to denote Christian faith in some sense. This Christian faith, which is only possible because of the faithfulness of Christ, is the ultimate goal of this process of the revelation of the righteousness of God. Similarly, Paul argues that righteousness will be reckoned to those who trust God, who raised the Messiah from the dead (4:24). For a summary of the objective reading of πίστις, see Keener, *Romans*, 58; Schreiner, *Romans*, 185–86. For more on Rom 1:16–17 and 3:21–26 as they relate to the revelation of God's righteousness in Christ's death and resurrection, see Campbell, *Rhetoric of Righteousness*, 22–69, 102–37.

86. For a similar argument that ἐκ πίστεως in Rom 5:1 refers to Christ's faithfulness and not to the faithfulness of Christ's followers, see Young, "Paul's Ethnic Discourse," 30–51. Also See Williams, "'Righteousness of God' in Romans," 241; Campbell, *Deliverance of God*, 677–711.

87. Campbell also argues that ἐκ πίστεως in 5:1 and τῇ πίστει in 5:2a refer to Christ's faithfulness rather than the individual believer's faith (*Deliverance of God*, 822–25).

(πίστιν φυλάξει) with you, or if in bestowing a kindness (χάριν διδούς) you did not bestow it absolutely and as from the very doing of it having at once received the full complete fruit (*Meditations* 9.42.4).

Seneca argues that if people practiced trust or faith in the exchange of services, there would be no need of laws (*Ben.* 3.15.1-3). Writing to Trajan, Pliny notes that he served faithfully as governor of Bithynia (*Ep.* 8.6.6-7).[88] Dio contends that the tyrant is an oppressor, not a good king (*3 Regn.* 40-41), for his "high-handed use of force is the ruin of others" (*3 Regn.* 48). Diogenes urges Alexander to be a good king by "putting his trust (πιστεύειν) in well-doing (εὐεργεσίᾳ) and devotion to righteousness (δίκαιον) and not in arms" (*4 Regn.* 65).

Read against this backdrop of benefaction, the prepositional phrase ἐκ πίστεως most likely suggests that the Messiah can bestow the gift of eschatological life because he is faithful. Due to his faithfulness, God vindicates the Messiah by raising him from the dead. So in Rom 5:1a, Paul summarizes the argument of Romans 1-4 by reiterating what God has done through the faithful Messiah, namely, God has publicly demonstrated his righteousness by resurrecting the Messiah, who was faithful even to the point of death. Christ's faithfulness, therefore, is the means by which both Jews and gentiles can be justified now even as they await their vindication (5:2b). Because the faithful and righteous Messiah has defeated humanity's most powerful enemies—sin and death—he is able to guarantee eschatological life to his followers; he is the wellspring of life.

The Messiah's Gift of Peace

The Messiah's gift of himself as humanity's substitute inaugurates the eschatological life and guarantees future vindication. Additionally, the Messiah's supreme benefaction brings the gift of *peace*. To have a better understanding of how Paul employs the concept of peace, we need to consider how the ideal Greco-Roman royal benefactors brought peace to their subjects, and the relationship between righteous rule and peace in the OT.

We have already seen in chapters 2 and 3 that royal benefactors were responsible for maintaining peace in the land. Cicero states that the

---

88. For further discussion of faith/trust in political relationships in the early Principate, see Morgan, *Roman Faith*, 85-95.

king's commitment to justice and to the welfare of his subjects leads him to secure freedom for the oppressed, provide help for the helpless, and protect the weak (*Off.* 2.12.41–42; Seneca, *Ep.* 73:8). Pliny praises Trajan for establishing the peace that created a conducive environment for agricultural prosperity (*Pan.* 29:1–5). Trajan is a lover of peace for he is committed to ending strife and overcoming enemies (*Pan.* 16:1–4). The Egyptians honored Ptolemy V for maintaining peace and stability and prevailing over all his enemies.[89]

Perhaps the leading emperor whose reign was associated with peace is Augustus. In *Res Gestae,* Augustus claims that he brought freedom from enemies, and established peace in the entire empire (1:1; 2:5; 6:13; 26–33). The emperor extinguished the flames of civil war and brought great prosperity to the empire. The poet Horace writes, "With Caesar [Augustus] in charge of affairs, peace will not be driven out by civic madness or violence, or by the anger that beats out swords and makes cities wretched by turning them against one another" (*Carm.* 4.15.5–20). Suetonius states that the emperor made Rome safe "for the future, so far as human foresight could provide for this" (*Aug.* 28). Philo praises Augustus as "the first and the greatest" (*Embassy* 22:148–49), and as "the averter of evil" who brought peace to the whole human race when it was facing utter destruction (21:144). Philo hails him for calming "torrential storms on every side" and for healing "the pestilences common to Greeks and barbarians" (21:145). In short, the *Pax Augusta* guaranteed the well-being, safety, freedom, and prosperity of Augustus's subjects.

Greco-Roman socio-political ideology is not the only context for interpreting peace in Romans 5. Paul's argument may also be illuminated by royal discourse in Second Temple Judaism and the OT. Philo writes that the art of shepherding equipped Joseph and Moses with the skills necessary for waging war against the enemy and establishing peace (*Joseph* 1:2–3; *Decalogue* 10:40–43; *Moses* 1.11.60–62). According to Josephus, the leading blessing that marked Solomon's reign was "peace and freedom from war and civil dissension" (*Ant.* 7:338). Solomon defeated all his enemies and brought great prosperity to the land. As we have argued in chapter 3, Philo and Josephus are influenced by Greco-Roman ideologies, but they are also rooted in their Jewish heritage.

The Davidic king is Yahweh's vicegerent, fighting his battles and maintaining peace and stability. In Ezekiel 34, the Lord promises that his

---

89. *OGIS* 90, lines 1–2, 9–10.

The Messiah's Supreme Royal Benefaction in Romans 5:1-11

"servant David" will nourish the people, restore peace and security, and serve as prince. His reign shall bring great prosperity to the people, and he shall deliver his subjects from their enemies and from the yoke of oppression and cause them to dwell securely in the land. The Psalter portrays the king as Yahweh's Messiah and son who establishes his universal and righteous reign by defeating and judging his enemies. Isaiah 32:17 states that the effect of righteousness will be peace, quietness, and trust forever.[90] The Isaianic Servant's vicarious death establishes many in righteousness and thereby brings healing and peace (Isa 53:5–6, 11–12). The parallels between Isaiah 53 and Rom 5:1 are striking. Like Romans, Isaiah 53 uses the terms δικαιόω (53:11) and εἰρήνη (53:5). Both texts also speak of righteousness and peace that come through the death of a royal figure. In Isaiah, peace is not simply the absence of war, but wholeness and prosperity which mark life under the Lord's righteous reign. Based on these primary texts, we may assert that Paul presents Jesus as the Davidic king who establishes his people in righteousness and enables them to enjoy peace with God.

The first main statement of Rom 5:1–11 is "we have peace with God" (εἰρήνην ἔχομεν πρὸς τὸν θεόν).[91] The verb ἔχομεν presents a textual problem which is likely to have been caused by itacism.[92] Some manuscripts have the present subjunctive ἔχωμεν ("let us have") instead of the indicative ἔχομεν ("we have"). The former implies that Paul is exhorting believers to enjoy peace with God while the latter means that Paul is stating an objective fact. Although the former reading has stronger external attestation, most interpreters continue to favor the indicative reading.[93] Moo summarizes the argument in favor of the indicative form thus:

> Most modern translations and commentators . . . adopt the indicative ἔχομεν. While this reading does not have a strong external support as the subjunctive . . . the context strongly favors a statement about what we have rather than an exhortation to enjoy what we have . . . The decision, then, lies in balancing the

---

90. Some of the interpreters who argue that Rom 5:1 alludes to Isaiah 32:17 are Dunn, *Romans 1–8*, 262; Fitzmyer, *Romans*, 395; Shum, *Paul's Use of Isaiah in Romans*, 193–96.

91. The preposition πρός denotes a sense of close personal or friendly relationship. See Harris, *Prepositions and Theology*, 189.

92. See Moir, "Orthography and Theology," 179–83.

93. For a helpful discussion of the text-critical evidence, see Metzger, *Textual Commentary*, 452.

claims of the external evidence and scribal probabilities on the one hand and Pauline usage and context on the other.[94]

But it could be that many interpreters are letting the disputable intrinsic probabilities trump the stronger external witnesses due to a questionable understanding of justification. As Campbell observes, "The grounds used to overrule the better-attested subjunctive are strongly correlated with the conviction that Paul is mobilizing some form of justification theory *and so could not possibly be indicating an uncertain or future situation at 5:1*" (italics original).[95] If we take "Pauline usage and context" seriously, as Moo urges, then justification is not yet a done-deal. As we have argued above, justification is heavily oriented towards the future for it anticipates resurrection from the dead. One of Paul's main concerns in this passage is to relieve his readers of any anxiety that might be caused by the coming judgment. It should, therefore, not be surprising that Paul is exhorting his readers to enjoy peace with God now even as they look forward to the eschaton when the Messiah will save them from the coming wrath (5:9).[96] In other words, the peace that Paul is exhorting believers to enjoy now is a foretaste of the peace that they will have in the future. The verb ἔχωμεν thus serves here both as an exhortation and a future indication.[97]

Peace with God comes "through our Lord Jesus the Messiah."[98] It is highly possible that the first readers of the epistle to the Romans interpreted Paul's argument on peace against the backdrop of royal benefaction, especially the *Pax Romana*.[99] We suggest that Paul is indeed depicting Jesus

---

94. Moo, *Epistle to the Romans*, 295–96n17.

95. Campbell, *Deliverance of God*, 822n124.

96. For further arguments supporting the subjunctive reading, see Fee, *God's Empowering Presence*, 495–96. For a reading that combines both the indicative and the subjunctive moods ("let us enjoy the peace we have"), see Martin, "Reconciliation," 42. Others who support the subjunctive form include Lightfoot, *Notes on Epistles of St. Paul*, 284; Sanday and Headlam, *Critical and Exegetical Commentary*, 120; Dodd, *Epistle of Paul to the Romans*, 72; Longenecker, *Epistle to the Romans*, 554–55.

97. See Campbell, *Deliverance of God*, 824. Campbell interprets the subjunctive "more as a future indication than a simple exhortation." But we think that Paul has both aspects in view. On the use of the subjunctive with a future sense, see Moule, *Idiom Book*, 21–23.

98. The preposition διά ("through") implies that the Messiah is the agent through whom peace is obtained.

99. On the *Pax Romana* and the writings of Paul, see Horsley, *Paul and Empire*; Georgi, *Theocracy in Paul's Praxis*; Faust, *Pax Christi et Pax Caesaris*. On whether Paul is subverting imperial ideology, see Bird, "One Who Will Arise," 146–65. Wright

Christ as a royal benefactor, but he is not just another Greco-Roman ruler. Like the Greco-Roman rulers, one of Jesus' benefactions to humanity is peace. Jesus secures this peace by defeating his enemies, namely, sin and death. But whereas the Greco-Roman rulers established temporal peace by defeating physical enemies, none of them could ever claim to have actually defeated sin and death. And given the eschatological emphasis in this passage, the present peace is a foretaste of what is to come. This means that the messianic peace is eternal rather temporal.

Why does humanity need peace with God? To answer this question, we need to revisit what Paul says in Romans 1–3. These chapters depict a people who are completely morally incapacitated and at war with God due to sin. In 1:18–32, Paul argues that gentiles are objects of God's wrath; God has handed them over to the slavery of sin (1:23, 25, 26). Their rebellion and refusal to honor God is the ground for the judgment that we see in Romans 1. It is a scene characterized by judgment and wrath rather than friendship and peace. God's judgment against human injustice is just because humanity is "without excuse" (1:20). Based on the apocalyptic cues in 1:18 ("revelation," "wrath," "from heaven"), Jipp argues that "the *present* revelation of God's wrath against injustice is a foretaste of God's eschatological judgment" (italics original).[100] Paul asserts that this eschatological judgment will be through Jesus Christ (2:16). God's judgment, mediated through the Messiah, will be impartial since he will render to each person according to his deeds (2:6). And since all humanity is "under sin" (3:9, 23), God's righteous judgment means that unless rescued, humanity is under divine wrath, and without peace with God.[101] Paul's definition of the gospel (1:3–4) as well as his declaration that divine righteousness has been revealed through Jesus Christ demonstrate that the Messiah is the appointed agent through whom humanity is rescued. So, when Paul declares in 5:1 that "peace with God" comes through "our Lord Jesus the Messiah," he implies that the Messiah delivers humanity from injustice

---

writes, "At every point, therefore, we should expect what we find: that for Paul, Jesus is Lord and Caesar is not" (*Paul in Fresh Perspective*, 69). Also see Crossan and Reed who state that "to proclaim Jesus as Son of God was deliberately denying Caesar his highest title" (*In Search of Paul*, 11).

100. Jipp, *Christ Is King*, 236. Also see Bell, *No One Seeks for God*, 14–15; Kensky, *Trying Man*, 182–90.

101. On human injustice versus divine justice in Romans, see Elliott, *Arrogance of Nations*, 73.

and the slavery of sin. The result is that those whom the Messiah rescues are no longer under divine wrath—they can indeed enjoy peace with God.

An issue that Paul needs to address is believers' eschatological anxiety. What is the basis of believers' eschatological assurance of peace? What will happen to them on the Day of Judgment when God's wrath is revealed? To answer these questions, we need to consider what Paul says in 5:6–11, but first let us once again underscore the unmistaken future orientation in this passage. We have already noted that justification points to the eschatological life, culminating in the resurrection of the body (5:1). Believers can enjoy peace with God now even as they boast in the hope of the glory of God (5:2). This hope will not put to shame (5:4–5). To affirm that believers have no basis for eschatological anxiety, Paul uses a standard type of argument, the "much more," in 5:9–11. Romans 5:9 focuses on wrath while 5:10–11 is concerned with reconciliation.

The point of 5:9 is quite straightforward: The Messiah's followers will be saved from the eschatological wrath. One of the implications here is that the reality of peace with God is not limited to the present life. The phrase πολλῷ μᾶλλον ("much more"), which is also repeated in 5:10, reflects a form of Greco-Roman rhetoric that argues "from the minor to the major" (*a minori ad maius*). In the Jewish rhetoric, the equivalent phrase *qal wayyōmer* ("light and heavy") holds that what applies in a light or a less important case will certainly apply in a heavy or a more important case. Paul, however, proceeds from the "heavy" to the "light."[102] The "major" case is that believers have been justified "now by his blood" (νῦν ἐν τῷ αἵματι αὐτου, 5:9a). The participle δικαιωθέντες ("having been justified") makes the connection to 5:1 explicit. Apart from 3:25, this is the only other occurrence of αἷμα in Romans in reference to the Messiah's self-sacrifice.[103] The noun αἷμα is a cultic depiction of the Messiah's death, implying that redemption comes at the cost of his life. Just as Paul states in 3:25 that the Messiah provides atonement by means of his blood, so he states in 5:9 that the Messiah secures justification by means of his blood.[104] And just as he says in 3:25 that the Messiah's sacrifice is the means by which God demonstrates his righteousness, so does he argue

---

102. Moo, *Epistle to the Romans*, 309–10; Wright, "Letter to the Romans," 519.

103. The only other occurrences of αἷμα in the Pauline corpus in relation to the death of Christ are 1 Cor 10:16; 11:25, 27; Col 1:20; Eph 1:7; and 2:13.

104. For further discussion on the relationship between justification and the Messiah's sacrifice, see Campbell, *Rhetoric of Righteousness*, 102–37; Carson, "Atonement in Romans 3:21–26," 119–39.

in 5:9 that believers' righteousness comes by the Messiah's blood. Paul further emphasizes the present eschatological reality by the adverb νῦν ("now"; so also 5:11). This adverb echoes 3:21, where Paul declares that God has intervened in the "eschatological now" through the Messiah to reveal his righteousness and provide redemption for humanity. The "major" case, which is also the more difficult and unthinkable, is that now there is deliverance from sin and death at the cost of the Messiah's death. God's initiative to deliver the Messiah over to death has brought the eschatological life to "now."

What remains (the "light" case) is relatively easier and obvious: "we shall be saved through him from wrath" (σωθησόμεθα δι' αὐτοῦ ἀπὸ τῆς ὀργῆς, 5:9b). This verse implies that the day of wrath is coming, but believers will not face wrath. The logic of Paul's argument is that if the Messiah can secure justification by his death, then there is absolute confidence that he will save his followers from wrath because he has conquered death. The Messiah's death overcomes the hostile powers of sin and death and thereby inaugurates eschatological life precisely by resurrection. If any follower of Jesus is anxious that God's wrath as described in Romans 1–3 still hangs over her and that she will face a terrible fate, then Paul's exhortation to her is simple: The Messiah will surely rescue you! The fact that God has demonstrated his love for us in the death of the Messiah (5:8) means that believers are objects of love, and not wrath (see Eph 2:1–7). For Paul, salvation is ultimately realized in the future. As believers live between the inaugurated eschatological life and its culmination, they have complete assurance that if the Messiah's death justifies the weak, ungodly, and sinners, then it is all the more certain that the Messiah's life will save those whom he has brought into the realm of righteousness.

Romans 5:10–11 makes a similar point concerning believers' eschatological assurance. There are striking parallels between 5:9 and 5:10:

Romans 5:9	Romans 5:10
	if while we were *enemies*
having been justified now	we were *reconciled* to God
by his blood	through the death of his Son
how much more	how much more having been *reconciled*

The terms highlighted above show Paul's aim in 5:10. As with the previous verse, he uses the argument from the "minor" to the "major" in the reversed order to declare that the Messiah's gift of peace means that eschatological anxiety has been alleviated. The Messiah has accomplished the most difficult task, namely, he has reconciled enemies to God. The verb καταλλάσσω ("reconcile") and its participial form occur only here in Romans; the noun form occurs once in 5:11.[105] But Paul has already used its counterpart εἰρήνη ("peace") in 5:1. The καταλλάσσειν-terminology occurs only once in the OT outside the apocrypha (LXX Jer 31:39). This suggests that the term is of Hellenistic origin. It connotes the exchange of hostility for peaceful relations.[106] The term is used in Greek secular literature mainly in politico-military contexts for peace-treaty initiatives.[107] In Second Temple Judaism, Philo, using related terms, depicts Moses as a mediator and reconciler who averted the wrath of God. Moses rescued the Israelites from God's impending wrath due to their idolatry:

> Struck with dismay, and compelled to believe the incredible tale, he yet took the part of mediator and reconciler (μεσίτης καὶ διαλλακτής) and did not hurry away at once, but first made prayers and supplications, begging that their sins might be forgiven. Then, when this protector and intercessor had softened the wrath of the Ruler, he wended his way back in mingled joy and dejection. He rejoiced that God accepted his prayers (*Moses* 2:166).

In *QE* 2:49, Philo interprets the Exodus 32 incident through the lens of benefaction. He comments that the idolatrous Israelites were "about to be condemned and waste away in corruption ... after receiving many benefactions and showing ingratitude in many ways." Moses remained on the mountain forty days "reconciling the Father to the nation by prayers and intercessions." Commenting on the same incident, Josephus writes, "When Moses in accordance with God's purpose had thus addressed them, the people were plunged in grief and affliction, and they besought Moses to intercede (καταλλάκτην) for them with God and to spare them that

---

105. On the theme of reconciliation in Paul, see Fitzmyer, "Reconciliation in Pauline Theology," 155–77; Fryer, "Reconciliation in Paul's Epistle to the Romans," 34–68; Martin, *Reconciliation*; Porter, "Peace, Reconciliation," 695–99; Porter, Καταλλάσσω *in Ancient Greek Literature*; Kim, "2 Cor 5:11–21," 360–84.

106. Porter, "Peace, Reconciliation," 695.

107. For a helpful linguistic background of the terminology, see Kim, "2 Cor 5:11–21," 361–62.

wandering in the wilderness and to give them cities" (*Ant.* 3:315). Both authors view Moses as an agent of reconciliation between Israel and God.

In the NT, the καταλλάσσειν-terminology is limited to the Pauline corpus, where it mostly describes the relationship between God and humans (Rom 5:10 [2x], 11; 11:15; 2 Cor 5:18, 19, 20; Eph 2:16; Col 1:20, 22).[108] Moreover, unlike what we find in the few extra-biblical references where the term speaks of God being reconciled to humans (e.g., 2 Macc 1:5; 5:20; 7:33; 8:29), in all the instances listed above, Paul speaks of the reconciliation of humans to God.[109] In view of its usage in Romans 5, Moo suggests that it denotes bringing together, or making peace between two hostile parties.[110] Fitzmyer defines reconciliation as "the restoration of the estranged and alienated person to friendship and intimacy with God."[111] If justification points to liberation from sin and death and being established in righteousness, then reconciliation emphasizes the end of enmity and the abiding friendship between God and the liberated community.

How does this reconciliation occur? It is "through the death of his son" (διὰ τοῦ θανάτου τοῦ υἱοῦ αὐτοῦ, 5:10a). This is the second mention of the Messiah's divine sonship since the definition of the gospel in 1:3–4—the first mention is in 1:9.[112] As Wright argues, Paul saves this messianic title "for the really weighty statements."[113] The one whose death reconciles humanity to God is the son of God. It was not unusual for ancient kings to justify their rule by making claim to divine status. Theocritus praises Ptolemy Philadelphus's divine birth, benefactions, and wealth and power bestowed by Zeus so that he may rule "the entire land and sea and all the roaring rivers" (*Id.* 17:1–135). Seneca states that the gods appoint the good king to uphold justice and care for the people (*Ben.* 4.32.1–3). The Egyptians honored Ptolemy V Epiphanes as "being a god, son of a god and a goddess" due to his benefactions to them.[114] Dio asserts that

---

108. It is only in 1 Cor 7:11 where the term describes husband-wife relationship.

109. Marshall, "Meaning of Reconciliation," 117–32.

110. Moo, *Epistle to the Romans*, 311.

111. Fitzmyer, *Romans*, 411. Elsewhere Fitzmyer writes, "The main effect of Christ's passion, death, and resurrection is the reconciliation of man to a state of peace and union with the Father" (*Pauline Theology*, 43–44).

112. The remaining references to Jesus' divine sonship in Romans are in Rom 8:3, 29, 32).

113. Wright, "Letter to the Romans," 520.

114. Danker, *Benefactor*, no. 31. Bird states, "The emperors, living and deceased, were worshiped since they provided benefaction and benevolence to their subjects

the good king receives his scepter from Zeus and uses it for the welfare of his people (*1 Regn.*12–13; cf. 84). As the vicegerent of the gods, the king is uniquely equipped to benefit the people (*2 Regn.* 26).[115] Smith rightly notes that the king's "beneficence is regarded as evidence of his divine nature."[116] Such beneficence is patterned after that of the gods. Virgil writes about Augustus thus: "And this in truth is he whom you so often hear promised you, Augustus Caesar, son of a god, who will again establish a golden age" (*Aen.* 6:791–93). A marble pedestal in Pergamum reads: "The Emperor, Caesar, son of a god, the god Augustus, of every land and sea the overseer."[117] A votive inscription for Nero describes him as "Son of the greatest of the gods, Tiberius Claudius."[118]

Divine sonship is also prevalent in kingship discourse in the OT. God promises David that he would establish his eternal dynasty through his son (2 Sam 7:1–17). David is referred to both as a servant (7:5, 8) and son (7:14), implying that the adopted son serves as Yahweh's surrogate. In Psalm 2:7, God tells the king, "You are my son, today I have begotten you." The same language of Yahweh begetting a son is also found in Ps 110:3. As Yahweh's son, the king serves as God's vicegerent who rules on his behalf. The king occupies an exalted position and serves as an agent of Yahweh's blessings to the people. He sits at Yahweh's right hand and shares his throne (Pss 2:6; 110:1). He is "the highest of the kings of the earth" (Ps 89:27); his splendor and majesty are great (Ps 21:5). He rules over all the nations of the earth (Pss 2:8, 10–11). All the nations of the earth shall bow before him (Ps 22:29; cf. v. 30). The rule of Yahweh's son is characterized by great prosperity. He satisfies the poor with bread, procures salvation for the people, and brings great joy to Zion (Ps 132:15–16). According to Psalm 144:13–14, the king transmits such blessings as full granaries, healthy and productive flock and cattle, and a peaceful existence.

In Rom 1:3–4 Paul declares that the Messiah, who descended from David, has been designated son-of-God-in-power by the Spirit and through the resurrection from the dead. The content of Paul's

---

who in turn lavished on them highest honors possible, climaxing in divine acclamation and cultic worship" (*Jesus the Eternal Son*, 40). For further discussion on how benefactions led to the worship of rulers, see Peppard, *Son of God*, 40.

115. On the Roman emperor as "Son of God," see Winter, *Divine Honours*, 67–71.
116. Smith, *Christ the Ideal King*, 41.
117. Deissmann, *Light from the Ancient East*, 347.
118. Deissmann, *Light from the Ancient East*, 347.

proclamation is the gospel of the son of God (1:9).[119] This royal son of God is the one whose sacrifice reconciles humanity to God. The king offers his own life as a gift to God's enemies to establish peace and harmony. As Hurtado states, Paul invokes divine-sonship rhetoric in 5:10 "to connote the connection between Jesus' death and the divine purpose which is so much the emphasis in this epistle."[120] The Messiah is God's agent with God's authority to accomplish God's purpose of redemption, reconciliation, and establishing a righteous and prosperous rule.

Transforming enemies into friends is the "major" task that the son of God has already accomplished. What remains is the "minor" task, namely, to save, not enemies, but friends from the coming wrath. If by his death the son of God has reconciled enemies to God, then now that he is alive, there is absolute certainty that he will save his followers and fulfill their hope of glory. In other words, dying for an enemy is more difficult and unthinkable than saving a friend. The death of the son of God demonstrates God's love and the Messiah's commitment to redeem the unworthy. This commitment neither ended with his death nor his resurrection; rather, it extends into the future when he will raise us from the dead and establish us in perfect righteousness. The assurance that this final stage of our redemption can never be aborted means that the peace that we are *now* enjoying with God extends into the future and anticipates our deliverance. For Paul, the Messiah's gift of peace to the unworthy completely eliminates anxieties that might be caused by the coming wrath of God.

The passage ends in 5:11 by proclaiming that believers "boast (καυχώμενοι) in God through our Lord Jesus the Messiah (διὰ τοῦ κυρίου ἡμῶν Ἰησοῦ Χριστοῦ) through whom we have now received reconciliation."[121] Every claim that the believer has, whether it concerns the present life or the future, is entirely based on God's decisive act to establish his righteous rule through his Messiah. Based on 5:1-2 and

---

119. On Jesus' divine sonship in Romans, see Hurtado, "Jesus' Divine Sonship," 217-33, here p. 223. Hurtado argues that Paul's use of divine-sonship language carries three major themes: (1) as an honorific of Jesus; (2) as a "*theocentric* force that emphasizes God's involvement in Jesus"; and (3) as a means of linking "the salvation of the elect with the status of Jesus." Also see Hurtado, "Son of God," 900-906. Other works on Jesus' divine sonship in Paul include Bousset, *Kyrios Christos*, 91-98, 206-10; Hengel, *Son of God*, 7-15; Tilling, *Paul's Divine Christology*.

120. Hurtado, "Jesus' Divine Sonship," 229.

121. For a summary of recent scholarship on boasting in Paul, see Gathercole, *Where Is Boasting?*, 10-16. Also see Barrett, "Boasting (καυχᾶσθαι κτλ.)," 363-68.

5:11a, the ground for boasting is God's initiative to provide redemption and reconciliation through the death and the resurrection of the Messiah. The person who can rightly boast is the one who is participating in the Messiah's pattern of dying and rising. What is impossible under the law, namely, boasting in God (see 2:17–24; 3:27), is now possible through our Lord Jesus the Messiah who has conquered death, and thereby secured eschatological life for his followers. Additionally, he is the one through whom there is reconciliation to God. As Gathercole writes, "God is now the ground for the boast because he has accomplished the reconciliation that has been won through the cross."[122] Boasting in God, then, is to celebrate the Messiah's victory which leads to reconciliation between the creator and humanity (cf. 1 Cor 1:31). Because of what the Messiah has done, believers can boast now in the present (νῦν) even as they anticipate God's eschatological verdict.[123] The fact that the references to justification (5:1) and to reconciliation (5:11) frame this passage implies that although they are distinct the two terms are inseparable. Having been liberated from the powers of sin and death, believers can celebrate their reconciliation to God. Furthermore, the fact that the reference to τοῦ κυρίου ἡμῶν Ἰησοῦ Χριστοῦ ("our Lord Jesus the Messiah") bookends this passage (5:1 and 5:11) points to Paul's explicit intention of declaring that believers' life is thoroughly defined by the Messiah's rule, a rule which restores a peaceful relationship between humanity and God.

The Messiah's Gift of Status

In addition to the gifts of life and peace, the Messiah's supreme benefaction also reverses believers' disgraceful status. In this work, we define status simply as one's social standing or hierarchy in the society.[124] There is a clear verticality in the ancient Greco-Roman society, whereby the elite occupy the upper ranks while the plebs are confined to lower status.[125] It is widely acknowledged that gift-giving has "implications for the

---

122. Gathercole, *Where Is Boasting?*, 259.

123. Barrett is probably right that νῦν in 5:11 "describes the anticipation in the present of God's verdict at the judgment, the peace of the Kingdom of God" (*Commentary on the Epistle to the Romans*, 109).

124. For a brief discussion of the meaning of "status," see Blanton, *Spiritual Economy*, 78.

125. Hellerman, *Reconstructing Honor*, 1–33.

negotiation of relative status."¹²⁶ As Blanton notes, "The asymmetric distribution of material goods reinforced the superior status of the 'big man' and confirmed the status of his subordinates."¹²⁷ In other words, gift-giving is a powerful means of establishing domination and influence. And as a means of enhancing social cohesion, gift-giving brings the giver and the receiver together, yet the exchange also separates them by exposing the different status between them. Benefactors always remain in the superior position even as they seek to guard that status through publicized reciprocity and continuous dependency of the beneficiaries.¹²⁸ Moreover, the elevated status of benefactors means that access to them and to their resources is often limited to their friends and relatives. Against this backdrop, Paul argues that the Messiah willingly shares in the fleshly existence of humanity and dies for us to reverse our disgraceful status (cf. Rom 8:3). One may plausibly assert that the Messiah's benefaction democratizes honor, whereby rather than being limited to the emperor and the elite, all followers of Christ are assured of an eternal honorable status before God.¹²⁹ To understand the Messiah's gift of status, we need to closely look at what Paul says about "access" (5:2), "grace" (5:2), and enmity (5:6–10).

Romans 5:2 states that it is through our Lord Jesus the Messiah that "we have access by faith into this grace in which we stand" (τὴν προσαγωγὴν ἐσχήκαμεν τῇ πίστει εἰς τὴν χάριν ταύτην ἐν ᾗ ἑστήκαμεν). The noun προσαγωγή means "a way of approach" or "access." It is used only three times in Paul in the NT (Rom 5:2; Eph 2:18; 3:12) and never used in the LXX.¹³⁰ The verb προσάγω occurs in Luke 9:41; Acts 16:20;

126. Blanton, *Spiritual Economy*, 76.

127. Blanton, *Spiritual Economy*, 76. According to Joubert gift-exchange produces "clear status demarcations, with the giver in the superior position" (*Paul as Benefactor*, 22).

128. The poet Martial illustrates this social dependence and inferior status as follows: "By chance I greeted you this morning by your real name, Caecilianus, instead of calling you 'my lord.' Do you want to know how much such freedom costs me? It robbed me of a hundred farthings" (*Epigr.* 6:88). Aristotle speaks of a virtue called μεγαλοπρέπεια ("magnificence"), which is displayed by the nobles who engage in such public benefactions as votive offerings, public buildings, sacrifices, building ships of war, and offering banquets among others (*Eth. nic.* 4.2.1). This means that the poor can never be magnificent since they lack the requisite financial means.

129. Thiessen rightly states that Greco-Roman rulership discourses "frequently promote a hierarchy that values the life of the ruler over the many lives of the ruled" ("Many for One," 449).

130. BDAG 876.

27:27; and 1 Pet 3:18. The LXX frequently uses the verb προσάγω to describe the offering of sacrifices (e.g., Lev 4:14). For one to approach God with an offering, they must be worthy and unblemished (cf. Exod 29:4, 8; Lev 21:18–19; Num 8:9–10). The noun προσαγωγή signifies privilege of approach to the royal chamber or a person of high rank.[131] This royal usage of προσαγωγή is further suggested by the noun χάρις, which is a key benefaction terminology. Xenophon (*Cyr.* 7.5.45) writes about how Cyrus expected his friends to act as intermediaries between him and his suppliants: "Now what I expected all such [supplicants] to do, if any one wanted anything from me, was to get into favor with you as my friends and ask you for an introduction (προσαγωγῆς)." When writing about how Cyrus distributed meat among his grandfather's servants, Xenophon states that King Astyages asked him whether he would also give any to Sacas his cupbearer. The king loved Sacas because of his role as a mediator: "Now Sacas, it seems, chanced to be a handsome fellow who had the office of introducing (προσάγειν) to Astyages those who had business with him and of keeping out those whom he thought it not expedient to grant access (προσάγειν)" (*Cyr.* 1.3.8; cf. 2.4.1).

Intermediary figures help people to secure access to the benefactions of the emperor.[132] The brokers have an intimate access to the ruler and receive benefits directly from him.[133] Those who serve as brokers are family members and friends of the emperor.[134] Peter Garnsey and Richard Saller rightly comment that this privilege of access to the ruler is only enjoyed by a few, including members of his household, relatives, and friends of high rank.[135] The friends of a ruler are always convinced that their requests would never be turned down.[136] Aristotle writes that conferring "favors and assistance on friends" (τὸ χαρίσασθαι καὶ βοηθῆσαι

---

131. Dunn, *Romans 1–8*, 248; Cranfield, *Critical and Exegetical Commentary*, 259; Osborne, *Romans*, 127; Longenecker, *Epistle to the Romans*, 558.

132. For further discussion on the place of brokerage in patron-client relations, see Eisenstadt and Roniger, *Patrons, Clients, and Friends*, 228–45; Wallace-Hadrill, "Patronage in Roman Society, 81–84; Saller, *Personal Patronage*, 4–5, 57–78; Crook, *Reconceptualising Conversion*, 72–79, 170–75.

133. Garnsey and Saller, *Roman Empire*, 174.

134. On "words" and "deeds" of the brokers as well as summaries of the types of brokerage found in the ancient world, see Collins, *Diakonia*, 96–149.

135. Garnsey and Saller, *Roman Empire*, 174.

136. Joubert indicates, "*Amicitia principum*, friendship with the emperor, was a sure way of gaining access to senatorial magistracies and other honourable positions" (*Paul as Benefactor*, 26).

φίλοις) is a great pleasure (*Pol.* 2.2.5-10). The king protects his friends (Dio, *1 Regn.* 20, 25, 30–32) even as his enemies live in fear of him (Dio, *1 Regn.* 25). The good king shares his pleasure with his friends and delights in their happiness (Dio, *3 Regn.* 95–96, 108–9). Pliny states that the emperor's friends enjoy the ownership of princely possessions (*Pan.* 50:7) because the emperor cannot withhold anything from a friend (86:1).

In view of this royal context, when Paul declares that through the Messiah believers "have gained access (προσαγωγήν) into this grace (χάριν) in which we stand" (Rom 5:2a), he means that the Messiah has brought his followers into his domain, whereby they can enjoy the benefits of his rule. The perfect tense verbs (ἐσχήκαμεν and ἐστήκαμεν) have an intensive force, expressing initial entrance into the Messiah's domain and its ongoing reality.[137] Having been delivered by the Messiah, the believer's existence is always before the heavenly throne. But what does Paul mean by χάρις?[138] Zeba A. Crook has identified four semantic ranges for the Greek word χάρις: "[T]o describe something beautiful or pleasing; to express gratitude for a benefaction received; to describe the quality of beneficence; and to refer to the concrete gift or benefaction itself."[139] Barclay suggests that the six common perfections of χάρις are superabundance, singularity, priority, incongruity, efficacy, and non-circularity.[140] For our purposes, it is important to underline that χάρις is used both for an initial gift and the gratitude of the beneficiaries.[141] Since we will discuss the latter use in the next section, the present section focuses on χάρις as a gift or favor given by the benefactor.

While urging Trajan to emulate the generosity of Heracles, Dio writes that Heracles considered gold and silver as worth nothing except "to be given away and bestowed" (δοῦναι καὶ χαρίσασθαι) upon others (1 *Regn.* 62). Because Heracles "believed that everything belonged to him exclusively and that gifts bestowed would call out the goodwill of the recipients," he gave gifts of money, lands, herds, kingdoms, and cities (*1 Regn.* 62–63). Seneca states that the gifts of the gods are "lavish and unceasing" (*Ben.* 1.1.9); every day the gods dispense the great largesse,

---

137. Dunn, *Romans 1–8*, 248.

138. The pronoun ταύτην suggests that Paul has a particular gift in view.

139. Crook, "Grace as Benefaction," 26–27.

140. Barclay, *Paul and the Gift*, 70–74.

141. Blundell observes that χάρις denotes something delightful that arouses desire and joy, and that it is used "both for an initial favor and its reciprocation as gratitude" (*Helping Friends*, 33).

including favorable winds and mighty rains (*Ben.* 4.25.1–3). The gods have entrusted to the king an exalted position that enables him to give many gifts (*Ben.* 5.4.2; *Clem.* 1.3.3). The civil law likewise affirms that everything belongs to the king (*Ben.* 7.4.2).[142] Apart from monetary aid and political offices, a ruler may bestow such gifts as citizenship, an exemption from taxes, distribution of grain, and funding public buildings (*Ben.* 6.19.2–5; 6.32.3–4; *Ep.* 73:8). The ruler's inexhaustible wealth (cf. *Ben.* 4.40.2) enables him to care for his subjects and come to their aid with timely assistance (*Ben.* 2.13.2–3).

Philo also shows close acquaintance with the terminology of χάρις within the benefaction system. He writes that "the highest truth" is that all things, including animals, plants, stars, heaven, sun, fire, air, water, and earth, are "the gift of God" (χάριν ὄντα θεοῦ) and that he has given all these things to the world (*Unchangeable* 23:107).[143] In *Virtues* 17:94, Philo describes all things that humans enjoy as "rich gifts" (πλουσίαις χάρισι) and "benefactions" (εὐεργεσίας) bestowed upon them by nature (cf. *Alleg. Interp.* 3.70.195–96). God is the creator who bestows "rich and unrestricted benefits (χάριτας) upon his creation" (*Creation* 4:23). Philo states that the term "'gifts' (δῶρα) brings out the sense of great and perfect boons, which God bestows (χαρίζεται) upon the perfect" (*Alleg. Interp.* 3.70.196). Commenting on how Noah found favor with God (Gen 6:8), Philo states:

> Now finding favor (χάριν εὑρεῖν) is not as some suppose equivalent only to being well-pleasing, but something of this kind besides. The righteous man exploring the nature of existences makes a surprising find, in this one discovery, that all things are a grace (χάριν) of God, and that creation has no gift of grace (χάρισμα) to bestow, for neither has it any possession, since all things are God's possession, and for this reason grace (χάριν) too belongs to him alone as a thing that is his very own. Thus, to those who ask what the origin of creation is the right answer would be, that it is the goodness and grace (ἀγαθότης καὶ χάρις) of God, which he bestowed (ἐχαρίσατο) on the race that stands next after him. For all things in the world and the world itself is a gift and act of kindness and grace (δωρεὰ ... εὐεργεσία καὶ χάρισμα) on God's part (*Alleg. Interp.* 3.24.78).

---

142. Alexander boasted about his unparalleled benefits to the people (Seneca, *Ben.* 5.6.1).

143. For further discussion of Philo's "ontological grace," see Barclay, "By the Grace of God," 141–43.

Divine favor fills the soul with delight: "Now when grace (χάριτος) fills the soul, that soul thereby rejoices and smiles and dances, for it is possessed and inspired" (*Drunkeness* 146).

Unlike Gaius who failed to benefit his subjects, Philo praises Augustus as the "great benefactor," "the source and fountain-head of the Augustan stock," "the first and the greatest," and "the common benefactor of all" (*Embassy* 22:148–49) because Augustus not only brought peace to the whole human race (*Embassy* 21:144) but also "dispensed their dues to each and all, who did not hoard his favors (τὰς χάριτας) but gave them to be common property, who kept nothing good and excellent hidden throughout his life" (*Embassy* 21:147). Josephus also uses the term χάρις to describe God's provision to the Israelites (*Ant.* 3:7). Moses exhorted the Israelites not to forget "the favors and the bounties (χάριτας καὶ δωρεάς), so great and unlooked for, which they had received from God" (*Ant.* 3:14). Josephus describes King Agrippa as one who was "by nature generous in his gifts (εὐεργετικὸς εἶναι ἐν δωρεαῖς) . . . He took pleasure in conferring favors (τῷ χαρίζεσθαι) . . . and he was a benefactor to all alike" (*Ant.* 19:328–30).

The preceding brief overview of χάρις in the ancient Greco-Roman and Second Temple Judaism contexts shows that the term denotes an act of generosity intended for the preservation of life. The gods give gifts to humans for their well-being. The rulers demonstrate care for their subjects by bestowing favors upon them. The fact that the favors of the rulers encompass every aspect of life means that the people's prosperity and well-being are dependent on the generosity of their ruler. This ancient context provides an important lens for interpreting Paul's argument on χάρις.[144] By stating that we stand "in grace," Paul asserts that Christ has provided his followers with everything they need for their sustenance and flourishing. To borrow Cicero's words, the Messiah is a beneficent ruler who has supplied his followers with "an abundance of the necessities of life" (*Off.* 2.21.74). Taken together with the language of access, χάρις as used in Rom 5:2 means that the Messiah is both the mediator and the king who brings his favor within the reach of his followers. Michael F. Bird comments that by grace Paul means that "we always have a VIP pass into the hallways of heavenly power."[145] Everything that the believer

---

144. Paul uses the term χάρις in the undisputed and disputed letters 97 times. He also uses χάρισμα 16 times, χαρίζεσθαι 13 times, χάριταν once, εὐχαριστεῖν 24 times, εὐχαριστία εὐχάριστος once, and ἀχάριστος once.

145. Bird, *Romans*, 163.

needs to bear fruit as a follower of the Messiah is available to her. Unlike the Greco-Roman benefaction system where access to the emperor is a privilege of just a few, the Messiah ushers all his followers into his royal chamber, the sphere of his dominion. Paul can even metaphorically say that believers "stand" in this realm. In other words, nothing can hinder or break believers' life-transforming and reality-defining benefaction of the Messiah.

But how does the Messiah provide access to his royal chamber? This is one of the questions that Paul addresses in 5:6–10. The Messiah lays down his own life as a gift and thereby provides the means by which his followers are brought into the realm of his kingdom. The cultic language that permeates these verses—Paul speaks of the Messiah's death four times and of his blood once—coupled with the use of προσαγωγή and χάρις in 5:2 strongly suggests that Paul depicts the Messiah as a royal benefactor who also fulfills the priestly role of offering sacrifice. Winter writes that as the high priest, the emperor was "to pray and sacrifice to the gods for the well-being of the Roman Empire."[146] The emperor's priestly title was *pontifex maximus*, which literally means the "greatest bridge builder." The Greek rendition of the title is ἀρχιερεύς ("high priest"). The title underscores the emperor's role as a mediator between the gods and the empire.

Richard Gordon observes that the emperor's priestly or sacrificial role is inextricably linked with his role as benefactor.[147] An inscription records Augustus's sacrifice and prayers as follows:

> Imperator Caesar Augustus sacrificed to the divine Moerae nine she-lambs, offered whole, in the Greek manner, and in the same manner, nine she-goats and he prayed as follows: Moerae, as it is written in your regard in those books, that each and everything may prosper for the Roman people I beseech you and pray that you increase the empire and majesty of the Roman people . . . at

---

146. Winter, *Divine Honours*, 15.

147. Gordon, "Veil of Power," 201–2. By engaging in sacrificial activity, the emperor serves as an exemplar to the elites in the Empire. Gordon (here p. 224) writes that priesthood serves "as a vehicle for the institutionalization towards the people of Rome, as a means of compelling the senatorial élite to imitate the emperor's generosity." Lendon aptly summarizes the emperor's role as a paradigmatic figure thus: "As the emperor, so the emperor's officials" (*Empire of Honour*, 16). The emperors also use priesthoods in the Roman colleges as symbolic capitals. That is to say, just like imperial benefaction, priesthoods are so highly valuable goods to the elite that the emperors use them as a means whereby he creates lasting relations of dependence and gratitude towards himself. See Gordon, "Veil of Power," 223.

war and at home . . . that you would bestow upon the Roman people . . . and the legions of the Roman people eternal safety, victory and health; and that you favor the Roman people . . . keep safe the state of the Roman people . . . be well disposed and propitious to the Roman people . . . myself, my family, my household.[148]

After Augustus's reign, all successive emperors until Gratian, who became emperor in 367 CE, held the office of *pontifex maximus*.[149] The emperor may thus be described as the hub and symbol of religious stability as well as the paradigm of virtuous devotion to the gods.[150] If Paul is suggesting that the Messiah performs the imperial role of offering sacrifice, then he does so in ways that play upon some aspects of Greco-Roman benefaction practices. For rather than offering animals as sacrifice, the Messiah offers his own life, not just as a paradigm of virtuous devotion to God, but to demonstrate God's love and bring deliverance to humanity. Paul states in 5:9 that this sacrifice is "by his blood" (ἐν τῷ αἵματι αὐτοῦ), which is a reference to the Messiah's painful death. The prepositional phrase "through the death of his son" (διὰ τοῦ θανάτου τοῦ υἱοῦ αὐτοῦ) in 5:10 is parallel to "by his blood" in 5:9. And one of the points of 5:10 is that the enemies (ἐχθροί) of God have been reconciled to him at the cost of his son's life.

The Messiah's offer of his life as χάρις completely reverses the disgraceful status of his followers. Benefactors applied the rule of censorship to benefit the worthy. Moreover, access to the emperor was limited to just a few, mainly their family members and friends. Those who could approach the emperor enjoyed a high social status. In contrast, Paul argues that the Messiah sacrifices his life for a people with absolutely no social standing. For anyone who has been described as weak, ungodly, sinner, and enemy does not qualify to come into the royal chamber. Paul's argument concerning the Messiah's benefaction must have surprised his readers who were intimately acquainted with the Greco-Roman benefaction system. Whereas in Greco-Roman practice benefactors sought to aid their friends, the Messiah comes to the rescue of God's enemies, the objects of divine wrath, and transforms them into God's friends.[151] Whereas

---

148. *ILS* 5050. Translated by Winter, *Divine Honours*, 54. Gordon states that about twenty of the 230 extant statues of Augustus represent him in the act of sacrificing ("Veil of Power," 212).

149. Cooley, *Res Gestae Divi Augusti*, 148.

150. See Hoklotubbe, *Civilized Piety*, 71.

151. Seneca writes that the reason for friendship is to have someone for whom to die: "For what purpose, then, do I make a man my friend? To have someone for whom

only a few people enjoyed access to the imperial throne, the Messiah's death brings all his followers into his royal courts. Unlike Greco-Roman practice where glory was the preserve of rulers and the elite, the supreme royal benefactor guarantees all his followers an eternal glorious status before God since they will all be raised from the dead, and will not face the eschatological wrath. The Messiah's gift of status brings friendship where there was hostility, glory where there was shame, righteousness where there was godlessness, empowerment where there was weakness, life where there was death, and love where there was wrath.

The Messiah's Gift of the Holy Spirit

The preceding discussion has established that Paul portrays the Messiah as the supreme royal benefactor who offers the ultimate gift of his own life to rescue a sinful and godless people. Because of this ultimate sacrifice, the Messiah's rule also dispenses the gifts of eschatological life, peace, and status. Another gift that comes with the Messiah's benefaction is the Holy Spirit (Rom 5:5). Structurally, 5:5 is an expansive comment on 5:4. The verse contains the first reference to the Holy Spirit as having been given to Christ's followers. In anticipation of a potential objection to his argument, Paul provides a reason why hope does not lead to shame. Within the framework of the Greco-Roman benefaction system, shame is mostly associated with the failure to render honor where it is due. Aristotle states that an honorable man fears disgrace (*Eth. nic.* 3.6.3). A thoughtful benefactor would do whatever he can to carefully dispense favors so that he may avoid shame (Seneca, *Ben.* 4.10.3). Dio condemns the people of Rhodes for their disgraceful conduct as seen in changing the inscriptions on older statues to honor newer benefactors. This is embarrassing to the former benefactors because it connotes obliteration of their memory from posterity and depriving "them of the rewards of virtue" (*Rhod.* 25). A benefactor whose memory does not perpetually abide with the progeny has essentially been defeated by death and thereby put to shame. Such a benefactor is a victim of ingratitude, which is the worst of all sins (Seneca, *Ben.* 1.10.4; 3.1.1; cf. 1.6.1; 5.20.4). The ingrates commit a shameful act as they deny benefactors their deserved memorialization. In brief, in the Greco-Roman benefaction system, shame comes when the

---

I may die, whom I may follow into exile, against whose death I may stake my own life, and pay the pledge, too" (*Ep.* 9:10).

beneficiaries fail to honor their benefactor and allow him to defeat death by abiding in the unending memory of posterity.

What Paul says about shame in Rom 5:5 is concerned with how to defeat death. Yet the argument is not about how the readers ought to perpetually memorialize the Messiah but how the supreme benefactor guarantees eternal honor and life to his followers. The question is: What is the warrant for complete assurance that hope, as strengthened by afflictions, will never lead to eschatological shame? To answer this question, we will discuss the main statement of the verse, followed by the supporting reason, and conclude with the agency of the Holy Spirit.

The main statement of the verse is that "and hope does not put to shame" (ἡ δὲ ἐλπὶς οὐ καταισχύνει).[152] Unlike what we find in the ancient benefaction, whereby only those who had access to wealth and excelled in generosity could somehow, though not in reality, avoid the shame of death, Paul demonstrates that believers are invited to share in the Messiah's glorious status and victory over death. In the context of Paul's argument, hope points to the certainty of resurrection from the dead. Is there any likelihood that in the last day, rather than being raised from the dead, Christ's followers will face God's wrath? Failure to be raised from the dead and share in Christ's perfect life and rule is the ultimate shame which humanity can ever face.[153] Paul asserts that for believers, there is absolutely no possibility that their hope will not be fulfilled.

The Pauline rhetoric of shame and endurance is in many ways similar to what we find among the OT prophets who resolve to wait patiently for God's salvation since they are convinced that God will not disappoint them (e.g., Isa 28:16; 50:7; 54:4 Mic 7:7; Hab 2:3; Zeph 3:8). Paul's words also echo the psalmist's confidence in God's faithful vindication of the righteous. LXX Ps 21:5–6 (22:4–5 MT) says, "In you our ancestors trusted; they trusted, and you delivered them. To you they cried, and they were saved; in you they trusted, and were not *put to shame*" (κατῃσχύνθησαν). LXX Ps 25:3 (24:3 MT) declares that "none who waits for you shall be *put to shame*" (καταισχυνθῶσιν). David cries out to the Lord in LXX Ps

---

152. The verb καταισχύνειν has a future connotation hence should probably be accented as a future tense (καταισχυνεῖ, "will put to shame"; see Moo, *Epistle to the Romans*, 312; Bryne, *Romans*, 170; Schreiner, *Romans*, 256) rather than as a present tense (καταισχύνει, "puts to shame"; see Cranfield, *Critical and Exegetical Commentary*, 261; Dunn, *Romans 1–8*, 252).

153. See Rom 10:11–13, where "not put to shame" describes the assurance of eschatological deliverance.

24:20 (25:20 MT) saying, "Guard my life and rescue me! Let me not be put to shame (καταισχυνθείην), for I take refuge in you." Likewise, in LXX Ps 30:2 (31:1 MT), David pleads with the Lord to deliver him and not let him be *put to shame* (cf. LXX 70:1).

The theme of shame is also evident in 2 Maccabees 7 where, contrary to the prevailing culture that may view painful humiliation as disgraceful, the martyrs ennoble righteous suffering in light of the eschatological hope of vindication and reward. Unlike the oppressors who view the confrontation purely from an earthly perspective, the martyrs view it ultimately as between the oppressors and God, on whose side the victims operate. The victims are confident that although they are martyred, God will vindicate and recompense them in the future. That is why the second brother can tell his prosecutor, "You cursed miscreant! You dispatch us from this life, but the King of the world shall raise us up, who have died for his laws, and revive us to life everlasting" (7:9). The martyrs display unwavering confidence in God and in his ability to accomplish divine purposes through adversity and to vindicate the righteous by the power of resurrection and glorification. As the martyrs enjoy the reward for their obedience to the laws, Antiochus IV and his descendants will be judged (7:17, 31–36). Just before he is tortured to death, the fifth brother declares to the king that although he does as he wills, he should not think that God has forsaken his own; ultimately God's sovereign power will torture the king and his seed as the martyrs enjoy eternal life and reward for their obedience to the laws.

Like what we find in the OT and in 2 Maccabees 7 (cf. Wis 2:12–20; 5:1–7), Paul is convinced that the hope of the righteous does not put to shame since the Lord will vindicate the righteous. Hope puts to shame if it is invalidated thereby leading the hopeful to ultimate embarrassment. In our verse, the concern is not with the Messiah, who has already conquered death hence was not put to shame, but with his allegiant followers. He is the supreme benefactor who assures his followers of victory over death.

The reason why hope does not put to shame is that "the love of God has been poured out in our hearts" (ἡ ἀγάπη τοῦ θεοῦ ἐκκέχυται ἐν ταῖς καρδίαις ἡμῶν).[154] This is the first reference to God's love in Romans.

---

154. Although τοῦ θεοῦ might be a plenary genitive ("the love that comes *from* God that produces our love *for* God), it is more likely a subjective genitive (the love that comes from God; contra Wright, "Letter to the Romans," 517) particularly given the passage's emphasis on the divine initiative as well as the fact that the certainty of the

Nowhere else in the NT is it written that God's love is poured out.[155] Many texts speak of the Spirit as the one who is poured out (Isa 32:15; 34:16; 44:3; Ezek 11:19; 36:26-27; 37:4-14; Joel 2:28-29; Acts 2:17, 18, 33; 10:45), but here it is love which is poured out. In Greco-Roman society, the ideal ruler shows commitment to his subjects by using his resources for their benefit. Due to his φιλανθρωπία or concern for the welfare of his subjects, such a ruler is called father, shepherd, guardian, savior, friend, and general. Aristotle writes that a beneficent king loves his subjects like an artist loves his own handiwork (*Eth. nic.* 9.7.4) and a mother her children (*Eth. nic.* 9.7.7). Seneca states that the ideal ruler "wears the countenance of a human being, all gentle and kindly" (*Ben.* 2.13.2) and he cares for his subjects (*Ben.* 2.13.2-3; *Clem.* 1.13.4). Dio notes that unlike a bad king who loves pleasure (*1 Regn.* 21), the ideal king must be a lover of humankind and care for his people just as a shepherd cares for the sheep (*1 Regn.* 15-20; *2 Regn.* 6; cf. *3 Regn.* 39, 55-57; *4 Regn.* 43-44). Philo writes that the good rulers "show a fatherly and sometimes more than fatherly affection" (*Spec. Laws* 4:184). Philo depicts Moses as an ideal ruler who never ignored "any opportunity that would advance the common well-being" (*Moses* 1.27.151). Contrary to the tyrant who ignores the sufferings of his subjects, the ideal ruler shows his love by toiling for the prosperity of his subjects. He gives gifts, delivers his subjects from their enemies, and maintains peace. Simply put, the ideal ruler is a benefactor who loves his subjects most (Cicero, *Off.* 1.15.47; see *Fam.* 3.5.1; 13.18.2).

When read within this framework of royal benefaction, Paul's assertion that God's love has been poured out in our hearts implies that the Messiah's rule demonstrates God's unwavering commitment to the prosperity of believers. The Messiah is the deliverer and shepherd whose substitutionary death reveals the extent of God's love for us (Rom 5:8). The truth of the causal clause of 5:5b is simple and yet profound: God loves us! The one who is suffering needs to constantly remember that God loves him, lest he develop bitterness toward God. And if indeed God loves us, and if the Messiah our Lord reigns, then hope cannot put us to

---

hope of the glory of God depends, not on the believer's love for God, but on what God has accomplished through the Messiah.

155. LXX Ps 44:3 uses "pour out" in reference to χάρις while Sir 18:11 uses it in reference to ἔλεος ("mercy"). Zech 12:10 speaks of the Lord pouring out "on the house David and on the inhabitants of Jerusalem a spirit of grace and pleas for mercy."

shame; rather, our anticipation of the resurrection of the dead is brightened by the afflictions of this life.

The verb "poured out" connotes a "lavish bestowal"[156] or an extravagant effusion.[157] The prepositional phrase "in our hearts" means that the love is "an inner, spiritual experience at the deepest level of our being."[158] But why does Paul introduce God's love at this point in his discourse? As Paul continues with his argument on suffering, he wants his readers to understand that their suffering does not suggest that God has forsaken them. In other words, neither does the absence of suffering suggest greater love of God nor does the presence of suffering imply divine indifference to the plight of believers. Moreover, righteous suffering is not a sign of the Lord's displeasure. The believer who is facing affliction should not think that God loves her less for God's love is constant in affliction just as it is unchanging in relative calm. The reality of God's love in sufferings implies that righteous suffering cannot be attributed to God's wrath occasioned by some supposed sins. If what is revealed against human wickedness is God's wrath (1:18—3:20), then what is poured out in the hearts of the redeemed is God's love.[159] The perspective that the believer adopts in sufferings is informed, not by the denial of God's wrath, but by the assurance of God's care and compassion, as revealed through the story of the Messiah. Although we were once children of wrath, we are now the recipients of God's transforming love (see Eph 2:1–5).

How is love poured out in our hearts? Paul's answer to this question is: "by the Holy Spirit who was given to us" (διὰ πνεύματος ἁγίου τοῦ δοθέντος ἡμῖν). The Holy Spirit is the agent that fills believers' hearts with the love of God.[160] As Schreiner writes, "The love of God is experienced when the Spirit is poured out in our hearts, suggesting that the

---

156. Kruse, *Paul's Letter to the Romans*, 231.
157. Moo, *Epistle to the Romans*, 304.
158. Osborne, *Romans*, 131.
159. In LXX Ps 68:25, the psalmist urges the Lord to pour out his wrath against the wicked while Ps 78:6 urges the Lord to pour out his wrath on the nations that do not call upon his name (cf. Jer 10:25). The Lord says in Hos 5:10 that he will pour out his wrath like water on the princes of Judah. Sirach 36:6 pleads with God to "raise up indignation" and "pour out wrath" against Israel's adversaries (cf. Zeph 3:8; Jer 6:11; 14:16; Ezek 7:8; 9:8; 14:19; 16:38). The verb is also used nine times in Rev 16:1–17 to depict the outpouring of God's wrath. Given these parallels, one may contend that Paul is implicitly contrasting the "old age," when we were objects of God's wrath, with the "new age," where we are now the recipients of God's love.

160. This means that the implied subject of the verb ἐκκέχυται is the Holy Spirit.

Spirit has the unique ministry of filling believers with the love of God."[161] The passive participle δοθέντος is a divine passive, which means that the implied subject is either God or the Messiah. Paul speaks of the Spirit of the Messiah (Rom 8:9), or the Spirit of Jesus the Messiah (Phil 1:19), but he mostly speaks of the Spirit of God (e.g., Rom 8:9, 11, 14; 15:19; 1 Cor 2:11, 14; 3:16; 6:11; 7:40; 12:3; 2 Cor 3:3, 17; Eph 4:30; Phil 3:3). In at least three places, he states that God sends or gives the Spirit (Gal 4:6; Eph 1:17; 1 Thess 4:8; cf. 1 Cor 2:12). The fact that Paul can state that the Spirit is of the Messiah just as he is of God cautions against suggesting that Paul never conceives of the giver of the Spirit as both God and Jesus.[162] More importantly, the gift of the Spirit has been given to believers as a mark that they belong to the new age inaugurated by the Messiah. In other words, the gift of the Spirit is one of the messianic blessings for the redeemed.

How does the gift of the Spirit guarantee our eschatological deliverance and eternal honorable status?[163] We can infer at least two points from Paul's argument. First, the Spirit testifies that believers belong to God. There is a special relationship between God and those on whom his Spirit rests. The portrait of the king in the OT reveals that as Yahweh's anointed, the king receives the Spirit, who empowers him to accomplish Yahweh's purposes. As one upon whom the Spirit rests, the king acts as a vicegerent of Yahweh. The Spirit not only assures the king of Yahweh's presence and care but also testifies to the king's divine sonship. Similarly, the prophets anticipated the outpouring of the Spirit to signify the dawn of the new age (Isa 32:15; 34:16; 44:3; Ezek 11:19; 36:26–27; 37:4–14; Joel 2:28–29). The death and resurrection of the Messiah inaugurate this new age, and the Spirit bears witness to believers that they indeed belong to Christ (Rom 8:9). Just as the king's special relationship to God was marked by anointing with the Spirit, so the believer's special relationship to God is marked by the gift of the Spirit. And since we eternally belong to God, he watches over us with steadfast love and care.

The second point is closely related to the first: The Spirit maps us onto the Messiah's pattern of dying and rising, hence granting us endurance in affliction and guaranteeing our glorification. It is not surprising

---

161. Schreiner, *Romans*, 257.

162. In Luke 24:49, Jesus promises his disciples that he will send the promise of his father upon them, while Acts 2:33 states that Jesus has poured out the Holy Spirit.

163. As a gift the Spirit is "given" (Rom 5:5; 2 Cor 1:22; 5:5), "supplied" (Gal 3:5), "sent" (Gal 4:6), and "received" by humans (Rom 8:15; 2 Cor 11:4; Gal 3:2).

that Paul speaks of the gift of the Spirit for the first time in Romans in the context of suffering and hope. This same Spirit of holiness was at work in the resurrection of Jesus (1:3–4). The Spirit assures us of God's love when suffering and enables us to view suffering in light of Christ's death and resurrection. Without the empowering presence of the Spirit, no one can conceive of suffering as an opportunity orchestrated by God for the believer's maturity. Moreover, it is through the Spirit that we can discern that afflictions ultimately strengthen the hope of glorification. Paul can therefore write that the Spirit is the seal and the "first installment," guaranteeing our future redemption and making our hope certain (Eph 1:13–14; 4:30; 2 Cor 1:22; 5:5).

Paul's emphasis in Rom 5:5 seems to be on the gift of the Spirit.[164] We may thus paraphrase the verse as follows: "The messianic gift of the Holy Spirit fills our heart with God's love and assures us of future vindication." Stated differently, the Spirit assures us that present affliction is not a preview of the eschatological shame; rather, present affliction is orchestrated by the one who loves us and who has invited us to proclaim his victorious reign by following his pattern of dying and rising. For Paul, the criterion for apportioning honor is not access to material wealth, but the possession of the Spirit.[165] Whoever lacks the Spirit will definitely be put to shame since his hope is an illusive and shallow optimism devoid of God's love. As Schreiner writes, "Believers know now in their hearts that they will be spared from God's wrath because they presently experience God's love for them through the ministry of the Holy Spirit."[166] The power that communicates God's love to believers, that sustains them in affliction, and that assures them of their glorification is that of the Holy Spirit.

Reciprocating the Messiah's Benefaction

We have seen that Paul articulates his aim of portraying Jesus Christ as the supreme royal benefactor by focusing on the Messiah's substitutionary death as well as the gifts of life, peace, status, and the Holy Spirit. Jesus

---

164. Osborne, *Romans*, 132: "The Holy Spirit is the supreme gift that makes it possible for us to know the gift of God's love."

165. Blanton, *Spiritual Economy*, 131: "Paul consistently opposed the 'standard' patronal paradigm that assigned relative rank in patron-client relationships on the basis of access to material wealth. In its place, he proposed an evaluative system in which spiritual rather than material resources constituted the more highly valued assets."

166. Schreiner, *Romans*, 257.

offers his own life for us sinners to deliver us from death and sin. His victory over death means that he alone can guarantee his followers eternal life, establish them in righteousness, and assure them of an eternal glorious status before God. It is also through the Messiah alone that humanity can have peace with God. And the gift of the Spirit assures Christ's followers of God's love for them. The present section examines Paul's theology of suffering as found in our passage in relation to the ethic of reciprocity. The main question is: How do the Messiah's followers respond to his benefaction when they are facing adversity? To answer this question, we need to analyze closely the connection between χάρις and "boasting" (καυχᾶσθαι). In Rom 5:2, Paul uses χάρις to define the realm of believers' existence, their new status as Christ's followers. Because we have been ushered into the royal chamber, our life is dependent on the Messiah's ultimate gift of his own life. Additionally, our standing in χάρις implies that we have been granted everything necessary for faith and life. But how does the fact of our unhindered access to the divine throne shape how we view suffering? Immediately after asserting that through the Messiah we have access into grace, Paul uses the term "boasting" (5:2b, 3, 11) to describe believers' life within the realm of χάρις. The implication in this carefully crafted rhetoric is that χάρις anticipates a specific form of response.

We have already seen that the term χάρις is used in the Greco-Roman context for an initial gift and its reciprocity. That Paul uses the term to denote a gift is hardly disputed; the question is whether Paul also retains the ethic of reciprocity in his construal of the Messiah's gift. A primary methodological premise in this work is that the Pauline χάρις should be interpreted in his immediate social context.[167] Abstracting χάρις from its Greco-Roman benefaction context mistakenly implies that χάρις is a timeless construct.[168] This in turn leads to a misunderstanding of Paul's argument on the Messiah's gift and how we ought to reciprocate that gift even in suffering. One of the problems with using "grace" to translate χάρις is that it might undermine the ethic of reciprocity which is intricately

---

167. Harrison, *Paul's Language of Grace*, 1–25.

168. For representative works that tend to interpret χάρις as a timeless construct, see Moffatt, *Grace in the New Testament*; Manson, "Grace in the New Testament," 33–60; Wobbe, *Der Charis-Gedanke bei Paulus*; Smith, *Bible Doctrine of Grace*; Grundmann, "Die Übermacht der Gnade," 50–72; Surburg, "Pauline Charis," 721–41; Doughty, "Priority of ΧΑΡΙΣ," 163–80; Berger, "Χάρις," 457–60; Boers, "Ἀγάπε and Χάρις in Paul's Thought," 693–713; Winger, "From Grace to Sin," 145–75.

linked to the ancient usage of the term.[169] When such qualifiers as free, pure, sheer, gratuitous, and altruistic are attached to an understanding of χάρις, the obvious implication is that the concept it conveys both negates reciprocal obligations and suggests a "timeless construct with minimal relevance to the social and theological framework of Graeco-Roman society."[170] Yet according to its usage in the ancient Mediterranean context, χάρις comes with inextricable ties of obligation.[171] Crook rightly argues that one does not need to build an unnecessary fence around χάρις "as if its value would be diluted by allowing for parallels between Pauline and Greco-Roman usage."[172] In other words, there is neither justification for abstracting the term from its historical context nor any solid basis for assuming that *every time* Paul uses χάρις he deviates from his societal conventions and eradicates reciprocity, obligation, and self-interest. Rather than treating χάρις as a timeless construct, there is need for keen attentiveness to how Paul engages first-century benefaction system, an engagement which is assimilative, innovative, and subversive.[173]

Harrison rightly asserts that "by the first century AD χάρις had become the central leitmotiv of the Hellenistic reciprocity system."[174] Within the benefaction system, every gift carries the obligation to reciprocate. That is to say, in the ancient world, χάρις is not merely conditioned (based on the worthiness of the recipients); it is also *obliging* (bearing subsequent demands).[175] Aristotle and Seneca speak of the three Graces that had been strategically set up to remind the people to reciprocate. The Graces are three because "there is one for bestowing a benefit, another for receiving it, and a third for returning it" (Seneca, *Ben.* 1.3.2–10). Seneca asserts that gift-giving lays the beneficiary under obligation to return a favor (*Ben.* 2.35.1, 4; 5.11.5). Cicero maintains that gift-giving

---

169. Crook, "Grace as Benefaction," 26. Crook identifies two problems with translating χάρις as grace: (1) theological reflection on the term eclipses its Greco-Roman usage, and (2) grace is itself a translation of the Vulgate's *gratia* rather than the Greek's χάρις.

170. Harrison, *Paul's Language of Grace*, 9–10.

171. For a helpful analysis of "the perfections" of χάρις, see Barclay, *Paul and the Gift*, 66–78.

172. Crook, "Grace as Benefaction," 26.

173. Some of the recent works that pay close attention to the ethic of reciprocity in Greco-Roman society and how Paul interacts with it include Pao, *Thanksgiving*; Harrison, *Paul's Language of Grace*; Crook, "Grace as Benefaction"; Barclay, *Paul and the Gift*.

174. Harrison, *Paul's Language of Grace*, 2.

175. Barclay, "Under Grace," 64.

is an investment that anticipates returns (*Off.* 2.20.69) and that people ought to do most for him who loves them most (*Off.* 1.15.47; cf. *Fam.* 3.5.1; 13.18.2). Demonstrating gratitude for gifts is the most urgent and mandatory duty (*Off.* 1.15.47). Dio states that a beneficent ruler delights in loyal hearts and the sweet praise of his friends (3 *Regn.* 110; 1 *Regn.* 31–32). Pliny notes that the people of Rome are indebted to Trajan due to his benefactions (*Pan.* 41:4). The people of Egypt are indebted to Rome and her people because of the benefactions they received from Trajan (*Pan.* 32:4). Reciprocity assumes various forms, ranging from counter gifts, gratitude, and honor to political and judicial support.

Similarly, statues and their accompanying honorary inscriptions publicize the benefactor's achievements, virtues, and the people's gratitude. As Danker writes, the honorific decree is the means by which the beneficiaries in Greco-Roman society express their gratitude and recognize "personal character or distinguished services."[176] The second-century BCE decree of Chalkis in honor of Archenus partly reads: "In order, therefore, that the people may manifestly return the appropriate favors (τὰς καταξίας ἀποδιδοὺς χάριτας) to men who are fair and good and the rest, seeing the gratitude (εὐχαριστίαν) of the city to the benefactors, may be zealous imitators of the good men."[177] A second-century BCE inscription from Pergamon states: "In order, therefore, that the people may appear foremost in reciprocating a benefaction (ἐγχάριτος ἀποδόσει) and be conspicuous in honoring those benefiting the People and its friends voluntarily and in committing the goodness of their deeds to eternal memory."[178] These and similar inscriptions reveal the use of χάρις in benefaction context to denote the initial favor and the people's reciprocity. The beneficiaries want everyone to witness their reciprocity to the benefactor. Thus, issuing decrees and inscribing them on bronze tablets demonstrate to all that the people know how to express gratitude to their benefactors for their favors.[179]

Failure to reciprocate is shameful and loathsome because it weakens social cohesion (Aristotle, *Eth. nic.* 2.23.8; 5.5.6–7). Ingrates are perverse and worthy of severe punishment. Ingratitude is not only the worst of all vices, but it also discourages benefactors from bestowing further favors.

176. Danker, *Benefactor*, 30.

177. *IG* XII(9) 899. Also see *IG* XI(4) 1061; XII(9) 239.

178. *OGIS* 248. For more examples of similar inscriptions, see Harrison, *Paul's Language of Grace*, 26–63.

179. Ma, *Statues and Cities*, 31–38, 56; Winter, *Seek the Welfare*, 27.

One way of avoiding ungrateful beneficiaries is by benefiting worthy people. In short, χάρις creates reciprocal ties of obligation between the benefactor and the beneficiaries (Cicero, *Off.* 1.17.56).[180] The subjects who have been benefited by the ruler ought to give loyalty and obedience to their beneficent ruler. As Crook notes, loyalty "was . . . a virtue of the system of . . . benefaction on every level."[181] Our interpretation of Paul's usage of χάρις and the messianic benefaction should take cognizance of the indispensable obligation to reciprocate.

We can discern the connection that Paul draws between χάρις and boasting in Romans 5 when we read the passage against the backdrop of the ethic of reciprocity. The argument of this section is straightforward: The Messiah's *incommensurate gift* (it is indiscriminately given to the unworthy) is also *conditional* (it demands obedient reciprocity). Or as Barclay puts it, the Messiah's gift is "*unconditioned* (based on no prior conditions) but not *unconditional* (carrying no subsequent demands)."[182] Incommensurability neither diminishes the value of the gift nor nullifies the obligation of the beneficiaries. On the contrary, the unworthiness of the beneficiary magnifies the need to show gratitude. For if a gift bestowed on worthy recipients demands a return, how much more the priceless one offered to ill-deserving beneficiaries! The question is not whether the beneficiaries of the Messiah's supreme benefaction ought to give him loyalty and obedience; rather, the question is: What shape does reciprocity to the Messiah's gift take, particularly in suffering? How do King Jesus' followers honor him for his benefaction when they are facing affliction?

Based on our passage, believers show gratitude to the Messiah, not by honorary inscriptions, statues, or seats of honor, but by "boasting" (5:2, 3, 11). Boasting implies that Christ's followers must submit faithfully to the rule of the Messiah and give him loyalty and obedience. The first object of boasting is the hope of the glory of God (5:2). As we have seen above, boasting in the hope of the glory of God points to the assurance of the resurrection life and deliverance from the eschatological wrath. But the period between the present life and the fulfillment of this hope is marked by afflictions. And Paul asserts that just as boasting characterizes the believer's anticipation of glorification, so does boasting characterize her "in afflictions" (ἐν θλίψεσιν). Afflictions, then, is the second object

---

180. Barclay, *Paul and the Gift*, 23, 63.
181. Crook, *Reconceptualising Conversion*, 214.
182. Crook, *Reconceptualising Conversion*, 64.

of boasting (5:3a).[183] The implication is that afflictions are intrinsically related to the believer's eschatological assurance.

By θλίψις, Paul refers to any kind of external pressures or affliction experienced by believers as they seek to live out their faith (cf. Eph 3:13; Col 1:24; 1 Thess 1:6).[184] These may include but are not limited to distress, persecution, famine, nakedness, danger, and sword (Rom 8:35). Moo argues that "all the evil that the Christian experiences reflects the conflict between 'this age,' dominated by Satan, and 'the age to come,' to which the Christian has been transferred by faith."[185] Because allegiance to King Jesus cannot be restricted to just some occasions, believers ought to view every kind of righteous suffering they might experience in light of their redemptive status in Christ. Although Matthew W. Bates' book *Salvation by Allegiance Alone* does not have a robust theology of suffering, he is right that Christians must show "embodied loyalty" or allegiance to Jesus the King even when suffering since "*present* glory is most clearly seen when we suffer in the Christ (2 Thess. 2:14), as suffering shows that we truly are participating in the Christ's death-unto-glorious-life" (italics original).[186]

At first, the assertion that believers reciprocate the Messiah's gift by boasting in afflictions may seem paradoxical, or even nonsensical. After all, beneficent rulers are expected to deliver their followers from danger, famine, pestilence, war, and any other form of affliction; they never design suffering for them and claim that suffering is an inevitable component of their life. Every ideal rule should be marked by prosperity, peace, order, and bounty, not by sufferings. Furthermore, Paul's assertion might be astonishing because future glorification implies that believers will never face afflictions again; Paul seems to hold hope and afflictions in tension.[187] But when read in the light of the trajectory of the Messiah and the call to participate faithfully in that trajectory, this assertion is not surprising.[188] Once again, what is true for the Messiah is also true for

---

183. The definite article (ταῖς) that precedes θλίψεσιν functions as a possessive pronoun, hence "our afflictions." The preposition ἐν introduces the object of our boasting (hence translated as "in") rather than the location of boasting (which would be translated as "in the midst of").

184. BDAG 457.

185. Moo, *Epistle to the Romans*, 303.

186. Bates, *Salvation by Allegiance Alone*, 5, 174.

187. Schreiner, *Romans*, 255.

188. The paradoxical thought of confident assurance in affliction is also found in Judaism. In 2 Macc 6:30, after Eleazar has been beaten almost to the point of death he

his followers; the path of suffering which the Messiah embraced without despairing or complaining is the same path that believers have to follow with complete confidence that the Messiah who has brought them into the realm of χάρις will supply them with everything they need to stand firm in suffering even as they anticipate glorification.

To boast in afflictions, therefore, connotes the unwavering confidence that Jesus is forever on his throne and that he can accomplish redemptive purposes through adversity and vindicate the righteous by the power of resurrection and glorification. From the human perspective, the last word in adversity might be defeat or shame or imprisonment or death, but from God's perspective the last word in adversity is glory and resurrection and peace. Just as divine orchestration led the Messiah to the cross, so does divine orchestration lead Christ's followers to suffering. We boast in afflictions, not in the sense of a passive turning of a blind eye to the pain of life, but in the sense of a settled conviction that afflictions are in the world by the Lord's design and that our response to suffering ought to proclaim the χάρις and the greatness of the Savior, who exercises sovereignty over the realms of life, death, and sufferings. Boasting in afflictions is another way of describing believers' obedient loyalty to Christ; it demonstrates the extent to which believers are willing to advertise allegiance to their supreme royal benefactor.[189]

If indeed suffering demands boasting, then it must bring benefits that outweigh the immediate pain which the sufferer undergoes. The question that Rom 5:3b–5 addresses is: Why do we boast in our afflictions? Paul's

---

says, "The Lord possesses all holy knowledge. He knows I could have escaped these terrible sufferings and death, yet he also knows that I gladly suffer these things, because I fear him." 4 Macc 7:22 states that it is a blessed thing to endure all kinds of sufferings for the sake of virtue. We also read in 4 Macc 10:20 that "[g]ladly do we lose our limbs in behalf of God" (also see 4 Macc 9:29–30; 11:22). 2 Bar. 52:5–7 encourages the righteous to rejoice in their present suffering and to make their souls ready for the reward awaiting them: "And concerning the righteous ones, what will they now do? Rejoice in the sufferings that you now suffer. For why do you look for the decline of your enemies? Prepare your souls for that which is kept for you, and make ready your souls for the reward which is preserved for you" (cf. 2 Bar 48:48–50). Jdth 8:25 says, "Let us give thanks to the Lord our God, who is putting us to the test." All this implies that suffering was never viewed as that which robs a person of inner confidence in God, a confidence that finds outward expression in facing adversity with unyielding courage.

189. Crook correctly asserts that "Paul presents his sufferings as a mark of his virtue as a client, a sign of his honor, and of the extent to which he has gone to obey the one who gave him this office [of apostleship]" ("Divine Benefactions," 26).

answer is that affliction is designed for the transformation of believers and for strengthening hope. The perfect participle εἰδότες ("because we know") introduces the causal clause which provides the reason for boasting in afflictions. Käsemann posits that Paul here appeals, not to a general truth, but to Christian experience.[190] Based on the parallels in Jas 1:2-4 and 1 Pet 1:6-7, Dunn suggests that "Paul is drawing here on a fairly well established pattern of Christian homily."[191] One might also conjecture that Paul is appealing to the Jewish experience of martyrdom. Whether the appeal is to Christian experience, or an established homiletical pattern, or martyrdom, the implication is that there is a settled certainty regarding what Paul is about to say. Given Paul's definition of the gospel in Rom 1:3-4, it is indisputable that this assurance is rooted in the pattern of Jesus Christ of facing affliction with complete trust in God's ability to vindicate the righteous.

We boast in afflictions because we know that "affliction produces[192] endurance, and endurance produces character, and character produces hope" (5:3b-4). Suffering is not an end in itself; rather, it is the onset of a chain of linked virtues.[193] "To endure" (ὑπομονή) was used in the Hellenistic world to describe those who courageously stood firm in the face of hostility and opposition.[194] "Endure" elsewhere in the NT denotes "bearing up" under trials (1 Cor 10:13) and unjust punishment (1 Pet 2:19) in the sense of holding out rather than caving in. The NT urges perseverance in the face of hostility since "the one who endures (ὑπομείνας) to the end will be saved" (Matt 10:22; cf. 24:13; Mark 13:13). The Synoptic apocalyptic material admonishes endurance in the context of false teaching and going astray in the last days (Matt 24:4, 11, 24; cf. 2 Tim 3:1-9; 4:3-4). The theme of ὑπομονή also recurs throughout Revelation, where the saints are encouraged to endure because they are guarding their faith in Christ and are faithful to the commandment of God (Rev 1:9; 2:2, 3:10; 13:10; 14:12). Thus, like the OT prophets and the NT apocalyptic texts, Paul wants his readers to understand that afflictions are valuable since they produce endurance, which is "a basic Christian

---

190. Käsemann, *Commentary on Romans*, 134.

191. Dunn, *Romans 1-8*, 251.

192. The verb here is κατεργάζομαι, which is a progressive present that implies that Paul is concerned with both the "process" and "result."

193. For a similar chain of linked virtues which suffering inaugurates, see 1 Pet 1:6-7 and Jas 1:2-4.

194. Hauck, "μένω, κτλ.," 574-88.

virtue and attitude"[195] that gives a believer an eschatological orientation in suffering and fills him with confidence in God's promise to complete the redemptive process through the Messiah. Endurance, therefore, is the continuous fruit of a celebratory and confident response in adversity, bearing in mind the Messiah's narrative of perseverance and his purpose of transforming his followers through affliction.

Endurance, in turn, produces δοκιμήν ("character"). The term denotes "the quality of being approved," hence "proven character" or "tested character." Dunn rightly notes that Paul regards "affliction as divinely appointed testing designed to prove and mature."[196] The implied metaphor of testing does not suggest that the Messiah designs suffering to discover the genuineness of faith; rather, it is meant to strengthen the believer's allegiance to the Messiah. Suffering is a divine pedagogy that grants believers deep insights into the nature and power of the Christ-event. The believer can view suffering as an indispensable opportunity for producing the moral integrity that marks the mature Christian.

But why is the transformation of believers' character necessary? Paul paints a horrible picture of a people marked by ingratitude, immorality, and idolatry in Rom 1:18—3:20. The Messiah redeems the undeserving sinners but he does not leave them in their morally deplorable condition. Instead, he designs afflictions for shaping their character so that through affliction they might attain true virtue. Those who were formerly morally incapacitated have now been ushered into the realm of χάρις and virtue, into the domain of Christ. Käsemann rightly asserts that Paul's concern here "is for the eschatological miracle of the humanization of man which is prefigured by the crucified Christ and in which the coming of the new world takes place."[197] The fact that the Messiah restores his followers' moral integrity through afflictions reveals why boasting is the appropriate response in suffering. Whereas formerly they were ungrateful, now believers can honor their Lord, not only because of the peace they are enjoying with God, but also in suffering.

After "character," Paul returns to the theme of hope: "and proven character [produces] hope" (ἡ δὲ δοκιμὴ ἐλπίδα). The eschatological hope that fills the good news of the coming of the Messiah serves as bookends to Paul's discussion on boasting in afflictions (5:2 and 5:5). Contrary to

---

195. Hauck, "μένω, κτλ.," 586.

196. Dunn, *Romans 1–8*, 251.

197. Käsemann, *Commentary on Romans*, 135.

what might be expected, afflictions strengthen rather than weaken believers' hope. Wright states, "When the patience is Christian patience, and the tried and tested character a Christian character, the result is neither shallow optimism nor settled fatalism, but hope."[198] Tested character produces hope because moral transformation shows that one has been delivered from the dominion of evil and brought into the domain of godliness. As the climax of this chain which is inaugurated by suffering, hope suggests that when suffering, Christ's followers look beyond the present age to the culmination of their redemption when they will be vindicated. There is some circularity in Paul's argument here. We can endure because we have hope, and at the same time endurance strengthens our hope "by making us continually reflect on the future realities guaranteed by God."[199] So afflictions, endurance, character, and hope are all woven together as a tapestry that defines Christian worldview.

How one responds to suffering reflects his understanding of the purpose of suffering in God's redemptive plan as well as the extent of his loyalty to the Messiah. For faithful followers of Christ, suffering is neither something to be avoided nor a sign of the Lord's displeasure. Boasting does not suggest that we face suffering with the Stoic indifference to disease, pain, and loss that enables one to "maintain a similar demeanor in every circumstance . . . in the throes of pain, upon the loss of a child, or in protracted illness."[200] Suffering ought not to be met with dismay, despair, resignation, bitterness toward God or others, or with doubting the Redeemer's faithfulness. Jesus' story of dying and rising means that we cannot view suffering negatively as something that impugns Christ's faithfulness to us. Paul's argument may seem to hold hope and afflictions in tension, yet his assertion that the latter strengthens the former implies that the two are inseparable. If boasting in the hope of the glory of God frees believers from eschatological anxiety, then boasting in afflictions frees them from despair and doubting the goodness of the Messiah.

The Messiah's supreme benefaction transforms believers' view of suffering. That suffering accrues benefits that ultimately strengthen hope means that the Messiah invites his followers to faithfully share in his pattern of suffering-unto-glory. Against the backdrop of the ethic of reciprocity, believers' boasting in suffering is their obedient response to

---

198. Wright, "Letter to the Romans," 517.
199. Osborne, *Romans*, 131.
200. Marcus Aurelius, *Meditations* 1:8.

Christ's beneficence and loyal enactment of his lordship. The Messiah's sovereignty over the realms of life, suffering, sin, and death enables his followers to faithfully participate in his pattern of dying and rising now even as they await glorification. And because our existence is defined by χάρις, we must always live in ways that are befitting our new identity in the Messiah. Suffering, then, reveals the depth of the believer's loyalty to the Messiah and provides an invaluable opportunity for maturity.

Summary of the Messiah's Supreme Royal Benefaction in Romans 5:1–11

This chapter has demonstrated that Paul's christological discourse engages the ancient Mediterranean practice of royal benefaction in both conventional and subversive ways. That Paul is at home within the world of the Greco-Roman royal benefaction system is evident through such motifs as peace, χάρις, access, glory, faith, friendship, love, sacrifice, hope, boasting, enmity, giving, shame, suffering, reconciliation, and "the good." Paul argues that the Messiah's supreme royal benefaction both guarantees believers' eternal glorious status before God and demands faithful response to his rule. To make this point, Paul discusses the Messiah's substitutionary death as the ultimate benefaction that in turn leads to the gifts of eschatological life, peace, status, and the Holy Spirit. Similarly, he also articulates how Christ's followers respond to χάρις, especially in suffering.

Like the Greco-Roman rulers, Jesus gives gifts, offers sacrifice, reveals God's love, transforms character, delivers from sin and death, and expects the beneficiaries to give him loyalty and obedience. Yet Jesus' benefaction is also surprising in many ways. First, Jesus inverts the dominant transcript by giving his own life as a gift. The one who dies for humanity is "our Lord Jesus the Messiah," "the Messiah," and "the son" of God; the righteous one offers his own life as a gift. Second, the Messiah offers his gift indiscriminately to the entire, sinful human race. The universality and incongruity of the gift do not minimize its value, for as Barclay comments, this gift "is no mere throwing away of life, but an expression of love, the deepest personal commitment."[201] Third, the timing of this gift is right, not because the giver has accurately assessed the worthiness and the willingness of the beneficiaries to reciprocate, but because it is intentionally given to the weak, ungodly, sinners, and enemies to rescue

---

201. Barclay, *Paul and the Gift*, 478.

them. In other words, the Messiah's gift is given in perfect cognizance of the moral incapacitation of the wrath-deserving humanity. Fourth, the Messiah's benefaction reverses the disgraceful status of his followers and promises them a glorious status. Indeed, there is neither reason for eschatological anxieties nor any likelihood that Christ's followers will be put to shame. Rather, they are confident that just as the Messiah conquered death, they too will resurrect to eternal life.

Lastly, the Messiah's benefaction demands appropriate response. In our passage, Paul is mainly concerned with the shape that this response takes in suffering. How believers respond to suffering reveals the extent of their faithfulness to the Messiah. The key term that defines how Christ's followers reciprocate his benefaction is "boasting." We boast in suffering because the Messiah designs suffering to transform character and strengthen the hope of glory. Those who have been brought into the realm of χάρις must faithfully participate in the Messiah's trajectory of dying and rising and fulfill their obligation to their Lord by boasting in hope and in affliction. If Jesus is a beneficent ruler who offers his own life as a gift, delivers humanity from sin and death, establishes a righteous dominion, brings peace, reverses the disgraceful status of his followers, and empowers his followers by the Holy Spirit, then his subjects must give him loyalty and obedience by fitting and faithful enactment of his rule.

Does Paul's argument in 5:12—8:39 draw upon the ancient system of royal benefaction? If so, how does Paul's argument therein develop the themes previewed in 5:1–11? The next chapter will answer these and similar questions.

5

The Messiah's Supreme Royal Benefaction in Romans 5:12—8:39

OUR STUDY OF ROM 5:1–11 in the preceding chapter demonstrates that Paul uses the ancient cultural script of royal benefaction to portray Jesus Christ as the supreme royal benefactor. The essence of royal benefaction is gift-giving and gratitude. The Messiah's gift is superior because he offers himself as a sacrifice to liberate a sinful humanity. He dies, not for "the good," but for the weak, ungodly, sinners, and enemies. The Messiah's benefaction is both cosmic, as it is offered to the entire human race, and incongruous, as it is indiscriminately bestowed on the unworthy.[1] This gift reverses the disgraceful status of humanity and guarantees eternal honor to the Messiah's followers. In view of the ethic of reciprocity, the beneficiaries of the Messiah's superior benefaction ought to faithfully submit to his lordship. The key word that Paul uses in 5:1–11 to define believers' appropriate response to the Messiah's benefaction is "boasting." Boasting in suffering implies a confident assurance that the Messiah designs suffering for redemptive purposes and that those whose existence is determined by χάρις must faithfully follow the Messiah's trajectory of dying and rising.

If 5:1–11 previews some of the themes of 5:12—8:39, then we should expect the motifs of gift-giving and gratitude in the latter passage. The present chapter argues that Paul's christological discourse as expressed through royal benefaction can be traced throughout Paul's larger

---

1. When I use the term "incongruous" I am indebted to Barclay, *Paul and the Gift*, 70–75.

The Messiah's Supreme Royal Benefaction in Romans 5:12—8:39

argument in 5:12—8:39. What are humanity's greatest enemies and how does the Messiah bring deliverance? What is the role of the Spirit in believers' new identity as God's sons? What does suffering with Christ mean and how does it relate to believers' destiny? To address these questions, the first section will discuss the Messiah's victory over sin and death. The aim here is to show that the Messiah's superabundant χάρις liberates humanity from the dominion of sin and death, and that those who have been liberated are under obligation to χάρις. The Spirit is at the center of believers' identity as Christ's loyal followers; thus, the second section will look at the Spirit in relation to the status of believers. Following Christ implies participating in his pattern of dying and rising; the third section, therefore, focuses on participating in the Messiah's suffering. We hope to show throughout this chapter that in 5:12—8:39 Paul develops further his argument in 5:1-11 that the Messiah's supreme benefaction guarantees eternal glorious status and demands appropriate reciprocal return of loyalty to his lordship.

The Messiah's Triumph over Sin and Death

The themes of creation, rebellion, and liberation dominate Rom 5:12-21 as Paul juxtaposes Adam and Christ in sharp binary terms. Each figure represents a domain marked by specific features. Adam's dominion is characterized by disobedience, sin, and death while Christ's dominion is characterized by obedience, righteousness, and life. Adam's disobedient lordship ushers in two powerful enemies—sin and death—from which humanity cannot free itself. But Christ's righteous rule defeats sin and death and liberates humanity. A key term that Paul uses in 5:12-21 and 6:1—8:39 to describe the dominion of Christ is χάρις.[2] The term occurs seven times in various forms in 5:12-21 (15 [3x], 16, 17, 20, 21) and seven times in Romans 6-8 (6:1, 14, 15, 17, 23; 7:25; 8:32). Moreover, Paul uses various forms of the synonym δωρεά ("gift") in 5:15-17 and the motif of "superabundance" (περισσεία) in 5:15, 17, 20. As we have seen in the previous chapters, χάρις is the central leitmotif of Greco-Roman benefaction.[3] So when Paul uses the term to characterize the rule of Christ, he

---

2. Cranfield suggests that χάρις sums up Paul's construal of the gospel (*Critical and Exegetical Commentary*, 71). Harrison states that "χάρις is undoubtedly Paul's preferred leitmotiv for any full-orbed description of divine beneficence" (*Paul's Language of Grace*, 212).

3. Harrison, *Paul's Language of Grace*, 2.

gives strong hints that he is portraying Jesus as a benefactor. Paul's goal throughout this discussion centered on χάρις is that the reign of χάρις leads to eternal life through Jesus the Messiah. To assert that χάρις exercises dominion over sin and death implies that χάρις is more than a transformative power; it is a conquering and renewing agent. The dominion of χάρις is the dominion of Jesus Christ, whose story culminates with his enthronement (cf. 1:3–4).[4] The Messiah's gift reverses the effects of Adam's dominion and brings humanity under obligation to his lordship.

We will proceed in this section by offering a brief discussion of how Philo and Josephus portray Adam. We have picked Philo and Josephus partly because we have already considered in chapter 3 some of their writings that are pertinent to our discussion, and partly because they are a few of the Second Temple Judaism writers whose interpretation of Genesis might illumine our reading of Rom 5:12–21. The goal here is to provide a framework for interpreting Paul's argument and to show that Paul's royal discourse employs the script of benefaction. Having established an interpretive framework, we will turn to Paul's discussion of the dominion of sin and death followed by how χάρις liberates humanity. Those who have been liberated are in turn expected to reciprocate by conducting themselves in a way that honors their benefactor. Thus the final section will focus on believers' obligation to χάρις. We will see that the Messiah's benefaction liberates humanity from the dominion of sin and death, guarantees an eternal status in God's family, and demands believers' loyalty to the Messiah.

Philo's Reading of Genesis 1–3

A look at how Philo reads Genesis 1–3 through the framework of benefaction may sharpen our understanding of the role that the cultural script of benefaction plays in Paul's argument.[5] Philo writes that Adam was "the first father of the race" and that because of all provisions of life that God had made, Adam's descendants "were to spend their days without

---

4. For a related work that contends that Paul uses "righteousness" in Rom 6:15–23 to connote Christ, see Southall, *Rediscovering Righteousness*, 83–147.

5. For a helpful discussion of Philo's interpretation of Genesis 1–3 in general and his portrayal of the first man in particular, see Levison, *Portraits of Adam*, 63–88. Also see Runia, *Philo of Alexandria*. For a general discussion of the theme of creation in Paul and Philo, see Worthington, *Creation in Paul and Philo*. Also helpful is Anderson, *Philo of Alexandria's Views*.

toil or trouble surrounded by lavish abundance of all that they needed" (*Creation* 79).[6] But they had to overcome the irrational pleasures of the soul, for if the soul were rightly ordered, then "God, being the lover of virtue and the lover of what is good and beautiful and also the lover of man (φιλάνθρωπον), would provide for our race good things all coming forth spontaneously and all in readiness" (*Creation* 81). But because Adam succumbed to the allures of passion, he could not avoid "due punishment of impious courses" (*Creation* 80). As a slave to passion, Adam "incurred labors and distress" and his "life was spent in unbroken toils in the pursuit of food and livelihood to save him from perishing by famine" (*Creation* 167–68). The evil that entered the Garden of Eden caused "the ever-flowing springs of the gifts of God" (τῶν τοῦ θεοῦ χαρίτων) to be closed (*Creation* 168). This metaphorical description of God's grace implies that prior to their disobedience, Adam and Eve enjoyed an abundance of God's provision. But now they constantly face life-threatening situations. God closed his ever-flowing springs so that they would not nourish "those felt to be undeserving (ἀναξίοις) of them" (*Creation* 168). The penalty for losing "the warfare in the soul" is "difficulty in obtaining the necessities of life" (*Creation* 80). This penalty affected the entire human race:

> If the human race had had to undergo the fitting penalty, it must needs have been wiped out by reason of its ingratitude to God its benefactor and preserver (τὴν πρὸς τὸν εὐεργέτην καὶ σωτῆρα θεὸν ἀχαριστίαν). But he being merciful took pity on it and moderated the punishment, suffering the race to continue, but no longer as before supplying it with food ready to its hand, that men might not, by indulging the twin evils of idleness and satiety, wax insolent in wrongdoing (*Creation* 169).

It is not just Adam and Eve who are slaves (*Creation* 167–68) but every person who acts like Adam. For if we yield to temptation as Adam did, our reason "is forthwith ensnared and becomes a subject instead of a ruler, a slave instead of a master, an alien instead of a citizen, and a mortal instead of an immortal" (*Creation* 165).

Philo also argues that humanity is suffering due to ingratitude. God is gracious, yet man has failed to show thankfulness. God, in his mercy, allows the human race to continue but without "food ready to its hand." Having become a slave to passion, the Adamic race can no longer enjoy

---

6. Also see *Creation* 136 where Philo designates Adam as "the first man" and "ancestor of our whole race."

the abundance of God's grace. In a Platonic and allegorical mold, Philo argues that man's rebellion resulted, not in the separation of the soul from the body, which is the death common to all humanity, but in the death of the soul, by which he means "the decay of virtue and the bringing in of wickedness" (*Alleg. Interp.* 1.32.106). This death is the imprisonment of the soul in the dungeon of "passions and wickedness (πάθεσι καὶ κακίαις) of all kinds" (*Alleg. Interp.* 1.33.106). For in the conflict between the body and the soul, the former prevails over the latter (*Alleg. Interp.* 1.33.106–7) so much that "the soul dies to the life of virtue, and is alive only to that of wickedness" (*Alleg. Interp.* 1.33.108). By succumbing to pleasure, the first man and his descendants have brought upon themselves "the life of mortality and wretchedness in lieu of that of immortality and bliss" (*Creation* 152). They have chosen "that fleeting and mortal existence which is not an existence but a period of time full of misery" (*Creation* 156). The soul can only be rescued when the body dies: "[S]hould we die, the soul lives forthwith its own proper life, and is released from the body, the baneful corpse to which it was tied" (*Alleg. Interp.* 1.33.108).

Elsewhere, Philo states that the Lord God gave man commandments and exhortations "in order that, should he obey the exhortations, he may be deemed worthy by God of his benefactions (ὑπὸ τοῦ θεοῦ εὐεργεσιῶν ἀξιωθείη); but that, should he rebel, he may be driven from the presence of the Lord who has a master's authority over him" (*Alleg. Interp.* 1.30.95–96). The implication here is that obedience keeps humanity within the realm of χάρις whereby they can enjoy God's blessings. But disobedience causes humanity to be driven from the presence of the Lord and to be deprived of the Lord's χάρις. Summarizing why God cast man out of the Garden of Eden (Gen 3:23), Philo writes:

> This is to show that, since "the Lord" as master and "God" as benefactor (ὡς δεσπότης ὁ κύριος καὶ ὡς εὐεργέτης ὁ θεός) had issued the commands, so in both capacities does he inflict punishment on him who had disobeyed (τὸν παρακούσαντα) them. For he dismisses the disobedient by the exercise of the very powers which he had exercised in urging him to obedience (*Alleg. Interp.* 1.30.96).

In brief, Philo reads the account of the fall of man as found in Genesis through the lens of divine benefaction even as he asserts in an allegorical manner and a Platonic fashion that the great conflict occurs in the soul. God is the "Lord" and "benefactor" who bestows gifts for humanity's enjoyment. In turn, humanity is expected to choose virtue, resist temptation, show gratitude, and obey God's commandment. But since man has succumbed to irrational passions, disobeyed, and failed to show gratitude (cf. *Alleg. Interp.* 1.31.99), God has cast him out of his presence; due to disobedience and disloyalty, he can no longer enjoy the abundance of God's χάρις. Instead, humanity must toil and face the imminent danger of perishing. Humanity's life after the fall is now marked by disobedience, death (by which Philo means slavery to passions and wickedness), and scarcity of life's necessities.

Josephus's Portrait of Adam

Josephus's reading of Genesis 3 bears some similarities to Philo's. Adam is "the man formed first out of earth" (*Ant.* 1:67; cf. 8:62); he enjoyed the fruit of land and the sea (*Ant.* 3:87). God had decreed for Adam and his descendants "to live a life of bliss, unmolested by all ill," and had through his providence ordained that "all things that contribute to enjoyment and pleasure were . . . to spring up for you spontaneously, without toil or distress of yours" (*Ant.* 1:46). These blessings would have ensured that "old age would not soon have overtaken you and your life would have been long" (*Ant.* 1:46). But Adam (and Eve) yielded to the serpent's deception and temptation to envy. Josephus characterizes Adam's act as unrighteousness, transgression, disobedience, and sin (*Ant.* 1:45–49). Adam is now bereft of virtue and plagued with an evil conscience (*Ant.* 1:47). God, therefore, punishes Adam by declaring that "the earth would no more produce anything of herself, but, in return for toil and grinding labor, would but afford some of her fruits and refuse others" (*Ant.* 1:49). Moreover, he "removed Adam and Eve from the Garden to another place" (*Ant.* 1:51).

Did Adam's sin affect his descendants? Josephus's account of the life of Cain and Abel shows that humanity would no longer enjoy the good life. Cain, who "was thoroughly depraved and had an eye only to gain," murdered his brother Abel (*Ant.* 1:52–66). Josephus employs decline narrative to underline the utter wickedness of Cain and his descendants:

> Thus, within Adam's lifetime, the descendants of Cain went to depths of depravity, and, inheriting and imitating one another's vices, each ended worse than the last. They rushed incontinently into battle and plunged into brigandage; or if anyone was too

timid for slaughter, he would display other forms of mad recklessness by insolence and greed (*Ant.* 1:66).

Adam himself died at the age of nine hundred and thirty (*Ant.* 1:68). Before he died, he bore many other children, among them Seth. Seth and his descendants, down to the seventh generation, embraced virtue and believed in "God as Lord of the universe," yet they too died (*Ant.* 1:68-72). The later generation "abandoned the customs of their fathers for a life of depravity. They no longer rendered to God his due honors, nor took account of justice towards men . . . and thereby drew upon themselves the enmity of God" (*Ant.* 1:72-73). Josephus's account implies that after Adam's sin, humanity's life is now marked by injustice, evil of every kind, and ultimately death. Even those who are virtuous cannot escape death. So whereas Josephus does not employ explicit benefaction language in his reading of Genesis, he like Philo, maintains that Adam's action was catastrophic, as it shortened humanity's lifespan, caused God to withhold his blessings, deprived man of God's companionship, and resulted in toil and pain. Because of sin, humanity can no longer enjoy the good life (cf. *Ant.* 1:14).

Philo's and Josephus's reading of Genesis offer important insights into Paul's argument on the dominion of sin and death as well as the dominion of χάρις. In the discussion that follows, we will see that there are significant parallels and contrasts between Paul's argument and Philo's and Josephus's characterization of Adam's sin and its consequences. Both Philo and Josephus also speak of the pervasive effect of humanity's disobedience, but as we shall see there is a marked difference, especially between Philo and Paul regarding the moral effect of Adam's sin. Similarly, the way both writers describe God's generosity using the motif of superabundance is analogous to how Paul depicts the dominion of χάρις.

The Dominion of Sin and Death

Like Philo and Josephus, Paul maintains that humanity is facing the predicament of sin and death. In Paul's perception, the two powers operative in the world are the power of sin leading to death (Rom 5:12-14, 20) and the power of grace leading to eternal life (5:17, 19, 21). In Rom 5:12-14, Paul states the problem, which is simply that sin entered the world through Adam; sin in turn resulted in death. There are at least two significant points that Paul makes in these verses and those that follow.

First, Paul carefully defines the realm in which God's grace erupts to highlight human unworthiness. Adam's realm is marked by sin and death (5:12). Paul depicts sin and death as cosmic powers that have subdued humanity.[7] He states twice that "death reigned" (ἐβασίλευσεν ὁ θάνατος, 5:14, 17) and once that "sin reigned in death" (ἐβασίλευσεν ἡ ἁμαρτία ἐν τῷ θανάτῳ, 5:21). To underscore the domineering effect of sin, Paul uses the term ἁμαρτία ("sin") and its cognates ten times (5:12 [3x], 13 [2x], 14, 16, 19, 20, 21), and the synonym παράπτωμα ("trespass") seven times (5:15 [2x], 16 [2x], 17, 18, 20). He also uses the nouns παράβασις ("transgression," 5:14) and παρακοή ("disobedience," 5:19). Moreover, Paul uses the term θάνατος ("death") and its cognates six times (5:12 [2x], 14, 15, 17, 21). The prevalence of these terms in this passage emphatically shows that humanity is held captive to sin and death and that they are completely unfit for the Messiah's gift. What humanity deserves is judgment leading to condemnation (5:16, 18).

Philo also speaks of the detrimental consequences of Adam's sin, but unlike Paul he does not view sin and death as cosmic powers.[8] Because Adam was overcome by passion, he incurred "due punishment of impious courses" (*Creation* 80). His life was now characterized by labors, distress, and "unbroken toils in the pursuit of food and livelihood to save him from perishing by famine" (*Creation* 167–68). Due to Adam's sin, the "ever-flowing springs of the gifts of God" (τῶν τοῦ θεοῦ χαρίτων) were closed, for Adam and his descendants were no longer deserving of them (*Creation* 168). Adam has been driven from the presence of God because his disobedience shows that he is not worthy of God's benefactions (*Alleg. Interp.* 1.30.95–96). The consequence of losing "the warfare in the soul" is "difficulty in obtaining the necessities of life" (*Creation* 80). Humanity no longer has "food ready to its hand" (*Creation* 169). Similarly, Philo states that Adam's disobedience leads to the death of the soul.[9] This happens when wickedness overpowers virtue in the soul so much that "the soul dies to the life of virtue, and is alive only to that of wickedness" (*Embassy* 1.33.108). Thus, both Philo and Paul view Adam's sin as an act of rebellion and disobedience that creates unworthiness. But unlike Philo who is influenced by Platonic dualism, Paul does not view

---

7. Croasmun rightly states that sin is a cosmic power that exercises great agency in the world (*Emergence of Sin*, 105). Also see Gaventa, "Cosmic Power of Sin," 113–35.

8. By "cosmic" we mean simply that which extends to the entire human world.

9. On the death of the soul in Philo, see Wasserman, *Death of the Soul*, 61–76; Conroy, "Philo's 'Death of the Soul,'" 23–40; Zeller, "Life and Death," 19–55.

death as the imprisonment of the soul in the dungeon of passions and wickedness. Rather, just like sin, death is a destructive power that morally incapacitates humanity (cf. Rom 6:14, 15–23). In Rom 1:18–32 and 3:9–20, Paul sets man's dilemma as a bodily predicament. Humanity is charged with immorality, idolatry, deception, murder, bitterness, and all sorts of evil. And in 7:14, the "I" is "fleshly sold under the power of sin." The "I" of 7:7–25 is "intrinsically morally incapacitated"[10] because he is under the power of Adam's dominion which is marked by sin and death. Therefore, when Paul argues that sin and death reign, he asserts that as Adam's dominion exerts its power through sin and death, it renders humanity fundamentally flawed and unworthy. No one is capable of laying claim to χάρις.

The second important point that Paul makes is the pervasive effect of sin and death. Sin and death exercise dominion over the entire human race. Sin and death invaded the world through one man, and "death spread to all men because all sinned" (5:12). Paul states in 5:17 that "because of one man's trespass, death reigned through that one man" (τῷ τοῦ ἑνὸς παραπτώματι ὁ θάνατος ἐβασίλευσεν διὰ τοῦ ἑνός). Adam's "one trespass resulted in condemnation for all people" (εἰς πάντας ἀνθρώπους εἰς κατάκριμα, 5:18), and by his disobedience "the many were made sinners" (ἁμαρτωλοὶ κατεστάθησαν οἱ πολλοί, 5:19). That Paul indicts the entire human race here just as he does in 1:18—3:20 is clear enough. What is contested is the precise role of Adam in relation to the spread of sin and death to his posterity.

A common way of reading 5:12–21 is through the lens of "corporate personality." Moo represents this reading when he writes:

> "[A]ll sinned" must be given some kind of "corporate" meaning: "sinning" not as voluntary acts of sin in "one's own person," but sinning "in and with" Adam . . . The point is . . . that the sin here attributed to the "all" is to be understood . . . as a sin that in some manner is identical to the sin committed by Adam. Paul can therefore say both "all die because all sin" and "all die because Adam sinned" with no hint of conflict because the sin of Adam *is* the sin of all. All people, therefore, stand condemned "in Adam," guilty by reason of the sin all committed "in him" (italics original).[11]

---

10. Jipp, *Christ Is King*, 183.
11. Moo, *Epistle to the Romans*, 326.

Moo adds that for Paul, Adam "was a corporate figure, whose sin could be regarded at the same time as the sin of all his descendants."[12] Notwithstanding its popularity, this reading is problematic because among other things it is mistakenly based on the assumption that Paul is concerned in this passage with how Adam and Christ "encompass humanity within themselves."[13] Paul, however, is concerned with two opposing kingdoms—that of sin and death, and that of χάρις and life. Adam represents the former while Christ the latter. Based on Paul's statement in 5:12 that "sin entered the world through one man, and death through sin," we may view Adam as the "epochal" entrance into his dominion of sin and death.[14] Paul does not say that "all sinned" *in Adam* in some figurative sense as "corporate personality" asserts, but that "in this way death spread to all men, because all sinned."[15] Constantine R. Campbell rightly comments:

> Paul is not suggesting that Adam's sin is imputed to all humanity, but that he opened the door to a dark domain through which all people subsequently walked, because "all sinned" in a concrete rather than figurative way. Consequently, Adam's role is that he marks the beginning of this dark domain; he held the door open as all humanity walked through.[16]

For Paul, humanity is enslaved to sin and death, not because everyone sinned "in Adam," but because "the many" are held captive to sin and death just as Adam was (5:15). Death reigned through Adam (5:17) because, as the "epochal figure" and "entry point," he holds the

---

12. Moo, *Epistle to the Romans*, 328.

13. Kreitzer, "Christ and Second Adam," 87. Critiquing the "corporate personality" reading, Campbell asks, "Why is all humanity outside Christ encompassed by Adam? Why is humanity incorporated into him? Why should Adam's actions be 'imputed' to all?" (*Paul and Union*, 344).

14. Campbell, *Paul and Union*, 344. Dunn comments, "Paul indicates that he wants this figure [Adam] to be seen not so much as an individual in his own right, but as a more than individual figure, what we might call an 'epochal figure'—that is, as the one who initiated the first major phase of human history and thereby determined the character of that phase for those belonging to it" (*Romans 1–8*, 289).

15. Cf. 2 Bar. 54:15, 19: "For if Adam sinned first and brought untimely death on all, each of those who descended from him, each individual has brought future pain upon himself. Adam is thus the cause for himself alone; each of us has become his own Adam, each for himself." The stress on personal responsibility cannot be clearer.

16. Campbell, *Paul and Union*, 345. Also see Dunn, *Romans 1–8*, 290.

gate open and ushers the entire human race into the domain of death.[17] Everyone is condemned (5:18) and "through the one man's disobedience the many were made sinners" (5:19) because, for Paul, all without exception entered into the domain of sin and death. Everyone is in the sphere of Adam "because all sinned" (5:12). Paul even adds in 5:13–14 that although sinners were not held accountable before the giving of the law, "death reigned (ἐβασίλευσεν ὁ θάνατος) from Adam to Moses even over those who did not sin in the likeness of the transgression of Adam." Moses marks a historical terminus which begins with Adam. From Adam to Moses, there was no law and therefore no transgression in the sense of breaking an explicit commandment. Yet, death still reigned from Adam to Moses.

We have seen above that Philo regards Adam as "the first father of the race," "the first man," and "the ancestor of our whole race" (*Creation* 79, 136). Due to all provisions of life that God had made, Adam's descendants "were to spend their days without toil or trouble surrounded by lavish abundance of all that they needed" (*Creation* 79). But Adam succumbed to passions and became a slave of wickedness. Like Paul, Philo writes about the pervasive effect of humanity's disobedience, but unlike Paul who views Adam as the entrance through which the entire human race inevitably becomes unworthy of grace, Philo asserts that "Adam creates the *possibility* of unworthiness" (italics original).[18] Only those who act *like* Adam and yield to temptation *like* Adam will have their reason ensnared and become "a subject instead of a ruler, a slave instead of a master, an alien instead of a citizen, and a mortal instead of an immortal" (*Creation* 165). Philo maintains that Adam's sin caused "the everlasting fountains of God's gifts" to be held back so that the unworthy would not receive them (*Creation* 168). The implication here is that although Adam is "the first father of the race," his disobedience does not determine the moral character of his descendants. Those who refuse to succumb to temptation are still capable of doing good, and hence worthy of God's gifts. For Paul, however, Adam's disobedience made many sinners (Rom 5:19) and "death spread to all men because all sinned" (Rom 5:12).

Paul's argument is in many ways similar to that of Josephus. Josephus characterizes Adam's act as unrighteousness, transgression, disobedience, and sin (*Ant.* 1:45–49). Because Adam gave in to the serpent's deception

---

17. Campbell, *Paul and Union*, 345.
18. McFarland, *God and Grace*, 124.

and temptation to envy, he is now plagued with an evil conscience (*Ant.* 1:47). Adam's descendants are God's enemies since they no longer honor God (*Ant.* 1:72–73). They cannot enjoy the good life; instead, their life is marked by injustice, evil, and ultimately death. Had Adam and his posterity obeyed God, they would not have been overtaken by old age and their life would have been long (*Ant.* 1:46). Thus, although Josephus does not explicitly state, like Paul, that death reigns, he views death as the ultimate punishment for disobedience. But Paul is more emphatic in his argument as he personifies sin and death and depicts them as enslaving powers that have held humanity sway. No one can do anything that would merit God's favor; instead, the entire human race must be rescued. This rescue comes through the reign of χάρις.

The Dominion of Grace

Paul begins Rom 5:15 with a contrastive declarative statement: "But the gift (χάρισμα) is not like the trespass."[19] This declaration elicits the question: How is the gift different from the trespass? Paul makes at least three points in response. First, the gift overflows. Three times Paul uses the motif of "superabundance" (περισσεία) to underscore both the generosity of the giver and the incommensurability of the gift. Thus, Paul states that "the grace (χάρις) of God and the gift (δωρεά) in the grace (χάρις) of the one man Jesus the Messiah abounded (ἐπερίσσευσεν) to the many" while the many were still dead (5:15). Romans 5:17 might be viewed as an expansive restatement of 5:15; Paul emphasizes in the former that "those who receive the abundance of grace and the gift of righteousness" (τὴν περισσείαν τῆς χάριτος καὶ τῆς δωρεᾶς τῆς δικαιοσύνης) have been rescued from the reign of death. And in 5:20, Paul asserts that "where sin increased, grace abounded all the more" (ὑπερεπερίσσευσεν ἡ χάρις).[20] There must be a reason why Paul emphasizes that χάρις overflows in the face of sin and death.

---

19. For the argument that 5:15a should be viewed as a rhetorical question rather than a contrastive declarative statement, see Caragounis, "Romans 5.15–16," 143; Porter, "Argument of Romans 5," 673–74; McFarland, *God and Grace*, 125–26; Jewett, *Romans*, 379–82.

20. On the language of abundance, also see 2 Cor 4:15; 8:7; 9:8; Eph 1:7b–8; 1 Tim 1:14. For another use of the rare verb ὑπερπερισσεύω, see 2 Cor 7:4.

The metaphor of superabundance is frequently used by Philo, who portrays God as a generous giver whose gifts overflow incessantly to the people:

> The title "God Eternal" is equivalent to "he that is, not sometimes gracious (χαριζόμενος) and sometimes not so, but continuously and always; he that without intermission bestows benefits (εὐεργετῶν); he that causes his gifts (δωρεῶν) to follow each other in ceaseless flow; he who makes his favors (χάριτας) come round in unbroken cycle, knitting them together by unifying forces; he who lets no opportunity of doing good go by (*Planting* 89–90).

Because God "loves to give" (φιλόδωρος), he bestows (χαρίζεται) good things on all and displays "his overflowing wealth" (τὸν περιττὸν πλοῦτον) to everyone (*Alleg. Interp.* 1:34). The fountain of God's gracious boons overflows in the world (*Drunkenness* 32). Commenting on Exod 16:4, Philo writes that the Israelites were to gather a day's portion of bread daily because it would be impossible to "contain all at once the abundant wealth of the gifts of God (τὸν πολὺν πλοῦτον τῶν τοῦ θεοῦ χαρίτων), but would be overwhelmed by them as by the rush of a torrent" (*Alleg. Interp.* 3:163). God is "the benefactor of the whole world who through his power gives out a bountiful abundance of goods (περιουσίας ἀγαθῶν ἐκδίδωσιν) to every part of the universe" (*Embassy* 118). God's abundant provision ensures that there "is not a single person in want, for his needs are supplied by the wealth of nature ... no one lacks, but everybody everywhere has an ample and more than ample sufficiency" (πολλὴν ἄγουσι περιουσίαν, *Virtues* 6).

Other ancient writers also speak of the abundance of gifts and the good life that the beneficent ruler promotes. Aristotle writes that because a king is better supplied "with goods of every kind than his subjects," he can advance the interests of his subjects (*Eth. nic.* 8.10.2). Such a king is a magnificent man whose gifts include votive offerings, sacrifices, public buildings, sponsoring games, equipping a ship of war, and giving a banquet to the public (*Eth. nic.* 4.2.11). He brings freedom to his subjects and delivers them from any imminent danger (*Pol.* 5.8.33–46). Cicero states that the man who is engaged in public service takes measures to ensure "an abundance of the necessities of life" (*Off.* 2.21.74). Because the good king is naturally inclined to generosity, he secures freedom for the oppressed, provides help for the helpless, protects the weak, sponsors games, hosts public banquets, supplies grains, ransoms prisoners, constructs temples, and engages in all sorts of works which serve the community (*Off.* 2.12.41–42; 2.17.58–60; 2.18.64). Seneca maintains that the ideal ruler's inexhaustible wealth leads him to humbly care for his subjects by using his power for their well-being and coming to their aid with timely assistance (*Ben.* 2.13.2–3). The gods entrust to the king an exalted position that enables him to give many gifts (*Ben.* 5.4.2; *Clem.* 1.3.3). Dio urges Trajan to emulate the limitless generosity of Heracles who "believed that everything belonged to him exclusively" and "made presents to many men, not only of money without limit and lands and herds of horses and cattle, but also of whole kingdoms and cities" (*1 Regn.* 62–63). The king is the savior and protector (σωτὴρ καὶ φύλαξ) of humanity (*3 Regn.* 6); he dispenses blessings "with the most lavish hand, as though the supply were inexhaustible" (*1 Regn.* 24). The ideal king "does not grow weary of showering gifts" (οὐδέποτε κάμνει χαριζόμενος) upon humanity (*3 Regn.* 73–81). Pliny's *Panegyricus* presents the ideal emperor as a universal benefactor who labors hard for the safety of humanity and whose gifts bring joy, relief, and prosperity to all. Horace praises Augustus for bringing peace to his subjects (*Saec.* 4.5.33–36) and enhancing abundant crop production (*Saec.* 4.5.37–41). And Josephus asserts that Agrippa's generosity endeared the people to him (*Ant.* 16:65; 18:144).

We also see in the OT that the good king's rule is characterized by prosperity. The king ensures abundant supply of "bread" (Ps 72:3, 6, 16; cf. Isa 25:6–9; Joel 2:24). His enthronement is likened to fresh rain falling on the earth and causing the land to produce abundant fruit (Ps 72:6; cf. 2 Sam 23:3–4; Hos 6:3; Mic 5:7). Due to abundant grain and gold, the people thrive like "the grass of the field" (Ps 72:16). According to Ps 132:15–16, Yahweh's son satisfies the poor with bread, procures salvation for the people, and brings great joy to Zion. The king transmits such blessings as full granaries, healthy and productive flock and cattle, and a peaceful existence (Ps 144:13–14).

Although Jewish and Greco-Roman writers do not always employ explicit "abundance" language, there is a consistent portrait of the ideal ruler as a generous giver of gifts. Such a ruler brings great joy and prosperity to the people even as he seeks to promote their welfare. When Paul is read within this ancient framework of royal benefaction, at least one parallel point and one significant contrast are evident. The similarity is that just as the ancient writers discussed above argue that the ideal ruler is generous, so Paul also uses the motif of "superabundance" to portray

God's generosity in the Messiah.[21] Brendan Byrne states, "Behind the act of Christ stood the overflowing power and generosity of the Creator."[22] Yet the Messianic abundance is unique because of the *singularity* of χάρις. Whereas all the ancient writers discussed above assert that abundant generosity is evident in *plurality* of gifts or benefactions, Paul consistently speaks in Rom 5:15–20 of a singular abundant gift. Paul's argument here must have surprised the ancient ear that was accustomed to associating generosity and abundance with multiplicity. What, then, does Paul mean when he declares that χάρις abounds?

Robert Jewett argues that Paul uses the verb περισσεύειν ("to abound") with the sense of "the removal of boundaries or limitations in the description of the gifts of the new age" and links the term to the "idea that the future age would reinstate the plentitude of paradise... He [Paul] believed that with the dawn of the new age, paradisal plenitude was flowing out into the world."[23] Jewett rightly reads Paul in light of the messianic age, but his suggestion that "abundance" points to "the *gifts* of the new age" (italics added) misses out on Paul's emphasis on the singularity of χάρις. Harrison posits that Paul avoids the plural χάριτες because of his monotheism: "God's grace would have been all too easily confused with the Greek goddesses, the *Charites*, if the plural was used."[24] But this explanation is doubtful, for Philo is also a monotheist yet, as we have seen above, he uses the plural χάριτες. It appears that Paul uses the singular because just as he has Adam's one destiny defining act of trespass, so does he have one destiny defining χάρις in view, namely God's gift of the Messiah.[25] Paul seems to echo Rom 5:8 where he states that God demonstrates his love for us through the death of the Messiah.

Χάρις is singular yet superabundant due to its incommensurability. In Greco-Roman society, gifts are often apportioned on the basis of merit. Virtue is rewarded with favors while impiety is punished by withholding gifts. Paul, however, stresses the incongruity of the Messiah's χάρις by declaring that it overflows in the face of sin and death. In the words of

---

21. See Rom 3:7; 15:13; 2 Cor 9:8.
22. Byrne, *Romans*, 179.
23. Jewett, *Romans*, 381.
24. Harrison, *Paul's Language of Grace*, 285.
25. Moo comments that in 5:15 χάρισμα denotes "the act of Christ himself considered as a 'work of grace.' Paul chooses this unusual way of designating the work of Christ to accentuate its gracious character and its power: Christ's act, being a work of God's grace (*Charis*), is far more potent than Adam's act" (*Epistle to the Romans*, 335).

Barclay, "God's grace through Christ is marked as extravagant precisely in its *incongruity* with the human condition" (italics original).[26] As we saw in our discussion of the Messiah's non-calculating atonement in the previous chapter, the Messiah takes full cognizance of human unworthiness but does not withhold his gift from the "weak," "ungodly," "sinners," and "enemies" (5:6–10). The Christ-gift overturns the norms of the ancient benefaction system according to which a gift must be commensurate with the worthiness of the receiver. The abundant divine gift that Paul describes in 5:12–21 is given, not on the basis of worth—whether racial, ethnic, social, or biological—but against the backdrop of humanity's imprisonment to sin and death. Barclay states, "The Christ-gift has arisen not in response to human obedience, but out of an avalanche of sin."[27] Orrey McFarland also underscores this emphasis on incommensurability when he writes, "Excess is primarily a result of incongruity, a lack of fit between Giver, gift, and recipient; the gift abounds because a righteous God gives to sinful humanity what it does not deserve."[28] The first point, then, that Paul makes in relation to the dominion of χάρις is that the gift of the Messiah erupts and overflows in the sphere marked by sin and death.

The second point that demonstrates that "the gift is not like the trespass" is that the gift comes through the agency of the Messiah.[29] We saw in chapters 2 and 3 that as the vicegerent of the gods, the king is the agent by which the gods dispense their gifts to humanity. He protects his people and delivers them from their enemies. Augustus, for instance, supplied "bread" and liberated "the people from the present fear and danger" (*Res Gestae* 5:2). He brought freedom from enemies leading to peace in the entire empire (*Res Gestae* 1:1; 2:5; 6:13; 26–33). We also see in the OT that the king is the agent of divine blessings to the people; he fights Yahweh's battles and delivers the people from their enemies. The king is a mighty warrior who triumphs over all his enemies and establishes a righteous dominion. Likewise, Paul repeatedly asserts that Jesus is the one who delivers humanity. According to Rom 5:15, Jesus the Messiah is the one man whose gift abounds to the many. In 5:17, Paul declares that "those who receive the abundance of grace and the gift of righteousness will

26. Barclay, *Paul and the Gift*, 495.
27. Barclay, "Under Grace," 65.
28. McFarland, *God and Grace*, 128.
29. We are using "agency" in the general sense of the person through whom something is accomplished. See BDAG 223–26; Campbell, *Paul and Union*, 238.

reign in life through the one man Jesus the Messiah" (διὰ τοῦ ἑνὸς Ἰησοῦ Χριστοῦ). In 5:18, Paul states that unlike Adam's one trespass, which leads to condemnation for all, the Messiah's one act of righteousness leads to acquittal of life for all. The Messiah is the one man whose obedience makes many righteous (5:19). Paul closes the chapter by declaring that "grace reigns through righteousness leading to eternal life through Jesus the Messiah our Lord" (διὰ Ἰησοῦ Χριστοῦ τοῦ κυρίου ἡμῶν, 5:21).[30] This repeated emphasis on the agency of the Messiah leaves no doubt that the reign of χάρις is the dominion of the Messiah and that the extravagant and incommensurate gift "happens precisely and exclusively in Jesus."[31] Just as Adam provides access into the domain of sin and death so Jesus provides access into the domain of grace and righteousness (cf. 5:2).

The last point that we want to discuss in regard to the dominion of χάρις is the effect of the Christ-gift. The ideal ruler brings freedom to his subjects and delivers them from any imminent external danger (Aristotle, *Pol.* 5.8.33–46; Dio, *3 Regn.* 6; Augustus, *Res Gestae* 5:2). He is referred to as a father, a shepherd, a guardian, a savior, and a general not only because of his generosity but also because he toils hard to protect his people and deliver them from their enemies. For Paul, the leading enemies of humanity are sin and death. The Christ-gift overpowers sin and death, delivers Christ's followers, and establishes them in righteousness. Just as in Rom 5:9 and 5:10, Paul uses the *a minori ad maius* arguments (πολλῷ μᾶλλον) in 5:15 and 5:17 to contrast the effect of Adam's act with that of Christ. Whereas Adam's act leads to the death of the many, "God's grace and the gift in the grace" (ἡ χάρις τοῦ θεοῦ καὶ ἡ δωρεὰ ἐν χάριτι) abounds to the many. The contrast shows that there is no balance between the gift and the trespass.[32] Rather, the gift reverses the effects of Adam's act by stopping the "relentless momentum of sin" and establishing "a counter-momentum leading out of sin into life."[33] The question, however, is: What is the relationship between ἡ χάρις and ἡ δωρεά (5:15b)?

Dunn is representative of those who take ἡ χάρις τοῦ θεοῦ καὶ ἡ δωρεά ("the grace of God and the gift") as a hendiadys, meaning that

---

30. For further discussion of the prepositional phrase διὰ . . . Χριστοῦ in Romans 5, see Campbell, *Paul and Union*, 239–42.

31. McFarland, *God and Grace*, 131.

32. Wright, "Letter to the Romans," 528.

33. Barclay, *Paul and the Gift*, 496. Barclay adds: "The gift does not start from a point of equilibrium, nor does it return matters to the status quo: it takes place in the context of multiplied sin to enable the very opposite of what is deserved."

"the grace of God" is "(merely) God's gracious disposition" while "the gift" denotes God's "gracious giving."[34] Based on this reading, this double expression may be rendered as "the gracious gift of God." But the fact that the article occurs before each of these nouns makes this reading doubtful. Moreover, Barclay notes: "The grace Paul speaks about here is not a general characteristic of God, but is tied to a specific event."[35] The more likely option is that ἡ χάρις and ἡ δωρεά each have distinct but related significance. Moo seems to favor this reading when he suggests that "grace" more likely "denotes the motive or manner in which God works, while 'the gift' is the specific manifestation of this grace—the righteous status and life conferred on 'the many.'"[36] But the problem with taking "grace" as denoting "motive or manner" is that by generalizing how God works (namely he works graciously), it fails to underscore the likelihood that Paul has in view a *specific act* of God. If Paul is concerned with "motive or manner," then this is underlined by the verb περισσεύειν. The articular noun ἡ χάρις points to one specific act that parallels, and yet surpasses, the one act of Adam. Most likely, ἡ χάρις τοῦ θεοῦ denotes God's gift of the Messiah while ἡ δωρεά denotes the gift of righteousness that comes through the Messiah's self-sacrifice and victorious resurrection. Based on this reading, the phrase "in the grace by the one man Jesus the Messiah" (ἐν χάριτι τῇ τοῦ ἑνὸς ἀνθρώπου Ἰησοῦ Χριστοῦ, 5:15b) not only parallels τὸ χάρισμα ("the gift") and ἡ χάρις τοῦ θεοῦ ("the grace of God," 5:15a) but it is also a more precise definition of the source of ἡ δωρεά.[37] The parallel means that χάρις is both God's gift of the Messiah and the Messiah's self-gift to humanity.[38] Otfried Hofius rightly comments that "the grace of God *is* as such the grace of our Lord Jesus Christ" (italics original).[39]

Romans 5:17 closely parallels 5:15 and more fully defines ἡ δωρεά. Paul writes that "those who receive the abundance of grace and the gift of righteousness (τῆς χάριτος καὶ τῆς δωρεᾶς τῆς δικαιοσύνης) shall reign in life through the one man Jesus the Messiah" (5:17). Paul here defines ἡ δωρεά as "the gift of righteousness" (ἡ δωρεά τῆς δικαιοσύνης). In other

---

34. Dunn, *Romans 1–8*, 279–80. Also see Käsemann, *Commentary on Romans*, 153–54.

35. Barclay, *Paul and the Gift*, 495.

36. Moo, *Epistle to the Romans*, 335n96.

37. Hofius, "Adam-Christ Antithesis," 188; McFarland, *God and Grace*, 127.

38. For Scripture references that suggest that the grace of God and the grace of Christ are one, see 2 Cor 6:1; 8:9; Gal 1:6; 2:21.

39. Hofius, "Adam-Christ Antithesis," 188.

words, ἡ δωρεά ("the gift," 5:15) parallels τῆς δωρεᾶς τῆς δικαιοσύνης ("the gift of righteousness," 5:17). The gift of righteousness (5:17b, 21b), therefore, is a result of χάρις. As Käsemann writes, grace denotes "the power which takes concrete shape in the gift as its result."[40] Paul has already noted in 5:1 and 5:9 that believers obtain righteousness through the Messiah who died for us (5:6-8). As we saw in the previous chapter, the gift of righteousness denotes the gift of eschatological life. Paul even states in 5:21b that χάρις reigns "through righteousness leading to eternal life through Jesus the Messiah our Lord." The Messiah is able to bestow this life because he has been vindicated by being raised from the dead. Unlike Adam whose disobedience (5:19) brings condemnation and death (5:16, 18), the Messiah's faithfulness (5:1) and obedience brings justification (5:16), makes the many righteous (5:19), and "results in justification of life for all" (5:18).[41] Because the obedient and righteous Messiah has defeated humanity's most powerful enemies—sin and death—he is able to guarantee eschatological life to his followers.

The dominion of χάρις overpowers that of sin and death because the Messiah astoundingly reverses what Adam inaugurated.[42] Adam sins as the epochal figure of the human race and thereby holds the gate open for all his descendants to walk into his realm of sin and death. Jesus, however, is the righteous and faithful Messiah who holds the gate open for all his descendants to enter into his kingdom of grace and life. Whereas Adam's act plunged the world into sin and death, Christ's act triumphs over sin and death and results in righteousness and life.[43] The Messiah's gift overflows in the sense that it triumphs over sin and death, and it is

---

40. Käsemann, *Commentary on Romans*, 154.

41. On ἐκ πίστεως in Rom 5:1 as referring to Christ's faithfulness, see Young, "Paul's Ethnic Discourse," 30–51.

42. Wright comments that "the gift of grace is nothing short of new creation, creation not merely out of nothing but out of anti-creation, out of death itself" ("Letter to the Romans," 528).

43. On how Christ triumphs over sin and death, see Jipp, *Christ Is King*, 185–86. Paul writes that death no longer exercises lordship over Jesus (Rom 6:9) because God "sent his son in the likeness of sinful flesh and as an offering for sin, he condemned sin in the flesh" (Rom 8:3b). Death exercised lordship over the Messiah when he took in his crucified body the negative effects of Adam's dominion. Jipp writes that since Christ is the representative of humanity, his crucifixion means that "humanity's weak fleshly bodily existence is 'crucified' (6:6a), 'destroyed' (6:6b), and 'condemned' (8:3)" (*Christ Is King*, 186). And because Christ has risen from the dead, death no longer has dominion over him. On Rom 8:3, see Bell, "Sacrifice and Christology," 1–27; Branick, "Sinful Flesh," 246–62.

given to sinful, mortal, and ill-deserving humanity. This χάρις is surprising because the Christ-gift is offered to unworthy recipients and because it establishes the beneficiaries in righteousness.[44] Having vanquished sin and death—the powers that held humanity captive—the Messiah now enables his followers to participate in the inaugurated eschatological life even as they anticipate their bodily resurrection. As those who have received χάρις, Christ's followers are obligated to give loyalty and obedience to their Lord. Thus, the section that follows examines how Paul depicts grace as obligatory.

Grace as Obligatory

If χάρις abounds in the face of humanity's unworthiness, then do Christ's followers need to maximize their unworthiness so that the Messiah's benefaction might overflow unceasingly (Rom 6:1)? Paul's readers might easily conclude, based on his argument that the gift is offered to the undeserving, that χάρις undercuts the moral order by becoming a license for sin. In response to this anticipated objection, Paul describes in Romans 6 what it means to live out "newness of life" (6:4) under the dominion of χάρις.[45] If the law cannot curb sinning (cf. 7:7-25), then the Christ-gift is the only means by which believers can triumph over sin.[46] As we will see in this section, Paul argues that living "under grace" (6:14) demands faithful and loyal response to the lordship of the Messiah. Stated differently, the Christ-gift obligates his followers to give him loyalty and obedience and thereby be faithful to their new status in Christ.[47] Commenting on 6:14, Barclay writes, "When Paul says that believers are 'under grace' he means that grace carries demands."[48] Käsemann notes that "obligation and service are indissolubly bound up with the gift. When God enters the arena, our experience is that he maintains his lordship even in his giving"

---

44. Concerning the Christ-gift's incommensurability, McFarland states, "As humanity is marked by Adam, the gift is always incongruous; the only place for the gift to be given, and the site in which the gift is worked out, is where sin reigns" (*God and Grace*, 131).

45. We understand the genitive ζωῆς as attributive, meaning new life. See Wallace, *Greek Grammar*, 89-90.

46. Moo, *Epistle to the Romans*, 356.

47. Under the ethic of reciprocity, by obligation we simply mean discharging one's duty to honor the benefactor by appropriate conduct.

48. Barclay, "Under Grace," 61.

because through his gifts "he subordinates us to his lordship and makes us responsible beings."[49]

We have seen from our examination of some of the relevant Greco-Roman and Jewish sources that the good ruler bestows gifts while the subjects discharge their obligation by conducting themselves in ways that honor their ruler. As Crook argues, loyalty to one's benefactor must be demonstrated by a set of behaviors that promote the benefactor's reputation.[50] The "gift" in Greco-Roman society comes with inalienable ties of loyalty. Cicero maintains that even a poor man who cannot return a favor in kind is still under obligation to be thankful if he is a good man (*Off.* 2.20.69). When one has discharged a debt, a moral obligation to show gratitude and loyalty still abides. The moral obligation does not end because "when I pay [a moral debt] I keep, and when I keep, I pay by the very act of keeping" (Cicero, *Planc.* 28:68). Such a debt is paid by good wishes and expressing deep affection that demands supporting the benefactor in their hour of peril and holding his "safety dear above all things" (Cicero, *Planc.* 28:69). Cicero basically asserts that based on the ethic of reciprocity, the recipient of a favor should be ready to do everything imaginable to reciprocate the benefactor's gift. The one whose life the benefactor has preserved should never forget his unending indebtedness (*Planc.* 28:69).

Seneca writes that gift-giving is "the exchange of obligations" (*Ben.* 2.18.1-2) and that the gift lays the beneficiary under obligation to return a favor (*Ben.* 1.14.4; 2.35.1; 2.35.4; 5.11.5; 6.10.2). The one accepting a benefit is receiving a debt that he should never be ashamed of acknowledging. Rather, he should publicize his gratitude, for the "man who returns his thanks only when witnesses have been removed shows himself ungrateful" (*Ben.* 2.23.2).[51] Even philosophy teaches men to honorably "avow the debt of benefits received, and honorably to pay them . . . Our philosopher will therefore acknowledge that he owes a large debt to the ruler who makes it possible, by his management and foresight, for him to enjoy rich leisure, control of his own time, and a tranquility uninterrupted by public employments" (*Ep.* 73:9-10). A passage in *De Beneficiis* that summarizes the gift as obligatory reads:

---

49. Käsemann, *New Testament Questions*, 174.

50. Crook, *Reconceptualising Conversion*, 199-250.

51. For further discussion on verbalized gratitude in the Greco-Roman world, see Peterman, *Paul's Gift*, 73-83.

> The greater the favor, the more earnestly must we express ourselves, resorting to such compliments as: "You [the benefactor] have laid more people under obligation than you think" (for every one rejoices to know that a benefit of his extends farther than he thought); "you do not know what it is that you have bestowed upon me, but you have a right to know how much more it is than you think" (he who is overwhelmed shows gratitude forthwith); "I shall never be able to repay to you my gratitude, but, at any rate, I shall not cease from declaring everywhere that I am unable to repay it" (2.24.4).

Xenophon notes that it is conventional that everyone ought to show goodwill to the one who gives gifts (*Anab.* 7.7.46). He portrays Cyrus the Great in *Cyropaedia* as a generous king who excels "more in kindness (φιλανθρωπίᾳ) than in generalship" (*Cyr.* 8.4.6–8). All nations are devoted to Cyrus as they seek to please him by their loyalty to him and gifts, including "the most valuable productions of their country, whether the fruits of the earth, or animals bred there, or manufactures of their own arts" (*Cyr.* 8.6.23).

Aristotle states that "the one who is benefited in purse or character must repay what he can, namely honor" (*Eth. nic.* 8.14.3; cf. 9.2.3–4). A proper understanding of the initial gift (χάρις) would cause the recipient to return a favor; one ought to return the services received, and "do so willingly; for one ought not to make a man one's friend if one is unwilling to return his favors" (*Eth. nic.* 8.13.9). Men are angry with "those who do not return their kindnesses nor requite them in full" (ἀντιποιοῦσιν εὖ, μηδὲ τὴν ἴσην ἀνταποδιδοῦσιν, *Rhet.* 2.2.17). These are people who are ungrateful (τοῖς χάριν μὴ ἀποδιδοῦσιν) and who ignore "all sense of obligation" (*Rhet.* 2.2.23–24). Writing to the people of Rhodes, Dio affirms:

> [T]here is nothing nobler or more just than to show honor to our good men and to keep in remembrance those who have served us well... For those who take seriously their obligations toward their benefactors and mete out just treatment to those who have loved them, all men regard as worthy of their favor (*Rhod.* 31:7–8).

Pliny notes that due to the aid that Trajan gave to Egypt when they were facing famine and starvation, Egypt is now obligated to Rome and her people (*Pan.* 32:1–4). Pliny asks Egypt to inquire no more about Trajan's generosity but to take the seed sowed in her "soft embrace and return it multiplied," remembering that "you have a debt to repay" (*Pan.* 32:4).

Like their Greco-Roman counterparts, Philo and Josephus also maintain that χάρις is obligatory. According to Philo, if a person is truly pious, then he will "attribute everything to God" (*Alleg. Interp.* 3.9.29).[52] Every good thing that a person has is not his own; everything belongs to God who gives (*Heir.* 103). If everything is God's, then whoever receives a gift should return χάρις for χάρις: "[C]ount that which is given a loan or trust and render it back to him who entrusted and leased it to you, thus as is fit and just requiting grace with grace" (χάριν χάριτι, *Heir.* 104–5).[53] Instead of arrogantly attributing the causation of good things to ourselves, Philo urges that we ought to bring to God the "firstfruit of your reaping," by which he means "not of the land but of ourselves, that we may mow and reap ourselves by consecrating every nourishing, excellent, and worthy growth" (*Dreams* 2.11.75–77). Those who fail to discharge their duty of reciprocity face dire consequences of their ingratitude (*Embassy* 60) and are "sure to lack defenders" (*Moses* 1.11.58). To avoid the consequences of ingratitude, the priest of Midian instructed his daughters to run after Moses and bring him home so that he might receive "some requital of the favor which we owe to him" (ὀφείλεται γὰρ αὐτῷ χάρις, *Moses* 1.11.59). Those who fail to honor the emperor deserve "utmost penalty for not tendering our requital with all due fullness" (*Flaccus* 7:50). Josephus writes that the king of Ethiopia was under obligation to Amenophis because of gratitude (χάριτι γὰρ ἦν αὐτῷ ὑποχείριος, *Ag. Ap.* 1:246). Eleazar expressed the Jews' obligation to Ptolemy and their willingness to reciprocate in every way possible: "Be assured that we shall submit to anything that is of benefit to you, even though it exceeds our nature, for we ought to make a return for the kindness (ἀμείβεσθαι γὰρ ἡμᾶς δεῖ τὰς σὰς εὐεργεσίας) which you have shown our fellow-citizens in various ways" (*Ant.* 12:53–56).

The foregoing brief survey of χάρις as obligatory or the ethic of reciprocity provides an important framework for reading Paul's argument on life "under grace." Harrison is right to posit that χάρις is "the leitmotiv of the first-century reciprocity system," but his assertion that God's

---

52. On Philo's view of God as cause and creator of all things, see McFarland, *God and Grace*, 26–37. Barclay states, "God's gracious causation of all that exists is of critical importance for Philo in distinguishing his philosophy from impious alternatives, and in motivating the central core of piety, gratitude to God" ("By the Grace of God, 142).

53. Moffatt observes that Philo "is never tired of speaking about God, and he never speaks very long about any aspect of God without introducing grace" (*Grace in the New Testament*, 48).

abundant grace subverts the obligation of reciprocity is less convincing.[54] Although he acknowledges that Paul endorses the conventions that the beneficiary is obliged to respond fittingly to benefaction, his discussion is confusing when he also contends that Paul's soteriology and pneumatology eschew loyalty oaths.[55] He adds that "the grace of Christ expected no requital."[56] But this is a misconstrual of how χάρις functions in Greco-Roman society. Critiquing Harrison's argument, McFarland writes, "It is strange that Harrison is at such pains to paint Paul's context and to say that he is best understood within that context, only to assert that he does not really fit on one of its most central aspects [namely the ethic of reciprocity]."[57] Paul argues in Romans 5–6 that those who have received the Messiah's overflowing χάρις *respond* by living a life commensurate with their new identity in Christ. It is a life that is not only appropriate and fitting but also loyal to the supreme benefactor. Paul's catchphrase for this miraculous reality is "newness of life" (καινότης ζωῆς) (6:4).

The Messiah's χάρις transforms the sinful humanity into a righteous people by mapping them onto the Messiah's death and resurrection (6:1–11). Paul describes the reality found in Christ as "newness of life" (6:4; cf. 7:6) because it entails creating life out of death. He uses the metaphor of baptism in 6:3–4 to describe the spiritual reality of believers' union with Christ. As Campbell writes, to be baptized into Christ's death is a figurative "description of the spiritual reality of dying with Christ."[58] Since Christ has been set free from sin by virtue of his death (6:7), and since he has been set free from death by virtue of his resurrection (6:9), his victory over sin and death inaugurates a new life for his followers. Just as Christ died to sin once and for all and is now alive to God, so those who are spiritually united with him reckon themselves "dead to sin but alive to God in Jesus the Messiah" (6:10–11). Believers' physical resurrection is a future phenomenon (6:5, 8), but newness of life begins now amidst the mortality of the body.[59] So "walking in newness of life" means living

---

54. Harrison, *Paul's Language of Grace*, 345–49.
55. Harrison, *Paul's Language of Grace*, 241, 287.
56. Harrison, *Paul's Language of Grace*, 266.
57. McFarland, *God and Grace*, 17.
58. Campbell, *Paul and Union*, 336.
59. Tannehill writes, "The believer participates in the new life in the present, but Paul is careful to make clear that it does not become the believer's possession. It is realized through a continual surrender of one's present activity to God, a walking in newness of life, and at the same time it remains God's gift for the future" (*Dying and*

appropriately as those who have received χάρις which makes it possible to partake in the Messiah's death and resurrection.[60]

We cannot abide in sin because our union with Christ in his death has rescued us from the tyranny of sin and brought us into the domain of righteousness (5:19; 6:1–11). Sin is a tyrant who entered the world (5:12), claims the obedience of humanity, reigns over humanity (5:21; 6:12, 14), enslaves its subjects (6:6), and dwells within them (7:17, 20). Due to its cosmic lordship, Paul can assert that all humans are "under sin" (3:9). But in Christ, humanity is liberated from the tyranny of sin so that they can serve a new master. The Messiah takes on the body of sin (8:3), dies, and he is liberated from sin by his resurrection (6:7–8).[61] Paul can, therefore, declare that "our old self was crucified with the Messiah so that the body commandeered by sin might be destroyed so that we would no longer be enslaved to sin" (6:6). To die with Christ marks the end of the slavery to sin and inaugurates the beginning of Christ's lordship over the believer.[62] Tannehill comments, "The Christian cannot lead a life of sin while under grace just because the new master, like the old, has a complete claim to his service and holds him in his power."[63] The metaphor of slavery, which Paul introduces here (6:6), and develops in 6:15–23, underscores how those who have been liberated from the dominion of sin to the dominion of χάρις are obligated to show loyalty to the Messiah, who is their new master.[64]

Paul uses the imagery of slavery in 6:15–23 in ways that are both conventional and surprising. He employs the concepts of obedience, manumission, and benefit to assert that believers are freed from the slavery of sin, which leads to death, to a better and superior slavery of

---

Rising, 12). Also see Timmins, Romans 7, 66–91.

60. Tannehill observes, "If the believer dies and rises with Christ, as Paul claims, Christ's death and resurrection are not merely events which produce benefits for the believer, but also events in which the believer himself partakes. The believer's new life is based upon his personal participation in these saving events" (Dying and Rising, 1).

61. For the argument that ὁ ἀποθανών ("the one who died") refers to Christ, see Campbell, Deliverance of God, 825–27.

62. Croasmun comments, "In the death of baptism, the cosmic Body of Sin is coming to nothing as its members fall off necrotic, having died with Christ in baptism and been raised to new life 'in Christ,' that is, in the Body of Christ" (Emergence of Sin, 121).

63. Tannehill, Dying and Rising, 17.

64. Paul uses the metaphor of slavery elsewhere in Romans both for himself (1:1) and the Roman believers (12:11; 14:4). Also see 1 Cor 7:22; Gal 1:10; Phil 1:1; cf. 1 Cor 6:20 and 7:23.

The Messiah's Supreme Royal Benefaction in Romans 5:12—8:39

righteousness, which leads to life. Emancipation from slavery to sin comes through "the gift of God . . . in Jesus the Messiah our Lord" (χάρισμα τοῦ θεοῦ . . . ἐν Χριστῷ Ἰησοῦ τῷ κυρίῳ ἡμῶν, 6:23). While a slave in Greco-Roman society could earn and save funds for future use, Paul asserts that there is nothing beneficial from enslavement to sin.[65] A slave of death bears fruit (καρπόν) that leads to shame (6:21). The "wages" (ὀψώνια) of slavery to sin is death (6:23). The dead are rescued, not by their own initiative, but by the miraculous and victorious intervention of the Messiah. In the Greco-Roman ethic of commensurability, no benefactor would give favors to anyone whose life is marked by wickedness. The Greco-Roman benefaction system and its ethic of reciprocity exalts the virtuous and shames the impious. The Messiah's gift is unconventional and indiscriminate because it is offered to the sinful and undeserving to free them from sin and death.

The fact that this liberating χάρις comes through the agency of Jesus means that the believer is obligated to her new master. For Paul, neutral freedom is an illusion since everyone is a slave to a master.[66] We are liberated from sin so that we might become slaves of righteousness or of God (6:18–22). We can no longer pledge allegiance to sin (6:12).[67] Rather, we are to consider ourselves "dead to sin and alive to God in Jesus the Messiah" (6:11). In 6:15–18 Paul repeatedly states that a slave must be obedient to the master. Since the Roman readers have experienced a change of ownership, they "have become obedient from the heart to the pattern of teaching to which you were committed" (6:17). Perhaps this change of ownership is what Paul alludes to when he uses the language of handing over (παραδίδωμι), namely, the pattern of teaching to which the readers are now submissive stipulates their obligation under the new lordship.

Paul can even use a commonplace illustration to urge his readers to a life of obedience: "For just as you once presented your members as slaves to impurity and to lawlessness leading to lawlessness, so now

---

65. Cf. *SIG*, 2nd ed. 845

66. For works that interpret the slavery metaphor against the backdrop of the slaves and freedmen of the emperor's household, see Weaver, *Familia Caesaris*; Meeks, *Origins of Christian Morality*, 169; Harrison, *Paul's Language of Grace*, 234–42. Also see Crook, *Reconceptualising Conversion*, 226–34.

67. There is a general consensus that Paul depicts sin in Romans 5–7 as a personified and cosmic actor, but that the Messiah has vanquished sin. On the personification of sin in Romans, Southall writes that "the personified actor Sin enters the world stage from offstage in order to go about its enslaving, deceiving, and domineering business of wreaking havoc in the world and in humanity" (*Rediscovering Righteousness*, 99).

present your members as slaves to righteousness leading to sanctification" (6:19).[68] In this verse and the next, Paul juxtaposes the slavery of sin and that of righteousness with the intent of portraying the dark side of the former and the bright side of the latter. He begins by challenging the believer to reckon his present status and fully surrender to the one who set him free. Slavery to sin results in ever-increasing wickedness (6:19). It is loathsome and embarrassing; in fact, it is so cruel that it leads to death. Having tasted life under the new master, the Roman readers are now ashamed of the fruit of the life they lived under the former master. It is possible that this retrospective shame has a positive role of making a slave of Christ more grateful for the Messiah's χάρις. Paul, then, is inviting his readers to delight in their new slavery because it produces holiness. Continuing in sin is inconsistent with the readers' present identity in Christ. Unlike the ancient practice whereby manumitted freedmen were still obligated to show loyalty to their benefactor, Paul asserts that believers owe exclusive loyalty to their new benefactor the Messiah.[69] Commenting on this imagery of slavery, Barclay states, "The gift of God in Jesus Christ has established not liberation from authority or demand, but a new allegiance, a new responsibility, a new 'slavery' under the rule of grace. Although not itself an imperative, grace is imperatival: it bears within itself the imperative to obey."[70] Thus, Paul's answer to the questions of 6:1 and 6:15 is that a believer does not abide in sin (μὴ γένοιτο) since the grace of God leads to obedience and holiness.[71]

Although Paul does not explicitly use the language of obligation (ὀφειλέτης) in 5:12—6:23, the way he configures life "under grace" (ὑπὸ χάριν) shows that the ones whose existence depends on the Messiah's gift ought to respond loyally to his rule.[72] In addition to the metaphors of baptism and slavery, such terms as "reckon," "obey," "newness of life," and "offer" point to a life which is governed by the power of the Messiah's

68. By "members" (μέλη), Paul probably has in mind body parts such as hands, feet, ears, eyes, and sexual organs (cf. Rom 3:10–18; 1 Cor 12:12–26). See Jewett, *Romans*, 410–11.

69. On manumission loyalty, see Crook, *Reconceptualizing Conversion*, 226–34.

70. Barclay, "Under Grace," 60. Campbell argues, "If the purpose of Christ's death—in part at least—is to bring a rebellious humanity into relationship with the holy God, it follows that, once reconciled, believers will live in a manner that befits such a relationship with such a God" (*Paul and Union*, 377).

71. Bird comments, "Grace is designed to get us out of that situation [of sin's domination], not to make us feel comfortable within it!" (*Romans*, 195).

72. See Rom 8:12 where Paul explicitly uses the language of obligation.

death and resurrection. Paul does not "ruthlessly" expunge the ethic of reciprocity from his construal of χάρις as Harrison asserts.[73] Instead, he urges the Roman readers to live in such a way that demonstrates that they are free from the power of sin and death and that they are allegiant to the Messiah. If we owe our existence to χάρις then we must render gratitude to the giver of χάρις. This is what Philo means when he asserts that people should return χάρις for χάρις (*Heir.* 104–5; cf. Seneca, *Ben.* 1.14.4; 2.2.11; 2.18.1–5; 2.35.1; 5.11.5; 6.10.2). Or as Josephus states, it is necessary to make a return for kindness (*Ant.* 12:53–56). Cicero, Seneca, Xenophon, Aristotle, and Pliny among others all agree that gifts create inalienable ties of loyalty and that the greater the gift the greater the obligation.

The fact that the Messiah's gift is indiscriminately given to ill-deserving humanity does not imply that the beneficiaries are thereby freed from the obligation to honor their supreme benefactor. To the contrary, they not only resist the allure of sin (cf. Rom 6:13–14) but also actively conform to the pattern of Christ's kingdom even as they are established in righteousness (cf. 6:17–18). It is important to underline that Paul portrays the body as the context of the conflict between sin and grace (6:13, 19). When the body was held captive by sin, it abounded in unrighteousness and could not honor God. In 1:18–32, Paul argues that humanity is at enmity with God due to dishonor. Instead of giving honor or thanksgiving (ἐδόξασαν ἢ ηὐχαρίστησαν) to God, humans "exchanged the glory of the immortal God (τὴν δόξαν τοῦ ἀφθάρτου θεοῦ) for images . . . [with the result that] God handed them over . . . to the dishonoring of their bodies (τοῦ ἀτιμάζεσθαι τὰ σώματα) . . . [and] to dishonorable passions" (πάθη ἀτιμίας, 1:21–26). Based on the pivotal role of "honor/dishonor" in Paul's logic, Pickett argues that dishonor "is both the reason humanity is at enmity with God, and the cause of the moral depravity which is deserving of God's wrath."[74] The body that does not honor God is given over to idolatry, immorality, and all sorts of vices (1:22–32; 7:5). Such a body is morally incapacitated and ultimately dead. In 1:31, Paul calls people who manifest moral incapacitation ἀσυνθέτους ("disloyal"). The "I" of 7:7–25 faces intrinsic moral incapacitation because he is under the dominion of sin and death.[75] Due to his ontological corruption, he

---

73. Harrison, *Paul's Language of Grace*, 348–49.
74. Pickett, "The Death of Christ," 730.
75. For further discussion of Rom 7:7–25, see Timmins, *Romans 7*; Jipp, "Educating the Divided Soul, 231–57; Wasserman, "Death of the Soul," 793–816; Engberg-Pedersen, "Reception of Graeco-Roman Culture," 32–57; Meyer, "Worm at the Core,"

cries out for deliverance: "Wretched man that I am! Who will rescue me from this body of death?" (τοῦ σώματος τοῦ θανάτου;) (7:24). To curb the passions of the body and to overcome death, humanity must be rescued by the Messiah. That is why Paul writes, "Thanks (χάρις) be to God through Jesus the Messiah our Lord" (7:25).[76] The Messiah's gift delivers believers and provides the empowerment to obey God.

Christ's followers are dead to sin (6:11), yet they still participate in the mortality that characterizes Adam's dominion. The resurrection life of Christ is at work in them, but they are not yet clothed with immortality. As they anticipate their own bodily resurrection, they cannot let sin reign in their mortal body to make them obey its passions (6:12). Although they formerly presented their members to sin "as weapons for unrighteousness," now they can obey Christ and present the members of their body to God "as weapons for righteousness" (6:13). The body which was once the site of dehumanizing disobedience and ungodliness has now become the site of obedience and the "inscription" that displays the glory of the Messiah and the power of χάρις to deliver and transform humanity. Barclay writes:

> Once appropriated by sin, the body is reappropriated by Christ. The very location where sin once held most visible sway, and where its former grip still draws our bodily selves towards death, is now the location where the "newness of life" breaks into action, displaying in counterintuitive patterns of behavior the miraculous Christ-life... In this tug-of-war between death and life, Christian obedience *in the body*, the former stronghold of sin, displays the fact that a miraculous counterforce is already at work.[77]

The Messiah's gift obliges believers to live worthily of χάρις, yet this does not mean that they can somehow manipulate him into conferring more favors. In Greco-Roman society, the public display of inscriptions in temples, marketplaces, or theaters is a means of honoring benefactors and a strategic way of exerting pressure on them to offer more gifts. That is why Rajak writes that "the honors were a not-too-subtle statement to the donor that he had a reputation that could be kept up only by further

---

62–84; Ziesler, "Role of the Tenth Commandment," 41–56.

76. This is a clear instant of returning χάρις for χάρις.

77. Barclay, "Under Grace," 69 (italics original).

The Messiah's Supreme Royal Benefaction in Romans 5:12—8:39   201

benefaction."[78] Honoring the Messiah, however, is not for the sake of earning additional favors. This is another aspect of the Greco-Roman ethic of reciprocity that the Messiah's supreme benefaction subverts. The Messiah has offered the gift of his own life to sinners (5:6–8) and his χάρις overflows to the unrighteous (5:15, 17, 20). As we have seen in chapter 4, the Messiah's followers "stand in χάρις" and are assured of rising from the dead. The Messiah has abundantly given us everything needed for faithful and fruitful allegiance to him. Thus, believers' reciprocity is not instrumental in securing additional favors; any notion that we can earn χάρις by reciprocity misses Paul's point in 5:15–17 concerning the singularity of χάρις. In 6:23, Paul writes that the singular "gift of God" (χάρισμα τοῦ θεοῦ) leads to "eternal life through Jesus the Messiah our Lord" (ζωὴ αἰώνιος ἐν Χριστῷ Ἰησοῦ τῷ κυρίῳ ἡμῶν). Christ's followers do not reciprocate in order to secure further gifts; rather, our reciprocity is the *appropriate conduct and fitting response* that reveals that we have indeed been liberated by the Messiah and that we are faithfully following our Lord. Our conduct ought to unquestionably reveal that we are loyal to Jesus Christ.

Believers' obedience and response to χάρις always point back to the crucified and risen Lord, who is the fountain of everything in this life. Therefore, we walk in "newness of life" (6:4); we reckon ourselves "dead to sin but alive to God in Jesus the Messiah" (6:11); we refuse to let sin exercise dominion over our mortal body to make it obey its passions (6:12); we do not present our "members to sin as weapons for unrighteousness" (6:13); we present ourselves to God as those who have Christ's resurrection life in us (6:13); we present our "members to God as weapons for righteousness" (6:13, 19); we are obedient to God's word (6:15–19); and we bear fruit that leads to sanctification and whose end is eternal life (6:22–23). We do all these things because χάρις so demands and because we are grateful to the source of our life and of everything good in this life (cf. 7:25). Bird writes that believers "are part of redemptive and transformative reality that invades the world in Jesus' death and resurrection, and that reality needs to be worked out in their own lives."[79] Working out this transformative reality means that Christ's followers must "apply and appropriate their new identity in Christ with Christ-honoring action."[80]

78. Rajak, "Benefactors," 308.
79. Bird, *Romans*, 218.
80. Bird, *Romans*, 219. Bird rightly states, "A theology of the Christian life that does not lay strenuous commands on the believer is based on a cheap version of grace

Bates calls this Messiah-honoring lifestyle "*embodied fidelity* to Jesus as Lord" (italics original).[81] We are not our own; we belong to the Messiah "who has been raised from the dead" (7:4). It is, then, not surprising that Paul portrays believers as obligated beneficiaries of the Messiah's χάρις. In the words of Bates, grace is not "at odds with the required behavioral changes (good deeds) associated with allegiant union to Jesus the king."[82] We reciprocate this gift by remaining faithful to our new identity in Christ and by conducting ourselves in a manner that demonstrates that indeed we have been liberated from the lordship of sin so that we may serve our supreme benefactor. What role does the Holy Spirit play in believers' new identity as Christ's loyal followers? This is the question that the next section discusses as we now turn to Romans 8.

The Holy Spirit and the Status of Believers

In chapter 4, we saw that Paul writes in Rom 5:5 for the first time that the Holy Spirit has been given to believers. Paul introduces the theme of the Spirit to support his argument that hope does not put Christ's followers to shame. The gift of the Spirit, through whom the love of God is poured out in the hearts of believers, gives confident assurance of resurrection. One of the questions we considered in our discussion of 5:5 is: How does the Spirit guarantee eschatological deliverance and eternal honorable status? In response, we noted two implicit points in Paul's argument. First, the Spirit assures us that we belong to God. Second, the Spirit maps us onto Christ's death and resurrection. In Romans 8, Paul picks up this theme of the Spirit and develops it further in order to substantiate his claim that the Messiah's superior gift eradicates eschatological anxiety and demands a Christ-honoring lifestyle. To proceed, we will first look at believers as God's pneumatic children. As God's children, believers are guaranteed an eternal status in God's family. Thus the second section focuses on the resurrection of God's children. We will conclude this section on the Spirit by looking at God's pneumatic sons' obligation to the Spirit.

---

that is itself based on an impoverished view of Christ."
81. Bates, *Salvation by Allegiance Alone*, 98.
82. Bates, *Salvation by Allegiance Alone*, 104.

Pneumatic Sonship

The main claim we are making in this section is that pneumatic descent from Christ results in eternal divine sonship. The portrait of the king in the OT shows that the reception of the Spirit by the king testifies to the king's sonship.[83] The king is henceforth not only a vicegerent of Yahweh but he is also assured of Yahweh's protection and care. There is, therefore, a special pneumatic relationship between the king and Yahweh. As Yahweh's anointed, the king receives Yahweh's Spirit.[84] The narratives of Saul and David show that the anointing is the occasion for the king's endowment with the Spirit of Yahweh (1 Sam 10:10; 16:13). Divine sonship means that the king occupies a glorious position and serves as an agent of divine blessings to the people. We have also seen from various Greco-Roman sources that a beneficent ruler is appointed by the gods, who entrust to him great resources for the welfare of the people. It is not unusual for the king to be honored as "son of a god" due to his benefactions. Virgil, for example, hails Augustus as "son of a god, who will again establish a golden age" (*Aen.* 6:791–93). Yet to our knowledge, there is nothing from antiquity that suggests that an emperor became a son of God by resurrection.[85] For Paul, Jesus is the risen son of God who is empowered by the Spirit and who gives his Spirit (Rom 8:9) to his followers so that they may participate in his messianic sonship.

Believers' sonship in God's family is patterned after the sonship of the Messiah. Paul declares in Rom 1:3–4 that the Messiah, who descended from David, has been installed as the son-of-God-in-power according to the Spirit and by virtue of the resurrection from the dead. Although some interpreters posit that this text implies an adoptionist Christology whereby Jesus receives divine sonship at his resurrection,[86] it seems

---

83. One may posit that this divine sonship implies that Yahweh has adopted the king as his son.

84. See Johnson, *Sacral Kingship*, 15–19.

85. For further discussion of the Roman emperors as "son of god," see Winter, *Divine Honours*, 67–71.

86. For representative works arguing for an adoptionist Christology, see Ehrman, *How Jesus Became God*, 221–22; Schmithals, *Theology of the First Christians*, 89–90. Critiquing an adoptionist Christology, Fee writes that "although it is true that if this [Rom 1:2–4] were the only text of its kind in the corpus, one could easily settle for an adoptionist Christology . . . [but] the rest of Romans itself will not allow such a view. Rather, Rom 1:4 should be understood as the Father's and Spirit's vindication of the eternal Son" (*Pauline Christology*, 544).

more convincing that Paul is concerned here, not with how Jesus *became* the eternal son of God, but with his *installation* as the son-of-God-in-power.[87] Paul sees a distinct feature between Jesus' pre-resurrection divine sonship and post-resurrection divine sonship. As Bird puts it, Paul implies in 1:3–4 that there is "a transition from one state of divine sonship to another state of divine sonship."[88] The description of Jesus as "from the seed of David" alludes to the OT promise that a descendant of David will be God's own son (2 Sam 7:10–14; Pss 89:4, 26, 35–37; 132:11–12, 17–18). In 1 Chr 17:11–13, God promises David that "I will raise up your offspring after you, one of your own sons, and I will establish his kingdom . . . I will be to him a father, and he shall be to me a son" (cf. 1 Chr 28:6). Similarly, in Ps 2:7 God says to the king, "You are my son, today I have begotten you." In LXX Ps 109:3 we read: "I have begotten you from the womb before the morning." Based on this background, when Paul says that Jesus is "from the seed of David," he means that Jesus is the royal Davidic deliverer, the son of David and the son of God.[89] The Messiah is already the son of God prior to his resurrection. The resurrection, however, marks the Messiah's transition from a fleshly human existence (cf. 8:3) to his installation as God's son *in power*. Paul writes in 1:4 that the installation of God's son is "according to the Spirit" (κατὰ πνεῦμα) by virtue of the resurrection from the dead. The implication is that the Spirit is "the power that distinctively characterizes Christ's condition of existence and operation originating from his resurrection."[90] The Messiah's sonship and enthronement evince the power of the Spirit to create life out of the situation of deadness.[91]

87. The participle ὁρισθέντος is a divine passive meaning "installed, designated, appointed." See BDAG 723; Bird, *Jesus the Eternal Son*, 14.

88. Bird, *Jesus the Eternal Son*, 15. Dunn notes that "the resurrection marked an enhanced, not initial bestowal, of Jesus' sonship—'Son of God *in power*'" (*Beginning from Jerusalem*, 217; italics original). Also see Bates, "Christology of Incarnation," 107–27; Jipp, *Christ Is King*, 167–79; Scott, *Adoption as Sons*, 223–44.

89. Cranfield states, "The position of the words τοῦ υἱοῦ αὐτοῦ . . . would seem to imply that the One who was born of the seed of David was already Son of God before, and independently of, the action denoted by the second participle" (*Critical and Exegetical Commentary*, 58). Similarly Hurtado writes, "The 'Son' here is God's unique agent, whose significance is set within the context of God's purposes" ("Jesus' Divine Sonship," 225).

90. Fatehi, *Spirit's Relation*, 254.

91. See Rom 8:2, 6 where Paul refers to the Spirit as "the Spirit of life." For a helpful discussion of Rom 8:2 and "the law of the Spirit of life," see Yates, *Spirit and Creation*, 135–42.

The Messiah's trajectory serves as a pattern for his followers since he is their representative. The son's descent from David "according to flesh" (κατὰ σάρκα) implies that he is Israel's royal representative. As Jipp states, Paul uses the term "σάρξ" (flesh) in 1:3 to mark Jesus out "as an actual man who shares in human existence and all the trappings that go with it."[92] We find a similar note in 8:3 where Paul writes that "God sent his own son in the likeness of sinful flesh" (cf. Gal 4:4; Phil 2:7). Commenting on Jesus' fleshly existence, Richard B. Gaffin notes:

> The phrase [according to the flesh] brings into view not only Christ's human nature but also and pointedly the order into which the assumption of humanity brought him, the environment with which this humanity is necessarily associated and from which it cannot be abstracted. The full thought of verse 3 is that by incarnation (by being born of the seed of David) the Son of God entered the sphere of σάρξ, the old aeon, the present evil age.[93]

The son's entrance into the realm of fleshly existence implies that he fully participates in the weakness, fragility, and decay that mark corporeality (cf. 1 Cor 15:42–43).[94] He has fully identified with the sinful humanity even to the point of executing "sin in his flesh" (τὴν ἁμαρτίαν ἐν τῇ σαρκί, Rom 8:3b).[95] But through the Spirit and by virtue of the resurrection from the dead, the son has transitioned to the stage marked by power and incorruptibility because death no longer exercises lordship over him (6:9–10). He not only shares in God's kingship and Spirit but his royal trajectory also marks out the trajectory of his followers because he is their royal representative. The enthroned and empowered God's son brings his followers into his royal domain whereby they can share in the benefits of his rule. Or, as Jipp puts it: "As simultaneously sharing in God's kingship as God's son *and* as representing Israel and sharing in its fleshly existence, Christ is uniquely positioned as the only one who can extend and share God's rule and its benefits with humanity."[96]

---

92. See Jipp, *Christ Is King*, 172.

93. Gaffin, *Resurrection and Redemption*, 109.

94. Cf. Bates, *Hermeneutics of the Apostolic Proclamation*, 92; Jipp, "Ancient, Modern, and Future Interpretations," 256.

95. Jipp state, "As a sin offering the Son is humanity's representative who *identifies* completely with human existence and whose body undergoes the judgment and sentence of death" (*Christ Is King*, 185; italics original).

96. Jipp, *Christ Is King*, 180. Emphasis original.

One of those benefits is membership in God's family. Paul declares in 8:9 that "if anyone does not have the Spirit of the Messiah, he does not belong to him." The converse is true; to have the Spirit of the Messiah means that one belongs to him and to God's family. Just as the reception of the Spirit assured the Davidic king of divine sonship, hence marking the king's special relationship to God, and just as Jesus was empowered by the Spirit of holiness by virtue of the resurrection from the dead, so the believer's familial relationship to God is marked by the gift of the Spirit.[97] Paul can then state that "those who are led by the Spirit of God are sons of God" (υἱοὶ θεοῦ εἰσιν, 8:14; cf. 8:19). To further highlight this familial relationship, Paul speaks twice of "adoption as sons" (υἱοθεσία, 8:15, 23), three times of "children of God" (τέκνα θεοῦ, 8:16, 17, 21), three times of "heirs" (κληρονόμοι, 8:17), and once of "brothers" (ἀδελφοῖς, 8:29).

In 8:15, Paul writes that "you have not received a spirit of slavery leading again to fear, but you have received a Spirit of adoption as sons, by which we cry out, 'Abba Father!'" The filial relationship that Paul depicts here is a result of believers' possession of the Spirit who enables them to participate in the reign of the empowered son. In 8:29, Paul refers to Jesus as "the firstborn among many brothers." According to LXX Psalm 88, the Davidic king is God's "firstborn son" (πρωτότοκον) and "the highest of the kings of the earth" (ὑψηλὸν παρὰ τοῖς βασιλεῦσιν τῆς γῆς, 88:28). This son cries out to Yahweh: "You are my father, my God, and the rock of my salvation" (88:27). The king clearly understands that there is an intimate father-son relation between him and God. Likewise, Paul depicts believers as sharing in the messianic sonship so much that just as the son cried out "Abba, Father" (Mark 14:36), so God's pneumatic sons can approach him with confidence as they cry out "Abba, Father!" Their relationship to God is marked by love rather than fear (cf. Rom 8:35, 39). The son who maps out the destiny of his followers also models how to approach our loving father. In Gal 4:6, Paul tells his readers that "because you are sons, God has sent the Spirit of his son into our hearts, crying out, 'Abba, Father.'" To participate in the sonship of the Messiah is to enjoy the same continuous loving relationship that the Messiah enjoys with the father. Moo states: "In crying out 'Abba, Father,' the believer not only gives voice to his or her consciousness of belonging to God as his child but also having a status comparable to that of Jesus himself."[98] And just as the status

---

97. See Peppard, *Son of God*, 138–40.

98. Moo, *Epistle to the Romans*, 502. Also see Rabens, *Holy Spirit and Ethics*, 226–27.

of Jesus as God's son cannot be broken, so those who have the Spirit of sonship are confident of their eternal membership in God's family. The Messiah's gift of the Spirit creates an intimate relationship between his followers and God and enables them to approach God as a loving father.

The Resurrection of the Sons of God

The gift of the Spirit is not only concerned with believers' filial relation to God but also with their resurrection. The ancient benefactors seek to overcome mortality by generosity and the resulting perpetual praise of the beneficiaries (Cicero, *Planc.* 2.17.60; cf. 2.18.63; *Inv.* 2.22.66; 2.53.161; *Off.* 2.6.22). Pliny writes that because Trajan excels in good deeds, he has won for himself eternal glory (*Pan.* 54:7—55:11). As we have seen in chapter 2, epigraphic memorialization assures the benefactors that posterity would always honor them. The Greco-Roman benefaction system and its ethic of reciprocity enables rulers to "conquer death" by having their names inscribed on bronze tablets as a sign of the people's gratitude. Paul is also concerned with how to conquer death, yet an important contrast is that for him, immortality is obtained, not by the unending praise of posterity, but by possessing the Spirit of the Messiah. The Messiah's eternal destiny is also the destiny of those who have his Spirit in them.

When humanity abandoned God and turned to idolatry (Rom 1:18–32), they fell short of glory (1:23; 3:23). As we have seen in chapter 4, this loss of glory relates to corruptibility and mortality.[99] Humanity is now faced with the monumental predicament of death. But the gift of the Spirit guarantees the Messiah's followers that they will resurrect to eternal life (8:11; cf. 2 Cor 1:22; 5:5; Eph 1:14). As Matthew Thiessen states, "Through the reception of the *pneuma*, those in Christ now have a share in his same indestructible resurrection life" (italics original).[100]

We may then describe the resurrection of Jesus as the inaugural step in the resurrection process that guarantees our own resurrection. The Messiah, whose first stage of royal trajectory was marked by corporeality (Rom 1:3), triumphed over death! In 1:4, Paul writes that Jesus has been "installed as the son-of-God-in-power according to the Spirit of holiness by means of the resurrection from the dead" (ἐξ ἀναστάσεως νεκρῶν). The

---

99. Blackwell rightly argues that glory in Romans denotes elevated honor and incorruptibility ("Immortal Glory," 285–308).

100. Thiessen, *Paul and the Gentile Problem*, 155.

fact that Paul uses a generalizing plural νεκρῶν ("from the dead ones") implies that the son's resurrection is the groundbreaking miracle that assures God's sons of their own eschatological resurrection. Wright writes, "What happened to Jesus, Paul believed, was the bringing forward into the present of this general resurrection, in one particular case, which still belonged organically to, and anticipated, the total 'resurrection of the dead.'"[101] Jesus is "the firstborn among many brothers" (Rom 8:29), "the firstborn from the dead" (Col 1:18; cf. Rev 1:5), and "the firstfruits" (1 Cor 15:23) who enters into glorification and resurrection life as the first from the dead ones.

Due to his victory over death, he is able to liberate his followers from mortality and grant them participation in his victorious reign. Just as Jesus has been installed as the son-of-God-in-power by the life-giving Spirit, so Jesus gives the Spirit as a gift to his followers (Rom 5:5) in anticipation of their indestructible life.[102] Christ gives life precisely by means of the Spirit. Paul can, therefore, refer to the Spirit as "the Spirit of life" (8:2), and declare that the mind governed by the Spirit is life and peace (8:6). The Spirit guarantees believers that they will be conformed to the likeness of the immortal and glorified son of God (Rom 8:29–30). This sharing in the son's likeness implies the resurrection of the body and participation in the Messiah's victorious reign.[103] Paul writes in Phil 3:20–21 that the Lord Jesus the Messiah "will transform the body of our humble state into conformity with the body of his glory" (μετασχηματίσει τὸ σῶμα τῆς ταπεινώσεως ἡμῶν σύμμορφον τῷ σώματι τῆς δόξης αὐτοῦ, cf. 1 Cor 15:49). As James D. Tabor comments, "The equation of Jesus the Son of God, with the *many* glorified sons of God to follow is God's means of bringing into existence a *family* (i.e., 'many brothers') of cosmic beings, the *Sons of God*, who share his heavenly *doxa*" (italics original).[104]

But why are God's sons in whom the Spirit dwells (Rom 8:9) still subject to death? Paul writes that they are bound to death "on account of sin"

---

101. Wright, "Letter to the Romans," 419.

102. See 1 Cor 15:45b where Paul writes that "the last Adam became a life-giving Spirit."

103. On the view that to be conformed to the image of the Son implies the resurrection of the body, see Kim, *Origin of Paul's Gospel*, 228, 321; Scott, *Adoption as Sons*, 247–56; Byrne, *'Sons of God'—'Seed of Abraham,'* 118. For a recent work that contends that to be conformed to the Son's image is to fulfill our vocation as God's vicegerents and to reign with the Messiah, see Jacob, *Conformed to the Image*.

104. Tabor, *Things Unutterable*, 11.

(8:10); although they are dead to sin in the sense that sin no longer holds them captive (6:11), they still possess the mortal body of the Adamic heritage. The resurrection life of Christ is at work in them through the Spirit who gives life, yet they have not yet been physically raised from the dead. Thus there is justification for viewing the believer as simultaneously dead and alive.[105] Barclay not only describes this reality as "the permanent paradox of grace in the life of a believer" but also argues that believers' ongoing mortality in this life puts them "into a state of permanent incongruity."[106] In other words, the Christ-gift is bestowed on those who are permanently marked by mortality due to sin, hence they are completely unworthy of God's favor. Christ's followers are on the one hand doomed to death because they exist in a body bound by mortality. On the other hand, they are eternally alive because of the miraculous new life originating from the resurrection of Jesus. The paradoxical depiction of the believer as dead-yet-living underlines a miraculous existential reality sustained by the Spirit. Christ's followers continue to face the situation of death until the final restoration when God will eventually give indestructible life to their mortal bodies through the Spirit who dwells in them.

Thus, one of the greatest paradoxes of the messianic age is that the mortal body is also the abode of the Spirit of life. Paul writes in 8:11 that "if the Spirit of him who raised Jesus from the dead dwells in you, then he who raised the Messiah from the dead will also give life to your mortal bodies through his Spirit who dwells in you." As believers await the redemption of their bodies, they are not anxious since they are following the trajectory of the Messiah.[107] The Spirit mediates the presence of the risen Lord to believers and reinvigorates their eagerness for immortality (8:23). And just as Paul declares in 1:4 that the Spirit is the means by which Jesus is installed as "the son-of-God-in-power" at the resurrection, so Paul declares in 8:11 that the Spirit is the means by which God will overcome our weak, fragile, and decaying existence and clothe us with immortality.[108] Just as the son was glorified, so the sons of God

---

105. Yates notes, "While the physical body awaits resurrection, the Christian is already alive in a fundamentally new way because of the indwelling of the life-giving spirit" (*Spirit and Creation*, 163).

106. Barclay, "Under Grace," 65–66.

107. Scott, *Adoption as Sons*, 222–23, 244–45, 256.

108. As Jipp states, Christ's resurrection serves as "the prototype for the rest of humanity" ("Ancient, Modern, and Future Interpretations," 257). Likewise, Scott comments, "Rom. 1:4 implies that the Son's resurrection is prototypical of the future

will share in the same glory as the resurrected son (8:29–30).[109] Based on 8:23, where Paul declares that those who have the firstfruits of the Spirit (ἀπαρχὴν τοῦ πνεύματος)[110] groan inwardly as they "eagerly await their adoption as sons, the redemption of our bodies" (υἱοθεσίαν ἀπεκδεχόμενοι, τὴν ἀπολύτρωσιν τοῦ σώματος ἡμῶν), we may describe this future stage of believers' liberation as the climactic adoption that demonstrates believers' victory over death by conformity to the Messiah's resurrection image and participating in his eternal dominion.[111]

As we have already argued, believers' eschatological adoption is guaranteed by the Spirit who indwells them and replicates Christ's pattern of dying and rising in them.[112] Their present pneumatic adoption guarantees their eschatological adoption to be effected by the Spirit. It is, therefore, not surprising that Paul declares that Christ's followers will not be put to shame (5:5), that the sons of God will one day be revealed (8:19), and that the creation anticipates "the freedom of the glory of the children of God" (8:21). We saw in chapters 2 and 3 that in Greco-Roman society, wealth is an important criterion for apportioning honor. Generous rulers obtain glory and "immortality" by benefiting their subjects, who in turn memorialize them in perpetuity. For Paul, however, the criterion for apportioning glory and overcoming mortality is not access to material wealth, but the possession of the Messiah's Spirit to whom believers are now obligated.

---

resurrection of the dead (ἀνάστασις νεκρῶν). Rom. 8 goes beyond this by arguing that those who are in Christ will participate in the resurrection and sonship of the Son by being adopted as sons of God at a Spirit-mediated resurrection. The correlation of Rom. 8 with Rom. 1:4 is thus complete and unmistakable: believers will share in the destiny of him who was 'appointed Son of God in power by the Holy Spirit at the resurrection of the dead" (*Adoption as Sons*, 244–45).

109. Eph 1:5 explicitly states that believers are predestined to adoption as sons.

110. The genitive "of the Spirit" (τοῦ πνεύματος) is most likely appositional rather than partitive. The latter would imply that believers do not yet have the Spirit in full. But if taken appositionally, then Paul is saying that the Spirit is the first installment or initial portion that anticipates the harvest of the bodily redemption at the resurrection by means of the Spirit (cf. 1 Cor 15:42–50).

111. On believers' eschatological adoption, see Blackwell, *Christosis*, 147–48; Macaskill, *Union with Christ*, 241.

112. Johnson, *Contested Issues*, 270. Scott writes, "For Rom. 8 shows that the present possession of the πνεῦμα υἱοθεσίας, the Spirit associated with adoption, guarantees the future participation of believers in the resurrection and universal sovereignty of the Son" (*Adoption as Sons*, 221).

The Obligation of God's Sons to the Spirit

The Spirit of Christ is at the center of believers' identity as God's sons and anticipated resurrection. Additionally, the Spirit also transforms and empowers believers so that their life may honor their supreme benefactor. Like other ancient gifts, the Messiah's gift comes with the expectation of reciprocity. The recipients of the divine favor are expected to live in ways that demonstrate their loyalty to the Messiah. In Romans 8, Paul depicts the appropriate response to the Messiah's benefaction as living "according to the Spirit" (8:4–5) and indebtedness to the Spirit (8:12–13). Humanity can overcome enslavement to passion and desire, not by adoption of the Jewish law (cf. 7:7–25), but by pneumatic empowerment.[113] Paul argues that the Spirit of life in the Messiah sets his readers free from the law of sin and death (8:2) so that they may please God (8:4–8). Those who have been liberated from the dominion of flesh (ἐν σαρκί) have been brought to the dominion of the Spirit (ἐν πνεύματι, 8:9) so that they may set their minds on "the things of the Spirit" (τὰ τοῦ πνεύματος, 8:5).[114]

A key phrase that Paul uses to define his readers' ethical life is "according to the Spirit" (κατὰ πνεῦμα) as opposed to "according to the flesh" (κατὰ σάρκα). Unlike 1:3, 8:3b, and 9:1–5 where σάρξ bears positive overtones, in 8:4–6 and 8:12–13 it has negative overtones. In 8:5–6, Paul describes two mutually exclusive mindsets and their respective outcomes. By mindset (φρόνημα), Paul refers to the sort of thinking that encapsulates one's disposition. To live "according to the flesh" is to set one's mind on the things of the flesh (τὰ τῆς σαρκὸς φρονοῦσιν) while to live "according to the Spirit" is to set one's mind on the things of the Spirit (τὰ τοῦ πνεύματος, 8:5) who dwells in us (8:10b–11).[115] The former leads to death (8:6a, 13a) while the latter leads to life and peace (8:6b).[116] Paul

113. On the argument that the "I" in Romans 7 is the Judaizing gentile and Paul's interlocutor in Romans 1–2, see Stowers, "Romans 7.7–25 as a Speech-in-Character," 180–202; Thiessen, *Paul and the Gentile Problem*, 148.

114. Thiessen rightly states that because gentiles have been freed from malevolent powers of this evil age, they are now marked by "an inner transformation that brings about the solution to the gentile moral problem that Paul caricatures in Rom 1:18–32. The gift of the *pneuma* now results in the moral capacity and ability for self-mastery. Gentiles now can effectively combat the works of the flesh" (*Paul and the Gentile Problem*, 160).

115. Gorman asserts that "to live 'according to' the Spirit is not merely to have an external norm, but a power within, a power that acts to override, indeed to replace, the power of 'the flesh,' the power of sin" (*Cruciformity*, 54).

116. Rom 8:13a, which says that "for if you live according to the flesh you will die,"

then adds that "the mind set on the flesh is hostile to God" (τὸ φρόνημα τῆς σαρκὸς ἔχθρα εἰς θεόν, 8:7) and that those who live in the realm of the flesh (ἐν σαρκὶ ὄντες) "cannot please God" (θεῷ ἀρέσαι οὐ δύνανται, 8:8). Christ's followers must set their minds on the things of the Spirit (8:5–6) and actively oppose the flesh (8:12–13; cf. Gal 5:16–26).

In Rom 1:18—3:20, Paul provides a window into what living κατὰ σάρκα entails. Humanity has not only refused to honor God but they have also turned to immorality and idolatry. They are worthless in their thinking and foolish in their hearts (1:21). God has handed them over "to the lusts of their hearts and to the dishonoring of their bodies" (ταῖς ἐπιθυμίαις τῶν καρδιῶν αὐτῶν εἰς ἀκαθαρσίαν τοῦ ἀτιμάζεσθαι τὰ σώματα αὐτῶν, 1:24). They are inflamed with dishonorable passions (1:26–27). Perhaps the clearest connection between 1:18–32 and what Paul describes in Romans 8 as a mind set on the flesh is the declaration in 1:28 that "God handed them over to a depraved mind, to do things which are not proper" (παρέδωκεν αὐτοὺς ὁ θεὸς εἰς ἀδόκιμον νοῦν, ποιεῖν τὰ μὴ καθήκοντα). The

---

is commonly interpreted as a warning to believers that they risk eternal separation from God if they continue to live according to the flesh. But this reading is questionable on at least three grounds. First, Rom 8 as a whole is concerned with eschatological assurance. Paul begins the chapter with "no condemnation" (8:1) and ends with the declaration that nothing "shall be able to separate us from the love of God, which is in Jesus the Messiah our Lord" (8:39). The entire chapter ought to be read within this framework of assurance. Second, within the chapter, Paul describes his readers as "sons of God" and "children of God" (8:14–21). As sons, the Spirit of God and of Christ lives in them (8:9), they have been adopted into the family of God (8:15), they are "heirs of God and co-heirs with the Messiah" (8:17), and they eagerly await the redemption of their bodies (8:23). Moreover, Paul does not speak of their glorification as a mere possibility, but as something that will certainly happen (8:29–30). Third, Paul has defined in 1:18—3:20 and 7:7–25 what living "according to the flesh" entails. The one who lives "according to the flesh" dishonors God, is ungrateful, immoral, idolatrous, murderous, and commits all sorts of wickedness. This person is "of the flesh, sold under sin" (7:14; cf. 3:9) and his body is imprisoned to death (7:24). How can he be liberated? Paul answers this question in 7:25: "But thanks be to God through Jesus the Messiah our Lord" (χάρις δὲ τῷ θεῷ διὰ Ἰησοῦ Χριστοῦ τοῦ κυρίου ἡμῶν). This response implies that those who are in the Messiah enjoy victory over the flesh and manifest the life-giving power of the Spirit. The preceding three points should inform how we interpret 8:13a. We suggest that when Paul says that "for if you live according to the flesh you will die," he has in mind not only sinful humanity as described in 1:18—3:20, but also the gentile who thinks that he can solve the problem of the flesh by Judaizing (7:7–25). Paul cannot declare that there is no basis for eschatological anxiety for God's sons and in the same breath affirm that those indwelt by the Spirit can still be damned. The rhetorical function of 8:13a is to urge the Romans to reckon that they are no longer in the domain of the flesh; consequently, they must live as those who have the life of Christ in them.

works of a depraved mind include all sorts of unrighteousness, wickedness, greed, evil, envy, murder, gossip, strife, deceit, malice, slander, hatred, pride, and disobedience (1:29–31). In 2:1—3:20, Paul argues that gentiles cannot Judaize their way out of moral incapacitation because "both Jews and gentiles are all under sin" (3:9). No one can please God by securing her own deliverance from the slavery of sin and death.

Liberation from "a depraved mind" comes by the Spirit. That is why Paul writes that the mind set on the Spirit is life and peace (8:6). Believers "walk/live according to the Spirit" (8:4) and "set their minds on the things of the Spirit" (8:5). The Spirit empowers Christ's followers to think in ways that are congruent with their new status in Christ. Walking "according to the Spirit" means that the Spirit empowers them to know, speak, and act in ways that are foreign to the natural, unregenerate person who lives κατὰ σάρκα. The one who has been transferred from the domain of the flesh to that of the Spirit is now able to please God.

In 8:12–14, Paul argues that our obligation to the Spirit is rooted in our identity as God's sons. As we have already seen, the language of obligation or debt is commonly used in benefaction contexts to underline the expectation to show gratitude for the benefits received. In Greco-Roman society, every gift comes with inalienable ties of reciprocity. Paul is at home within this benefaction context when he depicts believers as *not* debtors (ὀφειλέται) to the flesh, but by implication they are under obligation to the Spirit. Christ has not only given us the ultimate gift of himself that liberates us from sin and death, but he has also given us his own Spirit to empower us and restore our ethical capacity. To have the flesh as the controlling principle of one's life again would amount to ingratitude to God and a denial of one's new identity in Christ. As Jewett states, "The regulative principle for Christian family members is the Spirit of Christ."[117]

To be under obligation to the Spirit means that the Romans must discharge their duty by living in ways that are consistent with their identity as God's sons (cf. 8:14). New allegiance to the Spirit demands putting to death the deeds of the body (τοῦ σώματος, 8:13).[118] Paul's choice of the word σῶμα (body) here is not capricious; rather, the implication is that

---

117. Jewett, *Romans*, 493.

118. Tannehill rightly observes that "the Spirit has an active killing function" in the life of the believer (*Dying and Rising*, 80). Also relevant here is Crook, *Reconceptualising Conversion*, 199–250. Crook argues that loyalty to one's benefactor is a social quality that must be expressed in a set of behaviors and actions that increase the honor of one's benefactor or patron.

just as formerly the body was the stronghold of the flesh and its members weapons for unrighteousness, so now the body becomes the location for the manifestation of the transforming power of the Spirit. Although the body still faces the situation of death on account of sin (8:10) and longs for its redemption (8:23), the deeds that ought to mark it now are those of the life-giving Spirit. The Spirit who "sets us free from the law of sin and death" makes holy living possible and necessary. Moo rightly comments that holiness of life is achieved "by our constant living out the 'life' placed within us by the Spirit who has taken up residence within."[119]

Paul's insistence in 8:13 that it is by the Spirit that his readers can put to death the deeds of the body implies a complete reversal of the moral incapacitation that characterizes humanity in 1:18—3:20. Formerly, the body controlled by the flesh dishonored God by engaging in all sorts of wickedness, but now the body empowered by the Spirit pleases the Lord by bearing such fruit of the Spirit as "love, joy, peace, patience, kindness, goodness, faithfulness, gentleness, [and] self-control" (Gal 5:22–23). Those who profess the Messiah as king and who have the Messiah's Spirit living in them must live out their new identity as God's sons by continually overcoming the deeds of the body as the Spirit enables them.[120] It is only the Spirit that can empower believers to please the Lord by appropriately reciprocating the Messiah's benefaction. Thus, such key phrases as "live/walk according to the Spirit" and not "according to the flesh" (8:4–5), "please God" (8:8), "under obligation" (8:12), and "put to death the deeds of the body" (8:13) imply that loyalty to the Messiah is neither an optional extra nor a passive resignation. Rather, it calls for a steady and active devotion of the will as the Spirit empowers us to be true to our sonship and to respond to the Messiah's benefaction in ways that honor him.

Sharing in the Messiah's Suffering

In addition to the Spirit's role in believers' sonship, resurrection, and loyalty, another significant theme in Romans 8 is suffering. Paul previews the theme of suffering in Romans 5, where he argues that those who have been ushered into the Messiah's realm of χάρις "boast" in afflictions as they

---

119. Moo, *Epistle to the Romans*, 495–96.

120. Bates writes that "*pistis* is quite simply not *pistis* at all if it is not embodied and embedded in the allegiant community" (*Salvation by Allegiance Alone*, 121; italics original). Crook states, "Faith for Paul is not only often synonymous with allegiance or faithfulness, it is also an expression of exclusive loyalty" (*Reconceptualising Conversion*, 246).

seek to honor their supreme benefactor. God uses afflictions to develop endurance, form character, and strengthen hope. Given how God uses suffering to accomplish his redemptive purpose, boasting in suffering may be viewed as believers' faithful response to the Messiah's benefaction. So what we find in 5:3–5 is largely about believer's appropriate conduct in suffering. In Romans 8, Paul tackles at least two questions. First, what is the relationship between suffering and believers' eschatological status before God? Second, how does the inevitability of suffering confirm rather than repudiate the Messiah's love for his followers? In response, Paul argues that the Messiah's trajectory of suffering-unto-glory provides the interpretive lens and practical guidance that believers need in suffering.

The first reference to suffering in relation to believers in Romans 8 is in 8:17a where Paul presents suffering and glory as mutually related. The conjunction εἴπερ should probably be translated as "for it is indeed," "seeing that," or "since indeed" for it more likely introduces a fact that is accepted rather than a condition (cf. 8:9).[121] The clause should therefore be translated as "since indeed we suffer with him in order that we may also be glorified with him" (εἴπερ συμπάσχομεν ἵνα καὶ συνδοξασθῶμεν). Paul does not regard present suffering with Christ as a condition to sonship and future glory, but as an inevitable result for those who are in Christ. Cranfield's paraphrase of 8:17b eloquently captures this point: "[F]or the fact that we are now suffering with Him, so far from calling the reality of our heirship in question, is a pledge of our being glorified with Him hereafter."[122] This suffering points to how believers, through their union with Christ, have made Christ's story their own. Their participation in this story means that they will always be faithful to the Messiah as they face all sorts of hardships. Ben Witherington asserts, "One must follow the path Christ followed to glory, the path of self-sacrifice, or suffering with him and for him in the cause for which he suffered."[123]

Christ is the divine benefactor who invites his followers to share in his glory by means of suffering.[124] Greco-Roman benefactors use their great resources to deliver humanity from all kinds of sufferings, including

---

121. See Gieniusz, *Romans 8:18–30*, 74; Campbell, *Paul and Union*, 231; Cranfield, *Critical and Exegetical Commentary*, 407; Eastman, "Oneself in Another," 115; Jewett, *Romans*, 502; Smith, *Paul's Seven Explanations*, 178.

122. Cranfield, *Critical and Exegetical Commentary*, 407–8.

123. Witherington, *Paul's Letter to the Romans*, 219.

124. See Jacob, *Conformed to the Image*, 202–27. Jacob contends that sharing in Christ's glory is to participate in his universal sovereignty as son.

famine, war, and pestilence. A reign is peaceful and prosperous to the extent that it alleviates hardships and promotes happiness. No ancient royal benefactor would be memorialized for claiming to deliver his people by leading them to suffer greatly. Such a ruler would be termed as a tyrant, not a good king; he is neither generous nor philanthropic. Yet, the Messiah's unmatched generosity that is demonstrated through his identification with humanity (8:3) and substitutionary atonement (5:6–10) not only delivers humanity from sin and death, but also transforms how humanity views suffering. Just as the cross was Christ's pathway to glory, so those who suffer with Christ will also be glorified with Christ. And to reiterate, by glory Paul is describing the resurrection of the dead and the privilege of sharing in the Messiah's victorious rule. To be glorified with Christ is to be raised *in power* (1:3–4), clothed with immortality and incorruptibility, and to rule with him.

Paul's theology of suffering as seen here is very similar to that of Ignatius of Antioch.[125] Ignatius not only asserts that "Christianity is a matter of greatness when it is hated by the world" (*Romans* 6:3) but he is also desirous to "imitate the suffering of my God" (τοῦ πάθους τοῦ θεοῦ μου, 6:3) and to die as a martyr (4:1–2). Suffering in Christ is indeed the pathway to freedom: "But if I suffer, I will become a freed person who belongs to Jesus Christ, and I will rise up, free, in him" (4:3).[126] Like Paul, Ignatius contends that all Christians will face suffering even as they follow the example of Jesus. In *Magnesians* 5:2, he writes that "unless we voluntarily agree to die into his [Jesus Christ's] sufferings (τὸ ἀποθανεῖν εἰς τὸ αὐτοῦ πάθος), his life is not in us." Even the prophets also suffered due to their commitment to Christ: "The divine prophets themselves lived according to Christ Jesus. That is why they were persecuted, for they were inspired by his grace (ὑπὸ τῆς χάριτος αὐτοῦ) to convince unbelievers that God is one, and that he has revealed himself in his son Jesus Christ" (*Magnesians* 8:2). Ignatius also views Christian life as a contest: "Stand firm, as does an anvil which is beaten. It is the part of a noble athlete to be wounded, and yet to conquer. And especially, we ought to bear all things for the sake of God, that he also

---

125. This comparison is especially viable if the argument of Davies is right that Ignatius died in 113 CE ("Predicament of Ignatius of Antioch," 175–80).

126. Ignatius writes in *Romans* 5:3: "Now I am beginning to be a disciple. May nothing visible or invisible show any envy toward me, that I may attain to Jesus Christ. Fire and cross and packs of wild beasts, cuttings, and being torn apart, the scattering of bones, the mangling of limbs, the grinding of the whole body, the evil torments of the devil—let them come upon me, only that I may attain to Jesus Christ."

may bear with us" (*Polycarp* 3:1). Like Paul, Ignatius views suffering as the inevitable result of imitating Christ and faithful discipleship.

In Rom 8:18 Paul adds a comment that shows that although suffering and glory are mutually related, the former is a very slight thing in comparison with the latter: "For I consider that the sufferings of this present time are not worthy to be compared with the glory that is to be revealed to us" (Λογίζομαι γὰρ ὅτι οὐκ ἄξια τὰ παθήματα τοῦ νῦν καιροῦ πρὸς τὴν μέλλουσαν δόξαν ἀποκαλυφθῆναι εἰς ἡμᾶς). In 2 Cor 4:16–17, Paul writes that when believers face suffering, they do not lose heart because "although our outer self is decaying, our inner self is being renewed day by day. For our momentary, light affliction (παραυτίκα ἐλαφρὸν τῆς θλίψεως ἡμῶν) is producing for us an eternal weight of glory (αἰώνιον βάρος δόξης) far beyond all comparison." Afflictions are momentary but the glory that God is achieving for us through them is eternal. Suffering reminds us that the body is perishable, but it will be raised imperishable; suffering exposes us to shame and dishonor, but the resurrection life is marked by perfect glory; and suffering reveals the body's fragility, but the hope of glory declares that the body will be raised in power (cf. 1 Cor 15:42–44).

It is important to underline that this eschatological glory is the Messiah's undeserved gift to believers. In Greco-Roman society, "glory" is attained through benefactions, which are in turn reciprocated by loyalty and praise. That is why Plutarch writes that "the love of honor and beneficence (τὸ φιλότιμον καὶ φιλάνθρωπον) reaches out to eternity as it strives for the crown by deeds and benefactions (χάρισιν) that bring the doer a pleasure impossible to describe" (*Mor.* 1098E). Generous benefactors are honored because they deserve it. Paul, however, maintains that humanity's redemption is from start to end an incongruous gift. Believers will receive the eschatological glory, not because they are worthy, but because the Messiah loves them as unworthy sinners and has enabled them to participate in his resurrection life and victorious rule. Wright notes that the glory that is to be revealed to us implies that "the future revelation will bestow glory upon us . . . as a gift."[127] We see once again that the glorious destiny of the Messiah is also the destiny of his followers. As believers suffer, they are reminded that they are sharing in Christ's suffering and sonship. Union with Christ in suffering confirms rather than jeopardizes believers' eternal glorious status before God.[128]

127. Wright, "Letter to the Romans," 595.

128. Gieniusz comments that "the sufferings of the present time do not thwart the glory to be revealed" (*Romans 8:18-30*, 100).

To emphasize further the fact that suffering cannot thwart the eschatological glory, Paul turns to the question as to whether suffering can separate believers from the Messiah's love (8:31–39). Paul begins this closing passage of Romans 8 by affirming God's commitment to believers: "If God is for us, who is against us?" (8:31b). God has demonstrated that he is for us (ὑπὲρ ἡμῶν) by handing his son over for us (8:32, 39).[129] The questions that follow this affirmation of God's commitment are designed to alleviate any eschatological anxiety that Paul's readers might still have. One of those questions is: "Who shall separate us from the love of the Messiah?" (τίς ἡμᾶς χωρίσει ἀπὸ τῆς ἀγάπης τοῦ Χριστοῦ;) (8:35). To be severed from the Messiah's love is to forfeit salvation and therefore face the eschatological judgment.[130] Paul writes in 5:5 that God's love has been poured out in our hearts, and in 5:8 that God has demonstrated his own love for us by sending Christ to die for us "while we were still sinners." As we have seen, in Romans 5 Paul emphasizes humanity's unworthiness and the Messiah's incommensurate gift. In the present passage, Paul declares that the supreme benefactor who died for us (8:32), who was raised, and who is exalted at God's right hand, where he intercedes for humanity (8:34), is the Lord of love. He brings his unworthy followers into his dominion of love and keeps them therein forever.

Paul explicitly identifies the Messiah with the royal figure of LXX Ps 109:1: "Sit at my right hand, until I make your enemies a footstool for your feet." Christ's enthronement at God's right hand implies that he exercises sovereignty over all things (cf. Matt 20:21–23; Mark 10:37; 1 Cor 15:24–25; Eph 1:20–23). Those who have experienced the love of the Messiah share in his victorious rule (Rom 8:17). The Messiah's triumph is not just over sin and death, but over every imaginable danger that might beset God's people. The implied answer to the question "who shall separate us from the love of the Messiah?" is that "some agent" (τίς) will in fact attempt to stand against God's people, but it will all be futile because there is no power that is stronger than the Messiah's love (8:38–39). Moreover, these powers are impotent to "bring a charge against us" (8:33), or to "condemn" (8:34). Paul shows in 8:35 and 8:38–39 that "the powers of the dying age exercise themselves impotently yet still actually upon the church even as

---

129. On God's love as revealed through Jesus, Ziegler notes, "In the free and sovereign coming of the Son, in his self-giving unto death, and in his resurrection and ascension to the right hand of the Father, God's love has invaded and traversed the landscape of the fallen world concretely and with momentous effect" ("Love of God," 127).

130. See Jewett, *Romans*, 543.

they once did upon its Lord."[131] But Paul is emphatic that these powers cannot repossess those who have been liberated by the grace and love of the Messiah. That is why he declares in 8:39 that nothing "will be able to separate us from the love of God that is in the Messiah Jesus our Lord."[132]

What, then, is the present experience of those who are in the Messiah's dominion of love? They are under assault; they are assailed by all kinds of adversities. Whereas in 8:18 Paul speaks generally of the "sufferings of the present time," in 8:35 he is more specific as he provides a catalog of seven threats that conspire against Christ's followers: tribulation, distress, persecution, famine, nakedness, peril, and sword. Philip G. Ziegler writes as follows concerning this catalog of threats: "Whatever Christ's kingship entails, it does not insulate the community from the agonism of the clash of the ages; neither is the existence of such distress a mark of divine disfavor, as might perhaps anxiously be thought."[133] Paul's quotation of LXX Ps 43:23 in Rom 8:36 demonstrates that believers suffer for God's sake as they follow the trajectory of the Messiah who was handed over to death (8:32).[134] Just as the righteous Messiah was led as a "sheep to slaughter" (Isa 53:7), so believers are given over to death.[135]

Suffering, however, is not the end of the story; there is a resounding triumph! Paul states in 8:37 that "in all these things we mightily triumph through the one who loved us." The prior reference to the love of the Messiah (8:35) suggests that "the one who loved us" is Jesus. He suffered violence even to the point of death (8:32), yet he arose victoriously and all things are subject to him (8:34). Just as grace reigns over sin and death (Romans 5–6), so it is through the love of the Messiah

---

131. Ziegler, "Love of God," 120.

132. Jipp writes, "The Messiah's enthronement to a position of divine power (8:34; cf. 1:4) insures that there is simply no aspect of creation, no cosmic power belonging to Adam's dominion, that can return Christ's people to their former enslavement to the reign of sin and death" (*Christ Is King*, 196). Likewise, Käsemann states, "Redemption means nothing else but a change of lordship—indeed, a return from slavery to supra-earthly and earthly powers to the Father . . . Transferred into the kingdom of his beloved Son, we belong to a world that likewise has its lord and king" (*On Being a Disciple*, 198)

133. Ziegler, "Love of God," 120.

134. On Paul's use of LXX Ps 43:23, Hays writes: "Paul's point . . . is that Scripture prophesies suffering as the lot of those . . . who live in the eschatological interval between Christ's resurrection and the ultimate redemption of the world" (*Echoes of Scripture*, 58).

135. Hays, *Echoes of Scripture*, 63. Hays writes that Paul "hints and whispers all around Isaiah 53" with the implication that upon believers "is the chastisement that makes others whole, and with their stripes is creation healed."

that believers mightily prevail over every form of adversity. Jipp writes: "Christ's people are the ones who conquer, but this victory takes place by means of their participation in the Messiah's triumph."[136] Those who are in the Messiah belong to him forever. Their suffering is neither a sign of divine disfavor nor proof that they have been reclaimed by the powers of this world. Rather, they are following their supreme benefactor's pattern of suffering-unto-glory even as they are fully convinced that the one who loves them and who exercises sovereignty over all things has made an indissoluble final claim upon their destiny.

Summary of the Messiah's Supreme Royal Benefaction in Romans 5:12—8:39

The preceding argument shows that the Messiah's supreme royal benefaction overpowers sin and death and thereby guarantees believers' moral transformation and future resurrection. Believers are in turn expected to walk in "newness of life" by faithful response to the Messiah's lordship. The Messiah's death and resurrection are the means by which he overcomes sin and death. Throughout Rom 5:12—8:39, Paul argues that the historic events of the death, the resurrection, and the enthronement of the Messiah define life for believers. These events form the foundation for a new existence and continue to determine how believers engage in conflict with the powers of the old world. The Messiah invites his followers to share in his triumphant and beneficent reign.

Paul argues that the Messiah's benefaction is superior not only because it defeats sin and death, but it also reveals God's unmatched generosity. The gift of χάρις is superabundant, not due to its plurality, but precisely due to its singularity and incommensurability. This gift is Jesus himself who identifies with humanity and dies as their substitute. The Christ-gift abounds in the face of an avalanche of sin. The gift does not correspond to the unworthiness of the beneficiaries. Rather, it is bestowed on those who are condemned, and who are morally incapacitated. Once bestowed, the gift delivers humanity and guarantees their eternal destiny. The Messiah gives his Spirit to his followers so that they may become God's pneumatic children. Just as there is a filial relation between God and God's son, so God's pneumatic children enjoy an intimate relationship with him. Believers' present spiritual sonship assures them of

---

136. Jipp, *Christ Is King*, 197.

their eschatological sonship and the redemption of their bodies. And just as the Spirit of life was at work in the resurrection of the son, so the Spirit who indwells believers guarantees their victory over death; the Spirit will give life to the believer's mortal body. Unlike the ancient benefaction practice where glory was a preserve of the wealthy who won perpetual memorialization through generosity, Paul contends that the criterion for eternal glorious status before God is the possession of the Messiah's Spirit. It is through the Spirit that believers are mapped onto the Messiah's trajectory which is marked by suffering, death, resurrection, and sovereignty over all things.

To profess Jesus as the supreme royal benefactor implies that one must fulfill his obligation to honor him. The Messiah liberates believers from the dominion of sin and death so that they may live under the lordship of χάρις. They respond appropriately to the Messiah's benefaction by reckoning that they have been morally capacitated and that their mindset is now shaped by the Spirit. They, therefore, walk according to the Spirit, present the members of their body as weapons for righteousness, and recognize that sin no longer exercises lordship over them. Their conduct ought to show their unwavering loyalty to the Messiah. This reciprocity is not designed to win more gifts from the Messiah; rather, it demonstrates commitment to honoring the Lord and remaining true to one's identity within the family of God. As believers await their resurrection, Paul wants them to remember that there is no basis for eschatological anxiety because having been brought into the realm of the Messiah's χάρις, they will neither face condemnation nor experience severance from the Messiah's love.

6

Summary and Conclusion

THE GOAL OF THIS study has been to examine how Paul might be drawing upon the Greco-Roman system of royal benefaction in his messianic discourse in Rom 5:1–11 and how he develops in 5:12—8:39 some of the themes which he introduces in 5:1–11. Paul sets the tone of his Christology from the onset of Romans when he declares that he is a slave of Jesus the Messiah, and that the gospel is about the Davidic son, who has been enthroned as "the son-of-God-in-power . . . by the resurrection from the dead" (1:1–4). This son of David and son of God is "Jesus the Messiah our Lord" (1:4). In 15:7–13, Paul declares that Jesus is the root of Jesse about whose coming Isaiah prophesied. Thus, Paul's royal Christology forms an inclusio for the body of Romans (1:1–7 with 15:7–13). This framing pattern is also found in Romans 5–8. Paul states in 5:1 that peace with God comes through "our Lord Jesus the Messiah;" in 5:11, he writes that we boast through "our Lord Jesus the Messiah." At the end of Romans 5, Paul declares that χάρις reigns "through Jesus the Messiah our Lord." Paul's closing statement in Romans 6 is that "the gift of God is eternal life in the Messiah Jesus our Lord" (6:23). Romans 7 also ends in a similar way as Paul gives thanks to God "through Jesus the Messiah our Lord" (7:25). Likewise, Paul begins Romans 8 by declaring that there is no "condemnation for those who are in the Messiah Jesus" (8:1) and ends the chapter by affirming that nothing can separate believers from "the love of God that is in the Messiah Jesus our Lord" (8:39).

Wright observes that the christological formula sums up Paul's argument in Romans 5–8.[1]

Paul's framing pattern both reveals his explicit interest in royal Christology and suggests a significant interpretive clue. To have a better understanding of Romans, we need to accept Paul's invitation to read it as a messianic discourse. The question that follows is: How does Paul construct this discourse in 5:1–11, which previews 5:12—8:39? We have argued throughout this work that one of the resources Paul uses in his Christ-language is the ancient script of royal benefaction. Yet Paul is not merely interested in portraying Jesus as another benefactor who distributes gifts; rather, he argues that Jesus is the supreme royal benefactor whose commitment to believers guarantees their eternal glorious status before God and demands faithful response to his lordship even in suffering.

Royal Benefaction According to Greco-Roman and Jewish Writings

To prove our assertion that Paul's christological discourse draws upon the ancient system of royal benefaction, the introductory chapter was followed by chapters 2 and 3 which established the interpretive framework by focusing on the practice of royal benefaction as found in various Greco-Roman and Jewish writings as well as epigraphic evidence. Benefaction is a system of discriminatory gift exchange that seeks to promote social cohesion by the ethic of reciprocity. Differently defined, benefaction is the practice of gift-giving that thrives due to the benefactor's generosity and the beneficiaries' gratitude and loyalty. The ideal royal benefactor is appointed by the gods who have entrusted to him great resources for the welfare of the people. He demonstrates his generosity and philanthropy by bestowing benefactions. Such benefactions might include providing medical services, overcoming enemies, building cities, constructing temples, maintaining peace, supplying grain, sponsoring games, renovating public buildings, remitting taxes, cancelling debts, and lowering market price of commodities in time of need. Due to his love and care for the people, the ideal royal benefactor is often referred to as a father, a shepherd, a guardian, a savior, a general, and a friend. Like their Greco-Roman counterparts, the Jewish writers that we examined depict

---

1. Wright, "Letter to the Romans," 509. On the framing pattern in Romans 5–8, see Longenecker, *Epistle to the Romans*, 545.

the ideal ruler as Yahweh's representative who serves as an agent of blessings to the people. The king is Yahweh's anointed son who is empowered by the Spirit and whose reign is eternal. The king fights Yahweh's battles, delivers the oppressed, and rules with integrity. He establishes the people in righteousness and maintains peace and prosperity.

Benefaction in Greco-Roman society is discriminatory. The gift must be commensurate with the worthiness of the beneficiary. To give gifts indiscriminately is to act foolishly and to destroy social cohesion. Indiscriminate benefaction destroys social cohesion because it fails to reward the virtuous and punish the impious. The impious ought to be punished by withholding gifts from them. The benefactors are therefore urged to apply the rule of censorship and to strategically place their gifts. They should emulate a careful farmer who sows his seeds in productive soil to ensure plentiful harvest. And they ought to distribute favors like a skilled player who pitches the ball to skilled catchers. Giving to the wrong people (namely the base and the ungrateful) is not a sign of generosity; rather, it indicates thoughtlessness and indifference to excellence and reputation.

In addition to discrimination, gift-giving flourishes to the extent that the beneficiaries discharge their obligation to reciprocate. The ethic of reciprocity is the principle that the recipient of a favor should return χάρις for χάρις. Every gift comes with the expectation to reciprocate. Those who fail to show gratitude to the benefactor commit a shameful act and rob the benefactor of the honor due him. Ingratitude is the worst crime because it destroys social cohesion and rewards generosity with vice. A proper understanding of the initial favor as a debt would lead the beneficiaries to discharge their obligation to give loyalty and obedience to the benefactor. Three Graces had been strategically set up to remind the people of their obligation to reciprocate. The Graces dance in a ring to visualize a benefit passing from one hand to another, ultimately returning to the initial giver. If the ring, which symbolizes the circle of reciprocity, is broken, then the beauty of the dance also collapses. In other words, failure to reciprocate is detrimental to the practice of gift-giving as it amounts to rewarding generosity with disloyalty.[2] Honor and gratitude may be in the form of public praise, social or political support, statues, crowns, and seats of honor. Sometimes the beneficiary might even be willing to die for the sake of his benefactor. But the greatest way to express honor

---

2. See Crook, *Reconceptualizing Conversion*, 250. Crook rightly asserts that the system of benefaction or patronage was sustained by loyalty and that disloyalty dishonored the benefactor and could lead to the loss of benefactions.

and gratitude is through the honorary inscription. The inscription publicizes the benefactor's virtues, achievements, and honors voted him. It also testifies to the benefactor's victory over mortality through perpetual memorialization by posterity. The system of benefaction and the ethic of reciprocity that sustains it, therefore, provides a way for rulers to obtain lasting glory by having their names inscribed on bronze tablets and on the immortal love of posterity.

The Messiah's Supreme Royal Benefaction in Romans 5:1–11 and 5:12—8:39

Having described the system of ancient royal benefaction, chapters 4 and 5 looked at how Paul portrays Jesus as the supreme royal benefactor in Rom 5:1–11 and 5:12—8:39 respectively. Paul's intimate familiarity with the Greco-Roman benefaction system is evident through such motifs as peace, χάρις, access, glory, faith, friendship, love, sacrifice, hope, boasting, enmity, giving, shame, suffering, reconciliation, "the good," favor, superabundance, obligation, and obedience. Our discussion of 5:1–11 (chapter 4) and 5:12—8:39 (chapter 5) reveals that Paul presents Jesus as the supreme royal benefactor in both conventional and subversive ways.

Just as is expected of Greco-Roman benefactors, Paul maintains that the Messiah establishes peace and reconciliation, provides access into his royal presence, and gives χάρις to humanity. The Messiah delivers humanity from sin and death, brings boasting, offers sacrifice, and guarantees immortality and an honorable status to his followers. Similarly, as God's son, the Messiah reveals God's love and serves as an agent of divine blessings to humanity. He establishes his followers in righteousness and empowers them to obey God. And like what we find in the Greco-Roman benefaction system, the Messiah's χάρις demands appropriate conduct that honors him as the supreme benefactor.

Yet the Messiah's supreme royal benefaction subverts several aspects of the Greco-Roman benefaction system. First, the Messiah offers his own life as a gift, thereby he is both the giver and the gift. It is not unheard of in Greco-Roman society for a ruler to be willing to die for the sake of his people. The dominant script, however, is for the people to willingly face danger as an expression of love and devotion to their ruler. Paul subverts this dominant script when he declares that our Lord Jesus the Messiah and the son of God died for humanity. God handed his son over to death (8:32) to demonstrate his love for humanity (5:8).

Second, closely related to the preceding point is that the Messiah's gift of himself as χάρις is *singular*, and yet *superabundant*. In Greco-Roman society, abundance is usually associated with multiplicity of gifts. The generous ruler bestows many favors, for the more the favors the greater the honor won. But Paul declares in 5:15–20 that the one destiny defining χάρις is God's gift of the Messiah. The Messiah's χάρις is the generous offer, not of somethings, but someone, namely Godself.[3] This singular gift liberates humanity from the tyranny of sin and death, transforms humanity into friends and children of God, and enables participation in the life and reign of the Messiah.

Third, the Messiah's superabundant benefaction is indiscriminate. There is a profound mismatch (or "unfittingness") between the Messiah's gift and the unworthiness of humanity. Paul argues in 1:18—3:20 that the entire human race is sinful; both Jews and gentiles are "under sin" (3:9). To underline the complete unworthiness of those for whom the Messiah died, Paul refers to humanity as "weak," "ungodly," "sinners," and "enemies" (5:6–10). In 6:15–23, he describes believers' former life as slavery to sin. The body commandeered by sin (6:6) bore fruit of which believers are now ashamed (6:21). The Messiah died for those who are morally incapacitated (5:6–8) and who deserve condemnation (5:16–18). His χάρις does not reward the virtuous and punish the impious. He neither strategically places his χάρις to maximize the possibility of a return nor sows his seed in productive soil to ensure plentiful harvest. He does not dispense χάρις like a skilled player pitching the ball to a skilled catcher. Because he does not apply the rule of censorship, the Messiah would be scorned in Greco-Roman society for making his purse accessible to the base and for conferring his favor on the wrong people; he would be likened to a foolish farmer sowing his seed in worn-out and unproductive soil. According to the Greco-Roman benefaction system, the Messiah's indiscriminate benefaction, which abounds against the backdrop of an avalanche of sin, would be termed as foolish, disgraceful, and a threat to social cohesion.

But Paul declares that the Messiah's supreme benefaction is deliberately and wisely bestowed on a people who lack moral, social, or ethnic standing. Its wisdom and intentionality are evident in the fact that

---

3. Pickett states that "the gift which God gives in the death of Christ is Godself" ("Death of Christ," 739).

it is bestowed "at that time" (5:6), by which Paul implies the temporal appropriateness of the Messiah's death for the ungodly. Discriminatory gift-giving dictates that χάρις should be given *at the right time*, meaning *when* the beneficiary has demonstrated his worthiness. In Greco-Roman society, gifts are given to people *because of who they are*. Yet the Messiah died "at that time" in the sense that he offered his life with complete knowledge of human depravity. He never considered withholding his gift until such a time as would be more fitting to reward the virtuous. Based on the norms of the ancient benefaction, the Messiah's gift is foolish and untimely, but in the light of God's infinite wisdom and incommensurate generosity, the Messiah's gift is given *at the right time* to the worthless to rescue them from sin and death so that they may participate in the Messiah's eternal dominion. And unlike the Greco-Roman benefaction system whereby only a few people enjoy access to the ruler, the Messiah's gift indiscriminately ushers humanity into his royal chamber so that all may enjoy the benefits of his rule (5:2).

Fourth, the Messiah's benefaction reverses the disgraceful status of his followers and promises them an eternal glorious status before God. The Messiah gives χάρις to the morally incapacitated, but he does not leave them in that state. Instead, his gift liberates them from the slavery of sin and death and brings them into his kingdom of life. The Messiah's followers are now God's pneumatic sons because the Spirit of the Messiah dwells in them (8:9–16; cf. 5:5). And just as the Messiah is now "the son-of-God-in-power according to the Spirit of holiness by the resurrection from the dead" (1:4), so God's sons who have the Spirit of adoption are assured of rising from the dead. The destiny of the Messiah, who identified with humanity in his fleshly existence (1:3; 8:2) and died as their substitute (5:6–8), is also the destiny of God's children (8:17). The hope of the glory of God does not put to shame (5:5) because the Messiah's trajectory is also the believer's trajectory. Whereas in Greco-Roman society "lasting honor and immortality" can only be obtained by the wealthy through acts of kindness, Paul declares that it is the indwelling Spirit of the Messiah that guarantees the eschatological redemption (8:11; cf. 8:23) and deliverance from wrath (cf. 5:5, 9–10). Believers can "boast in the hope of the glory of God" (5:2a) because the Spirit who raised the Messiah from the dead (1:4) will give life to their mortal bodies (8:11).

The body needs to be brought to conformity to the image of the risen son (8:23, 29) because humanity's redemption is only complete when the body has been fully redeemed. The fact that the body has not yet been glorified implies that believers still inhabit a decaying world whereby their bodies still face conflict with the old powers. The body is dead on account of sin (8:10) but it is also the site of the miraculous power of the life-giving Spirit. Christ's followers have been liberated from the dominion of sin and death through their Spirit-mediated union with Christ. Their existence is both characterized by dying with Christ and the life-giving Spirit. The body continues to experience conflict with the power of sin and death in this life, but the indwelling Spirit guarantees its complete transformation and deliverance. As they await the redemption of the body (8:23), believers are not filled with eschatological anxiety since they are assured that rather than being enemies of God (cf. 5:10; 8:7), they are friends and sons of God (8:14–17). Similarly, having secured their peace with God (5:1, 10), the Messiah promises his followers that neither will they be condemned (5:10; 8:1, 31–34) nor will anything separate them from the Messiah's love (8:35–39). Unlike the Greco-Roman ruler whose benefaction secures neither his own actual immortality nor that of his subjects, the Messiah maps his followers onto his trajectory of death and resurrection, and thereby guarantees their eternal glorious status.

Fifth, the Messiah's benefaction is superior and surprising because it overturns the expectation of a heroic act of reciprocity. Many Greco-Roman writers affirm that no sacrifice is too great to pay for the sake of "the good" (ὁ ἀγαθός). The term ἀγαθός is often used to refer to the benefactor who wins great honor due to his generosity and concern for the welfare of others. In 5:7, Paul alludes to the rare but not inconceivable practice whereby the beneficiary of a favor would be willing to die on behalf of his benefactor. The Messiah, however, lays down his life neither for a just person nor "the good," but for the unworthy, and in so doing, he subverts an important aspect of the ethic of reciprocity.

Lastly, the Messiah's benefaction transforms believers' view of suffering. One of Paul's concerns in 5:3–5 and 8:17–39 is the shape that reciprocating the Messiah's benefaction takes in suffering. Believers' view of suffering is grounded in the Messiah's pattern of death and resurrection. The Messiah invites his followers to faithfully participate in his trajectory of suffering-unto-glory. The key word that Paul uses in 5:3–5 to define how believers respond appropriately to the Messiah's benefaction in suffering is "boasting." This boasting implies that believers have confidence not only in the Messiah's sovereignty over the realms of suffering, sin, death, and life, but it also underscores their willingness to give Christ loyalty and obedience even in adversity. Additionally, Christ's followers recognize that righteous suffering does not indicate the Messiah's disfavor; rather, just as God's son was handed over to death (8:32; cf. 5:6–10), so God's pneumatic children "are being put to death all day long" and "are considered as sheep to be slaughtered" for the sake of God (8:36; cf. Isa 53:7). But suffering is not the end of the believer's story. Paul argues that the Messiah designs suffering for shaping his followers' character and strengthening their hope of glory. Believers, who were formerly morally incapacitated, have been brought into the domain of χάρις whereby the Messiah orchestrates suffering to teach them endurance, establish them as godly, and remind them of glorification (5:3–5; 8:17).

What Paul says about believers' response in suffering might have surprised his readers because, according to the Greco-Roman practice of gift-giving, the ideal ruler is successful to the extent that he eliminates all forms of danger and suffering. The ruler who desires to be memorialized by posterity cannot claim to deliver people, and yet declare that suffering is inevitable under his reign. Such a ruler is tyrannical rather than benevolent and philanthropic. Paul's argument that suffering is a given, that believers must share in Christ's suffering, and that believers can indeed boast in suffering only makes sense in light of the death, the resurrection, and the enthronement of the Messiah. What is true for the supreme benefactor is also true for those who submit to his lordship. Suffering constantly reminds believers of the cosmic conflict, the Messiah's triumph, the call to participate in the Messiah's trajectory, and the need to continually rely on the Spirit's sustaining power.[4] Because the Messiah loves and is committed to his followers, one day he will vindicate them by the power of resurrection, when they will no longer face suffering and decay. Until then, believers must publicize their faithful allegiance to the Messiah even in adversity.

A point that we have highlighted above as a similarity between the Greco-Roman royal benefaction system and the Messiah's supreme benefaction is reciprocity. Whoever receives χάρις in Greco-Roman society understands that he must reciprocate by conducting himself in ways that honor the benefactor. Otherwise, he would be charged with ingratitude, which is a shameful act and the worst of all vices. Paul's theology of χάρις

---

4. Tannehill states, "Because they prevent the believer from trusting in himself and so falling back into the old life, suffering and death are positive aspects of God's rule over his own, and can be understood as participation in Christ's death. God has already conquered death, not by abolishing it (this is still future), but by commandeering it for his own purposes" (*Dying and Rising*, 77).

is inextricably embedded in this ancient context. For Paul, χάρις is indeed incongruous and unfitting (hence it is undeserved). Yet incommensurability does not nullify reciprocity; instead, χάρις demands appropriate conduct and loyal response. If a gift bestowed on the basis of worth obligates the beneficiary to express gratitude, then how much more the one given to the unworthy and upon which their eternal destiny depends! Paul explicitly writes in 1:5 that through the Messiah "we have received grace (ἐλάβομεν χάριν) and apostleship to bring about the obedience of faith (εἰς ὑπακοὴν πίστεως) among all the gentiles for his name's sake." For Paul, there is no doubt that those who have received χάρις must live in ways that are befitting their new identity in Christ. The Messiah has given us the unfitting gift that guarantees our eternal redemption; it is only appropriate to respond fittingly by faithful obedience to him.

This fitting response to χάρις is a major theme in Romans 6 and 8, where Paul defines life "under grace" and "according to the Spirit." The "newness of life" (6:4) that marks the believer is grounded in the Messiah's benefaction that overcomes humanity's intrinsic moral incapacitation and makes it possible and necessary to have a new mindset (8:4–9). Believers' disposition is now shaped by the Spirit rather than the flesh. As God's pneumatic sons, they are debtors to the Spirit (8:12–14).[5] It is by the Spirit that the Messiah restores their moral capacity so that they can offer the members of their body to God as weapons for righteousness (6:15–23). Paul even uses the metaphor of slavery to figure believers as bond-servants of Christ, meaning that they owe him faithful obedience (6:15–23). The Messiah's χάρις superabounds against the backdrop of an avalanche of sin (5:15–17), yet those who have been brought under χάρις cannot continue in sin because sin no longer exercises lordship over them (6:1–14).

How, then, should believers honor their supreme royal benefactor? Paul gives several imperatives that show that the believer's body is the site that displays "newness of life" and loyalty to the Messiah. Believers

---

5. Paul does not have any problem with figuring χάρις as obligatory. He identifies himself as a "debtor" (ὀφειλέτης, 1:14) because he has received χάρις that leads to the "obedience of faith among all the nations" (1:5; cf. 15:7–15). The Jerusalem collection is not an initial gift but a return gift (15:25–28). Paul writes that Macedonia and Achaia "are obliged (ὀφειλέται εἰσίν) to them [Jerusalem]. For if the gentiles have shared in their spiritual blessings (τοῖς πνευματικοῖς), they are obliged (ὀφείλουσιν) also to minister to them in material blessings (τοῖς σαρκικοῖς)" (15:27; cf. 13:8). Paul is simply operating with the principle that the recipient of a gift is under obligation to reciprocate fittingly.

are to reckon themselves "dead to sin but alive to God in Jesus the Messiah" (6:11); they should not let sin exercise dominion over their mortal body to make it obey its passions (6:12); they should not present their "members to sin as weapons for unrighteousness" (6:13); they should present themselves to God as those who have Christ's resurrection life in them (6:13); they should present their "members to God as weapons for righteousness" (6:13, 19); they should not let sin exercise lordship over them (6:14); and by the Spirit they put to death the deeds of the body (8:13). To live "under grace" is to bear fruit that leads to sanctification and whose end is eternal life (6:22–23). The goal of working out the reality of the Messiah's benefaction as the Spirit empowers us is to please God (8:8). The body, which still faces death and decay because of sin (8:10) and whose conflict with the powers of the Adamic dominion reminds the believer of the Messiah's incongruous χάρις, is also the "inscription" that displays gratitude to the Messiah for the gift of redemption. As believers await their eschatological redemption (8:23, 29), they must be true to their identity as God's children and the Messiah's followers. Their faithful allegiance to the Messiah is the proof that they have indeed been brought into the Messiah's dominion of χάρις.

It is important to clarify that believers' reciprocity is not designed to win more favors from the Lord. In Greco-Roman society, the public display of inscription both honors the benefactor and indirectly asks for more favors. Paul, however, argues that believers have been brought into the Messiah's royal domain (5:2) whereby they have everything necessary for bearing fruit to the Lord. Moreover, Paul maintains that the singular χάρις leads to eternal life through the Messiah (5:15–17; 6:23). Thus, rather than winning additional gifts, believers' Spirit-empowered reciprocity demonstrates that they belong to Christ and that they faithfully give him loyalty and obedience. For if the Messiah is indeed the supreme royal benefactor whose commitment to his followers guarantees their eternal glorious status before God, then it is only appropriate for his followers to respond fittingly to his benefaction by faithfully submitting to his lordship.

Fulfillment of the Aims of Study

Our main objective throughout this study has been to examine how Paul might be drawing upon the Greco-Roman royal benefaction system in

Rom 5:1–11 as well as 5:12—8:39 to accomplish his theological purpose of portraying Jesus Christ as the supreme royal benefactor so that the Roman readers might faithfully enact his rule now even as they anticipate glorification. To this end, this study has addressed three main textual conundrums in 5:1–11. First, at the lexical level, it has provided a reading that accounts for the benefaction motifs that permeate 5:1–11 and 5:12—8:39. Such motifs as peace, χάρις, access, glory, faith, friendship, immortality, love, sacrifice, hope, boasting, enmity, giving, shame, suffering, reconciliation, "the good," favor, superabundance, obligation, and obedience suggest that Paul is tapping into the Greco-Roman practice of royal benefaction. Our survey of Greco-Roman and Jewish sources has shown that the ancient writers often use these motifs as they discuss how rulers demonstrate their concern for the welfare of the people by bestowing favors and how the people render loyalty and obedience. Reading Paul in the light of his social context reveals that he employs benefaction language and that his royal discourse depicts Jesus Christ as the supreme royal benefactor to whom honor and obedience are due.

Second, this study looked at the relationship between χάρις as used in 5:2a and the Messiah's sacrifice as described in 5:6–10. In 5:2a, Paul uses the royal metaphor of "access" to declare that believers have been brought into the royal chamber. The Messiah provides privilege of approach into his realm of χάρις. The question that the reader is left with is: How does Jesus usher humanity into the royal chamber? We have argued that in response to this question, Paul describes the Messiah's self-sacrifice in 5:6–10. The Messiah provides access into χάρις by means of his own blood. He dies, not for "the good," but for sinners and enemies. Those who could not approach the divine throne due to their sinfulness now enjoy an intimate access to their Lord, who died for them. Their existence is always before the heavenly throne. The Messiah, who is both the gift and the mediator, liberates humanity from the lordship of sin and death, and provides everything necessary for his followers to be fruitful sharers in his rule even as they await their own resurrection.

Third, we have argued that the Messiah's supreme benefaction demands appropriate reciprocity or fitting response. In 5:1–11, Paul articulates the shape that this reciprocity takes in suffering. He uses the term "boasting" to characterize believers' confidence in the sovereignty of the Messiah as well as their call to participate in the Messiah's trajectory of dying and rising. Believers are to honor their supreme benefactor even in suffering. The fact that the Messiah designs suffering for the transformation of character and strengthening of hope (5:3–5) implies that suffering has a positive role within the Messiah's rule. The suffering that Paul writes about in Romans 5 and 8 neither indicates the Messiah's disfavor nor the believer's unfaithfulness to the Lord. Instead, what is true for the Messiah is also true for his followers. Thus, believers gladly suffer with the Messiah as they anticipate their glorification with him (8:17). Because Jesus is the supreme benefactor who offers his own life as χάρις to deliver humanity from sin and death, his followers must always give him loyalty and obedience by faithful response to his rule even in adversity.

Prospects for Further Research

This study has mainly focused on Rom 5:1–11 and provided an overview of 5:12—8:39. Even our analysis of the former passage is more illustrative than comprehensive. Further studies might examine at least two related problems. First, how does Paul depict Jesus as a cosmic royal benefactor? Greco-Roman rulers often present themselves as universal rulers who exercise sovereignty over all nations and creation. In Rom 1:5, Paul writes that we have received from the Messiah χάρις leading to the obedience of the nations. In 15:7–13, Paul states that the Messiah is the root of Jesse about whom Isaiah prophesied that he would come as the ruler and the hope of the nations. In 8:18–25, Paul speaks of the redemption of the creation, a redemption which is intricately tied to the glorification of God's sons and to the gift of the Spirit as the agent of creation's renewal. All this indicates the need to examine Paul's portrayal of the Messiah as a cosmic benefactor and how that relates to the Messiah's inheritance, believers' sharing in the Messiah's rule, and the obedience of the nations.

Second, is there the likelihood that Paul portrays Jesus as the supreme benefactor who also serves as a royal priest? From Augustus to Gratian, who became emperor in 367 CE, emperors held the office of *pontifex maximus* ("chief/high priest"). As a high priest, the emperors hold close proximity to the gods and secure the gods' gifts to the empire.[6] They also exemplify cultic devotion to the gods. Paul uses cultic language in Rom 5:6–10 as he describes the Messiah's self-sacrifice. In 8:34, he states that the Messiah is at God's right hand and that he intercedes for believers. Paul explicitly echoes LXX Ps 109:1, 4, where God's royal son is installed at God's right hand and designated priest. Priestly metaphors

---

6. Hoklotubbe, *Civilized Piety*, 71.

can also be found in Rom 12:1–2 and 15:14–29. Pauline scholarship would, therefore, profit from a study that examines the notion of a royal benefactor as a priestly figure and how that relates to the devotion expected of believers.

Throughout this work, we have looked at how Paul's christological discourse might be drawing upon the Greco-Roman royal benefaction system and the ethic of reciprocity that sustains it. As such, it provides a starting point for any of these prospects for further research. These further investigations might extend, challenge, and sharpen the argument herein.

Bibliography

Aalders, Gerhard Jean Daniël. *Political Thought in Hellenistic Times*. Amsterdam: A. M. Hakkert, 1975.
Adkins, A. W. H. *Merit and Responsibility: A Study in Greek Values*. Chicago: University of Chicago Press, 1975.
———. *Moral Values and Political Behaviour in Ancient Greece: From Homer to the End of the Fifth Century*. London: Chatto and Windus, 1972.
Agamben, Giorgio. *The Time That Remains: A Commentary on the Letter to the Romans*. Translated by Patricia Dailey. Stanford: Stanford University Press, 2005.
Alexander, T. Desmond. *The Servant King: The Bible's Portrait of the Messiah*. Vancouver: Regent College, 2003.
Allis, Oswald T. *The Unity of Isaiah: A Study in Prophecy*. Philadelphia: Presbyterian and Reformed, 1950.
Anderson, Gary A. *Charity: The Place of the Poor in the Biblical Tradition*. New Haven, CT: Yale University Press, 2013.
Arnim, Hans Friedrich August von. *Leben und Werke des Dio von Prusa, mit einer Einleitung: Sophistik, Rhetorik, Philosophie in ihrem Kampf um die Jugendbildung*. Berlin: Weidmann, 1898.
Atkins, E. M. "Cicero." In *The Cambridge History of Greek and Roman Political Thought*, edited by Christopher Rowe and Malcolm Schofield, 477–516. Cambridge: Cambridge University Press, 2000.
Attridge, Harold W. "Josephus and His Works." In *Jewish Writings of the Second Temple Period: Apocrypha, Pseudepigrapha, Qumran Sectarian Writings, Philo, Josephus*, edited by Michael E. Stone, 185–232. Assen: Van Gorcum, 1984.
Austin, Michel M. *The Hellenistic World from Alexander to the Roman Conquest: A Selection of Ancient Sources in Translation*. 2nd ed. Cambridge: Cambridge University Press, 2006.
Bakhtin, Mikhail M. "Toward a Methodology for the Human Sciences." In *Speech Genres and Other Late Essays*, edited by C. Emerson and M. Holquist, translated by V. W. McGee, 159–72. Austin: University of Texas Press, 1986.
Barclay, John M. G. "'By the Grace of God I Am What I Am': Grace and Agency in Philo and Paul." In *Divine and Human Agency in Paul and His Cultural Environment*, edited by John M. G. Barclay and Simon J. Gathercole, 140–57. JSNTSup 335. London: T. & T. Clark, 2006.
———. "Grace Within and Beyond Reason: Philo and Paul in Dialogue." In *Paul, Grace and Freedom: Essays in Honour of John K. Riches*, edited by Paul Middleton et al., 9–21. T. & T. Clark Biblical Studies. London: T. & T. Clark, 2009.

———. *Paul and the Gift*. Grand Rapids: Eerdmans, 2015.

———. "Under Grace: The Christ-Gift and the Construction of a Christian Habitus." In *Apocalyptic Paul: Cosmos and Anthropos in Romans 5–8*, edited by Beverly Roberts Gaventa, 59–76. Waco, TX: Baylor University Press, 2013.

———. "Unnerving Grace: Approaching Romans 9–11 from the Wisdom of Solomon." In *Between Gospel and election: Explorations in the interpretation of Romans 9–11*, edited by Florian Wilk et al., 91–110. WUNT 257. Tübingen: Mohr Siebeck, 2010.

Barraclough, Ray. "Philo's Politics: Roman Rule and Hellenistic Judaism." *ANRW* 21 (1972) 418–553.

Barrett, C. K. "Boasting (Καυχᾶσθαι Κτλ.) in the Pauline Epistles." In *L'Apôtre Paul: Personnalité, Style et Conception Du Ministère*, edited by A. Vanhoye, 363–68. BETL 73. Leuven: Leuven University Press, 1986.

———. *A Commentary on the Epistle to the Romans*. HNTC. San Francisco: Harper and Row, 1957.

———. *The Epistle to the Romans*. BNTC. Peabody, MA: Hendrickson, 1991.

Bassler, Jouette M. *Divine Impartiality: Paul and a Theological Axiom*. Chico, CA: Scholars, 1982.

Bates, Matthew W. "A Christology of Incarnation and Enthronement: Romans 1:3–4 as Unified, Nonadoptionist, and Nonconciliatory." *CBQ* 77 (2015) 107–27.

———. *The Hermeneutics of the Apostolic Proclamation: The Center of Paul's Method of Scriptural Interpretation*. Waco, TX: Baylor University Press, 2012.

———. *Salvation by Allegiance Alone: Rethinking Faith, Works, and the Gospel of Jesus the King*. Grand Rapids: Baker Academic, 2017.

Bauer, Walter, et al. *Greek-English Lexicon of the New Testament and Other Early Christian Literature*. 3rd ed. Chicago: University of Chicago Press, 2000.

Bell, Richard H. *No One Seeks for God: An Exegetical and Theological Study of Romans 1.18—3.20*. WUNT 106. Tübingen: Mohr Siebeck, 1998.

———. "Sacrifice and Christology in Paul." *JTS* 53 (2002) 1–27.

Berger, K. "Χάρις." In *Exegetical Dictionary of the New Testament*, edited by Horst Robert Balz and Gerhard Schneider, 3:457–60. Grand Rapids: Eerdmans, 1993.

Bilde, Per. *Flavius Josephus between Jerusalem and Rome: His Life, His Works and Their Importance*. Sheffield: Sheffield Aacdemic, 1988.

Bird, Michael F. *Jesus the Eternal Son: Answering Adoptionist Christology*. Grand Rapids: Eerdmans, 2017.

———. "'One Who Will Arise to Rule over the Nations': Paul's Letter to the Romans and the Roman Empire." In *Jesus Is Lord, Caesar Is Not: Evaluating Empire in New Testament Studies*, edited by Scot McKnight and Joseph B. Modica, 146–65. Downers Grove, IL: InterVarsity, 2013.

———. *Romans*. Edited by Tremper Longman III and Scot McKnight. SGBC. Grand Rapids: Zondervan, 2016.

Bird, Michael F., and Preston M. Sprinkle, eds. *The Faith of Jesus Christ: Exegetical, Biblical, and Theological Studies*. Peabody, MA: Hendrickson, 2010.

Blackwell, Ben C. *Christosis: Pauline Soteriology in Light of Deification in Irenaeus and Cyril of Alexandria*. Tübingen: Mohr Siebeck, 2011.

———, ed. *Reading Romans in Context: Paul and Second Temple Judaism*. Grand Rapids: Zondervan, 2015.

Blackwell, Benjamin C., et al., eds. *Paul and the Apocalyptic Imagination*. Minneapolis: Fortress, 2016.

Blackwell, Benjamin C. "Immortal Glory and the Problem of Death in Romans 3.23." *JSNT* 32 (2010) 285–308.
Blanton, Thomas R. "The Benefactor's Account-Book: The Rhetoric of Gift Reciprocation According to Seneca and Paul." *NTS* 59 (2013) 396–414.
———. *A Spiritual Economy: Gift Exchange in the Letters of Paul of Tarsus*. New Haven, CT: Yale University Press, 2017.
Blenkinsopp, Joseph. "The Sacrificial Life and Death of the Servant (Isaiah 52:13—53:12)." *VT* 66 (2016) 1–14.
Blocher, Henri. *Songs of the Servant: Isaiah's Good News*. London: InterVarsity, 1975.
Block, Daniel I. "Bringing Back David: Ezekiel's Messianic Hope." In *The Lord's Anointed: Interpretation of Old Testament Messianic Texts*, edited by Philip E. Satterthwaite et al., 167–88. Grand Rapids: Baker, 1995.
———. "My Servant David: Ancient Israel's Vision of the Messiah." In *Israel's Messiah in the Bible and the Dead Sea Scrolls*, edited by Richard S. Hess and M. Daniel Carroll, 17–56. Grand Rapids: Baker, 2003.
Blundell, Mary Whitlock. *Helping Friends and Harming Enemies: A Study in Sophocles and Greek Ethics*. Cambridge: Cambridge University Press, 1989.
Boatwright, Mary Taliaferro. *Hadrian and the Cities of the Roman Empire*. Princeton: Princeton University Press, 2000.
Bodel, John. "A Brief Guide to Some Standard Collections." In *Epigraphic Evidence: Ancient History from Inscriptions*, edited by John Bodel, 153–74. Approaching the Ancient World. London: Routledge, 2001.
Boers, Hendrikus. "Ἀγάπε and Χάρις in Paul's Thought." *CBQ* 59 (1997) 693–713.
———. "The Structure of Rom 5:1–11." In *Text und Geschichte: Facetten theologischen Arbeitens aus dem Freundes—und Schülerkreis: Dieter Lührmann zum 60 Geburtstag*, edited by Stefan Maser and Egbert Schlarb, 1–18. Marburg: N. G. Elwert, 1999.
Borgen, Peder. "Philo of Alexandria." In *Jewish Writings of the Second Temple Period: Apocrypha, Pseudepigrapha, Qumran Sectarian Writings, Philo*, edited by Michael E. Stone, 233–82. Assen: Van Gorcum, 1984.
———. *Philo of Alexandria: An Exegete for His Time*. NovTSup 86. Leiden: Brill, 1997.
Born, Lester K. "Perfect Prince According to the Latin Panegyrists." *AJP* 55 (1934) 20–35.
Bourdieu, Pierre. *Le Sens Pratique*. Paris: Minuit, 1980.
———. "Marginalia: Some Additional Notes on the Gift." In *The Logic of the Gift: Toward an Ethic of Generosity*, edited by Alan D. Schrift, 231–41. New York: Routledge, 1997.
Branick, Vincent P. "The Sinful Flesh of the Son of God (Rom 8:3): A Key Image of Pauline Theology." *CBQ* 47 (1985) 246–62.
Braund, David. *Rome and the Friendly King: The Character of the Client Kingship*. London: Croom Helm, 1984.
Bray, Gerald. *Biblical Interpretation: Past and Present*. Downers Grove, IL: InterVarsity, 1996.
Bringmann, Klaus. "The King as Benefactor: Some Remarks on Ideal Kingship in the Age of Hellenism." In *Images and Ideologies: Self-Definition in the Hellenistic World*, edited by A. W. Bulloch et al., 7–24. Hellenistic Culture and Society 12. Berkeley: University of California Press, 1993.
Briones, David E. "Mutual Brokers of Grace: A Study in 2 Corinthians 1.3–11." *NTS* 56 (2010) 536–56.

———. *Paul's Financial Policy: A Socio-Theological Approach*. London: Bloomsbury, 2013.
Burk, Denny. "The Righteousness of God (Dikaiosunē Theou) and Verbal Genitives: A Grammatical Clarification." *JSNT* 34 (2012) 346–60.
Byrne, Brendan. *Romans*. Collegeville: Liturgical, 1996.
———. *Sons of God, Seed of Abraham: A Study of the Idea of the Sonship of God of All Christians in Paul against the Jewish Background*. AnBib 83. Rome: Biblical Institute, 1979.
Campbell, Constantine R. *Paul and Union with Christ: An Exegetical and Theological Study*. Grand Rapids: Zondervan, 2012.
Campbell, Douglas A. *The Deliverance of God: An Apocalyptic Rereading of Justification in Paul*. Grand Rapids: Eerdmans, 2009.
———. *The Rhetoric of Righteousness in Romans 3.21–26*. JSNTSup 65. Sheffield: JSOT, 1992.
———. "The Story of Jesus in Romans and Galatians." In *Narrative Dynamics in Paul: A Critical Assessment*, edited by Bruce W. Longenecker, 97–124. Louisville: Westminster John Knox, 2002.
Caragounis, Chrys C. "Romans 5.15–16 in the Context of 5.12–21: Contrast or Comparison?" *NTS* 31 (1985) 142–48.
Carson, D. A. "Atonement in Romans 3:21–26: 'God Presented Him as a Propitiation.'" In *The Glory of the Atonement: Biblical, Historical and Practical Perspectives: Essays in Honor of Roger Nicole*, edited by Roger R. Nicole et al., 119–39. Downers Grove, IL: InterVarsity, 2004.
Chapman, Stephen B. *1 Samuel as Christian Scripture: A Theological Commentary*. Grand Rapids: Eerdmans, 2016.
Clarke, Andrew D. "The Good and the Just in Romans 5:7." *TynBul* 41 (1990) 128–42.
Clines, David J. A. *I, He, We and They: A Literary Approach to Isaiah 53*. Sheffield: Sheffield Academic, 1983.
Cohen, Shaye J. D. *Josephus in Galilee and Rome: His Vita and Development as a Historian*. Columbia Studies in the Classical Tradition 8. Leiden: Brill, 1979.
Collins, Adela Yarbro, and John J. Collins. *King and Messiah as Son of God: Divine, Human, and Angelic Messianic Figures in Biblical and Related Literature*. Grand Rapids: Eerdmans, 2008.
Collins, John J. *The Scepter and the Star: Messianism in Light of the Dead Sea Scrolls*. 2nd ed. Grand Rapids: Eerdmans, 2010.
Collins, John N. *Diakonia: Re-Interpreting the Ancient Sources*. New York: Oxford University Press, 1990.
Conroy, J. T. "Philo's 'Death of the Soul': Is This Only a Metaphor?" *SPhilo* 23 (2011) 23–40.
Cooley, Alison E. *Res Gestae Divi Augusti: Text, Translation, and Commentary*. Cambridge: Cambridge University Press, 2009.
Cranfield, C. E. B. *A Critical and Exegetical Commentary on the Epistle to the Romans: Introduction and Commentary on Romans I–VIII*. ICC. Edinburgh: T. & T. Clark, 1975.
Cremer, Hermann. *Die paulinische Rechtfertigungslehre im Zusammenhange ihrer geschichtlichen Voraussetzungen*. Gütersloh: Bertelsmann, 1900.
Croasmun, Matthew. *The Emergence of Sin: The Cosmic Tyrant in Romans*. New York: Oxford University Press, 2017.

Crook, Zeba A. "The Divine Benefactions of Paul the Client." *Journal of Greco-Roman Christianity and Judaism* 2 (2001) 9–26.

———. "Grace as Benefaction in Galatians 2:9, 1 Corinthians 3:10, and Romans 12:3; 15:15." In *Social Sciences and Biblical Translation*, edited by Dietmar Neufeld, 25–38. SBLSymS 41. Atlanta: Society of Biblical Literature, 2008.

———. *Reconceptualising Conversion: Patronage, Loyalty, and Conversion in the Religions of the Ancient Mediterranean*. BZNW 130. Berlin: Walter de Gruyter, 2004.

Crossan, John Dominic, and Jonathan Reed. *In Search of Paul: How Jesus's Apostle Opposed Rome's Empire with God's Kingdom: A New Vision of Paul's Words and World*. San Francisco: Harper San Francisco, 2004.

Cullmann, Oscar. *The Christology of the New Testament*. London: SCM, 1963.

Dahl, Nils A. *The Crucified Messiah, and Other Essays*. Minneapolis: Augsburg, 1974.

———. "Two Notes on Romans 5." *ST* 5 (1952) 37–48.

Danker, Frederick W. *Benefactor: Epigraphic Study of a Graeco-Roman and New Testament Semantic Field*. St. Louis: Clayton, 1982.

———. "The Endangered Benefactor in Luke–Acts." *SBLSP* 20 (1981) 39–48.

Danker, Frederick W., and Robert Jewett. "Jesus as the Apocalyptic Benefactor in Second Thessalonians." In *The Thessalonian Correspondence*, edited by Raymond F. Collins, 486–98. BETL 87. Leuvain: Leuven University Press, 1990.

Das, A. Andrew. *Solving the Romans Debate*. Minneapolis: Fortress, 2007.

Davies, Stevan L. "Predicament of Ignatius of Antioch." *VC* 30 (1976) 175–80.

Davis, Norman, and Colin M. Kraay. *The Hellenistic Kingdoms: Portrait Coins and History*. London: Thames and Hudson, 1973.

De Blois, L. "Traditional Virtues and New Spiritual Qualities in Third Century Views of Empire, Emperorship and Practical Politics." *Mnemosyne* 47 (1994) 166–76.

Deissmann, Adolf. *Light from the Ancient East: The New Testament Illustrated by Recently Discovered Texts of the Graeco-Roman World*. Translated by Lionel R. M. Strachan. Grand Rapids: Baker, 1965.

Derrida, Jacques. "The Time of the King." In *The Logic of the Gift: Toward an Ethic of Generosity*, edited by Alan D. Schrift, 121–47. New York: Routledge, 1997.

DeSilva, David Arthur. *Honor, Patronage, Kinship and Purity: Unlocking New Testament Culture*. Downers Grove, IL: InterVarsity, 2000.

———. *Introducing the Apocrypha: Message, Context, and Significance*. Grand Rapids: Baker Academic, 2002.

Desmond, William D. *Philosopher-Kings of Antiquity*. London: Continuum International, 2011.

Di Lella, Alexander A. *The Hebrew Text of Sirach: A Text-Critical and Historical Study*. The Hague: Mouton, 1966.

———. "The Newly Discovered Sixth Manuscript of Ben Sira from the Cairo Geniza." *Bib* 69 (1988) 226–38.

Dodd, C. H. *The Epistle of Paul to the Romans*. MNTC 6. Collins: Fontana, 1959.

Donfried, Karl P., ed. *The Romans Debate*. Rev. and Expanded ed. Peabody, MA: Hendrickson, 1991.

Doughty, Darrell J. "Priority of ΧΑΡΙΣ: An Investigation of the Theological Language of Paul." *NTS* 19 (1973) 163–80.

Downs, David J. "Is God Paul's Patron?: The Economy of Patronage in Pauline Theology." In *Engaging Economics: New Testament Scenarios and Early Christian Reception*, edited by Bruce W. Longenecker and Kelly D. Liebengood, 129–56. Grand Rapids: Eerdmans, 2009.

Duhm, Bernhard. *Das Buch Jesaja*. HKAT. Göttingen: Vandenhoeck & Ruprecht, 1892.
Dunn, James D. G. *Beginning from Jerusalem: Christianity in the Making*. Vol. 2. Grand Rapids: Eerdmans, 2009.
———. *Romans 1–8*. Vol. 38A. WBC. Nashville: Thomas Nelson, 1988.
Eastman, Susan. "Oneself in Another: Participation and the Spirit in Romans 8." In *"In Christ" in Paul: Explorations in Paul's Theology of Union and Participation*, edited by Michael J. Thate et al., 103–25. WUNT 384. Tübingen: Mohr Siebeck, 2014.
Eaton, John H. *Kingship and the Psalms*. SBT 32. London: SCM, 1976.
Ehrenberg, Victor, and A. H. M. Jones. *Documents Illustrating the Reigns of Augustus and Tiberius*. Oxford: Clarendon, 1955.
Ehrman, Bart D. *How Jesus Became God: The Exaltation of a Jewish Preacher from Galilee*. New York: HarperOne, 2014.
Eilers, Claude. *Roman Patrons of Greek Cities*. Oxford: Oxford University Press, 2002.
Eisenstadt, S. N., and Luis Roniger. *Patrons, Clients, and Friends: Interpersonal Relations and the Structure of Trust in Society*. Cambridge: Cambridge University Press, 1984.
Elliott, John H. "Patronage and Clientage." In *The Social Sciences and New Testament Interpretation*, edited by Richard L. Rohrbaugh, 144–56. Peabody, MA: Hendrickson, 1996.
Elliott, Neil. *The Arrogance of Nations: Reading Romans in the Shadow of Empire*. Minneapolis: Fortress, 2008.
———. *The Rhetoric of Romans: Argumentative Constraint and Strategy and Paul's Dialogue with Judaism*. JSOT Supplement Series 45. Sheffield: Sheffield Academic, 1990.
Elliott, Neil, and Mark Reasoner, eds. *Documents and Images for the Study of Paul*. Minneapolis: Fortress, 2011.
Engberg-Pedersen, Troels. "Gift-Giving and Friendship: Seneca and Paul in Romans 1–8 on the Logic of God's Χάρις and Its Human Response." *HTR* 101 (2008) 15–44.
———. "Gift-Giving and God's Charis: Bourdieu, Seneca and Paul in Romans 1–8." In *The Letter to the Romans*, edited by Udo Schnelle, 95–111. BETL 226. Leuven: Peeters, 2009.
———. "The Reception of Graeco-Roman Culture in the New Testament: The Case of Romans 7:7–25." In *The New Testament as Reception*, edited by Mogens Müller and Henrik Tronier, 32–57. JSNTSup 230. London: Sheffield Academic, 2002.
Erskine, A. "The Romans as Common Benefactors." *Historia* 43 (1994) 70–87.
Fatehi, Mehrdad. *The Spirit's Relation to the Risen Lord in Paul: An Examination of Its Christological Implications*. WUNT 128. Tübingen: Mohr Siebeck, 2000.
Faust, Eberhard. *Pax Christi et Pax Caesaris: Religionsgeschichtliche, traditionsgeschichtliche und sozialgeschichtliche Studien zum Epheserbrief*. NTOA 24. Göttingen: Vandenhoeck & Ruprecht, 1993.
Fears, J. Rufus. "The Cult of Virtues and Roman Imperial Ideology." In *Aufstieg und Niedergang der römischen Welt*, 827–948. Berlin: Walter de Gruyter, 1981.
Fee, Gordon D. *God's Empowering Presence: The Holy Spirit in the Letters of Paul*. Peabody, MA: Hendrickson, 1994.
———. *Pauline Christology: An Exegetical-Theological Study*. Peabody, MA: Hendrickson, 2007.
Feldman, Louis H. "Josephus' Portrait of Solomon." *HUCA* 66 (1995) 103–67.
———. *Philo's Portrayal of Moses in the Context of Ancient Judaism*. Notre Dame: University of Notre Dame Press, 2007.

———. "Philo's View of Moses' Birth and Upbringing." *CBQ* 64 (2002) 258–81.
Ferguson, Everett. *Backgrounds of Early Christianity*. 3rd ed. Grand Rapids: Eerdmans, 2003.
Finley, Moses I. *The Ancient Economy*. Berkeley: University of California Press, 1999.
Fitzmyer, Joseph A. *Pauline Theology: A Brief Sketch*. Englewood Cliffs: Prentice-Hall, 1967.
———. "Reconciliation in Pauline Theology." In *No Famine in the Land: Studies in Honor of John L. McKenzie*, edited by James W. Flanagan and Anita W. Robinson, 155–77. Missoula: Scholars, 1975.
———. *The One Who Is to Come*. Grand Rapids: Eerdmans, 2007.
———. *Romans: A New Translation with Introduction and Commentary*. AB 33. New York: Doubleday, 1993.
Friedländer, Ludwig. *Roman Life and Manners under the Early Empire*. Translated by Leonard A. Magnus. Vol. 1. London: Routledge & Kegan Paul, 1965.
Fryer, N. S. L. "Reconciliation in Paul's Epistle to the Romans." *Neot* 15 (1981) 34–68.
Gaffin, Richard B. *Resurrection and Redemption: A Study in Paul's Soteriology*. Phillipsburg: Presbyterian and Reformed, 1987.
Galinsky, Karl. *Augustan Culture: An Interpretive Introduction*. Princeton: Princeton University Press, 1996.
Gardner, Gregg. "Jewish Leadership and Hellenistic Civic Benefaction in the Second Century B.C.E." *JBL* 126 (2007) 327–43.
Garnsey, Peter. "The Generosity of Veyne." *JRS* 81 (1991) 164–68.
Garnsey, Peter, and Greg Woolf. "Patronage of the Rural Poor in the Roman World." In *Patronage in Ancient Society*, edited by Andrew Wallace-Hadrill, 153–70. Leicester-Nottingham Studies in Ancient Society. London: Routledge, 1989.
Garnsey, Peter, and Richard Saller. *The Roman Empire: Economy, Society and Culture*. Berkeley: University of California Press, 2015.
Gathercole, Simon J. *Defending Substitution: An Essay on Atonement in Paul*. ASBT. Grand Rapids: Baker Academic, 2015.
———. *Where Is Boasting?: Early Jewish Soteriology and Paul's Response in Romans 1–5*. Grand Rapids: Eerdmans, 2002.
Gaventa, Beverly Roberts, ed. *Apocalyptic Paul: Cosmos and Anthropos in Romans 5–8*. Waco, TX: Baylor University Press, 2013.
———. "God Handed Them Over: Reading Romans 1:18–32 Apocalyptically." *ABR* 53 (2005) 42–53.
———. "Neither Height nor Depth: Discerning the Cosmology of Romans." *SJT* 64 (2011) 265–78.
———. *Our Mother Saint Paul*. Louisville: Westminster John Knox, 2007.
———. *When in Romans: An Invitation to Linger with the Gospel According to Paul*. Grand Rapids: Baker Academic, 2016.
Gentry, Peter J. "The Atonement in Isaiah's Fourth Servant Song (Isaiah 52:13—53:12)." *SBJT* 11 (2007) 20–47.
Georgi, Dieter. *Theocracy in Paul's Praxis and Theology*. Minneapolis: Fortress, 1991.
Gerbrandt, Gerald Eddie. *Kingship According to Deuteronomistic History*. SBLDS 87. Atlanta: Scholars, 1986.
Gieniusz, Andrzej. *Romans 8:18–30: "Suffering Does Not Thwart the Future Glory."* Atlanta: Scholars, 1999.

Gill, Christopher. "Stoic Writers of the Imperial Era." In *The Cambridge History of Greek and Roman Political Thought*, edited by Christopher Rowe and Malcolm Schofield, 597–615. Cambridge: Cambridge University Press, 2000.

Gill, Christopher et al., eds. *Reciprocity in Ancient Greece*. Oxford: Oxford University Press, 1998.

Goldsworthy, Adrian Keith. *Pax Romana: War, Peace, and Conquest in the Roman World*. New Haven, CT: Yale University Press, 2016.

Goodenough, Erwin R. *The Politics of Philo Judaeus: Practice and Theory*. Hildesheim: Georg Olms, 1967.

Goppelt, Leonhard. *Typos: The Typological Interpretation of the Old Testament in the New*. Translated by Donald H. Madvig. Grand Rapids: Eerdmans, 1982.

Gordon, Richard. "From Republic to Principate: Priesthood, Religion and Ideology." In *Pagan Priests: Religion and Power in the Ancient World*, edited by Mary Beard and John North, 179–98. Ithaca: Cornell University Press, 1990.

———. "The Veil of Power: Emperors, Sacrificers and Benefactors." In *Pagan Priests: Religion and Power in the Ancient World*, edited by Mary Beard and John North, 201–31. Ithaca: Cornell University Press, 1990.

Gorman, Michael J. *Cruciformity: Paul's Narrative Spirituality of the Cross*. Grand Rapids: Eerdmans, 2001.

Gradel, Ittai. *Emperor Worship and Roman Religion*. Oxford: Clarendon, 2002.

Grant, Michael. *Herod the Great*. New York: American Heritage, 1971.

Gregory, Bradley C. "Abraham as the Jewish Ideal: Exegetical Traditions in Sirach 44:19–21." *CBQ* 70 (2008) 66–81.

Griffin, Miriam T. "De Beneficiis and Roman Society." *JRS* 93 (2003) 92–113.

———. *Seneca: A Philosopher in Politics*. Oxford: Clarendon, 1976.

Griffin, Miriam T., and Brad Inwood. *Lucius Annaeus Seneca: On Benefits*. Chicago: University of Chicago Press, 2011.

Grindheim, Sigurd. "The Kingdom of God in Romans." *Bib* 98 (2017) 72–90.

Groningen, Gerard van. *Messianic Revelation in the Old Testament*. Grand Rapids: Baker, 1990.

Grundmann, Walter. "Die Übermacht der Gnade: Eine Studie zur Theologie des Paulus." *NovT* 2 (1957) 50–72.

Gundry, Judith. "'Or Who Gave First to Him, so That He Shall Receive Recompense?' (Rom 11,35): Divine Benefaction and Human Boasting in Paul and Philo." In *The Letter to the Romans*, edited by Udo Schnelle, 171–95. BETL 226. Leuven: Peeters, 2009.

Hadas-Lebel, Mireille. *Flavius Josephus: Eyewitness to Rome's First-Century Conquest of Judea*. Translated by Richard Miller. New York: Macmillan, 1993.

———. *Philo of Alexandria: A Thinker in the Jewish Diaspora*. Leiden: Brill, 2012.

Hahn, Scott W. *The Kingdom of God as Liturgical Empire: A Theological Commentary on 1–2 Chronicles*. Grand Rapids: Baker Academic, 2012.

Hammond Bammel, Caroline P. "Patristic Exegesis of Romans 5:7." *JTS* 47 (1996) 532–42.

Hands, A. R. *Charities and Social Aid in Greece and Rome*. Ithaca: Cornell University Press, 1968.

Hardwick, Michael E. *Josephus as an Historical Source in Patristic Literature through Eusebius*. BJS 128. Atlanta: Scholars, 1988.

Harland, Philip A. *Associations, Synagogues, and Congregations: Claiming a Place in Ancient Mediterranean Society*. Minneapolis: Fortress, 2003.

Harris, Murray J. *Prepositions and Theology in the Greek New Testament: An Essential Reference Resource for Exegesis*. Grand Rapids: Zondervan, 2012.

Harrison, James R. "Paul and the 'Social Relations' of Death at Rome." In *Paul and His Social Relations*, edited by Stanley E. Porter and Christopher D. Land, 85–123. Pauline Studies 7. Leiden: Brill, 2013.

———. *Paul's Language of Grace in Its Graeco-Roman Context*. WUNT 172. Tübingen: Mohr Siebeck, 2003.

Hays, Richard B. "Christ Prays the Psalms: Paul's Use of an Early Christian Exegetical Convention." In *Future of Christology: Essays in Honor of Leander E Keck*, edited by Abraham J. Malherbe and Wayne A. Meeks, 122–36. Minneapolis: Fortress, 1993.

———. *Echoes of Scripture in the Letters of Paul*. New Haven, CT: Yale University Press, 1989.

———. "'The Righteous One' as Eschatological Deliverer: A Case Study in Paul's Apocalyptic Hermeneutics." In *Apocalyptic and the New Testament: Essays in Honor of J. Louis Martyn*, edited by Joel Marcus and Marion L. Soards, 191–215. JSNTSup 24. Sheffield: JSOT, 1989.

Heim, Knut. "The Perfect King of Psalm 72." In *The Lord's Anointed: Interpretation of Old Testament Messianic Texts*, edited by Philip. E. Satterthwaite et al., 223–48. Grand Rapids: Baker, 1995.

Hellerman, Joseph H. *Reconstructing Honor in Roman Philippi: Carmen Christi as Cursus Pudorum*. SNTSMS 132. Cambridge: Cambridge University Press, 2005.

Hendrix, Holland Lee. "Benefactor/Patron Networks in the Urban Environment: Evidence from Thessalonica." *Semeia* 56 (1991) 39–58.

Hengel, Martin. *Between Jesus and Paul: Studies in the Earliest History of Christianity*. Philadelphia: Fortress, 1983.

———. *The Son of God: The Origin of Christology and the History of Jewish-Hellenistic Religion*. Philadelphia: Fortress, 1976.

Hess, Richard S. "The Image of the Messiah in the Old Testament." In *Images of Christ: Ancient and Modern*, edited by Stanley E. Porter et al., 22–33. RILP 2. Sheffield: Sheffield Academic, 1997.

———. "Splitting the Adam: The Usage of 'Ādām in Genesis I–V." In *Studies in the Pentateuch*, 1–15. VTSup 41. Leiden: Brill, 1990.

Hinnant, Charles H. "The Patriarchal Narratives of Genesis and the Ethos of Gift Exchange." In *The Question of the Gift: Essays across Disciplines*, edited by Mark Osteen, 105–17. London: Routledge, 2014.

Hofius, Otfried. "The Adam-Christ Antithesis and the Law: Reflections on Romans 5:12–21." In *Paul and the Mosaic Law*, edited by James D. G. Dunn, 165–205. Grand Rapids: Eerdmans, 2001.

Hoklotubbe, T. Christopher. *Civilized Piety: The Rhetoric of Pietas in the Pastoral Epistles and the Roman Empire*. Waco, TX: Baylor University Press, 2017.

Horbury, William. *Jewish Messianism and the Cult of Christ*. London: SCM, 1998.

Horsley, G. H. R., and S. R. Llewelyn, eds. *New Documents Illustrating Early Christianity*. 10 vols. Sydnet: Macquarie University, 1981.

Horsley, Richard A., ed. *Paul and Empire: Religion and Power in Roman Imperial Society*. Harrisburg: Trinity, 1997.

———, ed. *Paul and the Roman Imperial Order*. Harrisburg: Trinity, 2004.

Hugenberger, Gordon P. "The Servant of the Lord in the 'Servant Songs' of Isaiah." In *The Lord's Anointed: Interpretation of Old Testament Messianic Texts*, edited by Philip E. Satterthwaite et al., 105–40. Grand Rapids: Baker, 1995.

Hurtado, Larry W. "Jesus' Divine Sonship in Paul's Letter to the Romans." In *Romans and the People of God: Essays in Honor of Gordon D. Fee on the Occasion of His 65th Birthday*, edited by Sven Soderlund and N. T Wright, 217–33. Grand Rapids: Eerdmans, 1999.

———. "Son of God." In *Dictionary of Paul and His Letters*, edited by Gerald F. Hawthorne et al., 900–906. Downers Grove, IL: InterVarsity, 1993.

Inwood, Brad. "Politics and Paradox in Seneca's De Beneficiis." In *Justice and Generosity: Studies in Hellenistic Social and Political Philosophy*, edited by André Laks and Malcolm Schofield, 241–65. Cambridge: Cambridge University Press, 1995.

———. *Reading Seneca: Stoic Philosophy at Rome*. Oxford: Clarendon, 2005.

Irigaray, Luce. "Selections from the Logic of Practice." In *The Logic of the Gift: Toward an Ethic of Generosity*, edited by Alan D. Schrift, 190–230. New York: Routledge, 1997.

Jacob, Haley G. *Conformed to the Image of His Son: Reconsidering Paul's Theology of Glory in Romans*. Downers Grove, IL: IVP Academic, 2018.

Jewett, Robert. *Paul's Anthropological Terms: A Study of Their Use in Conflict Settings*. Leiden: Brill, 1971.

———. *Romans: A Commentary*. Edited by Eldon J. Epp. Minneapolis: Fortress, 2007.

Jipp, Joshua W. "Ancient, Modern, and Future Interpretations of Romans 1:3–4: Reception History and Biblical Interpretation." *JTI* 3 (2009) 241–59.

———. *Christ Is King: Paul's Royal Ideology*. Minneapolis: Fortress, 2015.

———. "Educating the Divided Soul in Paul and Plato: Reading Romans 7:7–25 and Plato's Republic." In *Paul: Jew, Greek, and Roman*, edited by Stanley E. Porter, 231–57. Leiden: Brill, 2008.

———. "Rereading the Story of Abraham, Isaac, and 'Us' in Romans 4." *JSNT* 32 (2009) 217–42.

Johnson, Aubrey R. *Sacral Kingship in Ancient Israel*. Cardiff: University of Wales Press, 1967.

Johnson, Luke Timothy. *Among the Gentiles: Greco-Roman Religion and Christianity*. New Haven, CT: Yale University Press, 2009.

———. *Contested Issues in Christian Origins and the New Testament: Collected Essays*. NovTSup 146. Leiden: Brill, 2013.

Jones, Christopher Prestige. *The Roman World of Dio Chrysostom*. Cambridge, MA: Harvard University Press, 1978.

Joseph, Alison L. *Portrait of the Kings: The Davidic Prototype in Deuteronomistic Poetics*. Minneapolis: Fortress, 2015.

Joubert, Stephan. "Coming to Terms with a Neglected Aspect of Ancient Mediterranean Reciprocity: Seneca's Views on Benefit-Exchange in De Beneficiis as the Framework for a Model of Social Exchange." In *Social Scientific Models for Interpreting the Bible: Essays by the Context Group in Honor of Bruce J. Malina*, edited by John Pilch, 47–63. Leiden: Brill, 2001.

———. "One Form of Social Exchange or Two?: 'euergetism,' Patronage, and Testament Studies." *BTB* 31 (2001) 17–25.

———. "Patrocinium and Euergetism: Similar or Different Reciprocal Relationships? Eavesdropping on the Current Debate amongst Biblical Scholars." In *The New Testament in the Graeco-Roman World: Articles in Honour of Abe Malherbe*, edited by Marius Nel et al., 171–95. Zürich: LIT, 2015.

———. *Paul as Benefactor: Reciprocity, Strategy and Theological Reflection in Paul's Collection*. WUNT 124. Tübingen: Mohr Siebeck, 2000.

Judge, E. A. "The Conflict of Educational Aims in New Testament Thought." *Journal of Christian Education* 9 (1966) 32–45.

———. *The First Christians in the Roman World: Augustan and New Testament Essays*. Edited by James R. Harrison. Tübingen: Mohr Siebeck, 2008.

Kaiser, Walter C. *The Messiah in the Old Testament*. Grand Rapids: Zondervan, 1995.

———. "Psalm 72: An Historical and Messianic Current Example of Antiochene Hermeneutical Theoria." *JETS* 52 (2009) 257–70.

Käsemann, Ernst. *Commentary on Romans*. Grand Rapids: Eerdmans, 1980.

———. *New Testament Questions of Today*. Philadelphia: Fortress, 1969.

———. *On Being a Disciple of the Crucified Nazarene: Unpublished Lectures and Sermons*. Translated by R. A. Harrisville. Grand Rapids: Eerdmans, 2010.

Kaye, Bruce Norman. *The Argument of Romans: With Special Reference to Chapter 6*. Austin: Schola, 1979.

Kensky, Meira Z. *Trying Man, Trying God: The Divine Courtroom in Early Jewish and Christian Literature*. WUNT 289. Tübingen: Mohr Siebeck, 2010.

Keppie, L. J. F. *Understanding Roman Inscriptions*. Baltimore: Johns Hopkins University Press, 1991.

Kidd, Reggie M. *Wealth and Beneficence in the Pastoral Epistles: A "Bourgeois" Form of Early Christianity?* Atlanta: Scholars, 1990.

Kim, Seyoon. "2 Cor 5:11–21 and the Origin of Paul's Concept of 'Reconciliation.'" *NovT* 39 (1997) 360–84.

———. *The Origin of Paul's Gospel*. Eugene, OR: Wipf & Stock, 2007.

Koester, Helmut. *Ancient Christian Gospels: Their History and Development*. London: SCM, 1990.

Konstan, David. *Friendship in the Classical World*. Cambridge: Cambridge University Press, 1997.

Krasser, H. "P. Caecilius Secundus, C. (Pliny the Younger)." In *Brill's New Pauly Encyclopaedia of the Ancient World: Antiquity*, edited by Hubert Cancik and Helmuth Schneider, 11:390–92. Leiden: Brill, 2007.

Kreitzer, L. Joseph. "Christ and Second Adam in Paul." *CV* 32 (1989) 55–101.

Kruse, Colin G. *Paul's Letter to the Romans*. Grand Rapids: Eerdmans, 2012.

Kümmel, Werner Georg. *Exegetical Method: A Student's Handbook*. New York: Seabury, 1981.

Lambert, Stephen D. "What Was the Point of Inscribed Honorific Decrees in Classical Athens?" In *Sociable Man: Essays on Ancient Greek Social Behaviour in Honour of Nick Fisher*, edited by Stephen D. Lambert, 69–92. Swansea: Classical, 2011.

Landau, Y. "Martyrdom in Paul's Religious Ethics: An Exegetical Commentary on Romans 5:7." *Imm* 15 (1982) 24–38.

Lau, Te-Li. *The Politics of Peace: Ephesians, Dio Chrysostom, and the Confucian Four Books*. Leiden: Brill, 2010.

Leithart, Peter J. *Gratitude: An Intellectual History*. Waco, TX: Baylor University Press, 2014.

Lemche, Niels Peter. "From Patronage Society to Patronage Society." In *Origins of the Ancient Israelite States*, edited by V. Fritz and P. R. Davies, 106–20. Sheffield: Sheffield Academic, 1996.

———. "Kings and Clients: On Loyalty between the Ruler and the Ruled in Ancient 'Israel.'" *Semeia* 66 (1994) 119–32.

Lendon, J. E. *Empire of Honour: The Art of Government in the Roman World*. Oxford: Clarendon, 1997.

Levison, John R. *Portraits of Adam in Early Judaism: From Sirach to 2 Baruch.* Edited by James H. Charlesworth. JSPSup 1. Sheffield: JSOT, 1987.

Lightfoot, Joseph B. *Notes on Epistles of St. Paul from Unpublished Commentaries.* London: Macmillan, 1895.

Linebaugh, Jonathan A. *God, Grace, and Righteousness in Wisdom of Solomon and Paul's Letter to the Romans: Texts in Conversation.* WUNT 152. Boston: Brill, 2013.

Lomas, Kathryn, and Tim Cornell, eds. *Bread and Circuses: Euergetism and Municipal Patronage in Roman Italy.* London: Routledge, 2003.

Longenecker, Bruce W. *Remember the Poor: Paul, Poverty, and the Greco-Roman World.* Cambridge: Eerdmans, 2010.

Longenecker, Richard N. *The Epistle to the Romans: A Commentary on the Greek Text.* NIGTC. Grand Rapids: Eerdmans, 2016.

———. "The Focus of Romans: The Central Role of 5:1—8:39 in the Argument of the Letter." In *Romans and the People of God: Essays in Honor of Gordon D. Fee on the Occasion of His 65th Birthday,* edited by Sven Soderlund and N. T. Wright, 49–69. Grand Rapids: Eerdmans, 1999.

Lowe, Bruce A. "Oh Διά! How Is Romans 4:25 to Be Understood?" *JTS* 57 (2006) 149–57.

———. "Paul, Patronage and Benefaction: A 'Semiotic' Reconsideration." In *Paul and His Social Relations,* edited by Stanley E. Porter and Christopher D. Land, 57–84. Pauline Studies 7. Leiden: Brill, 2013.

Lynch, Matthew. *Monotheism and Institutions in the Book of Chronicles Temple, Priesthood, and Kingship in Post-Exilic Perspective.* Tübingen: Mohr-Siebeck, 2014.

Ma, John. *Statues and Cities: Honorific Portraits and Civic Identity in the Hellenistic World.* Oxford: Oxford University Press, 2013.

Maartens, P. J. "The Relevance of 'context' and 'Interpretation' to the Semiotic Relations of Romans 5:1–11." *Neot* 29 (1995) 75–108.

Macaskill, Grant. *Union with Christ in the New Testament.* Oxford: Oxford University Press, 2013.

MacLachlan, Bonnie. *The Age of Grace: Charis in Early Greek Poetry.* Princeton: Princeton University Press, 1993.

MacMullen, Ramsay. "The Epigraphic Habit in the Roman Empire." *AJP* 103 (1982) 233–46.

———. "Personal Power in the Roman Empire." *AJP* 107 (1986) 512–24.

Malina, Bruce J., and Jerome H. Neyrey. *Portraits of Paul: An Archaeology of Ancient Personality.* Louisville: Westminster John Knox, 1996.

Manson, William. "Grace in the New Testament." In *The Doctrine of Grace,* edited by William Thomas Whitley, 33–60. London: SCM, 1932.

Marshall, I. Howard. "The Meaning of Reconciliation." In *Unity and Diversity in New Testament Theology: Essays in Honor of George E. Ladd,* edited by Robert A. Guelich, 117–32. Grand Rapids: Eerdmans, 1978.

Martin, Dale B. *Slavery as Salvation: The Metaphor of Slavery in Pauline Christianity.* New Haven, CT: Yale University Press, 1990.

Martin, Ralph P. *Reconciliation: A Study of Paul's Theology.* Eugene, OR: Wipf and Stock, 1997.

———. "Reconciliation: Romans 5:1–11." In *Romans and the People of God: Essays in Honor of Gordon D. Fee on the Occasion of His 65th Birthday,* edited by Sven Soderlund and N. T. Wright, 36–48. Grand Rapids: Eerdmans, 1999.

Martin, Troy W. "The Good as God (Romans 5.7)." *JSNT* 25 (2002) 55–70.

Marttila, Marko. "David in the Wisdom of Ben Sira." *SJOT* 25 (2011) 29–48.

Bibliography

Mason, Steve. *Josephus, Judea, and Christian Origins: Methods and Categories*. Peabody, MA: Hendrickson, 2009.

Matera, Frank J. *God's Saving Grace: A Pauline Theology*. Grand Rapids: Eerdmans, 2012.

Matthews, Victor H. "The Unwanted Gift: Implications of Obligatory Gift Giving in Ancient Israel." *Semeia* 87 (1999) 91–104.

Mauss, Marcel. "Essai sur le Don: Forme et Raison de L'échange dans les Sociétés Archaïques." *Sociologie et Anthropologie* (1950) 145–279.

———. *The Gift: The Form and Reason for Exchange in Archaic Societies*. Translated by W. D. Hall. London: Routledge, 1990.

McCarter, P. Kyle. "The Apology of David." *JBL* 99 (1980) 489–504.

McDonald, Patricia M. "Romans 5:1–11 as a Rhetorical Bridge." *JSNT* 40 (1990) 81–96.

McFarland, Orrey. *God and Grace in Philo and Paul*. Leiden: Brill, 2016.

McKeon, Richard. *Introduction to Aristotle*. New York: The Modern Library, 1947.

McKnight, Scot, and Joseph B. Modica, eds. *Jesus Is Lord, Caesar Is Not: Evaluating Empire in New Testament Studies*. Downers Grove, IL: InterVarsity, 2013.

McLaren, James S. *Turbulent Times?: Josephus and Scholarship on Judaea in the First Century CE*. JSPSup 29. Sheffield: Sheffield Academic, 1998.

McLean, Bradley H. *An Introduction to Greek Epigraphy of the Hellenistic and Roman Periods from Alexander the Great down to the Reign of Constantine (323 BC–AD 337)*. Ann Arbor: University of Michigan Press, 2002.

Meeks, Wayne A. "Moses as God and King." In *Religions in Antiquity: Essays in Memory of Erwin Ramsdell Goodenough*, edited by Jacob Neusner, 354–71. Leiden: Brill, 1968.

———. *The Origins of Christian Morality: The First Two Centuries*. New Haven, CT: Yale University Press, 1993.

Meggitt, Justin J. *Paul, Poverty and Survival*. Edinburgh: T. & T. Clark, 1998.

Mettinger, Tryggve N. D. *King and Messiah: The Civil and Sacral Legitimation of the Israelite Kings*. Lund: Gleerup, 1976.

Metzger, Bruce M. *A Textual Commentary on the Greek New Testament: A Companion Volume to the United Bible Societies' Greek New Testament*. Stuttgart: Deutsche Bibelgesellschaft, 1994.

Meyer, Elizabeth A. "Explaining the Epigraphic Habit in the Roman Empire: The Evidence of Epitaphs." *JRS* 80 (1990) 74–96.

Meyer, Paul W. "The Worm at the Core of the Apple: Exegetical Reflections on Romans 7." In *The Conversation Continues: Studies in Paul and John in Honor of J. Louis Martyn*, edited by Robert T. Fortna and Beverly Roberts Gaventa, 62–84. Nashville: Abingdon, 1990.

Mikalson, Jon D. *Greek Popular Religion in Greek Philosophy*. Oxford: Oxford University Press, 2010.

Millar, Fergus. *The Emperor in the Roman World, 31 BC–AD 337*. Ithaca: Cornell University Press, 1977.

Millett, Paul. *Lending and Borrowing in Ancient Athens*. Cambridge: Cambridge University Press, 1991.

Mitchell, David C. "Lord, Remember David: G. H. Wilson and the Message of the Psalter." *VT* 56 (2006) 526–48.

Moffatt, James. *Grace in the New Testament*. London: Hodder & Stoughton, 1931.

Moir, Ian A. "Orthography and Theology: The Omicron-Omega Interchange in Romans 5:1 and Elsewhere." In *New Testament Textual Criticism; Its Significance for Exegesis: Essays in Honor of Bruce M. Metzger*, edited by E. J. Epp and G. D. Fee, 179–83. Oxford: Clarendon, 1981.

Moles, John L. "The Date and Purpose of the Fourth Kingship Oration of Dio Chrysostom." *Classical Antiquity* 2 (1983) 251–78.
Mondésert, Claude. "Philo of Alexandria." In *The Cambridge History of Judaism*, edited by W. D. Davies et al., 3:877–900. Cambridge: Cambridge University Press, 1984.
Moo, Douglas J. *The Epistle to the Romans*. NICNT. Grand Rapids: Eerdmans, 1996.
Morgan, Teresa. *Roman Faith and Christian Faith: Pistis and Fides in the Early Roman Empire and Early Churches*. Oxford: Oxford University Press, 2015.
Mott, Stephen C. "The Power of Giving and Receiving: Reciprocity in Hellenistic Benevolence." In *Current Issues in Biblical and Patristic Interpretation: Studies in Honor of Merrill C. Tenney*, edited by Gerald F. Hawthorne, 60–72. Grand Rapids: Eerdmans, 1975.
Moule, C. F. D. *An Idiom Book of New Testament Greek*. Cambridge: Cambridge University Press, 1959.
Mowinckel, Sigmund. *The Psalms in Israel's Worship*. Translated by D. R. Ap-Thomas. Rev. ed. Grand Rapids: Eerdmans, 2004.
Moxnes, Halvor. "Patron-Client Relations and the New Community in Luke-Acts." In *Social World of Luke-Acts: Model for Interpretation*, edited by Jerome H. Neyrey, 241–68. Peabody, MA: Hendrickson, 1991.
Nelson, Milward Douglas. *The Syriac Version of the Wisdom of Ben Sira Compared to the Greek and Hebrew Materials*. Atlanta: Scholars, 1987.
Neyrey, Jerome H. "God, Benefactor and Patron: The Major Cultural Model for Interpreting the Deity in Greco-Roman Antiquity." *JSNT* 27 (2005) 465–92.
———. "'Josephus' Vita and the Encomium: A Native Model of Personality." *JSJ* 25 (1994) 177–206.
———. "Lost in Translation: Did It Matter If Christians 'Thanked' God or 'Gave God Glory'?" *CBQ* 71 (2009) 1–23.
Novenson, Matthew V. *The Grammar of Messianism: An Ancient Jewish Political Idiom and Its Users*. New York: Oxford University Press, 2017.
———. "The Jewish Messiahs, the Pauline Christ, and the Gentile Question." *JBL* 128 (2009) 357–73.
Pao, David W. *Thanksgiving: An Investigation of a Pauline Theme*. Leicester: Apollos, 2002.
Peppard, Michael. *The Son of God in the Roman World: Divine Sonship in Its Social and Political Context*. New York: Oxford University Press, 2011.
Peterman, Gerald W. *Paul's Gift from Philippi: Conventions of Gift-Exchange and Christian Giving*. Cambridge: Cambridge University Press, 1997.
Pfoh, Emanuel. "Some Remarks on Patronage in Syria-Palestine During the Late Bronze Age." *JESHO* 52 (2009) 363–81.
Philip, Finny. *The Origins of Pauline Pneumatology: The Eschatological Bestowal of the Spirit upon Gentiles in Judaism and in the Early Development of Paul's Theology*. WUNT 194. Tübingen: Mohr Siebeck, 2005.
Pickett, Raymond. "The Death of Christ as Divine Patronage in Romans 5:1–11." *SBLSP* 32 (1993) 726–39.
Pohl, William C. "A Messianic Reading of Psalm 89: A Canonical and Intertextual Study." *JETS* 58 (2015) 507–25.
Porter, Stanley E. "The Argument of Romans 5: Can a Rhetorical Question Make a Difference?" *JBL* 110 (1991) 655–77.
———. *Καταλλάσσω in Ancient Greek Literature: With Reference to the Pauline Writings*. EFN 5. Cordoba: Ediciones el Almendro, 1994.

———. "Peace, Reconciliation." In *Dictionary of Paul and His Letters*, edited by Gerald F. Hawthorne et al., 695–99. IVP Bible Dictionary Series. Downers Grove, IL: InterVarsity, 1993.

Price, Simon R. F. *Rituals and Power: The Roman Imperial Cult in Asia Minor*. Cambridge: Cambridge University Press, 1984.

Pulcini, Theodore. "In Right Relationship with God: Present Experience and Future Fulfillment: An Exegesis of Romans 5:1–11." *SVTQ* 36 (1992) 61–85.

Rabens, Volker. *The Holy Spirit and Ethics in Paul: Transformation and Empowering for Religious-Ethical Life*. Minneapolis: Mohr Siebeck, 2014.

Rae, Murray. "Texts in Context: Scripture and the Divine Economy." *JTI* 1 (2007) 23–45.

Rajak, Tessa. "Benefactors in the Greco-Jewish Diaspora." In *Geschichte, Tradition, Reflexion: Festschrift für Martin Hengel*, edited by Peter Schäfer, 305–19. Tübingen: Mohr Siebeck, 1996.

Rappaport, Uriel. "Josephus' Personality and the Credibility of His Narrative." In *Making History: Josephus and Historical Method*, edited by Zuleika Rodgers, 68–81. JSJSup 110. Leiden: Brill, 2007.

Rawson, Beryl. "Children as Cultural Symbols: Imperial Ideology in the Second Century." In *Childhood, Class, and Kin in the Roman World*, edited by Suzanne Dixon, 21–42. New York: Routledge, 2001.

Reed, Jeffrey T. "Discourse Analysis as New Testament Hermeneutic: A Retrospective and Prospective Appraisal." *JETS* 39 (1996) 223–40.

Reumann, John. *Righteousness in the New Testament: Justification in the United States Lutheran-Roman Catholic Dialogue*. Philadelphia: Fortress, 1982.

Rey, Jean-Sébastien, and Jan Joosten, eds. *The Texts and Versions of the Book of Ben Sira: Transmission and Interpretation*. Supplements to the Journal for the Study of Judaism 150. Leiden: Brill, 2011.

Richardson, Peter. *Herod: King of the Jews and Friend of the Romans*. Columbia: University of South Carolina Press, 1996.

Ridley, Ronald T. *The Emperor's Retrospect: Augustus' Res Gestae in Epigraphy, Historiography, and Commentary*. Leuven: Peeters, 2003.

Roberts, J. J. M. "The Enthronement of Yhwh and David: The Abiding Theological Significance of the Kingship Language of the Psalms." *CBQ* 64 (2002) 675–86.

Rodríguez, Rafael. *If You Call Yourself a Jew: Reappraising Paul's Letter to the Romans*. Cambridge: James Clarke, 2015.

Rodríguez, Rafael, and Matthew Thiessen, eds. *The So-Called Jew in Paul's Letter to the Romans*. Minneapolis: Fortress, 2016.

Rohrbaugh, Richard L. "Introduction." In *The Social Sciences and New Testament Interpretation*, edited by Richard L. Rohrbaugh, 1–18. Peabody, MA: Hendrickson, 1996.

Rose, Wolter H. *Zemah and Zerubbabel: Messianic Expectations in the Early Postexilic Period*. JSOTSup. Sheffield: Sheffield Academic, 2000.

Ross, William David. "The Development of Aristotle's Thought: Dawes Hicks Lecture on Philosophy British Academy." *Proceedings of the British Academy* 43 (1957) 63–78.

Rowe, Christopher, and Malcolm Schofield, eds. *The Cambridge History of Greek and Roman Political Thought*. Cambridge: Cambridge University Press, 2000.

Runia, David T. *Philo of Alexandria on the Creation of the Cosmos According to Moses*. Leiden: Brill, 2001.

Sahlins, Marshall David. *Stone Age Economics.* New York: Aldine, 1972.
Saller, Richard P. "Patronage and Friendship in Early Imperial Rome: Drawing the Distinction." In *Patronage in Ancient Society*, edited by Andrew Wallace-Hadrill, 49–62. Leicester-Nottingham Studies in Ancient Society. London: Routledge, 1989.
———. *Personal Patronage under the Early Empire.* Cambridge: Cambridge University Press, 2002.
———. "Status and Patronage." In *The Cambridge Ancient History*, edited by A. Bowman et al., 11:817–54. Cambridge: Cambridge University Press, 2000.
Sanday, William, and Arthur C. Headlam. *A Critical and Exegetical Commentary on the Epistle to the Romans.* ICC. New York: Scribner, 1895.
Sanders, E. P. *Paul and Palestinian Judaism: A Comparison of Patterns of Religion.* Philadelphia: Fortress, 1977.
Satterthwaite, Philip E. "David in the Books of Samuel: A Messianic Expectation?" In *The Lord's Anointed: Interpretation of Old Testament Messianic Texts*, edited by Philip E. Satterthwaite et al., 41–65. Grand Rapids: Baker, 1995.
Schlatter, Adolf. "The Theology of the New Testament and Dogmatics." In *The Nature of New Testament Theology: The Contribution of William Wrede and Adolf Schlatter*, edited by Robert Morgan, 117–66. London: SCM, 1973.
Schmithals, Walter. *The Theology of the First Christians.* Louisville: Westminster John Knox, 1997.
Schmitt, Mary. "Peace and Wrath in Paul's Epistle to the Romans." *The Conrad Grebel Review* 32 (2014) 67–79.
Schofield, Malcolm. "Aristotle: An Introduction." In *The Cambridge History of Greek and Roman Political Thought*, edited by Christopher Rowe and Malcolm Schofield, 310–95. Cambridge: Cambridge University Press, 2000.
Schreiner, Thomas R. *Romans.* Grand Rapids: Baker, 1998.
Schultz, Richard. "The King in the Book of Isaiah." In *The Lord's Anointed: Interpretation of Old Testament Messianic Texts*, edited by Philip E. Satterthwaite et al., 141–65. Tyndale House Studies. Grand Rapids: Baker, 1995.
Schwartz, Daniel R. *Agrippa I: The Last King of Judaea.* Texte und Studien zum antiken Judentum 23. Tübingen: Mohr Siebeck, 1990.
Schwartz, Seth. *Were the Jews a Mediterranean Society?: Reciprocity and Solidarity in Ancient Judaism.* Princeton: Princeton University Press, 2010.
Scott, James C. *Domination and the Arts of Resistance: Hidden Transcripts.* New Haven, CT: Yale University Press, 1990.
Scott, James M. *Adoption as Sons of God: An Exegetical Investigation into the Background of ΥΙΟΘΕΣΙΑ in the Pauline Corpus.* WUNT 48. Tübingen: Mohr Siebeck, 1992.
Seeley, David. *The Noble Death: Graeco-Roman Martyrology and Paul's Concept of Salvation.* Sheffield: JSOT, 1990.
Seifrid, Mark A. *Justification by Faith: The Origin and Development of a Central Pauline Theme.* NovTSup 68. Leiden: Brill, 1992.
———. "Righteousness Language in the Hebrew Scriptures and Early Judaism." In *Justification and Variegated Nomism: The Complexities of Second Temple Judaism*, edited by D. A. Carson et al., 1:415–42. WUNT 140. Tübingen: Mohr Siebeck, 2001.
Seland, Torrey, ed. *Reading Philo: A Handbook to Philo of Alexandria.* Grand Rapids: Eerdmans, 2014.
Seneca, Lucius Annaeus. *On Benefits.* Translated by Miriam T. Griffin and Brad Inwood. Chicago: University of Chicago Press, 2011.

Sherwin-White, A. N., and Simon R. F. Price. "Pliny the Younger." In *The Oxford Classical Dictionary*, edited by Simon Hornblower and Antony Spawforth, 1198. Oxford: Oxford University Press, 2003.

Shum, Shiu-Lun. *Paul's Use of Isaiah in Romans: A Comparative Study of Paul's Letter to the Romans and the Sibylline and Qumran Sectarian Texts*. WUNT 156. Tübingen: Mohr Siebeck, 2002.

Skehan, Patrick William. "Strophic Structure in Psalm 72 (71)." *Bib* 40 (1959) 302–8.

Smith, Barry D. *Paul's Seven Explanations of the Suffering of the Righteous*. SBL. New York: Peter Lang, 2002.

Smith, Charles Ryder. *The Bible Doctrine of Grace and Related Doctrines*. London: Epworth, 1956.

Smith, Julien. *Christ the Ideal King: Cultural Context, Rhetorical Strategy, and the Power of Divine Monarchy in Ephesians*. WUNT 313. Tübingen: Mohr Siebeck, 2011.

Spicq, Ceslas. *Theological Lexicon of the New Testament*. Translated by James D. Ernest. 3 vols. Peabody, MA: Hendrickson, 1994.

Spilsbury, Paul. "God and Israel in Josephus: A Patron-Client Relationship." In *Understanding Josephus: Seven Perspectives*, edited by Steve Mason, 172–91. JSPSup 32. Sheffield: Sheffield Academic, 1998.

Stansell, Gary. "The Gift in Ancient Israel." *Semeia* 87 (1999) 65–90.

Starling, David. "The Messianic Hope in the Psalms." *RTR* 58 (1999) 121–34.

Stegemann, Ekkehard W., and Wolfgang Stegemann. *Urchristliche Sozialgeschichte: Die Anfänge im Judentum und die Christusgemeinden in der mediterranen Welt*. Stuttgart: W. Kohlhammer:, 1995.

Stendahl, Krister. *Final Account: Paul's Letter to the Romans*. Minneapolis: Fortress, 1995.

Sterling, G. E. "Philo." In *Dictionary of New Testament Background*, edited by Craig A. Evans and Stanley E. Porter, 789–93. Downers Grove, IL: InterVarsity, 2000.

Stevenson, Gregory M. "Conceptual Background to Golden Crown Imagery in the Apocalypse of John (4:4, 10; 14:14)." *JBL* 114 (1995) 257.

Stevenson, T. R. "The Ideal Benefactor and the Father Analogy in Greek and Roman Thought." *CQ* 42 (1992) 421–36.

Story, Cullen. "Another Look at the Fourth Servant Song of Second Isaiah." *HBT* 31 (2009) 100–110.

Stowers, Stanley K. *A Rereading of Romans: Justice, Jews, and Gentiles*. New Haven, CT: Yale University Press, 1994.

———. "Romans 7.7–25 as a Speech-in-Character (Προσωποποιία)." In *Paul in His Hellenistic Context*, edited by Troels Engberg-Pedersen, 180–202. Minneapolis: Fortress, 1995.

Surburg, Raymond F. "Pauline Charis: A Philological, Exegetical, and Dogmatical Study." *CTM* 29 (1958) 721–41.

Swain, Simon. *Hellenism and Empire: Language, Classicism, and Power in the Greek World, AD 50–250*. Oxford: Clarendon, 1996.

———. "Reception and Interpretation." In *Dio Chrysostom: Politics, Letters, and Philosophy*, edited by Simon Swain, 13–50. Oxford: Oxford University Press, 2000.

Tabor, James D. *Things Unutterable: Paul's Ascent to Paradise in Its Greco-Roman, Judaic, and Early Christian Contexts*. Lanham: University Press of America, 1986.

Tannehill, Robert C. *Dying and Rising with Christ: A Study in Pauline Theology*. Eugene, OR: Wipf & Stock, 2006.

Theobald, Michael. *Die überströmende Gnade: Studien zu einem paulinischen Motivfeld*. Würzburg: Echter Verlag, 1982.

Thiessen, Matthew. "The Many for One or One for the Many?: Reading Mark 10:45 in the Roman Empire." *HTR* 109 (2016) 447–66.

———. *Paul and the Gentile Problem*. New York: Oxford University Press, 2016.

Throntveit, Mark A. "The Idealization of Solomon as the Glorification of God in the Chronicler's Royal Speeches and Royal Prayers." In *The Age of Solomon: Scholarship at the Turn of the Millennium*, edited by Lowell K. Handy, 411–27. Studies in the History and Culture of the Ancient Near East 11. Leiden: Brill, 1997.

———. *When Kings Speak: Royal Speech and Royal Prayer in Chronicles*. SBLDS 93. Atlanta: Scholars, 1987.

Tilling, Chris. *Paul's Divine Christology*. Grand Rapids: Eerdmans, 2015.

Timmins, Will N. *Romans 7 and Christian Identity: A Study of the "I" in Its Literary Context*. SNTSMS 170. Cambridge: Cambridge University Press, 2017.

Treat, Jeremy R. *The Crucified King: Atonement and Kingdom in Biblical and Systematic Theology*. Grand Rapids: Zondervan, 2014.

Verbrugge, Verlyn D. *Paul and Money: A Biblical and Theological Analysis of the Apostle's Teachings and Practices*. Grand Rapids: Zondervan, 2015.

Vermeule, Cornelius C. *Roman Imperial Art in Greece and Asia Minor*. Cambridge: Belknap Press of Harvard University Press, 1968.

Versteeg, J. P. *Adam in the New Testament: Mere Teaching Model or First Historical Man?* Translated by Richard B. Gaffin Jr. Phillipsburg: P&R, 2012.

Veyne, Paul. *Bread and Circuses: Historical Sociology and Political Pluralism*. Translated by B. Pearce. London: Penguin Books, 1990.

Villalba i Varneda, Pere. *The Historical Method of Flavius Josephus*. ALGHJ 19. Leiden: Brill, 1986.

Wagenvoort, Hendrik. *Pietas: Selected Studies in Roman Religion*. Leiden: Brill, 1980.

Wagner, J. Ross. "The Christ, Servant of Jew and Gentile: A Fresh Approach to Romans 15:8–9." *JBL* 116 (1997) 473.

Walbank, F. W. "Monarchies and Monarchic Ideas." In *The Cambridge Ancient History*, edited by A. E. Astin et al., 7:62–100. Cambridge: Cambridge University Press, 1984.

Walker, Donald Dale. *Paul's Offer of Leniency (2 Cor 10:1): Populist Ideology and Rhetoric in a Pauline Letter Fragment*. WUNT 152. Tübingen: Mohr Siebeck, 2002.

Wallace, Daniel B. *Greek Grammar beyond the Basics: An Exegetical Syntax of the New Testament with Scripture, Subject, and Greek Word Indexes*. Grand Rapids: Zondervan, 1996.

Wallace-Hadrill, Andrew. "Patronage in Roman Society: From Republic to Empire." In *Patronage in Ancient Society*, edited by Andrew Wallace-Hadrill. New York: Routledge, 1989.

Walton, John H. "The Imagery of the Substitute King Ritual in Isaiah's Fourth Servant Song." *JBL* 122 (2003) 734–43.

Wasserman, Emma. "The Death of the Soul in Romans 7: Revisiting Paul's Anthropology in Light of Hellenistic Moral Psychology." *JBL* 126 (2007) 793–816.

———. *The Death of the Soul in Romans 7: Sin, Death, and the Law in Light of Hellenistic Moral Psychology*. WUNT 256. Tübingen: Mohr Siebeck, 2008.

Watts, James W. *Psalm and Story: Inset Hymns in Hebrew Narrative*. Sheffield: JSOT, 1992.

Weaver, P. R. C. *Familia Caesaris: A Social Study of the Emperor's Freedmen and Slaves.* Cambridge: Cambridge University Press, 1972.

Welles, C. Bradford. *Royal Correspondence in the Hellenistic Period: A Study in Greek Epigraphy.* Chicago: Ares, 1974.

Wengst, Klaus. *Pax Romana and the Peace of Jesus Christ.* Translated by J. Bowden. Philadelphia: Fortress, 1987.

Westbrook, Raymond. "Patronage in the Ancient Near East." *JESHO* 48 (2005) 210–33.

Westerholm, Stephen. "Righteousness, Cosmic and Microcosmic." In *Apocalyptic Paul: Cosmos and Anthropos in Romans 5–8*, edited by Beverly Roberts Gaventa, 21–38. Waco, TX: Baylor University Press, 2013.

Westermann, Claus. *Isaiah 40–66: A Commentary.* Philadelphia: Westminster, 1969.

Westfall, Cynthia Long. *A Discourse Analysis of the Letter to the Hebrews: The Relationship between Form and Meaning.* London: T. & T. Clark, 2005.

Wetter, Gillis P. *Charis: Ein Beitrag zur Geschichte des ältesten Christentums.* Leipzig: Hinrichs Buchhandlung, 1913.

Wetzel, James. *Augustine and the Limits of Virtue.* Cambridge: Cambridge University Press, 1992.

Wheatley, Alan Brent. *Patronage in Early Christianity: Its Use and Transformation from Jesus to Paul of Samosata.* Eugene, OR: Pickwick, 2011.

Whitelam, Keith W. "Israelite Kingship: The Royal Ideology and Its Opponents." In *The World of Ancient Israel: Sociological, Anthropological and Political Perspectives*, edited by Ronald E. Clements, 119–40. Cambridge: Cambridge University Press, 1989.

Whitlark, Jason. "Enabling Charis: Transformation of the Convention of Reciprocity by Philo and in Ephesians." *PRSt* 30 (2003) 325–57.

Whitsett, Christopher G. "Son of God, Seed of David: Paul's Messianic Exegesis in Romans 1:3–4." *JBL* 119 (2000) 661–81.

Whybray, Roger N. "Ben Sira in History." In *Treasures of Wisdom: Studies in Ben Sira and the Book of Wisdom*, edited by Núria Calduch-Benages and J. Vermeylen, 137–45. BETL 143. Leuven: Leuven University Press, 1999.

Williams, Sam K. "The 'Righteousness of God' in Romans." *JBL* 99 (1980) 241–90

Wilson, Gerald Henry. "The Use of Royal Psalms at the 'Seams' of the Hebrew Psalter." *JSOT* 35 (1986) 85–94.

Winger, Michael. "From Grace to Sin: Names and Abstractions in Paul's Letters." *NovT* 41 (1999) 145–75.

Winter, Bruce W. *Divine Honours for the Caesars: The First Christians' Responses.* Grand Rapids: Eerdmans, 2015.

———. *Seek the Welfare of the City: Christians as Benefactors and Citizens.* Grand Rapids: Eerdmans, 1994.

Wisse, Frederik. "Righteous Man and the Good Man in Romans 5:7." *NTS* 19 (1972) 91–93.

Witherington, Ben. *Paul's Letter to the Romans: A Socio-Rhetorical Commentary.* Grand Rapids: Eerdmans, 2004.

Wobbe, Joseph. *Der Charis-Gedanke bei Paulus: Ein Beitrag zur neutestamentlichen Theologie.* Münster: Aschendorff, 1932.

Woodhead, A. G. *The Study of Greek Inscriptions.* 2nd ed. Norman: University of Oklahoma Press, 1992.

Woolf, Greg. "Monumental Writing and the Expansion of Roman Society in the Early Empire." *JRS* 86 (1996) 22–39.

Worthington, Jonathan D. *Creation in Paul and Philo: The Beginning and Before*. WUNT 317. Tübingen: Mohr Siebeck, 2011.

Wright, Benjamin G. *No Small Difference: Sirach's Relationship to Its Hebrew Parent Text*. Atlanta: Scholars, 1989.

Wright, N. T. *The Climax of the Covenant: Christ and the Law in Pauline Theology*. Minneapolis: Fortress, 1992.

———. "The Letter to the Romans." In *The New Interpreter's Bible: General Articles and Introduction, Commentary, and Reflections for Each Book of the Bible, Including the Apocryphal/Deuterocanonical Books*, 10:393–770. Nashville: Abingdon, 2002.

———. *Paul and the Faithfulness of God*. Vol. 2. Christian Origins and the Question of God. Minneapolis: Fortress, 2013.

———. *Paul in Fresh Perspective*. Minneapolis: Fortress, 2009.

Yadin, Yigael. *The Ben Sira Scroll from Masada*. Jerusalem: Israel Exploration Society, 1965.

Yates, John W. *The Spirit and Creation in Paul*. WUNT 2.251. Tübingen: Mohr Siebeck, 2008.

Young, Stephen L. "Paul's Ethnic Discourse on 'Faith': Christ's Faithfulness and Gentile Access to the Judean God in Romans 3:21—5:1." *HTR* 108 (2015) 30–51.

———. "Romans 1.1–5 and Paul's Christological Use of Hab. 2.4 in Rom. 1.17: An Underutilized Consideration in the Debate." *JSNT* 34 (2012) 277–85.

Zanker, Paul. *The Power of Images in the Age of Augustus*. Translated by Alan Shapiro. Ann Arbor: University of Michigan Press, 1990.

Zeller, D. "The Life and Death of the Soul in Philo of Alexandria: The Use and Origin of a Metaphor." *SPhilo* 7 (1995) 19–55.

Ziegler, Philip G. "The Love of God Is a Sovereign Thing: The Witness of Romans 8:31–39 and the Royal Office of Jesus Christ." In *Apocalyptic Paul: Cosmos and Anthropos in Romans 5–8*, edited by Beverly Roberts Gaventa, 111–30. Waco, TX: Baylor University, 2013.

Ziesler, John A. *The Meaning of Righteousness in Paul: A Linguistic and Theological Enquiry*. Cambridge: Cambridge University Press, 1972.

———. "The Role of the Tenth Commandment in Romans 7." *JSNT* 33 (1988) 41–56.

Zuiderhoek, Arjan. *The Politics of Munificence in the Roman Empire: Citizens, Elites, and Benefactors in Asia Minor*. Cambridge: Cambridge University Press, 2009.

Zvi, Miriam Pucci Ben. "Josephus' Account of the Destruction of the Temple." In *Flavius Josephus: Interpretation and History*, edited by Jack Pastor et al., 53–63. JSJSup 146. Leiden: Brill, 2011.

www.ingramcontent.com/pod-product-compliance
Lightning Source LLC
Chambersburg PA
CBHW071248230426
43668CB00011B/1639